Introduction to the Profession of Counseling

FIFTH EDITION

Frank A. Nugent
Professor Emeritus, Western Washington University

Karyn Dayle Jones
University of Central Florida

Merrill
is an imprint of

Upper Saddle River, New Jersey
Columbus, Ohio

Library of Congress Cataloging-in-Publication Data

Nugent, Frank A.

  Introduction to the profession of counseling / Frank A. Nugent. -- 5th ed.

    p. cm.

  ISBN-13: 978-0-13-514430-5

  ISBN-10:   0-13-514430-2

1. Counseling--Textbooks.   I. Jones, Karyn Dayle.   II. Title.

  BF637.C6N83 2009

  158′.3--dc22

                           2008003353

Vice President and Executive Publisher: Jeffery W. Johnston
Publisher: Kevin M. Davis
Acquisitions Editor: Meredith D. Fossel
Editorial Assistant: Maren Vigilante
Senior Managing Editor: Pamela D. Bennett
Senior Project Manager: Linda Hillis Bayma
Production Coordination: Vishal Harshvardhan, Aptara, Inc.
Design Coordinator: Diane C. Lorenzo
Cover Designer: Jeff Vanik
Cover Image: SuperStock
Operations Specialist: Susan Hannahs
Director of Marketing: Quinn Perkson
Marketing Manager: Kris Ellis-Levy
Marketing Coordinator: Brian Mounts

This book was set in Garamond by Aptara, Inc. It was printed and bound by Courier Westford, Inc. The cover was printed by Phoenix Color Corp.

Pearson Education Ltd., London
Pearson Education Singapore, Pte. Ltd.
Pearson Education Canada, Inc.
Pearson Education–Japan
Pearson Education Australia PTY, Limited

Pearson Education North Asia Ltd., Hong Kong
Pearson Educación de Mexico, S.A. de C.V.
Pearson Education Malaysia, Pte. Ltd.
Pearson Education Upper Saddle River, New Jersey

Merrill
is an imprint of

10 9 8 7 6 5
ISBN-13: 978-0-13-514430-5
ISBN-10:   0-13-514430-2

To Our Students

Preface

This book presents a comprehensive introduction to professional counseling, a profession that helps individuals, groups, and families work through troubles arising from problems experienced in everyday life. Beginning in the early part of the 20th century, the counseling profession has progressed to encompass a number of specializations and practices to help a diverse population with varied issues and concerns. Counselors work in schools, mental health agencies, hospitals, churches, colleges and universities, and private practice. They provide services to children, adolescents, and adults who experience depression, anxiety, life transitions, trauma, substance abuse, academic or work-related problems, grief and loss, family conflict, relationship problems, and much, much more. Counselors employ techniques from a wide variety of counseling approaches based on psychodynamic, humanistic, and cognitive–behavioral theories.

Counselors receive education and training in graduate programs in counselor education or psychology. Training programs may focus on a person's holistic concerns—the need to nurture one's body, mind, spirit, and soul in a multicultural society. Training standards, licensure, and certification requirements continue to be raised, and collaboration and teamwork continue to increase among counselors and other health care professionals.

Over the decades, as the counseling profession has adapted to the changing needs of society, it has developed approaches to theory and practice that give counselors the flexibility and depth necessary to work with people living in a multicultural society faced with a broad spectrum of concerns and conflicts.

OVERVIEW

The following is a summary of the text:

- *Part 1: Foundations of Counseling:* The first chapter provides a definition of professional counseling and presents a historical overview of the profession. The chapters on professional, ethical, and legal issues and on the effective counselor emphasize the profession's responsibility to maintain, monitor, and improve effective counseling practice. The chapter on counseling in a multicultural world emphasizes the importance of recognizing diversity and embracing a multicultural approach in counseling.

- *Part 2: Theories:*   Counseling and human development theories and techniques, as they apply to counseling, are given comprehensive coverage. These include psychodynamic theories, humanistic theories, cognitive–behavioral theories, and other theories and approaches commonly used in the counseling profession.

- *Part 3: The Counseling Activities:*   This section of the text provides descriptions of the primary activities of counselors. The section begins with assessment, testing, and diagnosis, a critical part of the overall counseling process. Separate chapters on individual counseling, group counseling, and consultation follow. Discussion is presented about the counseling process, with an emphasis on the importance of the counseling relationship.

- *Part 4: Counseling Specialties:*   This last part features discussions of how counseling theories, techniques, and professional guidelines are applied in each of the various settings: schools, colleges, and communities. In addition, chapters on counseling specialties such as marriage and family counseling, career counseling, substance abuse counseling, and gerontological counseling are presented.

NEW FEATURES OF THE FIFTH EDITION

To address the burgeoning needs and trends of professional counseling, significant revisions and expansions have been made throughout the book. The issue of technology and online counseling has been addressed in several chapters throughout the text. Because of the ongoing emphasis and importance of multiculturalism in the counseling profession, the chapter on counseling in a multicultural world has been moved to Part 1: Foundations of Counseling. A new section entitled "Counseling Activities" has been added to encompass the chapters describing the most common work activities of counselors. A new chapter on consultation has been included, focusing on consultation in schools, mental health agencies, and organizational settings. We also combined the chapters on counseling in elementary schools and counseling in middle and secondary schools from the previous edition into one chapter entitled "Counseling Programs in Schools." Other new features of the fifth edition include the following:

- *Part 1:* Augmented the coverage of trends in the counseling profession; updated information on accreditation of training programs and licensing and certification requirements; updated discussion of professional, ethical, and legal issues in counseling to reflect the 2005 Code of Ethics of the American Counseling Association (ACA); updated and expanded information on multicultural counseling.

- *Part 2:* Amended information about human development theories as they relate to the counseling profession; updated material about the role of theories in guiding, evaluating, and improving the practice of counseling.

- *Part 3:* The chapters in this section focus primarily on the most common activities performed by counselors. In the chapter on assessment, revised information on *DSM-IV-TR* and added material on the initial interview. A new chapter on consultation has been added in this section.

- *Part 4:* Revised information about the profession of school counseling and added information about the American School Counseling Association (ASCA) National Model for School Counseling Programs. Revamped and expanded the chapter on mental health and community counseling, focusing on the current roles and activities of mental health and community counselors.

This text is intended for undergraduate and graduate students in introductory courses in counseling. Because of its strong emphasis on applying theory to practice, it can also supplement counseling practicum or internship seminars for graduate students, as well as those courses designed for continuing professional education for practicing counselors. Students in health-related training programs, such as social work and psychiatric nursing, will also benefit from the kind of instructional material that this text offers. For professionals who need to study for licensure or certification exams, this text is an excellent resource because it provides comprehensive coverage of all areas included in the exams.

ACKNOWLEDGMENTS

We very much appreciate those who reviewed the fifth edition and made comments and suggestions for improvement: Thomas Mercer Collier, Jr., Old Dominion University; Maria Darcy, University of West Florida; David Duran, California Polytechnic State University, San Luis Obispo; Beverly A. Farrow, Marshall University; and Rita Marinoble, California State University, Sacramento.

We also express our appreciation for the encouragement and support of Pearson/ Merrill publisher Kevin Davis, editor Meredith D. Fossel, and the ongoing help from editorial assistant Maren Vigilante.

About the Authors

Frank A. Nugent

Frank A. Nugent, PhD, Professor Emeritus of Psychology, Western Washington University (WWU), Bellingham, has more than 50 years' experience in professional counseling. Over the years, he has served as a counselor in schools and universities, as a counseling psychologist in private practice, and as a counselor educator, supervisor, and psychology professor. In 1993, the Washington State Counseling Association presented him with the Hank Bertness Award in recognition of his contributions to mental health and to the counseling profession during his long career.

Nugent received his MA in vocational counseling at Columbia University (1947), where he worked under Donald Super. Nugent worked, in turn, as a supervising counselor at the University of California–Berkeley and Stanford University Counseling Centers and as a counselor at Pleasant Hill High School in California. He completed his PhD in counseling psychology at the University of California–Berkeley (1959). Among Nugent's contributions is the creation of the student counseling center at Western Washington University, where he served as director from 1962 to 1973. He also initiated and coordinated for WWU's Psychology Department both the MEd program in school counseling in 1963 and the MS degree in mental health counseling in 1978. As president of the board for the Whatcom County Mental Health Clinic and, later, for the Lake Whatcom Residential Treatment Center, he helped spearhead the development of new facilities for both agencies.

At the state level, Nugent was influential in gaining certification for school counselors and was recognized for promoting professional and ethical standards for both school and mental health counselors at the state and national levels. He served as president of the Washington State Psychological Association in 1968–69 and was initiator, cofounder, and first president of the Washington Mental Health Counselors Association in 1980. At that time, he spearheaded the drive to obtain state licensing for mental health counselors.

Nugent received a Fulbright Senior Research Scholarship in 1982 to study counseling in Germany. After retirement, he continued teaching part time in WWU's psychology department; he also helped develop WWU's gerontology certificate program and taught courses in the extended-day program on the psychology of aging.

Karyn Dayle Jones

Karyn Dayle Jones, PhD, is an associate professor in counselor education at the University of Central Florida. She has 18 years of experience in the counseling profession and has been a counselor educator for 10 years. Jones has authored or coauthored several book chapters and refereed publications and has given many professional presentations in the field of counseling and counselor education. She is the past president of the Counseling Association for Humanistic Education and Development, a division of the American Counseling Association.

Jones is a Florida Licensed Mental Health Counselor, National Certified Counselor, and Certified Reality Therapist, and she has worked as a counselor in mental health agencies, schools, and private practice. Jones received her MA in mental health counseling from Rollins College (1991) and her PhD in counselor education from the University of South Carolina (1996). She has clinical experience providing individual, group, and family counseling to children, adolescents, and adults for such issues as child abuse, substance abuse, custody, and other disorders.

Brief Contents

Contents

16   Counseling Programs in Colleges and Universities   275

Note: Every effort has been made to provide accurate and current Internet information in this book. However, the Internet and information posted on it are constantly changing, so it is inevitable that some of the Internet addresses listed in this textbook will change.

Part One
Foundations of Counseling

CHAPTER 1

The Profession of Counseling: History and Trends

T he demand for counseling services continues to grow and spread in schools, colleges, and communities. Counselors help individuals work through issues and situational conflicts in a complex, multicultural society. Conflicts arise when individuals have difficulty fulfilling both their own needs and the expectations of others. Sometimes conflicts emerge because of contradictions or uncertainty regarding a person's motivations, attitudes, or feelings. Individuals may have mixed feelings about career choice or about attending college. Conflicts may result from discord between individuals and important persons in their lives. Parents and children may have contradictory values or different role expectations. Financial problems or the illness of a loved one may inhibit the pursuit of a person's life goals.

Counselors help clients cope with changing family values, family breakups, shifting job markets, and national crises. Increasing numbers of people lack such essentials as food and shelter, creating pressures that may lead to depression, drug and alcohol abuse, and street crimes. Persons with feelings of loneliness or indifference may have difficulty coping effectively with their own needs or with society's demands. Families with child abuse, domestic violence, and substance abuse need both counseling and support services. Counselors provide a full range of services for individuals, couples, families, adolescents, and children who need help and support.

After studying this chapter, you will be able to

- Describe professional counseling, the services that counselors provide, and the clients whom counselors serve.
- Understand the history of the profession of counseling.
- Recognize the current trends in counseling.

1

WHAT IS PROFESSIONAL COUNSELING?

Professional counseling is a service in which counselors work with individuals, couples, or families for the purpose of promoting optimal mental health and functioning. Regardless of where they work, counselors help persons of various multicultural backgrounds resolve conflicts, solve problems, or make decisions in a social, cultural context.

Counselors are prepared to engage in multiple roles to meet the variety of counseling services required by the public. Their primary role is counseling individuals, groups, or families regarding personal, interpersonal, social, cultural, or career concerns. Professional counseling is a process during which counselor and client develop an effective relationship, one that enables the client to work through difficulties.

Professional counselors have master's degrees or doctorates in counseling; they may be licensed or certified by state legislatures or certified as counselors by national professional counseling associations. Professional counselors are usually trained in one or more of the following types of counseling specialties:

school counseling	rehabilitation counseling
marriage and family therapy	substance abuse counseling
mental health counseling	career counseling
college and university	creative or expressive arts
pastoral counseling	play therapy

A BRIEF HISTORY OF THE COUNSELING PROFESSION

As a result of efforts by individuals and organizations throughout the last hundred years, counseling has attained the status of a national profession through national preparation standards, accreditation of preparation programs, credentialing of practitioners at both the state and national levels, ethical standards for its membership, and advancement of its research knowledge base (Sweeney, 2001). Professional counseling is historically connected to both education and psychology and each had an impact on the development of counseling as a profession. This section will provide an overview of the historical antecedents of counseling as a profession.

1900–1920: The Beginnings of Counseling

Vocational Counseling

In 1908, Frank Parsons opened a vocational bureau, the first of its kind, to offer counseling to those looking for work. It was more than just a placement center that listed job openings. Unusual for his time, Parsons believed that persons have the right to choose their own vocations rather than, say, follow their fathers' line of work, assisting on the farm or in the factory. He implemented this idea by creating the role of *vocational counselor.* By listening to what young persons (generally adolescent boys) had to say about themselves, he countered the prevailing authoritarian attitude that told young people what to do (Parsons, 1909). His belief in the value of listening to their desires and feelings regarding what they wanted to do vocationally was a forerunner of what was to become the essential feature of counseling.

In helping the client self-explore, Parsons developed a unique methodology—that of a self-inventory, perhaps the first questionnaire of its kind. Comprehensive in scope, it probed a person's interests, aptitudes, limitations, moral character, appearance, bodily characteristics, motivations, and disposition. It was a take-home survey with which the applicant could solicit help from family, friends, and teachers (Parsons, 1909). By today's standards, it was primitive and unwieldy—the many pages of questions would take hours, if not days, to complete. Questions were simplistic; for example, applicants were asked to mark whether they were honest or dishonest, bold or bashful, sensible or foolish. Interpretation of overall responses was time consuming and difficult.

But Parsons's concept that a self-survey could be useful in matching one's characteristics to a suitable vocation was unique. Moreover, he believed in the importance of counselor–client interaction; together, they interpreted the results of the self-survey, reviewed the consistencies and inconsistencies in the survey responses, and looked for meaningful patterns. Through such interaction they determined the client's appropriate vocation.

Impressed by Parsons's work, the superintendent of schools in Boston designated 117 teachers as vocational counselors in Boston's elementary and secondary schools. By 1910, approximately 30 cities had programs in vocational planning and job placement. Training in vocational counseling began at Harvard University in 1911. In 1913, the National Vocational Guidance Association was founded (Brewer, 1942).

Parsons and others used the terms *counseling* and *guidance* synonymously, and both "counselor–client" interaction and "advice giving" were used. But after Parsons's death in 1909 and after World War I, interest in this method of self-exploration virtually disappeared and was replaced by occupational information centers. This move was supported by funds from the federal government through the 1917 Smith–Hughes Act—funds primarily for developing vocational guidance in schools.

1920–1940: The Early Years

The Testing Movement

The field of psychometrics blossomed and flourished from 1920 to 1940, and along with it emerged psychologists whose primary tasks were developing, administering, and interpreting tests. During World War I, the first group of standardized tests were developed when the U.S. Army asked psychologists to develop assessment devices to screen out emotionally and intellectually unfit draftees, to place draftees in appropriate jobs, and to select qualified persons for officer training. Psychologists' efforts led to the development of verbal and nonverbal group intelligence tests (the Army Alpha and Beta) and to Woodworth's Personal Data Sheet.

Group testing and group assessment proliferated and became a significant force in the growth and direction of applied psychological testing and vocational counseling and guidance (Osipow & Fitzgerald, 1996). The practice of testing became known as *psychometrics* and those who administered and interpreted the tests, *psychometrists.*

Tests were developed to cover all aspects of human behavior—intelligence, personality, various aptitudes, and achievement. Arthur Otis, for example, in 1922 developed the Otis Group Intelligence Scale; E. K. Strong, in 1927, published the Strong Vocational Interest Blank; Clark Hull, in 1928, issued his landmark text describing aptitude testing; and Starke Hathaway developed the Minnesota Multiphasic Personality Inventory during the 1930s, publishing it in 1941. The use of standardized tests took hold in psychological, sociological, educational, and vocational guidance services. Business and industry, as well, used tests as a means to screen applicants for jobs.

Educational Guidance in Schools

Progressive education, which was introduced into schools in the 1920s by philosopher John Dewey, exerted a strong influence on school curricula (Woodring, 1953). Proponents believed that schools had the responsibility not only to guide children in their personal, social, and moral development but also to modify the school environment for optimal learning. Insisting that all school children should receive a well-rounded education, they emphasized broadening school curricula to include personal and social development, as well as academic knowledge and vocational skills.

Leading educator John Brewer, in his landmark book *Education as Guidance* (1932), claimed that guidance and education were synonymous. He proposed that the objective of education is to develop skills in living. Schools should guide young people in individual and cooperative activities, and learning should include citizenship, recreation, personal well-being, and moral development. Teachers were considered guidance specialists who should incorporate life skills into their subject matter. Teachers were to help students "relate themselves to the life of the local community and to that of the nation and the world" (Strang, 1953, p. 143).

Vocational Guidance

During the 1920s, most vocational guidance centers were incorporated into school districts and faded from the community as separate agencies. They reemerged in the community during the Depression in the 1930s, however, to assist the large numbers of unemployed. According to Super (1942), schools had proved to be inadequate settings for vocational guidance because they "were unable to see beyond the narrow confines of the school" (p. 260).

Child Guidance Clinics and the Beginnings of Counseling

In 1921, child guidance demonstration clinics were established in several strategic cities as a result of increased public interest in the mental health of children. An interdisciplinary team of psychiatrists, psychologists, and social workers worked with children and parents (Goldenberg & Goldenberg, 2007; Levy, 1971). The team's major task was the testing and diagnosis of children with learning problems and adults with symptoms of mental illness (Hershenson, Power, & Waldo, 2003). Treatment was primarily that of modifying or changing the environment (e.g., placing the child in a foster home) or psychoanalysis by psychiatrists.

Some child guidance clinics practiced relationship therapy as developed by psychiatrist Otto Rank (1936) and popularized by others, such as psychiatrist Frederick Allen and social worker Jessie Taft (Rogers, 1939, 1942). Some clinics also used play therapy as practiced by child therapists such as Fredrick Allen, Dorothy Baruch, Melanie Klein, and David Levy (Rogers, 1939, 1942). This trend in the use of relationship therapy was given impetus by the changes in psychoanalytic treatment made by Alfred Adler and Karen Horney, two dissenters of Freud.

During the 1930s, Carl Rogers (1939), a clinical psychologist at a child guidance clinic in Rochester, New York, was also practicing one of the new therapies called *expressive therapy* with children. Although his initial period of training and practice was primarily psychometrics, as was customary then for clinical psychologists, he developed a strong interest in the new relationship therapies (Rogers, 1939, 1942). They, in turn, influenced his theory of nondirective and client-centered counseling, which he presented in the following decade.

College Counseling

In 1939, E. G. Williamson published *How to Counsel Students: A Manual of Techniques for Clinical Counselors,* which contained the first theory developed specifically for counseling. This book was an outcome of his work at the University of Minnesota's student counseling center, the first of its kind in the country, at which students were given educational and vocational counseling. Williamson's clinical counseling theory was based on the assumption that personality consists of measurable traits that can be related to occupational choice and success. His term *clinical counseling* paralleled the diagnostic approach that prevailed at this time among clinical psychologists, social workers, and guidance specialists. The popularity of Williamson's theory of clinical counseling as applied to vocational counseling can be attributed, in part, to the testing movement that was flourishing in social agencies and schools.

1940–1960: Emergence of Professional Counseling

Client-Centered Counseling

A new direction developed in counseling in the 1940s prescriptive after Carl Rogers published *Counseling and Psychotherapy* (1942), in which he proposed his *nondirective, client-centered therapy.* A clinical psychologist with many years of experience in child guidance clinics in the 1930s, Rogers, as described earlier, had been influenced by a process theory of therapy in which the client develops primarily through an evolving relationship with the counselor (Rogers, 1939, 1942). Out of this experience, Rogers developed an approach he called *nondirective* to counteract the directive approach prevalent among practitioners at educational and vocational guidance clinics. He later changed the term *nondirective* to *client-centered* (1951, 1961, 1973).

Like other clinical psychologists of his time, Rogers had been steeped in testing and diagnosis. But while practicing in this mode, he also indicated his doubts about relying only on testing as a way of diagnosing. Rogers's approach differed significantly from Williamson's traditional model of guidance or clinical counseling described earlier. Williamson's method was to gather data, evaluate, and diagnose the problem first and then to "treat" or "counsel" the client. In later years, Williamson's system came to be known colloquially as the "test 'em and tell 'em" method (Romano & Skovolt, 1998, p.463). Debates over the relative merits of Williamson's diagnostic prescriptive method versus the Rogerian client-centered approach continued throughout this period.

Other influences also contributed to a shift in counseling and therapeutic practice at this time. As a result of the Nazi dictatorship, the Holocaust, and the war, many prominent European existentialists and neo-Freudian psychoanalysts immigrated to the United States—Otto Rank, Alfred Adler, Karen Horney, Erich Fromm, Erik Erikson, and Victor Frankl. Their approaches counteracted the prevailing American scientific assessment of individual differences, the trait factor theory of personality, behaviorism, and classical Freudian psychoanalysis. Their presence in America influenced such leading American psychological theorists as Rollo May, Abraham Maslow, and Carl Rogers.

Deinstitutionalization and Psychopharmacological Interventions

In the 1950s, public attention was drawn to the inhumane care received by patients in state mental hospitals. For well over a century, the mental hospital (i.e., asylum) had been the primary mode of care for the mentally ill. Awareness of the deplorable living conditions, abusive treatment, and ineffective therapies led to *deinstitutionalization,* the name given to the policy of moving people with severe mental illness out of large state institutions and then permanently closing most of those institutions.

The 1950s also inaugurated the psychopharmacological treatment of mental illness. In 1952, the antipsychotic drug chlorpromazine (Thorazine) was introduced and became the medication of choice in the treatment of schizophrenia. Thorazine lessened psychotic symptoms for many patients, so they were released from state mental hospitals back to their families and communities. In addition, two classes of antidepressants (tricyclics and monoamine oxidase inhibitors [MAOIs]) and lithium (a mood stabilizer used to treat bipolar disorder) were developed during that time. The emergence of these medications played a critical role in changing and improving the treatment of a variety of mental conditions that, up to this point, required inpatient care.

1960–1980: Growth In Professional Counseling

Community Counseling and Mental Health Counseling

While psychotropic medications advanced the deinstitutionalization movement, the passing of the Community Mental Health Centers Act (CMHC Act) of 1963 also focused on shifting treatment for people with severe mental illness from state mental hospitals to "least restrictive environments" within communities (Accordino, Porter, & Morse, 2001; Bachrach & Clark, 1996; Broskowski & Eaddy, 1994). The objectives of the CMHC Act were for community mental health centers to provide services through inpatient treatment, outpatient treatment, partial hospitalization programs, emergency/crisis treatment, and consultation/education (Hadley, Culhane, Mazade, & Manderscheid, 1994). The CMHC Act paved the way for large numbers of counselors to work in community mental health centers.

Responding to the demand for counselors for these centers, counselor education programs devoted greater attention to preparing master's level counselors to work in community mental health settings. Most community counseling programs began after 1970 (Stadler and Stahl, 1979), and the first textbooks written on community counseling were published in the 1970s (Amos & Williams, 1972; Lewis & Lewis, 1977). The term *community counselor* was coined by Lewis and Lewis (1977, 1989) to describe the work of counselors in a variety of environments (Gladding & Veach, 2003).

Because, during the early years, community counselors were not trained in the disciplines of social work, psychology, or medicine (psychiatry), they were considered "paraprofessionals"—without a professional organizational home and unqualified for the traditional credentials or licensure (Beck, 1999; Pistole & Roberts, 2002). Despite this perceived shortcoming, they were soon recognized as being among the primary providers of care in community mental health agencies (Brooks & Gerstein, 1990).

School Counseling

Counseling had boomed during the late 1950s and 1960s, with growth primarily in secondary schools. The number of secondary school counselors had escalated from 6,700 in the early 1950s to more than 30,000 in 1965 (Aubrey, 1982). Elementary school counseling emerged later, after the passage of the Elementary and Secondary Education Act of 1965, which authorized grants to school districts for developing elementary school counseling. Even so, those numbers increased more slowly throughout the country than the numbers of secondary school counselors; by the early 1970s, the number of elementary school counselors had increased to nearly 8,000 (Schmidt, 2003).

Counseling Centers Spread on College Campuses

During the 1960s, increasing numbers of universities offered free counseling services to students who were experiencing problems that interfered with their academic work. By this time, Nugent was the director of Western Washington University's counseling center:

> At Western Washington University (WWU) I founded a program in 1962 that was modeled after my experience as a counselor at the UC–Berkeley and Stanford University counseling centers—a program in which counseling was voluntary and confidential, separated from the college administrative and diagnostic testing center, and a program that included weekly case conferences. Our consulting psychiatrist, Buell Kingsley, was eager to work with normally functioning clients and to practice the new model of therapy that de-emphasized diagnosis and

avoided pathologizing client behavior. Prior to coming to Bellingham, Kingsley had left his psychoanalytic practice on the East Coast to intern at the Child Guidance Clinic in Philadelphia, known for practicing relationship therapy developed by Frederick Allen, who had worked under Otto Rank (Rogers, 1942). Kingsley came to Bellingham's fledgling mental health clinic only on condition that the psychiatric social worker he interned under, Barbara Smith, be hired as well (B. Smith, personal communication, March 2000). After I arrived at WWU, we hired Kingsley as our counseling center's psychiatric consultant and formed a liaison with the nearby mental health clinic. Kingsley's and Smith's experience with the new family systems and relational therapies made a significant impact during the 1960s and 1970s in the community and at WWU's college counseling center, where Kingsley's relational approach offset the approaches of behaviorist staff members.

Development of Professional Associations

Professional associations were very important to the counseling profession at this time, because the newly formed, fledgling profession was in need of a unifying force that could define its role, nurture its development, and set and implement standards of training. In 1952, the American Personnel and Guidance Association (APGA) was formed by the joining of four independent associations: The National Vocational Guidance Association (NVGA), the National Association of Guidance and Counselor Trainers (NAGCT), the Student Personnel Association for Teacher Education (SPATE), and the American College Personnel Association. In 1983, APGA changed its name to the American Association of Counseling and Development, and then, in 1992, it adopted its current name, the American Counseling Association (ACA). ACA is associated with a comprehensive network of 19 divisions and 56 branches.

Counseling Theories Multiply in the 1960s and 1970s

The profession of counseling showed a remarkable ability to adapt to the many new theoretical, therapeutic approaches. Humanistic approaches—Maslow's theory of self-actualization, the Rogerian client-centered or person-centered approach, and Gestalt therapy—spread rapidly, contending with the prevailing psychoanalytic and behavioristic schools of psychology. The phrase *third force in psychology* was used to describe humanism as distinct from behaviorism and psychoanalysis.

Out of this grew what came to be known as the *human potential movement.* The emphasis on personal growth became very popular and accessible with the emergence of group counseling. Encounter groups, promoted by Rogers (1970), and sensitivity training groups sought to raise consciousness and generated an intense experiential atmosphere that released pent-up emotions.

At the same time, behaviorism had become very popular in academic circles. John Krumboltz (1966) edited a book on behavioral counseling with the significant title *Revolution in Counseling.* The opposing views of humanists and behaviorists regarding human nature prompted Carl Rogers and B. F. Skinner to hold debates.

Rogers's client-centered counseling and Skinner's behaviorism, despite their opposing view, had been developed into therapeutic systems that could be used by practitioners.

These two camps agreed only in their rejection of the third camp, psychoanalytic, whose followers were generally lumped under one person: Sigmund Freud. At that time, psychoanalytic dissenters of Freud—psychosocial analysts Alfred Adler, Erich Fromm, Karen Horney, Otto Rank, Rollo May, and Erik Erikson, not to mention Carl Jung—were virtually ignored.

In the meantime, the polarized and narrow Rogerian and Skinnerian views were quietly being offset by other forces that soon would soften their extreme views and add substantially to the theoretical and practical base for effective counseling and therapy. Cognitive theories soon became influential in psychology, the first of which was Albert Ellis's rational emotive therapy (1973). Although Ellis called his book *Humanistic Psychotherapy,* he added a new dimension to humanistic practice by acknowledging that reasoning and emotions are related processes and that one's emotional problems result from illogical or distorted thoughts.

Other developments going on during this period that would later influence the counseling and therapy profession were psychosocial analyst Erik Erikson's life-span developmental theory, George Kelly's personal construct therapy, Alfred Adler's work with families, family systems theories, and the analytical psychology of Carl Jung and his followers.

1980–2000: Coming of Age

Since the 1980s and 1990s, professional counselors have become well established in both schools and the community. Well-trained counselors who have master's degrees have become the norm in many school districts, and almost all states have licensure laws for mental health counselors practicing in the community. Moreover, counseling theories and practices have expanded to cover diverse elements of the population, addressing the special characteristics of women, men, gays, lesbians, and various cultural and ethnic groups. Comprehensive neighborhood health centers that coordinate counseling, medical, and social services have emerged throughout the country, serving primarily the situational needs of those who are poor or uninsured. The overall success of counseling can be attributed to its unique ability to adapt to a wide range of diverse populations in a pluralistic society.

Counseling practice has broadened still further its range of theoretical approaches. The 1980s brought a host of new theories, including cognitive theories, and in the 1990s there was a resurgence of psychodynamic therapies, modified for the contemporary world, brought on by an increase in the number of cases of trauma, violence, addictions, and crises. As counselors and therapists work with an ever-widening range of clients and client needs, they acknowledge that adhering to a single model of therapy or developmental theory is inadequate. Increasing numbers of counselors and therapists have been moving toward an integrative theory of development and an integrative theoretical approach to therapeutic practice.

Pluralism and the Environment

In the 1980s, awareness of the pluralistic nature of American society increased. Many books and articles on multicultural counseling were published during the 1980s (see chapter 14).

McGoldrick, Pearce, and Giordano (1982), for instance, published *Ethnicity and Family Therapy*, in which they describe the need for family counselors to be aware of the special characteristics of more than a dozen ethnic groups when working with families. Counselors are cautioned about their potential biases and are encouraged to become aware of differing social and cultural beliefs and the special characteristics of each of the various ethnic groups.

During the 1990s, professional counselors continued to recognize the depth and complexity of counseling individuals living in a multicultural society (see chapter 14). The American Counseling Association (ACA) set up a task force and published special editions of journals covering counseling practices with various ethnic groups, women and men, and lesbians and gay men. Multicultural counseling competencies developed by Sue, Arredondo, and McDavis (1992) were adopted in the 1990s by leading professional counseling associations: the Association of Multicultural Counseling and Development (AMCD) in 1995; the Association for Counselor Education and Supervision (ACES) in 1996; and the International Association of Marriage and Family Counseling (IAMFC) in 1997.

Professional Associations

To further upgrade master's degree training programs, in 1981 the Council for Accreditation of Counseling and Related Educational Programs (CACREP) was established. CACREP is an independent agency recognized by the Council for Higher Education Accreditation to accredit master's degree programs in a variety of counseling specialties, including career counseling, college counseling, community counseling, marriage and family therapy, mental health counseling, and school counseling, as well as doctoral programs in counselor education. CACREP's core curriculum is used as the basis for the educational requirements of most state licensure laws for counseling.

In 1982, at a time when state legislatures were slow to pass licensing laws for counselors, APGA (later known as the American Association for Counseling and Development [AACD], and now ACA) established the National Board for Certified Counselors (NBCC). This board certified counselors who met standards of training set by the association. And although it did not have the legal status of state licensing, it did help assure consumers that certified counselors met certain training standards. Since the early 1980s, the number of states passing licensing laws for counselors who have master's degrees has increased. By 2007, 48 states (except California and Nevada) and Puerto Rico and the District of Columbia have state licensure laws, the most recent being New York (January 1, 2006) (American Counseling Association, 2007).

School Counseling

As school counselors who have master's degrees in counseling have become more common, they have been increasingly asked to intervene in student crises resulting from substance abuse, gang violence, family conflicts, and teenage pregnancies. In many places, school counselors are faced with violent outbreaks in which students are victims or witnesses. In response, school counselors have had to learn how to intervene in the aftermath of violence, as well as to assess violence-prone students and to be ready to intervene accordingly.

In many school districts, crises have become so prevalent that counselors have often been prevented from serving the normal developmental needs of students (see chapter 17). In an attempt to counter this problem, many school districts nationwide designed and implemented comprehensive school counseling programs. These programs actually began in the 1970s, but spread slowly. During the 1990s, as guidelines became available, school districts throughout the country gradually started adopting programs. That trend has continued into the new millennium in both elementary and secondary schools (Baker, 2000). Such comprehensive programs have helped to enable counselors to provide the important services of individual and group counseling, classroom guidance, coordination, and consultation.

Managed Care and Mental Health Counseling

As a result of escalating health costs, diminishing financial resources, and an increased demand for services, managed health care systems such as health maintenance organizations (HMOs) have proliferated; in fact, according to Kiesler (2000), 88% of U.S. citizens with private insurance are enrolled in behavioral health plans nationwide. The advent of managed health care into community mental health has caused great upheaval among counselors and other mental health professionals (Danzinger & Welfel, 2001). Managed care presents numerous ethical challenges for mental health professionals. For example, when client diagnoses do not fall within reimbursement guidelines, mental health professionals feel pressure to choose between honest and accurate diagnosis without third-party reimbursement payment and deceptive diagnosis (usually giving a more severe diagnosis) in order to gain reimbursement (Cooper & Gottlieb, 2000). In addition, managed care has been perceived as dictating counseling practice by emphasizing the use of brief counseling or solution-focused approaches in counseling.

College Counseling

Since the 1990s, college counseling centers have had increased cases of clients with severe psychiatric problems, increased cases of alcohol abuse and sexual assault, and more demand for crisis intervention. Issues such as clinical depression, anxiety, suicide risk, and substance abuse, as well as disorders involving psychosis and other severe pathology, are now relatively common among student clients in college counseling centers. Thus, psychological testing, diagnosis, and treatment planning are the norm at many centers. College counseling centers provide more time-limited, brief counseling rather than long-term, in-depth psychotherapy. Outreach programs such as drug and alcohol abuse prevention, multicultural awareness, eating disorder prevention, and stress reduction are often provided by many centers. Although career issues are commonly related to or affected by clinical problems, career counseling has been separated from many college counseling centers.

Introduction of the Internet to the Counseling Field

The use of the Internet in the counseling field began in the 1990s and is now present in all aspects of counseling services, including information search and retrieval, assessment and diagnosis, psychoeducation, supervision, consultation, record keeping, and actual counseling itself (i.e., online counseling, also known as Internet counseling or Web counseling) (Guterman & Kirk, 1999; Riemer-Reiss, 2000; Sampson, Kolodinski, & Greeno, 1997). The Internet has proved to be effective in many areas of counseling services, but some controversy still exists over its appropriateness and efficacy for various aspects of the field.

The primary concerns about Internet counseling involve the confidentiality and privacy of client information. In addition, critics question the ability of counselors to develop effective counseling relationships with clients, and counselor availability may be a concern if a client is experiencing a crisis or trauma. Despite these concerns, Internet counseling continues to grow. Professional organizations have attempted to address the potential problems of Internet counseling by adapting the ethical codes of conduct for counselors.

The New Millennium: Trends in Counseling

The past 100 years have seen the birth and growth of the counseling profession. Now, in the early 21st century, the profession is replete with multiple theories that provide different perspectives on human behavior, has a growing and comprehensive research base, has established advanced training programs and credentialing, and has ongoing development of new and refined intervention strategies to respond to clients from a variety of cultural backgrounds (Herr, 2004).

Challenges exist for counselors in the new millennium (Herr, 2004, p. 17). The changing family patterns in the United States demonstrate the decrease in the number of nuclear and intact traditional families. The growing pluralism of cultural traditions, languages, and ethnic and racial backgrounds of Americans is now the rule, not the exception. And increasing numbers of persons—children, youth, and adults—are being identified as *at risk*, meaning that they are vulnerable to social, academic, and occupational failure.

Mental Health and Community Counseling

Within mental health and community counseling, controversies exist about professional identity. Unlike the 1970s, when the profession argued over the virtues of behaviorism versus humanism, the profession now struggles with continuing to embrace development and overall client wellness versus the more pathological orientation of other mental health fields. Historically, counselors were committed to a developmental, strengths-oriented approach to assessing and counseling clients. Influences from other mental health fields (e.g., psychiatry, psychology), the emphasis on accountability and evidence-based practice, and market forces (i.e., the decisions about which mental health services are funded) have influenced counselors toward a more remedial and pathological orientation (McAuliffe & Eriksen, 1999).

Some counselor educators still believe that counselors should follow a developmental model and should not diagnose and treat pathology (Hohenshil, 1993), thus differentiating counselors from psychologists and psychiatrists. However, the norm today is that virtually all counselors who have master's degrees (marriage and family, mental health, and community) must diagnose clients using the *Diagnostic and Statistical Manual of Mental Disorders* (*DSM-IV-TR*) and follow an evidence-based treatment plan (Mead et al., 1997).

School Counseling

A primary issue for school counseling in the new millennium is that of professional identity. For many years, school counseling has lacked consistent identity from state to state, district to district, even school to school, across the United States. To answer the question, "What do school counselors do?" the ASCA created the *ASCA National Model: A Framework for School Counseling Programs* (ASCA, 2003). It serves as a framework to guide states, districts, and individual schools in designing, developing, implementing, and evaluating a comprehensive, developmental, and systemic school counseling program. The model clearly describes school counselors' duties and responsibilities related to designing and implementing a comprehensive school counseling program.

The early years of the 21st century also brought about profound changes in education. In 2001, the No Child Left Behind (NCLB) Act (U.S. Department of Education, 2002a) was passed. In order to make schools accountable for student learning, and to ensure that at-risk youth are not "left behind" academically (U.S. Department of Education, 2002b), the legislation made federal funding for education contingent on students' school-wide performance on academic tests. The legislation also had an impact on the role of the school counselors, and many are now given administration assignments for the NCLB program (e.g., test coordination, proctoring, test security), allowing them less time for dealing with the emotional/social needs of students (Dollarhide & Lemberger, 2006).

Technology and Counseling

Advances in computer technology and Internet accessibility continue to affect the counseling profession in many ways. Technology has required counselors to augment and extend their skills (e.g., use of the Internet, computer-mediated assessment and record keeping, video conferencing, online counseling) (Herr, 2004). Today, it is difficult to find mental health agencies and private practices that are not using technology in one form or another (Baltimore, 2002). In addition, computer-mediated communication is transforming school counseling by changing the nature of interactions among counselors, school personnel, parents, counselor educators, students, and field supervisors (Wilczenski & Coomey, 2006). In terms of counselor training, Internet-based courses in counselor education programs have expanded in scope and content, especially for courses that do not include significant clinical components (Layne & Hohenshil, 2005).

The delivery of technology-assisted distance counseling, including Internet counseling, continues to grow and evolve. Although Internet counseling is not a desirable alternative for all clients or all counselors, there are some unique advantages that many find attractive (Layne & Hohenshil, 2005). Because of the growth of Internet counseling and other technology-assisted distance counseling, various certifying bodies and accreditation agencies have developed standards and guidelines for ethical online counseling practice. The NBCC and the Center for Credentialing and Education (CCE) created a document entitled "The Practice of Internet Counseling" that contains a statement of principles for guiding the evolving practice of Internet counseling. The CCE also recently established a new credential for counselors practicing various forms of distance counseling: the Distance Credentialed Counselor (DCC). CACREP (2001) focused attention on the appropriate use of technology in the 2001 standards. In addition, the 2005 ACA Code of Ethics greatly expanded its codes on technology applications, broadening the ethical use of technology in research, record keeping, and the provision of services to consumers (Code A.12.; ACA, 2005).

SUMMARY

Over the last hundred years, counseling has attained and clarified its professional identity. The development of national preparation standards, accreditation of preparation programs, credentialing of practitioners at both the state and national levels, ethical standards for the profession, and advancement of the research knowledge base have all contributed to its growth as a profession (Sweeney, 2001).

Historically, counseling has progressed from its beginnings as primarily vocational counseling to a variety of specialties within the profession. Professional counselors can specialize in school counseling, mental health counseling, community counseling, marriage and family counseling, play therapy, substance abuse, and on and on.

The demand for counselors continues to increase. According to the *Occupational Outlook Handbook*, produced by the Bureau of Labor Statistics, the U.S. government's job forecasting agency, the "overall employment of counselors is expected to grow faster than the average for all occupations through 2014" (U.S. Department of Labor, 2006). Students in counselor education programs can expect job opportunities to be very good because the number of job openings that arise are expected to exceed the number of graduates of counseling programs.

PROJECTS AND ACTIVITIES

1. Survey several mental health agencies in your community. Find out how many staff members hold degrees in the various professions, including counseling, social work, psychology, or psychiatry.
2. Attend a meeting of your local, regional, or state counseling association. What issues are of current interest in the association?
3. Set up a panel of counselors from schools, colleges, and community agencies, all of whom have had training in counseling. Ask the panelists these questions: What are your major responsibilities? How do these responsibilities tie in with your training? What gaps do you see in services to the general public?

4. Search the Internet for local community mental health agencies in your area. What population do they serve and what types of services do they offer?

5. Interview a counselor at the college you attend who has been employed there for 15 to 20 years. Ask how the counselor perceives the changes that have occurred at the college and among college students and what changes are anticipated.

6. Search the Internet and find two sites that provide online counseling. Review the information provided to prospective clients and explore the site as much as you can without signing up as a client. Evaluate the degree to which the professionals providing the online service are complying with either the NBCC guidelines for Web counseling or the ACA guidelines for Internet online counseling.

CHAPTER 2

Professional, Ethical, and Legal Issues

Being an effective counselor includes "having knowledge of and the ability to integrate a code of ethics into one's professional practice" (Kocet, 2006, p. 228). Practicing ethically is especially important in the counseling profession when professionals,
by the nature of the relationship, have power over their clients and the potential to do
harm (Haug, 1999). Because professional counselors have knowledge and skills beyond
those of ordinary citizens, counselors are charged with the responsibility of practicing in
a manner that is helpful and not harmful to their clients.

The purpose of this chapter is to familiarize students with key concepts related to
professional, ethical, and legal issues in the counseling profession. After studying this
chapter, you will

- Understand the role of professional associations in professional and ethical issues in
counseling.
- Have knowledge about the various requirements for counselor training and credentialing.
- Be familiar with the ACA Code of Ethics and its role in professional practice.
- Be aware of legal issues related to the counseling profession.

PROFESSIONALISM, ETHICS, AND LEGAL ISSUES

Professionalism, ethics, and legal issues are interrelated terms in the counseling profession, but with different meanings. Remley and Herlihy (2007) defined the term
professionalism in the counseling field as an internal motivation to perform at the level of
best practices that represent the ideals of the profession, enhance its image, and promote
its development (p. 47). *Ethics* are standards of conduct or practice deemed "acceptable
or good practice according to agreed-upon rules or standards of practice established by a

profession" (Cottone & Tarvydas, 2003, p. 4). Professional organizations develop "codes of ethics" to articulate the standards of practice for that particular profession (Kocet, 2006, p. 228). *Legal issues* refer to laws related to the counseling profession. In the counseling field, laws dictate the "minimum" standards of behavior that society will tolerate, whereas ethics represent the "ideal" standards expected by the profession (Remley & Herlihy, 2007, p. 3).

Kitchener (1984) developed a critical evaluation model to link ethics and professional practice. This model is based on four underlying moral principles involved in counselor–client relationships: autonomy, beneficence, nonmaleficence, and justice. *Autonomy* means that clients have the right to self-determination, *beneficence* refers to counselors' intent to foster growth in clients, *nonmaleficence* means that counselors avoid taking actions that can harm clients, and *justice,* or fairness, refers to treating clients equally regardless of race, gender, age, or social or economic differences. Others have since built on Kitchener's model (see Corey et al. [2007] and Cottone & Tarvydas [2003]). These four underlying principles are helpful for counselors in ethical decision making and underlie the codes of ethics developed by professional associations for the counseling profession.

Professional Associations

The primary professional association whose definitions and standards are specifically designed for counselors is the American Counseling Association (ACA). ACA began in 1952, originally named the American Personnel and Guidance Association (APGA), with the union of four independent associations: the National Vocational Guidance Association (NVGA), the National Association of Guidance and Counselor Trainers (NAGCT), the Student Personnel Association for Teacher Education (SPATE), and the American College Personnel Association (ACPA). The American Personnel and Guidance Association later changed names in 1983 to the American Association for Counseling and Development (AACD). Then, on July 1, 1992, the association changed its name again to the American Counseling Association to reflect the common bond among association members and to reinforce their unity of purpose.

ACA services professional counselors in the United States and in 50 other countries, including Europe, Latin America, the Philippines, and the Virgin Islands. In addition, ACA is associated with a comprehensive network of 19 divisions and 56 branches (see Table 2.1 for a list of ACA divisions).

In the early 1960s, ACA (then known as the American Personnel and Guidance Association [APGA]), in conjunction with the American School Counseling Association (ASCA) and the Association for Counselor Education and Supervision (ACES), developed definitions and training standards for the school counselor role. APGA also drew up a code of ethics in 1961 to cover counselors in all settings. In the late 1970s and the 1980s, the association worked with its affiliate, the American Mental Health Counselors Association (AMHCA), to attain licensure and certification for mental health counselors in the community. ACA also adopted a process of accrediting graduate counseling programs developed by ACES. This accreditation is conducted by the Council for Accreditation of Counseling and Related Educational Programs (CACREP).

TABLE 2.1
ACA Divisions

Association for Assessment in Counseling and Education (AACE)
Promotes the effective use of assessment in the counseling profession.

Association for Adult Development and Aging (AADA)
Focuses on professional development and advocacy related to adult development and aging issues.

Association for Creativity in Counseling (ACC)
Promotes greater awareness, advocacy, and understanding of creative and diverse approaches in counseling.

American College Counseling Association (ACCA)
Focuses on fostering student development in colleges, universities, and community colleges.

Association for Counselors and Educators in Government (ACEG)
Dedicated to counseling clients and their families in local, state, and federal government or in military-related agencies.

Association for Counselor Education and Supervision (ACES)
Emphasizes the need for quality education and supervision of counselors in all work settings.

Association for Lesbian, Gay, Bisexual, and Transgender Issues in Counseling (ALGBTIC)
Promotes greater awareness and understanding of gay, lesbian, bisexual, and transgender (GLBT) issues among members of the counseling and related professions.

Association for Multicultural Counseling and Development (AMCD)
Seeks to develop programs specifically to improve ethnic and racial empathy and understanding.

American Mental Health Counselors Association (AMHCA)
Seeks to enhance the profession of mental health counseling through licensing, advocacy, education, and professional development.

American Rehabilitation Counseling Association (ARCA)
Focuses on enhancing the development of people with disabilities throughout their life span and promoting excellence in the rehabilitation counseling profession.

American School Counselor Association (ASCA)
Supports school counselors' efforts to help students focus on academic, personal/social, and career development.

Association for Spiritual, Ethical, and Religious Values in Counseling (ASERVIC)
Supports spiritual, ethical, religious, and other human values as essential to the full development of the person and to the discipline of counseling.

Association for Specialists in Group Work (ASGW)
Promotes quality in group work training, practice, and research, both nationally and internationally.

Counseling Association for Humanistic Education and Development (C-AHEAD)
Promotes humanistically oriented counseling practices.

Counselors for Social Justice (CSJ)
Focuses on social justice and social action in the counseling profession.

TABLE 2.1
Continued

International Association of Addictions and Offender Counselors (IAAOC)
Provides leadership in and advancement of the professions of addiction and offender counseling.

International Association of Marriage and Family Counselors (IAMFC)
Promotes excellence in the practice of couples and family counseling.

National Career Development Association (NCDA)
Promotes career development for all people over the life span.

National Employment Counseling Association (NECA)
Dedicated to helping people prepare for, enter, understand, and progress in the world of work.

ACA publishes the *Journal of Counseling & Development* and *Counseling Today,* which contain articles and information pertinent to the counseling field. The organization also sponsors yearly conventions, at which workshops and papers are presented. In addition, ACA coordinates national task forces to study and make recommendations about counseling policy and practice, and it lobbies the U.S. Congress to pass legislation to upgrade and fund counseling programs.

Counselor Training

Accreditation of Counselor Training Programs

In order to maintain high standards that are consistent in counselor training programs throughout the country, various professional associations have established certain criteria for master's level counselor training programs and accreditation procedures. Accreditation programs include the Council for the Accreditation of Counseling and Related Programs (CACREP), the Council on Rehabilitation Education (CORE), the Commission for Accreditation of Marriage and Family Therapy Education (COAMFTE), and the American Association of Pastoral Counselors (AAPC) (Clawson et al., 2003).

Accreditation of counselor training programs is a voluntary process initiated by counselor education departments. Each accrediting program requires a separate application for each specialty area, and procedures for each generally take at least 2 years. A counseling training program must meet the guidelines set by the agency and must go through a process of self-evaluation before inviting a team of agency evaluators for an on-site visit. Accreditation must be renewed and reevaluated every 2 to 5 years (Clawson et al., 2003).

Graduates from an accredited counselor training program have certain obvious advantages: Employers prefer to hire graduates of accredited programs; graduates tend to be given preference when applying for an advanced degree; in many states, licensure has the same requirements as accreditation; and national professional counselor certification requirements are essentially the same as those of accrediting agencies (Remley & Herlihy, 2007).

CACREP. In 1981, ACA founded the Council for the Accreditation of Counseling and Related Programs (CACREP); it is the largest accrediting body for evaluating graduate counseling training programs. CACREP accredits master's degree programs in career counseling; college counseling; community counseling; gerontological counseling; marital, couple, and family counseling; mental health counseling; school counseling; and student affairs. It accredits doctoral programs in counselor education and supervision.

To become accredited, a master's program must include the following CACREP standards (Clawson et al., 2003):

- At least 2 years and 48 to 60 academic semester hours, depending on the specialty.
- Eight core curricular experiences consisting of professional identity, social and cultural diversity, human growth and development, career development, helping relationships, group work, assessment, and research and program evaluation.
- Practicum and internship experiences for all students.

Doctoral programs require more hours of supervised internship and more intensive coverage of core areas.

CORE. The Council on Rehabilitation Education (CORE) is composed of representatives from five different national rehabilitation associations (Clawson et al., 2003). It accredits master's degree rehabilitation programs focusing on the effective delivery of rehabilitation services to individuals with disabilities. Courses include professional identity; social and cultural diversity; human growth and development; employment and career development; counseling and consultation; group work; assessment; research and program evaluation; medical, functional, and environmental aspects of disability; and rehabilitation services and resources. Additional requirements include a supervised practicum and internship.

COAMFTE. The Commission for Accreditation of Marriage and Family Therapy Education (COAMFTE) certifies training programs in marriage and family therapy at the master's, doctoral, and postgraduate degree levels. Graduates from COAMFTE-accredited programs are qualified to diagnose and treat mental and emotional disorders, whether cognitive, affective, or behavioral, within the context of marriage and family systems.

AAPC. The American Association of Pastoral Counselors (AAPC) certifies master's degree pastoral programs, accredits pastoral counseling centers, and approves training programs. Master's degree programs require approximately 67 semester hours of counseling and related course work, 100 practicum hours, and 333 internship hours (Clawson et al., 2003).

Counselor Credentialing: Licensing and Certification

Graduates of counselor training programs have several different types of credentialing available to verify that they have attained a certain level of professional preparation: (a) licensing by state legislatures, (b) certification in specialty areas by state agencies, and (c) certification by national certification boards sponsored by national professional counseling associations.

Licensure

A *license* is permission to either do a particular thing or use a particular title. States pass licensure laws as a way to protect the health, safety, and welfare of its citizens. Once a state legislature has passed a counseling licensure law, it becomes illegal for any individual who is not licensed by the state to call themselves a licensed counselor or to engage in the activities of a licensed counselor. The title of their profession varies by state, e.g., Licensed Professional Counselor (LPC), Licensed Professional Clinical Counselor (LPCC), or Licensed Mental Health Counselor (LMHC). State legislatures in 48 states (except California and Nevada), the District of Columbia, and Puerto Rico require counselors to be licensed in order to engage in private practice in that state. The advantage of being licensed by the state is that only licensed counselors are qualified for third-party reimbursement and are accepted as mental health providers by managed care organizations. Counselors working in educational institutions or state or community agencies are not required to be licensed by the state to practice in those settings.

Certification

A *certificate* is verification that a counselor has met certain qualifications for education and/or work experience, or a certain score on a specified examination. Unlike state licensure boards, state certification boards authorize certification for particular counseling specialties rather than for general counseling practice. Two areas commonly certified by states are school counseling and substance abuse counseling (Remley & Herlihy, 2007).

All 50 states credential school counselors; each state department of education determines the educational requirements and professional experience required to be employed in that state as a counselor in the public schools. Most states require a master's degree in school counseling that includes a practicum in a school setting. Overall, throughout the country, credentialing requirements for school counselors are less stringent and uniform than are licensure laws for counselors in the community.

For substance abuse counseling, state agencies have different levels of counselor certification available for those who don't have master's degrees in counseling. The National Board of Certified Counselors (NBCC), under the sponsorship of ACA, and the Commission of Rehabilitation Counselor Certification (CRCC) both offer national certification for counselors. These national professional certifications were set up before state licensing of counselors came into being, as a way of establishing standards for counselor training.

Currently, NBCC offers four professional certifications: (a) National Certified Counselor (NCC) for work in all settings, (b) National Certified School Counselor (NCSC), (c) Certified Clinical Mental Health Counselor (CCMHC), and (d) Master Addictions

Counselor (MAC). The requirements for NCC certification are a master's degree in counseling with post-master's supervised experience and a written exam. The other specialized certifications require additional training and experience within the specialty.

There are both disadvantages and advantages for counselors who are nationally certified by NBCC. National certificate is not the same as licensure; to engage in private practice, counselors must still be licensed in their state. Moreover, national certification does not qualify counselors to receive third-party health insurance payments or to be accepted as mental health providers by managed care organizations. On the other hand, nationally certified counselors have the advantage of being recognized as qualified counselors in all states. Furthermore, national certification recognizes those with counselor specialties, whereas state licensing does not. Many counselors decide to become both state licensed and nationally certified, thus acquiring the advantages of both.

PROFESSIONAL CODES OF ETHICS AND STANDARDS

Professional codes of ethics and standards are developed by professional associations to protect the public from unethical or incompetent professionals, as well as to protect the profession from unethical practices by any of its members (Herlihy & Corey, 2005). The ACA Code of Ethics (2005) applies to counselors. Similar codes have been set by APA (2002), the American Association for Marriage and Family Therapy (AAMFT) (2001), and the National Association of Social Workers (NASW) (1999). Because the ACA Code is most representative of general counseling practice, this section highlights the major issues addressed in the ACA Code of Ethics.

Ethics Regarding the Counseling Relationship

When establishing a relationship, the counselor's primary responsibility is "to respect the dignity and to promote the welfare of clients" (Section A.1.). Counselors work jointly with clients to encourage clients' positive growth and development.

Dual or Multiple Relationships

Dual or *multiple relationships* refer to counselors engaging in nonprofessional interactions or relationships (i.e., outside of counseling sessions) with current or former clients. Traditionally, counselors were advised to avoid dual/multiple relationships whenever possible. However, recent ethics scholars challenge this notion and say that dual/multiple relationships, sometimes known as *boundary crossings,* are normal and can actually be meaningful in the counseling relationship, particularly in rural or certain cultural communities (Glosoff, Corey, & Herlihy, 2006; Moleski & Kiselica, 2005). For example, as Kocet (2006) described, "in some smaller communities, a client may also be the only mechanic in town or a client who has been attending counseling to work on improving her relationship with her partner invites the counselor to attend her wedding" (p. 231).

The ACA Code of Ethics (2005) advises that counselors avoid nonprofessional interactions with current and former clients when possible; however, counselors may engage in nonprofessional interactions (excluding sexual or romantic interactions) if the interaction may be potentially beneficial to the client (Standards A.5.c. and A.5.d.). Examples of potentially beneficial interactions include attending a formal ceremony (e.g., a wedding/commitment ceremony or graduation); purchasing a service or product provided by a client or former client (except unrestricted bartering); hospital visits to a client's ill family member; or mutual membership in a professional association, organization, or community (Kocet, 2006, p. 231).

Sexual Involvement with Clients

Counselor–client sexual intimacy is forbidden in the ethical codes of all therapeutic professions (Corey et al., 2007). The ACA Code of Ethics states, "Sexual or romantic counselor–client interactions or relationships with current clients, their romantic partners, or their family members are prohibited" (Standard A.5.a). In addition, the Code prohibits counselors from engaging in sexual or romantic counselor–client interactions or relationships with former clients, their romantic partners, or their family members for a period of 5 years following the last professional contact (Standard A.5.b.).

The harm to clients who become sexually involved with counselors is "deep, lasting, and occasionally permanent" (Remley & Herlihy, 2007, p. 197). Effects can range from mistrust of opposite-sex relationships to hospitalization and, in some cases, suicide (Corey et al., 2007). Other effects on clients include feelings of guilt, negative feelings about the counseling experience in general, a deterioration of their sexual relationship with their primary partner, and even symptoms of posttraumatic stress disorder.

Counselors and therapists who sexually exploit clients not only can be sued for malpractice, but also can be jailed on felony charges and lose their licenses, their insurance coverage, or their jobs (Corey et al., 2007).

Counselor Values

Values are standards or ethical guidelines that influence an individual's or group's behavior, attitudes, and decisions. A person's particular lifestyle is based on a value system derived from his or her particular religious, philosophical, social, cultural, and political background. Values are fostered by families, cultural groups, religious organizations, and schools, or they may be arrived at through an individual's personal searching. Value issues come up in counseling when clients have mixed motivations about choices they must make or when their choices conflict with the values of family members, peers, or society.

A counselor's job is to help clients search for various alternative behaviors or attitudes and decide which best contribute to their personal satisfaction and development and still permit effective social interaction. The counselor's task is complex because this search may involve several value systems: those of the clients, the counselor, the school, the society, the clients' peer groups, and the clients' families. These value systems may all be different, even the values of the parents. Counseling is further complicated because the counselor cannot always keep personal values out of counseling sessions. A counselor's particular lifestyle and general behavior suggest clues to his or her beliefs about values in general. A counselor should express personal values when appropriate, but allow clients to make their own decisions about alternative values (Corey et al., 2007).

One crucial area of potential values conflict lies in counselor reactions to a client's race, ethnicity, gender, or sexual orientation. The ACA Code of Ethics specifically states that counselors should respect differences in diverse cultural backgrounds and "actively attempt to understand the diverse cultural backgrounds of the clients they serve" (ACA, 2005, p. 4).

According to the ethical codes, counselors must be aware that their own biases might unduly influence a client. In such situations, counselors should decide whether to continue working with the client or refer the client to another counselor. For example, counselors who have certain religious beliefs against abortion find themselves in a moral bind when a pregnant client contemplates abortion. Counselors must determine whether their moral convictions permit an objective discussion of the issue. If not, the counselors should refer the client to another counselor. Similarly, counselors must not try to persuade a client who opposes abortion to consider abortion as a wise alternative.

Freedom of Choice and Informed Consent

Both freedom of choice and informed consent relate to the voluntary nature of counseling. The ACA Code of Ethics (2005) states, "Clients have the *freedom to choose* [emphasis added] whether to enter into or remain in a counseling relationship and need adequate information about the counseling process and the counselor" (Standard A.2.a). Besides ethical considerations regarding voluntary counseling, experience has shown that most persons profit more from counseling when they are free to choose, or voluntarily seek out, counseling. Many counseling theorists and practitioners consider motivation to change behavior, especially intrinsic motivation, a first essential step toward a successful counseling outcome.

Informed consent requires that counselors inform clients of the goals of counseling, the services that will be provided, potential benefits and risks, fees, length of counseling, limits of confidentiality, qualifications of the counselor, procedures and techniques to be used, and clients' right of access to their files. With this information, clients can make informed judgments about whether to enter counseling with a particular counselor. Some state licensing laws require counselors to display disclosure statements that spell out these considerations, as well as make a copy of the statement available to clients upon request.

Clients need to be aware of information provided to insurance companies. For example, for an insurance company to cover any costs of counseling services, the client's problems must fit into a particular category of *mental disorder*. Mental disorder categories are based on psychiatric categories of diagnosable disorders listed in the American Psychiatric Association's *Diagnostic and Statistical Manual of Mental Disorders* (*DSM-IV-TR;*

APA, 2000). Counselors must take steps to ensure that clients understand the implications of a diagnosis of a mental disorder and obtain consent from clients when it is necessary to diagnose them for insurance reimbursement. Diagnoses should be shared with clients once agreement is reached. Through sharing, the diagnoses become a part of therapy, and clients' rights are protected.

Ethics Regarding Confidentiality, Privileged Communication, and Privacy

Respecting Clients' Rights

Trust is the cornerstone of the counseling relationship. As such, keeping client information private is vital in establishing and maintaining client trust and respecting clients' rights. Three terms are frequently used when discussing clients' rights: privacy, confidentiality, and privileged communication. These terms are sometimes used interchangeably, but the concepts have important differences. *Privacy* is the broadest of the three terms alluding to persons' rights to decide what personal information will be shared with or withheld from others (Remley & Herlihy, 2007). *Confidentiality* is an ethical concept that more specifically refers to counselors not disclosing to others what a client has said in counseling sessions without the permission of the client. *Privileged communication* is a legal term referring to confidential communication that one cannot be forced legally to divulge. More about privileged communication is discussed later in the chapter.

Guaranteed confidentiality enables clients to develop trust in the counseling relationship and to disclose and explore painful or forbidden feelings and experiences during the healing process. In the ACA Code of Ethics, the importance of confidentiality is described as follows: "Counselors do not share confidential information without client consent or without sound legal or ethical justification" (Standard B.1.c).

Some counselors say that they are better able to understand and help a client when they share information about the client with teachers or parents or with staff members of other agencies. They claim that because they are doing this to benefit their client, they see no need to request client consent, which the client might refuse to give. This behavior is not only unethical, but also counterproductive to professional practice. Too often, counselors who have taken someone else into their confidence are shocked to find that the client in question is later informed of the interaction by that very person. When counselors think that sharing client information with others will be helpful to the client, they can indicate that to the client. Requesting a client's cooperation keeps that person involved, enhances trust, and makes sharing a productive part of therapy. If the client refuses, exploring the reasons for client reluctance can also prove productive.

Exceptions to Voluntary and Confidential Counseling

In certain cases, individuals may lose their freedom of choice regarding counseling and have to submit to involuntary assessment and/or treatment if the counselor thinks that they may hurt themselves or others. When a client is dangerously suicidal, psychotic, homicidal, or otherwise dangerous to others, the counselor has to break confidentiality and call on other mental health professionals who can determine whether involuntary treatment is necessary. The counselor is also legally bound to report cases of child abuse or to testify in court when summoned. If a counselor is in doubt about the necessity of breaking client confidences, consultation with other professionals is recommended, with action taken only after careful deliberation. Counselors inform clients of the limitations of confidentiality during the informed consent process.

In public schools, a student's behavior may become so disruptive or debilitating, the learning problems so acute, or the home situation so poor that administrators may decide that psychological intervention is necessary to determine administrative or therapeutic action. In such cases, the student and family lose the right to choose. School counselors work closely with school psychologists in deciding the best psychological intervention strategies for the student in trouble (Gibson & Mitchell, 2007).

When clients disclose that they have a contagious or life-threatening disease (such as AIDS), counselors may be justified in warning unprotected third parties when clients have not informed and refuse to inform partners about their condition (see Standard B.2.b).

Counselors must protect the confidentiality of clients who are minors or adults who cannot give informed consent (Standards B.5.a., B.5.b., and B.5.c.). Counselors inform parents and legal guardians about the confidential nature of the counseling relationship. In addition, counselors need to help minors or adults incapable of giving consent understand how information will be shared and used by others.

Counselors' Professional Responsibilities

Awareness of Degree of Competence

The ACA Code of Ethics addresses the need for counselors to be aware of their level of competence. They must not attempt to counsel individuals who have problems that require knowledge or skills beyond the counselors' qualifications (Standard C.2.a). If a counselor is uncertain about his or her ability to work with a particular client or becomes uncertain after seeing the client a few times, the counselor should consult with another professional or refer the client to another counselor.

Counselor Impairment

Counselors work with clients on a variety of significant and heart-wrenching issues, such as sexual abuse, grief and loss, and natural disasters to name a few (Kocet, 2006). Almost every counselor will experience stress from working with clients with severe and complex issues. Unfortunately, counselors may become impaired when they are unable to efficiently cope with stress and become unable to perform their responsibilities appropriately and effectively (Corey et al., 2007).

The ACA Code of Ethics directs counselors to seek assistance with problems that reach the level of professional impairment. "Counselors are alert to the signs of impairment from their own physical, mental, or emotional problems and refrain from offering or providing professional services when such impairment is likely to harm a client or others" (Standard C.2.g.). In addition, the Code asserts the need for counselors to assist other counselors in recognizing their own professional impairment and to provide consultation and assistance when warranted.

LEGAL ISSUES

Privileged Communication

Both counselors and clients have certain legal rights, responsibilities, and limitations. *Privileged communication* is defined as "the legal right which exists by statute and which protects the client from having his confidences revealed publicly from the witness stand during legal proceedings without his permission" (Shah, 1969, p. 57). Basically, this means that a judge cannot order privileged information to be revealed in court. Privileged communication is meant to preserve a well-established relationship so that the client can talk freely without fear of disclosure in court. Privileged communication exists in the following relationships: attorney–client, physician–patient, mental health provider–client, husband–wife, and clergy–parishioner.

Counselors should have a clear understanding of the difference between ethical confidentiality and the confidentiality involved in privileged communication. Privileged communication is specific to counselors testifying in a court of law. It is a legal right granted to clients by a state law, rather than a right guaranteed by a professional association's ethical code. Privileged communication is the *client's* right, not the counselor's.

The general rule is that counselors must keep client disclosures confidential; however, *exceptions* to this rule occur frequently in the course of counseling (Glosoff, Herlihy, & Spence, 2000; Remley & Herlihy, 2007) and include the following:

When a Client Is a Danger to Self or Others

If a counselor determines that a client has the potential of harming another person, the counselor must take steps necessary to prevent harm. In the now-famous case of *Tarasoff v. Regents of the University of California* (1976), a client at the university student health services told his psychologist that he intended to kill his fiancée. The psychologist contacted the police, who questioned the client and then released him as not dangerous. Subsequently, the client killed his fiancée. The fiancée's parents sued the board of regents and the employees of the university. The suit was dismissed in a lower court, but the California Supreme Court ruled in favor of the parents, saying that the psychologist should have warned the client's fiancée.

This issue stirred controversy throughout the mental health community. Many believe that the police overrode a psychologist's opinion about a psychological condition that was beyond the expertise of the police. Furthermore, the police, not the psychologist, should be responsible for warning a potential victim. In that way, policing stays in the hands of the police, and therapy remains with mental health providers.

In any case, when a client is dangerous to others, intervention by the authorities is necessary if the client is unresponsive to treatment. Because states vary considerably regarding the legal "duty to warn," counselors should know their state laws and whether they must warn, to whom a warning should be given, and under what circumstances (Glosoff et al., 2000, p. 457). Consultation with other professionals is suggested when counselors are in doubt about their legal responsibility.

When a counselor determines that a client is suicidal, the counselor must take specific steps to protect the client from harm to self. The first step is evaluating the client's level of risk of suicide. Clients who are at high risk of suicide have frequent and intense suicidal *ideation* (ideas or images); a suicide plan that is specific, lethal, and available; few social supports; questionable self-control; and other risk factors (Granello & Granello, 2007, p. 240). Under these circumstances, the client needs psychiatric hospitalization. All states have legal procedures for mental health professionals to initiate involuntary psychiatric assessment and hospitalization for a client. Counselors should have knowledge of their specific state laws with regard to the steps involved in protecting clients from harm to self.

Suspected Abuse of a Child or Vulnerable Adult

Counselors are faced with a dilemma when clients, in confidence, reveal that abuse of a child or vulnerable adult is occurring either to them or to someone else. The counselor must report the abuse to child protective services. Laws in all 50 states and the District of Columbia require that a person who suspects child abuse must report it, usually to child protective services, although states vary in detail. Failure to report child abuse is a misdemeanor.

Child abuse includes physical injury, mental injury, sexual abuse, and neglect. The person reporting is given immunity from any civil or criminal liability for breaking confidentiality. When teachers suspect child abuse, it is their legal responsibility to report it to the child protective agency; the counselor should not do the reporting for teachers. This arrangement frees the counselor to develop a counseling relationship with the child and the parents after the reporting is done.

Legal Disputes (Malpractice)

The most frequently cited category of exceptions to confidentiality is disputes between client and counselor (Glosoff et al., 2000). This refers to situations in which a client files a complaint, either in court or with licensing boards, against his or her counselor for practicing in a manner that leads to injury to the client (Remley & Herlihy, 2007). When this occurs, the law automatically waives the privilege associated with counseling relationships. The following ethical issues pose the highest risks of malpractice lawsuits:

- Failure to protect clients from harm to self (e.g., attempted or completed suicide) (McAdams & Foster, 2000)
- Violation of clients' personal rights (e.g., sexual relationships with clients) (Remley & Herlihy, 2007)
- Failure to protect others from clients (failure to protect someone who is in danger)

Counselors can protect themselves from malpractice suits by becoming aware of and abiding by all the preventive measures possible. The following are some of the numerous suggestions offered by Corey et al. (2007): practicing within one's professional competence; honoring confidentiality; issuing a formal disclosure stating the limitations of expertise; consulting with other professionals whenever necessary; staying aware of informed consent laws; declaring the pros and cons of treatment approaches; stating, before treatment, fee and fee collection policies; following necessary termination processes; avoiding dual relationships; and keeping accurate, detailed records.

Court-Ordered Disclosures

Counselors can be subpoenaed and required to testify in court about privileged communications with clients. This often happens in child custody cases or cases in which psychological evaluations were ordered by the court. When subpoenaed to release confidential client information, counselors may ask the court to waive the requirement and then explain to the court the potential harm that could be done to the counseling relationship. If the judge still requires the counselor to disclose, only essential information should be revealed (Standard B.2.d.; Remley & Herlihy, 2007).

Client Waiver of the Privilege

Because privileged communication is a client's right, the client has the right to waive the privilege and allow counselors to disclose client information to others. This usually happens when a client asks his or her counselor to provide information about the counseling relationship to a specific third party (Remley & Herlihy, 2007), such as a psychiatrist, medical doctor, attorney, or others.

Minors' Rights

The ACA Code of Ethics outlines the need for counselors to protect the rights of clients who are minors (Standards B.5.a., B.5.b., and B.5.c.). Children and adolescents have been granted the rights to informed consent and privileged communication in counseling, but in practice, these rights remain confusing and complex. To compound the confusion, minors' rights and responsibilities in school differ from those in the community. Thus, minors' rights to seek treatment and to be accorded confidentiality in schools and in the community are discussed separately here.

Minors' Rights in School Counseling

Although opinions in the literature differ, the general consensus is that children have a right to voluntary counseling in schools, even without parental permission. When parents enroll their children in school, they know that their children will be participating in a number of obligatory and optional services, and one of those optional services is counseling (Remley & Herlihy, 2007). Schmidt (1987) presented the case of a fourth grader in counseling whose mother objected to the counseling sessions on religious grounds. The director of counseling in the district concluded that the school ethically and legally should continue counseling if the child wished to continue, even if the parent objected. Acceptance of children asking for and receiving counseling in schools has increased because of the recognition in child abuse laws that children need protection from parents who harm or neglect them.

The American School Counseling Association (ASCA) published *Ethical Standards for School Counselors,* focusing specifically on counseling children in the schools (ASCA, 2004). Regarding informed consent, the ASCA Ethical Standards for School Counselors state that professional school counselors must "inform students of the purposes, goals, techniques, and rules of procedure under which they may receive counseling at or before the time when the counseling relationship is entered" (Standard A.2.a.). When young children are allowed the same opportunities for informed consent and free choice that are given to older children and adults, their involvement in counseling and their sense of responsibility for their own behavior can increase. Relationships among teachers, parents, counselors, and children can also improve.

Managing confidentiality with minors in a school is often more complex than counseling children in other settings. School counselors must balance their ethical and legal responsibilities to their client (the child), the client's parents, and the school system (Glosoff, 2002). According to ASCA ethical standards, school counselors must keep client information confidential unless disclosure is required to prevent clear and imminent danger to the student or others or when legal requirements demand that confidential information be revealed (Standard A.2.b.). School counselors need to inform children about the limits of confidentiality. Some issues that may compel counselors to breach confidentiality regardless of the child's preference include suicide risk, use of drugs, threat of harm to others, and signs of serious mental illness. If a child does not want confidential information disclosed, the counselor can discuss the matter with the child to discover the reasons for the objection, the information that is disputed, and the possible consequences of giving out that information.

In many cases, school counselors find it important to involve parents in family consultation or family counseling because children's problems generally are part of family interactions. Most parents are cooperative and pleased that counseling is available, but some parents are concerned about their children seeing counselors on their own and about confidentiality. Counselors who meet with parents to discuss the value of such an approach can usually reduce parental doubts and resistance.

According to the ASCA Ethical Standards for School Counselors (2004), professional school counselors maintain and secure the records necessary for providing services to students as required by laws, regulations, institutional procedures, and confidentiality guidelines; however, the school counselor keeps sole possession of the records separate from students' general educational records (Standards A.8.a. and A.8.b.). Although a student's school records are open to parental review, counseling records are exempt.

Minors' Rights in Community Counseling

Throughout the country, minors generally must have parental consent or must be ordered by the court to see a counselor in the community. According to Lawrence and Robinson Kurpius (2000), exceptions to this law may vary from state to state and may include mature minors (usually those over age 16), emancipated minors (those over 16 who are self-sufficient and living away from home), minors whose lives are at risk (parents must be informed as soon as possible), minors who seek drug treatment, minors with sexually transmitted diseases, and minors over 12 who have been sexually assaulted.

Like school counselors, counselors who provide counseling services to children in the community need to keep client information confidential with the appropriate ethical and legal exceptions. The ACA Code of Ethics (2005) states that counselors must inform parents and legal guardians about the role of counselors and about the confidential nature of the counseling relationship (Standard B.5.b.).

In certain states, special rules pertain to minors of divorced parents: Consent is required of the custodial parent only, and information is released to noncustodial parents only with the custodial parent's consent.

RESEARCH AND PROGRAM EVALUATION

A professional group offering a public service has a responsibility to assess the quality of the service, the degree to which it is helping the public, and its overall effectiveness. In counseling, these assessments generally take the form of research and program evaluations, which differ in their contributions to assessment of the profession. *Research* studies the effectiveness of counseling theories and techniques with clients. *Program evaluation* studies the usefulness and efficiency of a counseling program in the community from a practical and budgetary standpoint. Program evaluators, who usually are practicing counselors or counselor educators, determine the utility and efficiency of programs and attach values to their findings. They assess programs through questionnaires, surveys, evaluative interviews, and observations. The main questions that they address are, is the program serving the intended populations? and is the program efficient and effective? (Posavac & Carey, 2002). Decisions about initiating or changing programs arise from evaluations. At times, *accountability* becomes part of the evaluation. For example, directors may be asked to justify whether their programs warrant funding with taxpayers' monies from state or local budgeting agencies.

Training on how to conduct research and program evaluation is included in an effective counseling curriculum. Evaluation and accountability procedures, policies, and problems fit well in supervised internship experiences. Each of these assessment activities, however, raises professional and ethical issues.

Counselors who conduct research or program evaluation need to understand the possible negative impact of such activities on clients. The ACA Code of Ethics (2005) states that counselors who conduct research with human participants are responsible for their welfare and should take reasonable precautions to avoid causing them psychological or emotional harm (Standard G.1.d.).

Clients who are asked to participate in research or program evaluation have the right to be fully informed about the proposed study and the right to decide whether they want to participate. Failure to honor these rights is unethical (Corey et al., 2007). Similarly, it is unethical to deceive research subjects by withholding pertinent material or by otherwise manipulating them so that they are more apt to participate in a study. An example of unethical deception occurs when a family therapist, to determine progress in later sessions, tapes families in the first session without their knowledge.

INTERNET COUNSELING

The rapidly increasing use of Internet counseling—also called *online counseling, e-therapy, e-counseling,* or *cyber counseling*—has presented new and complex ethical challenges (Remley & Herlihy, 2007). Internet counseling generally refers to mental health services provided online. The majority of online counseling takes place via e-mail (Stofle, 2001), but services may also be offered by instant messaging and video conferencing.

Ethical dilemmas associated with Internet counseling are many and include (a) difficulties in maintaining client confidentiality and rights to privacy; (b) increased opportunities for counselor and client anonymity, resulting in potential misrepresentation of counselor credentials and client symptoms; (c) difficulties in determining the appropriateness of online counseling for particular client problems; (d) inability to effectively deal with client crisis online; and (e) potential for miscommunication due to lack of non-verbals and the time delay inherent in online communication (Cook & Doyle, 2002; Remley & Herlihy, 2007; Rochlen, Zack, & Speyer, 2004).

Professional counseling associations have developed guidelines and codes to address the ethical issues of Internet counseling. The National Board for Certified Counselors (NBCC) and the Center for Credentialing and Education (CCE) created a document entitled *The Practice of Internet Counseling* that contains a statement of principles for guiding the evolving practice of Internet counseling (NBCC & CCE, 2001). CACREP (2001) focused attention on the appropriate use of technology in the 2001 Standards. In addition, the 2005 ACA Code of Ethics greatly expanded its codes on technology applications, broadening the ethical use of technology in research, record keeping, and the provision of services to consumers (ACA, 2005).

Regarding confidentiality, the ACA Code directs Internet counselors to use encrypted Web sites and e-mail communications when possible to help ensure confidentiality (Standard A.12.g.). Furthermore, counselors must inform clients when encryption measures are not possible.

The ACA Code of Ethics (2005) is clear about the need for counselors to determine whether online counseling is appropriate for a particular client. The Code states that counselors should determine whether clients are intellectually, emotionally, and physically able to use online counseling (Standard A.12.b.). When Internet counseling is inappropriate for prospective clients, counselors should encourage them to seek counseling through a traditional face-to-face counseling relationship.

SUMMARY

Ethical codes are designed to protect the client and to monitor the profession. Ethical codes focus on issues that involve the counselor–client relationship, such as dual relationships, sexual involvement, and counselor biases; clients' rights, such as informed consent and confidentiality; and counselor responsibilities, such as competency awareness, responsibility to the workplace, and self-monitoring.

Legal considerations involve the issue of privileged communication and actions that counselors must take when a client is a danger to self or others, when there is suspected abuse of a child or vulnerable adult, when legal disputes occur, and for court-ordered disclosures.

Certain ethical and legal codes protect minors' rights of free choice and informed consent and confidentiality. However, minors' rights and responsibilities in school may differ from those in the community.

Counselors have a professional responsibility to assess the quality of their services. A primary way of doing this is through program evaluations that measure the usefulness and efficiency of a program and through research studies that assess the effectiveness of counseling theories and techniques with clients.

The increasing use of Internet counseling has presented new and complex ethical issues. Counselors offering online services need to maintain client confidentiality, represent themselves and their credentials accurately, and refer clients to face-to-face counseling if problems are too complicated for online counseling. Professional organizations strongly suggest that counselors carefully abide by the ethical standards for online counseling.

PROJECTS AND ACTIVITIES

1. Write or telephone the president or executive secretary of your regional or state professional association, and ask about procedures for reporting unethical behavior of association members. Find out what sanctions, if any, can be applied. Also explore whether your state department of education has policies on unethical behavior by school counselors.

2. Organize a panel of counselors with master's and doctoral degrees in counseling who are working in private practice, schools, colleges, and community agencies. Ask them to discuss professional licensure and certification.

3. Select several agencies with different emphases, such as a child guidance clinic, a halfway house, a crisis clinic, and a public school. Find out whether they employ any paraprofessionals. If so, compare their training programs and duties. How do these duties compare with those of professional persons?

4. In the following three cases, assume that you are a school counselor or a licensed community counselor. In each case, write a response indicating what you would say or do. Note: Cases A, B, and C were written by Dr. Elvet G. Jones, Professor Emeritus of Psychology at Western Washington University–Bellingham.

- Case A: A principal (or agency head) who was once a professional counselor confers with you and tells you that because drug problems in your area have now reached "epidemic proportions," it would be wise for you to let him know about any client who comes to you with such a problem. What do you say to this principal (or agency head)?

- Case B: A 17-year-old comes to see you for the first time. He appears very depressed. He tells you that on May 16, his 18th birthday, he plans to commit suicide; he also tells you in great detail why and how he intends to do so. He furthermore says that he is telling you this because he wants to be sure that no one is accused of doing him in and that because he does not belong to any church and has no priest or minister, you are the only person he is telling. In light of your role as a counselor and considering the ACA Code of Ethics, how do you proceed in this case?

- Case C: The personnel director at a large, local business calls you about a former client, now 19 years of age. She apparently is on a trip out of the country with her entire family for at least a month and cannot be reached, but she is being seriously considered for a good job, and the director wants to make a decision within 30 days. What the director wants from you is an evaluation of the woman's personal and emotional adjustment. How do you respond to this request for information that could lead to this young woman's getting a good job?

5. Search the Internet for online counseling services from a mental health counselor. Does the site offer information as suggested by the ACA Code of Ethics? Identify which ethical issues it addresses (e.g., confidentiality, informed consent, counselor competence). How would you assess the site in terms of the ethical guidelines?

CHAPTER 3

The Effective Counselor

What does it take to become an effective counselor? Many researchers and authors have studied the profession to identify specific traits and behaviors of counselors who are capable and competent. First and foremost, an effective counselor has a positive, accepting view of other people (Young, 2005). Effective counselors are well-adjusted individuals with good self-esteem who are committed to their own continued growth and development. They have the personal qualities that enable them to develop trusting counseling relationships with clients.

In addition to personal characteristics, effective counselors have the knowledge and skills necessary to guide or encourage clients during the counseling process. Effective counselors are knowledgeable about the major counseling theoretical orientations: humanistic, cognitive–behavioral, psychodynamic, brief, and constructivist approaches. They are aware of the different helping strategies inherent in each of these orientations, and they select strategies that fit their theoretical orientation and the needs of their clients. In addition, counselors use a variety of listening skills to establish a trusting relationship that encourages clients to clarify problems and begin self-exploration.

After studying this chapter, you will

- Have knowledge of the personal qualities of effective counselors.
- Be acquainted with fundamental counseling theories and strategies.
- Learn about the basic interviewing skills and techniques of effective counselors.

PERSONAL QUALITIES

Effective counselors are well-integrated individuals committed to their own continued growth. They tend to be open to new experiences, aware of their own motivations, values, vulnerabilities, and unmet needs. They know when to seek counseling themselves to maintain growth and meaning in life. These qualities enable counselors to empathize with and support clients struggling through the often-painful steps of self-examination and self-exploration necessary for change and development.

In the 1950s, Carl Rogers (1951, 1957) proposed that counselors establish effective relationships with their clients that would lead to client self-actualization. He presented three core characteristics essential to an effective counselor–client relationship:

1. Empathy
2. Congruence (genuineness)
3. Unconditional positive regard (acceptance)

Empathy refers to one's ability to recognize, perceive, and feel the emotions of another. Rogers (1957) described empathy as sensing "the client's private world as if it were your own, but without ever losing the 'as if' quality." Empathy enables counselors to understand a client's inner world and convey that understanding to the client (Gladding, 2007).

Congruence, also known as *genuineness,* refers to the basic integrity of counselors that permits them to be authentic and honest with clients. Counselors are congruent when they are "freely and deeply" themselves in the counseling relationship—when they are transparent and give up roles and facades (Rogers, 1980).

Unconditional positive regard involves warm, accepting, and nonjudgmental attitudes toward clients. It means that the counselor experiences a positive, acceptant attitude toward whatever the client is at that moment—that there are no *conditions* of acceptance (Rogers, 1957).

Carkhuff (1969, 1971) proposed two additional core characteristics: respect and immediacy. *Respect* refers to the counselor's high regard for a client's worth as a person. *Immediacy* refers to the counselor's sensitivity to what the client is experiencing at the moment. It also refers to the overall relationship between counselor and client in the "here and now."

Counseling theorists have presented other qualities that also contribute to an effective counselor, such as self-awareness, interpersonal awareness, objectivity, personal integrity, open-mindedness, flexibility, and trustworthiness (Corey, Corey, & Callanan, 2007). *Self-awareness* refers to a counselor's understanding and acceptance of his or her own feelings, attitudes, and values; recognition and acceptance of his or her own vulnerabilities and personal inadequacies; and awareness of the impact that these have on others.

Interpersonal awareness, objectivity, and *personal integrity* refer to the counselor's ability to understand a client's struggles and pain. Counselors do not overidentify with or become oversolicitous of their clients, nor do they underestimate and ignore their clients' feelings. Counselors who are aware of their own inadequacies, vulnerabilities, and defenses do not project their own unresolved emotions on their clients; they are able to accept clients' emotional reactions toward them objectively. They are also aware of their position of power with vulnerable, dependent clients and do not abuse it by attempting to control or manipulate client behavior. In addition, they are comfortable with intimacy, but are aware of appropriate boundaries in the counseling relationship.

Open-minded counselors are open to new ideas and experiences that stimulate personal and professional growth. They are alert to preconceived notions that they may have about a client's experiences, feelings, and values, and they are accepting of a client's views that are different from their own. Counselors who are open minded and unbiased tend to maintain clearer and more accurate perceptions of clients' feelings and actions.

Counselors who are *flexible* are not bound to one theoretical view, nor do they impose one set of techniques on all clients at all times in all contexts. They are thus able to work with a wide range of clients and client problems.

Trustworthy counselors hold confidences shared by clients. They do not deceive clients by misrepresenting their areas of expertise or their theoretical views about counseling, nor do they experiment with new or untried techniques outside their areas of expertise. If a counselor wants to try a new technique within his or her specialty, the counselor should first get the consent of the client.

Effective counselors are also aware of value differences between themselves and their clients when the clients present value conflicts. Counselors help clients seek resolutions that are consistent with the clients' self-growth and effective interactions in society. Counselors do not impose their own values on clients.

Awareness of Diverse Cultures

Counselors should become aware of their own cultural values and beliefs and the ways that they differ from those held by others, especially their clients (Sue & Sue, 2003). Counselors face situations, customs, and worldviews that differ from their own that could affect counseling effectiveness. Undoubtedly, counselor identity affects counseling intervention, and therefore should be understood in relation to both self and others (Baruth & Manning, 2007).

The ACA Code of Ethics (2005) requires counselors to be culturally competent and to actively attempt to understand the diverse cultural backgrounds of the clients that they serve. Counselors demonstrate awareness of diverse cultures (recognizing both one's own and others' cultural identities), acquire and use knowledge about others' cultures, and incorporate counseling skills in a culturally respectful manner (Eriksen & Kress, 2005; Frame & Williams, 2005; Kocet, 2006; Welfel, 2006). Standard A.2.c. of the ACA Code addresses the importance of counselors communicating in a manner that can be understood by clients as developmentally and culturally appropriate (ACA, 2005, p. 4).

Effective counselors are open and responsive to the different socialization and cultural processes and the different views about human nature that exist among the diverse cultures in our multicultural society.

Personal Growth and Professional Development

Many people now entering the counseling profession have probably had some sort of counseling themselves. A successful therapeutic experience enables counselors to understand the process of growth and transformation expected in a counseling relationship. If personal counseling were an expected part of their professional development, counselors-in-training would more likely become aware of their own limitations and strengths; they would experience the process of delving into themselves, which could help them relate to clients in more authentic or nonexploitative ways. By learning how to recognize their own unmet needs, counselors-in-training prepare themselves to deal with their own reactions when they are working with clients. All counselors would benefit from intermittent or periodic counseling as they experience transitions, losses, or conflicts in their own lives. Maintaining self-awareness is necessary to remain effective with clients.

Many opportunities exist for counselors to expand their self-awareness and learn new perspectives about relating to clients. Regular supervision with an experienced counselor and case presentations within a supervision group can help counselors become aware of personal issues and acquaint them with counseling approaches different from their own. In addition, professional development through conferences and workshops can help counselors stay current with the best practices in the profession, as well as receive continuing education credit. Professional associations offer a multitude of workshops at their annual conferences, in addition to continuing education opportunities online.

Avoiding Burnout

Most counselors who experience short periods of heightened stress are aware of their condition, are able to work through difficult periods, and can manage to function effectively. If counselors are unaware of or unable to cope with the stresses of their lives, if they continue feeling anxious and become worn out, and if they become ineffective with their clients, they are suffering from *burnout*.

When burnout occurs, counselors feel overwhelmed and exhausted, with little energy left for their clients. They may begin to feel cynical and "manifest negative attitudes about self and work" (Remley & Herlihy, 2007, p. 161). If counselors do not heed and attend to these symptoms, *impairment* is likely to occur. Impaired counselors are counselors who may be unaware of, and unable to cope with or resolve, emotional stress, resulting in an inability to relate to clients in an effective manner and a likelihood that their ineffectiveness may harm clients. At this stage, since client welfare is at stake, counselors may have to suspend their professional responsibilities until they regain their equilibrium. The ACA Code of Ethics (2005) is very clear on this point:

> Counselors are alert to the signs of impairment from their own physical, mental, or emotional problems and refrain from offering or providing professional services when such impairment is likely to harm a client or others. They seek assistance for problems that reach the level of professional impairment, and, if necessary, they limit, suspend, or terminate their professional responsibilities until such time it is determined that they may safely resume their work. (Standard C.2.g)

Various conditions lead to counselor burnout or impairment:

- Ongoing feelings of frustration and unresolved personal issues while working with clients
- A highly demanding, poor work environment
- Difficulty with unresolved personal conflicts or crises

Corey (2005) challenges those practitioners who think that counselor burnout is just part of the job. He contends that many counselors who suffer from burnout or impairment tend to blame outside conditions in their lives rather than focusing on their own personal strengths, resources, and limitations. He comments that such an attitude often contributes to general feelings of hopelessness and powerlessness. He believes that it is essential that counselors recognize that they can be instrumental in bringing about changes, both in their environment and in themselves.

Effective counselors must be aware of their own countertransference, which inevitably arises during counseling. *Countertransference* refers to a counselor's projected emotional reaction to or behavior toward the client; unless resolved adequately, countertransference can be detrimental to the counseling relationship and lead to counselor burnout (Gladding, 2007).

Effective counselors notice signs of potential burnout and take the following steps to alter the situation:

- Confront and attempt to improve stressful working conditions
- Evaluate whether personal issues are interfering with counseling relationships
- Learn their limits and set limits with others
- Engage in professional consultation
- Attend professional workshops to sharpen competencies
- Participate in professional growth activities
- Seek professional counseling
- Broaden interests beyond work

Counselors can establish regular case conferences with peers and attend counseling workshops where they can share strategies about working with difficult client problems. Regarding stressful working conditions, counselors can also discuss with colleagues ways of reducing overload. At the same time, they can educate heads of agencies or supervisors about the consequences of counselor burnout, including its impact on client welfare and agency effectiveness. Counselors can discuss with their supervisors countertransference issues, doubts, or uncertainties about a counseling approach, as well as concerns about taking on too much responsibility for clients. In addition, such conferences can help counselors resolve personal issues, doubts about themselves and their competencies, or personal conflicts that are impeding their work.

PROFESSIONAL COMPETENCIES

Professional competencies considered essential for counselors fall into four major categories: (a) knowledge about counseling theories and strategies, (b) interviewing skills, (c) assessment and diagnostic skills, and (d) sound ethical judgment.

Knowledge about Counseling Theories and Strategies

It is important for counselors to be aware of the differences among the various theoretical approaches and the value of using these approaches with different client circumstances. It is necessary for counselors to learn all major theories before they decide to specialize in one theoretical orientation, and they must learn the various strategies that these theories propose (see chapter 6). Humanists, for example, use strategies to increase clients' insights about themselves and their environment. Among the humanists, Rogerians use interviewing and relationship skills to help clients self-actualize, and Gestaltists use strategies such as visual imagery, body work, or confrontation to provoke feeling responses in clients. Cognitive–behaviorists use strategies such as reinforcement, social modeling, cognitive restructuring, and reframing to correct clients' distorted perceptions about the nature of their problems. Psychodynamic therapists help clients integrate conscious and unconscious processes by helping them become aware of the dynamic, intrapsychic processes underlying their perceptions and interactions.

Although counselors and therapists may eventually specialize in applying certain strategies based on one particular theoretical view, many counselors tend to be *eclectic* and draw upon techniques from a variety of theoretical orientations, depending on the nature of the problem, varying client characteristics, the social context and environment, and the counselor's work setting (Cheston, 2000; McClure et al., 2005). Although an eclectic approach allows counselors more flexibility, practitioners without a firm theoretical foundation—often the case with inexperienced or minimally trained counselors or therapists—can be dangerous. Such persons are apt to be injudicious in using techniques that go beyond their expertise and training; and when inappropriately applied, techniques that are otherwise potentially beneficial to clients can become damaging. Counselors can avoid the dangers inherent in an eclectic approach by integrating various techniques into a theoretical model (see chapter 6).

An *integrative* theoretical approach is acquired over time as counselors develop a broad and comprehensive understanding of counseling theories and strategies. Through practice, as well as participation in periodic postgraduate training programs, counselors gradually draw on techniques from the different theoretical approaches that are consistent with their fundamental assumptions about human growth and development. They are cautious about using a technique unless they have acquired sufficient training and expertise, but they are willing to take intensive training to learn new strategies that fit their own theoretical model (see chapter 6).

Effective counselors also know when to refer clients to specialists—when client problems require techniques that go beyond their expertise. For example, a counselor who thinks that a particular client needs to explore deeper childhood issues involving sexual trauma would refer the client to a therapist who specializes in treating childhood trauma. Similarly, a counselor whose client has agoraphobic reactions might refer the client to a cognitive therapist specializing in the treatment of phobias.

Interviewing Skills

A significant part of counselor training is the development of effective interviewing skills—a basic component of the counseling process. Several authors have been most active in describing the types and uses of interviewing skills that contribute to an effective counseling process (Egan, 2007; Ivey & Ivey, 2007; Young, 2005). Most emphasize the counseling relationship and present specific interviewing skills that can be taught to counselors.

Listening and Attending Skills: Establishing a Relationship

Listening and attending skills, though important throughout the counseling session, are particularly necessary during the beginning stage because they are central to establishing a relationship (see Table 3.1). When counselors listen intently, clients get the feeling that what they are saying is important. They then feel encouraged to talk more about themselves—the first step in self-exploration. The counselor who is listening attentively is less likely to make premature judgments about the client or the client's problem or to give premature advice—interferences that would spoil the counseling process.

Listening and attending skills serve two different but related functions: The counselor uses *listening skills* to gain information and encourage clients to talk about themselves, as well as to help clients express how they perceive themselves and their problems (open and closed questions and encouraging). In contrast, the counselor uses *attending skills* to understand and clarify a client's feelings and to convey the counselor's feelings of understanding to the client (paraphrasing, reflection of feeling, and summarization). Counselors

TABLE 3.1
The Basic Listening Sequence

Skill	Description	Function in Interview
Open questions	"What": facts "How": process or feelings "Why": reasons "Could": general picture	Brings out major data and facilitates conversation.
Closed questions	Usually begin with "do," "is," "are," and can be answered in a few words.	Quickly obtains specific data; closes off lengthy answers.
Encouraging	Repeating back to client a few of the client's main words.	Encourages detailed elaboration of the specific words and their meanings.
Paraphrasing	Repeating back the essence of a client's words and thoughts using the client's own main words.	Acts as promoter for discussion; shows understanding; checks on clarity of counselor understanding.
Reflection of feeling	Selective attention to emotional content of interview.	Results in clarification of emotion underlying key facts; promotes discussion of feelings.
Summarization	Repeating back of client's facts and feelings (and reasons) to client in an organized form.	Clarifies where the interview has come to date; useful in beginning interview, periodically throughout the session, and to close session.

who attend closely to their clients also use appropriate eye contact, body language, and tone of voice (Ivey & Ivey, 2007; Ivey et al., 2007).

When using listening and attending skills from a multicultural perspective, counselors shift the focus from facilitating client self-expression or self-understanding to facilitating client understanding of self in a situational context. Counselors should listen for family and contextual issues that affect client expression of self (Ivey et al., 2007). Attending skills, for example, require an awareness of what is appropriate within a client's culture. With some clients, for example, direct eye contact is personally or culturally inappropriate, the use of body language is different, and vocal tone may vary (Ivey & Ivey, 2007).

Facilitative Skills: Influencing Skills and Strategies

Once the relationship has developed, additional skills are necessary to help clients explore ways to change behavior. Ivey and Ivey's (2007) *influencing skills* allow counselors to help clients more deeply explore their problems and take actions that will lead to change (see Table 3.2). Three general influencing techniques are confrontation, focusing, and reflection of meaning. These techniques help inspire and empower clients to change undesirable attitudes and behaviors and alter their interactions in detrimental environments. Although influencing skills are meant to encourage the client to take action, counselors should not allow their own needs to interfere. In other words, they should not determine for the client what that action should be.

Confrontation is a facilitative tool used to increase client insight and motivation in order to change self-defeating behaviors. Young (2005) describes confrontations as "interventions that point out discrepancies in client beliefs, behaviors, words, or nonverbal messages" (p. 182). The counselor may confront clients when they show persistent discrepancies between what they say and how they behave or when they give mixed or garbled messages about their feelings and actions. The intention of confrontation is to invite clients to face themselves realistically in order to examine behaviors or attitudes that are blocking their growth and development (Egan, 2007; Young, 2005).

Egan (2007) prefers the term *challenge* to *confrontation* in order to avoid the idea of a client–counselor battle. Young (2005) cautions that confrontation, though a powerful tool to elicit change, must always be used judiciously and not used in a harsh, critical manner with a client. Ivey and Ivey (2007) describe effective confrontation as supporting clients while challenging discrepancies or mixed messages in their comments. All authors agree that if confrontations are done in a way that damages self-esteem or humiliates or shames the client, the client's defenses will become even more impenetrable.

Counselors also use *focusing skills* to direct discussion to areas that they believe will improve clients' perspectives about themselves, their problems, and the influence of others in their environment. Counselors usually focus first on their clients and their clients' problems; later, counselors change the focus to others in the clients' lives, to the counselor–client relationship, or to cultural–environmental or contextual (i.e., situational or historical) conditions (Ivey & Ivey, 2007).

In some instances, counselors may find it helpful to refer briefly to their own beliefs and experiences, a technique called *self-disclosure*. Sharing something about themselves can deepen counselor–client relationships or facilitate client insight or action. Counselors

TABLE 3.2
Influencing Skills

Skill	Description	Function in Interview
Interpretation/reframing	Provides an alternative frame of reference from which the client may view a situation. May be drawn from a theory or from one's own personal observations. *Interpretation may be viewed as the core influencing skill.*	Attempts to provide the client with a new way to view the situation. The interpretation provides the client with a clear-cut alternative percep- tion of "reality." This perception may enable a change of view that in turn may result in changes in thoughts, constructs, or behaviors.
Directive	Tells the client what action to take. May be a simple suggestion stated in command form or may be a sophisticated technique from a specific theory.	Clearly indicates to clients what action counselors or therapists wish them to take. The prediction with a directive is that the client will do what is suggested.
Advice/information	Provides suggestions, instructional ideas, homework, advice on how to act, think, or behave.	Used sparingly, may provide client with new and useful information. Specific vocational information is an example of use of this skill.
Self-disclosure	The interviewer shares personal experience from the past or may share present reactions to the client.	Emphasizes counselor "I" state- ments. This skill is closely allied to feedback and may build trust and openness, leading to a more mutual relationship with the client.
Feedback	Provides clients with specific data on how they are seen by the counselor or by others.	Provides concrete data that may help clients realize how others per- ceive behavior and thinking pat- terns, thus enabling an alternative self-perception.
Logical consequences	Shows client the logical outcome of thinking and behavior—if/then.	Provides an alternative frame of reference for the client. This skill helps clients anticipate the conse- quences or results of their actions.
Influencing summary	Summarizes counselor comments; most often used in combination with the attending summarization.	Clarifies what has happened in the interview and summarizes what the therapist has said. This skill is designed to help generalization from the interview to daily life.

might say, "I get angry at my husband at times," or "I, too, had troubles concentrating in college, but I settled down once I picked a major." Some research shows that a small to moderate amount of counselor self-disclosure has a positive effect on clients and the relationship (Barrett & Berman, 2001; Knox et al., 1997). However, counselors must be judicious in the timing, depth, and length of time spent in self-disclosure. The sharing must be directed toward helping the client progress and must not occur because the counselor is anxious about the client's feelings or because the counselor overidentifies with the client.

Link to Theoretical Orientation

Counselors and therapists vary in how they use interviewing skills during counseling sessions, depending on their theoretical orientations (Ivey et al., 2007). All counselors use listening and attending skills, but they differ in the use of questions: Humanists tend not to use questions; cognitive/behaviorists, on the other hand, frequently ask questions. Humanists avoid using reframing skills, whereas cognitive/behaviorists commonly use feedback, interpretation, reframing skills, and confrontation. Psychodynamic therapists primarily use interpretation, with little attempt to encourage clients to apply new insights and learning to daily life.

Assessment Skills

The main purpose of assessment is to gather information that will be useful in planning counseling goals that will guide the helper and client (Young, 2005, p. 200). The assessment process occurs throughout the counseling relationship, but the initial interview with the client contributes important information to counselors. Information can also be gathered through tests, observations, and contact with the client's family, friends, previous mental health providers, and other collateral contacts. Other purposes of the assessment process include

- Determining the client's presenting problem
- Making an accurate diagnosis
- Gathering information to aid in the development of a treatment plan
- Gathering baseline data to measure the client's progress in counseling.
- Determining a client's suitability for a certain treatment program or modality

Sound Ethical Judgment

Effective counselors work with clients in an ethical and professional manner. Although counselors-in-training learn the codes of ethics of professional behavior, the codes give only guidelines. Counselors must rely on their own good judgment in knowing how to use those guidelines. As discussed in chapter 2, counselors must promote the welfare of clients, avoid nonprofessional interactions with current and former clients when possible, avoid sexual or romantic counselor–client interactions, exercise professional and ethical behavior in maintaining confidential relationships, and be aware of signs of professional impairment.

Effective training programs use case studies and case conferences to acquaint students with ethical dilemmas and to give them practice in exercising good judgment. When faced with perplexing ethical dilemmas, effective counselors consult with professional colleagues to help them resolve these dilemmas. Counselors who function best in their professional practice also work at resolving their own unmet needs and learn to cope with their own emotional conflicts. In addition, as discussed earlier, effective counselors recognize that they are ethically responsible for recognizing their own signs of stress and must take steps to deal with or prevent undue stress that could impair their ability to work with clients (ACA, 2005, C.2.g).

PROFESSIONAL COLLABORATION

Making referrals and forming liaisons with other health care agencies has always been an essential part of the counseling practice. This interaction has evolved over the years into collaborative programs in which health care professionals from different agencies share or cluster their facilities, not only to cut down on costs, but also to encourage collaboration among health care professionals.

The need for health care professionals to work collaboratively has escalated in recent years because of ever more complex sources of stress—psychological, economic, social, and physical—that affect people's lives. In the community, comprehensive neighborhood health care clinics combine into one facility the various services provided by counselors, social workers, rehabilitation counselors, physicians, and psychiatrists. Community mental health agencies provide broad-spectrum mental health services to children, adults, and families in both inpatient and outpatient settings; partner with local substance abuse treatment programs to address co-occurring mental health/substance abuse problems; and work with hospitals to address clients' medical needs.

In a special issue of *Professional School Counseling* on collaboration between school counselors and community mental health workers, Sink (2000) comments: "Our profession can forge proactive links among schools, homes, and communities by embracing 'comprehensive' multifaceted school-wide and community-wide models" (p. ii). In response to research indicating the value of collaborative programs in preventing violence in the schools, Cunningham and Sandu (2000) proposed a school–community team of school counselors, community mental health workers, law enforcement agencies, churches, and other community-based providers to develop and implement a comprehensive violence prevention program. In a similar vein, Luongo (2000) recommended that families in which children or youth are using drugs, are victims of abuse, or are violent can best be served by the integrated efforts of school counselors, child welfare workers, juvenile justice personnel, and behavioral health services workers.

Although college and university counseling centers have typically kept networking efforts on campus, many centers are beginning to extend off campus to connect with community health care providers. Almost half of colleges and universities with counseling centers offer psychiatric services on campus (Gallagher, 2006). Palladino (2005) described how university–urban school collaboration is useful in improving elementary students' career awareness and self-awareness; enhancing collaborative relationships among university faculty, graduate students, and school professionals; facilitating graduate student professional development and training; and initiating collaborative research. Most notable has been the emergence of collaborative programs in which schools, colleges, and community agencies have arranged to share the same facility, or to form a cluster of facilities, in order to work together more closely.

THE WHOLE COUNSELOR

Counselors-in-practice become effective when they are able to integrate personality characteristics, personal growth experiences, and professional competencies into a cohesive counseling approach consistent with their values in life. In other words, the effective counselor cannot be wholly described through lists of personal characteristics or professional competencies. Counselors are effective when they integrate personal attributes and professional competencies in an ethical manner that benefits clients. They are not self-satisfied, intransigent, or egocentric about who they are and what they know. Instead, they are open and flexible to new ideas and new techniques based on sound judgment and moral principles that safeguard client welfare, all the while resisting impulsive shifts in pursuit of current fads.

SUMMARY

Effective counselors are well-integrated individuals committed to their own continued growth and development. They have personal qualities and professional competencies that enable them to develop trusting counseling relationships that foster mutual counselor–client interactions and encourage therapeutic developmental changes.

The personal qualities of effective counselors include warmth, congruency, and positive regard, supplemented by self-awareness, open-mindedness, flexibility, objectivity, trustworthiness, and personal integrity.

Professional competencies acquired by effective counselors include the knowledge and skills necessary to help them guide or encourage clients during the counseling process. Effective counselors are knowledgeable about the major counseling theoretical orientations: humanistic, cognitive–behavioral, psychodynamic, brief, and constructivist approaches. They are aware of the different helping strategies inherent in each of these orientations, and they select strategies that fit their theoretical orientation and the needs of their clients. In addition, counselors use a variety of listening skills to establish a trusting relationship that encourages clients to clarify problems and begin self-exploration.

Effective counselors abide by ethical standards that ensure their clients' integrity and welfare: maintaining client confidentiality, refraining from imposing their own values on clients, and refusing to exploit clients to satisfy the counselor's needs. To remain effective, mature counselors engage in self-growth activities and personal counseling intermittently, thus maintaining and enhancing their self-awareness.

PROJECTS AND ACTIVITIES

1. Interview a professional counselor and ask what he or she believes are important characteristics in effective counselors. What is the counselor's theoretical approach and what techniques does he or she use most often?

2. Role-play two beginning interviews: one in which the client is nontalkative and the other in which a client with the same presenting problem is talkative. Note the differences in listening skills required.

3. Discuss and differentiate how counselors use listening and attending skills and influencing skills.

4. Identify and list personal and self-growth activities that may help counselors increase their effectiveness in counseling.

5. In small groups in class, discuss your cultural heritage (e.g., culture, race, ethnicity, and religion) and discuss how who you are and how you relate to others can either facilitate or inhibit your helpfulness as a counselor.

CHAPTER 4

Counseling in a Multicultural World

Multicultural counseling emphasizes an ecological framework in which knowledge of culture, race, ethnicity, gender, sexual orientation, age, family history, spirituality, values, and attitudes are fundamental to understanding a client in counseling (Robinson, 2005). If counselors are to provide effective services to a culturally diverse population, they must acquire awareness and knowledge, as well as develop culturally effective counseling approaches (Sue & Sue, 2007). The ACA Code of Ethics (2005) emphasizes the importance of multiculturalism by stating in its preamble that counselors "recognize diversity and embrace a cross-cultural approach in support of the worth, dignity, potential, and uniqueness of people within their social and cultural contexts" (p. 3). Competence in multicultural counseling requires special training as part of overall counselor training.

After studying this chapter, you will

- Acquire knowledge of the basic terminology related to multicultural counseling, including culture, race, ethnicity, gender, and sexual orientation.
- Become aware of how counselors' assumptions, values, and biases can affect clients in counseling.
- Gain knowledge of distinct populations and issues that have an impact on counseling in a culturally diverse world.

CULTURE, RACE, AND ETHNICITY

The primary aim of multicultural counseling is for counselors to recognize and appreciate that differences exist among people and clients. Counselors who attempt to understand clients' diverse backgrounds need to strive to comprehend many different aspects and characteristics of their culture. A prerequisite to this is for counselors to have knowledge of the basic concepts of culture, race, and ethnicity.

Culture

Culture is often difficult to specifically define because of its broad nature and the myriad terms used to describe the concept. *Culture* may involve such factors as individuals' belief systems, behaviors and perceptions, race, ethnicity, gender, age, sexual orientation, language, spirituality, socioeconomic status, educational attainment, and traditions (Baruth & Manning, 2007; Robinson, 2005). Ingraham and Meyers (2000) define *culture* as an organized set of thoughts, beliefs, and norms for interaction and communication among people, which may influence cognitions, behaviors, and perceptions. Culture is not static, but should be considered abstract and fluid as people constantly recreate themselves and their contexts.

Race

Traditionally, the term *race* has been based on a group of people's appearance or distinguishable physical traits (Robinson, 2005). Baruth and Manning (2007) define *race* as a way that a group of people "defines itself or is defined by others as being different from other groups because of assumed innate physical characteristics" (p. 7). Categories of race are considered sociopolitical constructs and should not be interpreted as being scientific or anthropological in nature (U.S. Census Bureau, 2007a). The U.S. Census Bureau identifies five categories of race: American Indian or Alaska Native, Asian, Black or African American, Native Hawaiian or Other Pacific Islander, and White. Racial identity alone contributes little to understanding a client's ethnicity or overall cultural background.

Ethnicity

The term *ethnicity* is used to describe a "culturally distinct population whose members share a collective identity and a common heritage" (Baruth & Manning, 2007, p. 7). Ethnicity also connotes a shared culture, language, behavior, religion, nationality, or geographic origin. The U.S. government considers race and ethnicity two distinct concepts and formally acknowledges two ethnicities: "Hispanic or Latino" and "Not Hispanic or Latino" (U.S. Census Bureau, 2001).

MULTICULTURAL COUNSELING

Multicultural counseling (sometimes called *cross-cultural counseling*) has become a major force in the counseling profession. Baruth and Manning (2007) define *multicultural counseling* as, "Professional intervention and counseling relationships in which the counselor and the client belong to different cultural groups, subscribe to different worldviews, and have distinguishing differences such as gender, sexual orientation, disabilities, social class, and lifespan period" (p. 18). All counseling is, to some degree, multicultural because in every counseling relationship counselors and clients bring different cultural values and influences and different social roles into the sessions.

Counselors need to be aware of their own cultural heritage and how it has shaped their cultural beliefs, attitudes, and values, especially as it applies to counseling other people. Ultimately, counselors cannot understand others' cultural beliefs and worldviews until they understand their own (Baruth & Manning, 2007). In addition, counselors' perceptions of clients' cultural backgrounds undoubtedly affect treatment strategies. Counselors need to understand their own cultural characteristics, values, and biases and how these orientations may interfere with providing the best service to clients.

Multicultural Counselor Competencies

Competence in multicultural counseling underscores the recognition of clients' cultures and then develops a set of skills, knowledge, and policies to provide effective services (Sue & Sue, 2007). The term *competence* places the responsibility on counselors and other practitioners and challenges them to deliver culturally appropriate services. Counseling services tailored to culture would be more inviting, would encourage clients from diverse backgrounds to seek treatment, and would improve their outcome in treatment (U.S. Department of Health and Human Services [DHHS], 2001). The Association for Multicultural Counseling and Development (AMCD) approved counselor competency standards for work with multicultural clients. The following summary is taken from Robinson (2005):

- *Culturally competent counselors are aware of their own assumptions, values, and biases.* Counselors explore the beliefs and values of their own cultural heritage and the impact that heritage has made on them. They are aware of how their own biases can affect minority clients and acknowledge and respect the differences that exist between their attitudes and values and those of clients of differing cultures. When in doubt, they consult with other culturally competent professionals.
- *Culturally competent counselors understand the worldviews of culturally diverse clients; the counselors become knowledgeable about their cultural background, way of life, and everyday living experiences.* Counselors possess or acquire specific knowledge about the cultural values, attitudes, and beliefs of a client's cultural group. They are also aware of societal discriminations that can influence the client's personal development, career choices, psychological problems, and attitudes about counseling.
- *Culturally competent counselors use only those intervention strategies and techniques that are appropriate to the client's cultural values and customs.* Counselors acquire a wide repertoire of appropriate interviewing skills and strategies. They consider the cultural characteristics of clients in their selection and interpretation of assessment and treatment measures and develop an awareness of possible biases in these measures. When counselors become aware of such biases in their professional work, they act as agents of social change to eliminate such practices. Counselors make use of community resources culturally relevant to the client, such as the client's church or neighborhood cultural center.

COUNSELING CLIENTS OF SPECIFIC CULTURAL GROUPS

Cultural diversity among the population in the United States will continue to grow. In 2005, the U.S. Census Bureau (2006b) reported that as many as one third of the total 300 million U.S. residents now claim "minority" heritage. Undoubtedly, counselors will work with clients with differing cultural backgrounds, customs, traditions, and values. The skills that counselors bring to the multicultural counseling situation will depend a great deal on their knowledge of cultures different from their own.

The culture of clients influences many aspects of mental health and patterns of help seeking. A client's culture may affect how that client describes his or her emotional symptoms to a counselor. Asian American clients, for example, are more likely to report their physical problems, such as dizziness, while not reporting their emotional symptoms (U.S. DHHS, 2001). Culture also affects how an individual copes with their symptoms, how supportive their families and communities are, whether and where they seek help (counselor, physician, clergy, traditional healer), and how well they do in treatment (U.S. DHHS, 2001). It is important that counselors be aware that the cultural values of various cultural groups affect the counseling approach and outcomes.

For the purposes of this chapter, we chose to concentrate on four cultural groups: African American, Asian American, Hispanic American, and Native American Indian. However, counselors also need to be aware that members within each group often come from different geographic locations or countries of origin, may speak different languages, and may adhere to different customs (Atkinson et al., 1998). Thus, this is only a general overview.

Counseling African American Clients

In the United States, African Americans are the second largest cultural group, totaling approximately 35 million people (U.S. Census Bureau, 2007d). African Americans are a heterogeneous group. Some grew up in the rural South, others in northern cities; some are recent immigrants from Latin America or Africa. The African American population is also tremendously diverse in terms of social class, geographical location, and educational attainment, among other demographic characteristics (Baruth & Manning, 2007).

As a group, African Americans are resourceful, having survived centuries of discrimination and oppression. Their strengths lie in kinship bonds and loyalty to family (Gladding & Newsome, 2004). Family boundaries often include an extended family of aunts, uncles, and other relatives. In addition, children are readily accepted into the family, regardless of the marital status of their parents. African Americans are more likely than non-Hispanic Whites to live with and care for grandchildren (U.S. Census Bureau, 2007d).

Work and education are highly valued. Most African Americans are high school graduates, and more than 1 out of every 6 has a bachelor's degree or higher (U.S. Census Bureau, 2007d). Parents expect children to take advantage of education and may seek mental health services because the parents are very concerned about their children's progress in school.

Although improvements have been made in the last several decades, African Americans continue to experience significant levels of poverty. The percentage of African

Americans living in poverty (25%) is twice that of the total population (12%) (U.S. Census Bureau, 2005).

Baruth and Manning (2007) emphasize that religion plays an important part in the lives of African Americans, with the church playing a vital role in providing support or other resources. They strongly recommend that counselors consider the clergy and church networks to be supportive resources for families in crisis.

Regardless of the socioeconomic status of an African American client, counselors must be aware of possible feelings of powerlessness and rage because of environmental barriers related to discrimination. African Americans of higher socioeconomic status bring in problems similar to those of non-Hispanic White clients, which often include self-actualization, improvement of self-esteem, career concerns, and family problems. Lower-income African Americans are often concerned about factors related to physical and economic survival, such as poverty, unemployment, housing, and health care. In addition, problems may include depression, alcohol and drug abuse, poor academic performance, and juvenile delinquency. Behind all of this is often a desire to improve their quality of life.

Counseling Asian American Clients

The Asian American population is about 13 million (U.S. Census Bureau, 2007c), and Asian Americans are one of the fastest growing groups in the United States. Projections are that Asian Americans will number almost 18 million in 2020 (U.S. Census Bureau, 2007c). Although the Asian American population is small compared with other minority groups, they represent a rapidly growing diverse culture in America. Table 4.1 shows the states with the greatest numbers of Asian Americans.

Asian Americans are not a homogeneous group, although they are often perceived as such. Asian Americans are of many different heritages, each with a distinct culture; many

TABLE 4.1
States with the Largest Asian American Populations

State	Population
California	4.1 million*
New York	1.2 million*
Texas	677,620
New Jersey	564,802
Hawaii	529,000
Illinois	500,739

*Population numbers are rounded up to the nearest hundred thousand.
Source: U.S. Census Bureau. (2004a). Annual estimates of the population by race alone or in combination and Hispanic or Latino origin for the United States and states. Washington, DC: Author.

Asian Americans have origins in China, India, Philippines, Indonesia, Japan, Korea, Laos, Malaysia, Pakistan, Sri Lanka, Taiwan, Thailand, and Vietnam. Asian Americans in the United States have, as a group, great linguistic diversity and speak more than 100 languages and dialects. About 35% of Asian Americans and Pacific Islanders live in households where there is limited English proficiency in those over age 14 (President's Advisory Commission on Asian Americans and Pacific Islanders, 2001).

Large differences exist within Asian American groups in terms of employment and socioeconomic status. Among Asian groups, Chinese (52%) and Japanese (48.4%) were more likely to work in management or professional occupations. Those from India or the Phillipines had the highest median household income of all Asian American groups, whereas the poverty rate was highest among Koreans, Vietnamese, and Chinese (U.S. Census Bureau, 2007c). Compared with the non-Hispanic White population, Asian Americans have a greater proportion of college graduates and higher median incomes, and more were employed in management or professional occupations (U.S. Census Bureau, 2007c).

Within Asian American communities, a strong emphasis is placed on the specific role of each family member. The personal needs of the individual are superseded by the needs of both the elders and the family. Shame is used to reinforce family expectations about appropriate behavior (Maki & Kitano, 2007; Sue & Sue, 2007).

Asian Americans generally tend to underutilize mental health services, perhaps due to the strong stigma related to mental illness or due to their view of emotional problems as shameful and distressing. In a study of the counseling preferences of Asian American college students, Atkinson et al. (1998) found that they underuse personal counseling services, although they tend to use vocational counseling services more than do college students in the general population.

When Asian Americans do seek counseling, they may resist talking about themselves or displaying emotions (Sue & Sue, 2007). The problems brought to counseling by Asian Americans of higher socioeconomic status often relate to career choice, educational opportunities, independence versus loyalty to family, pressure to succeed, and social isolation (Baruth & Manning, 2007). Immigrant groups typically have problems related to language, depression, unemployment, and housing—problems also typical of other low-income groups.

When working with first-generation Asian American clients, counselors must be aware of cultural values that influence the clients' views about mental health. Clients' religious beliefs and traditions are closely tied to their attitudes about mental health and mental illness (Sue & Sue, 2007). Because many Asian American clients are familiar with the use of mediation or negotiation to solve problems, they often respond well to counselors who use such processes. These clients also share the Asian value that family unity comes before the individual's welfare. Counselors need to be aware of these influences when helping clients resolve family conflicts (Maki & Kitano, 2007).

Counseling Hispanic American Clients

The 20th century has witnessed the mass migration of Hispanics, or Latinos, to the United States (Robinson, 2005); and today, the Hispanic American population of 44.3 million represents the largest ethnic minority in the United States. Hispanic Americans are a very diverse group, coming from Mexico (64%); Puerto Rico (10%); Cuba, El Salvador, and the Dominican Republic (3%); and other Central American countries and South America (23%) (U.S. Census Bureau, 2006a). California, Texas, Florida, and New York have the largest Hispanic American population.

Approximately 23% of Hispanic Americans live in poverty (U.S. Census Bureau, 2004b). Alcohol and drug abuse, as well as unemployment, are serious problems for low-income Hispanic Americans. School dropout rates are high, often because of language barriers, which interfere with school–family interactions. Hispanic families encourage their children to speak Spanish at home and at school as a means of maintaining cultural identification, whereas school officials generally insist that they speak English (Sue & Sue, 2007).

Counselors need to understand common cultural values among Hispanic Americans (Table 4.2). Although frequently misunderstood as being related to men's sexual prowess and women's objectification, *machismo* is part of Latino culture; it describes stoicism, the masculine traits of "dignity, *respeto* (respect), and, in some instances, dominance within the family" (Robinson, 2005, p. 82). *Respeto* is a core conviction that all people (particularly those in authority) deserve to be treated with respect and courtesy. As such, elders and parents are expected to receive respect from younger people. *Familism* refers to "faith in friends and family," meaning that family and networks of friends are highly valued in the Latino culture (Robinson, 2005, p. 82). Mental health services are sometimes underused by Hispanic Americans because strong family caring reduces the need for outside help (Baruth & Manning, 2007). Casas, Vasquez, and Ruiz de Esparza (2007) say,

> In traditional Hispanic culture, the family unit (including the extended family) is given great importance; consequently, in that cultural context it is "normal" to deal with the reality and necessity of valuing the welfare of the family higher than one's individual welfare. (p. 142)

TABLE 4.2
Common Cultural Values among Hispanic Americans

Dignidad	Refers to having personal honor, self-respect, and self-pride as demonstrated through dignified behavior, responsibility, and hard work.
Familism	Emphasizes the deep importance of family; obedience and respect toward parents and elders; honesty, helpfulness, generosity, and loyalty toward the family; responsibility, sacrifice, and hard work for the benefit of the family.
Machismo	Refers to *manhood*, the courage to fight; the masculine traits of dignity, respect, and in some instances, dominance within the family.
Personalismo	Focuses on the value of interpersonal relationships; loyalty, honesty, generosity toward one's friends; hospitality toward others; willingness to help others.
Respeto	Emphasizes that all people (particularly elders, parents, and other authority figures) deserve to be treated with respect and courtesy; it includes qualities such as humility, deference, submissiveness, and obedience.
Simpatico	Refers to being charming, congenial, agreeable, open, and outgoing.

Hispanic families also traditionally emphasize interdependence over independence and cooperation over competition. Family structures are often hierarchical, which may include deference to elders and males, rigidly defined gender roles, and a belief in the inherent superiority of males (Baruth & Manning, 2007; Robinson, 2005). Latino families are likely to live within family units rather than to live alone, and children tend to remain with the family until they marry (U.S. DHHS, 2001).

Language and communication differences can lead to academic and employment problems. The communication problem is not a first-generation problem; many second- and third-generation Hispanic Americans continue to have difficulty with English, and children and teens tend to speak Spanish or "Spanglish" (a blend of Spanish and English words) in the home (Baruth & Manning, 2007). In addition to language differences, some Hispanic American communication styles are dissimilar to those of the predominant European American culture. For example, many Hispanic Americans tend to speak softly, avoid eye contact when listening to or speaking with persons perceived as having high status, and interject less.

Baruth and Manning (2007) identify several problems commonly experienced by Hispanic Americans that might warrant counseling intervention:

- Problems caused by discrimination, prejudice, and lack of appropriate social skills for coping in a predominantly European American society.
- Frustrations caused by maintaining allegiance to traditional Hispanic values (e.g., familism, respeto, machismo, personalism) while trying to acculturate into a predominantly European American society.
- Conflicts caused by women's changing roles as women move from traditional roles to more independent roles.
- The belief that all Hispanic Americans, regardless of geographic origin, have the same cultural characteristics.
- Language problems and communication barriers.

Counseling Native American Indian Clients

The terms *Native American Indian, Native American,* and *American Indian* are used interchangeably in the literature:

> As most scholars, students, and North, Central, and South American Indians know, the term *American Indian* is an imposed ethnic label, an ethnic gloss used to refer to nations of peoples who presumably share some common physiognomic and sociocultural characteristics. . . . The contentious label continues to be used, to the extent that almost all indigenous peoples of the Western Hemisphere are referred to as *Indians.* (Trimble & Jumper-Thurman, 2007, p. 56)

According to the U.S. Census Bureau (2007b), in 2004, approximately 2.1 million people in the United States declared themselves to be either Native American Indians or Alaska Natives. Among Native Americans, Cherokee was the largest tribal grouping, with a population of 331,000 or 15% of the Native American population. Navajo was the second largest tribal grouping, with a population of 230,000 or 11% of the Native American and Alaska Native–alone population. Table 4.3 shows the population of several of the Native American tribal groups.

TABLE 4.3
Native American Population Based on Tribal Group

Tribal Group	Population	Percentage
Alaska Athabascan (Alaska Native)	12,370	0.6
Aleut (Alaska Native)	11,037	0.5
Apache	66,048	3.1
Blackfeet	39,508	1.8
Cherokee	331,491	15.4
Cheyenne	15,715	0.7
Chickasaw	12,773	0.6
Chippewa	92,041	4.3
Choctaw	55,107	2.6
Creek	27,243	1.3
Eskimo (Alaska Native)	35,951	1.7
Iroquois	50,982	2.4
Lumbee	59,433	2.8
Navajo	230,401	10.7
Osage	13,982	0.6
Ottawa	12,824	0.6
Paiute	14,944	0.7
Pima	48,709	2.3
Potawatomi	14,952	0.7
Pueblo	69,203	3.2
Seminole	12,578	0.6
Sioux	67,666	3.1
Tlingit–Haida (Alaska Native)	18,677	0.9
Tohono O'Odham	20,577	1.0
Yaqui	16,169	0.8
Yuman	10,419	0.5

Source: U.S. Census Bureau. (2007b). The American community—American Indians and Alaska Natives: 2004. Retrieved August 25, 2007, from http://www.census.gov/prod/2007pubs/acs-07.pdf

Because most Indian tribes are recognized as nations by treaties with the U.S. government, they have certain sovereign rights and are under federal jurisdiction. Conflicts among local, state, and federal governments regarding the rights and jurisdictions of Native Americans occur in many areas. For instance, these jurisdictional conflicts can lead to confusion about who will fund mental health services, with the frequent result being a lack of adequate funding.

According to Baruth and Manning (2007), Native Americans, who are lowest on the socioeconomic scale, have very serious problems with survival, poverty, and unemployment, which often relate to discrimination and stereotyping. About 1 out of every 4 Native Americans and Alaska Natives live below the poverty level, compared with about 1 out of every 10 non-Hispanic Whites (U.S. Census Bureau, 2007b). On reservations, unemployment, poverty, and school dropout rates are significantly higher than the national average. Native Americans resist Anglo-American education when it ignores Indian culture. Native Americans have higher rates of suicide than the national averages.

Alcoholism is a major concern faced by Native Americans. Almost 11% of Native Americans and Alaskan Natives reported having a past-year alcohol use disorder, compared with 7.6% of other racial groups (Substance Abuse and Mental Health Services Administration [SAMHSA], 2007). Domestic violence is also a huge problem, with the rate of abuse for Native American women 3½ times larger than the national average (Sue & Sue, 2007).

Many problems that Native Americans have are affected by a change in socioeconomic status and upward mobility. Those who have college degrees not only have problems similar to those of middle-class Whites, but they also often find themselves in conflict with members of their tribes. They are often seen as having abandoned their people and their heritage.

Counselors should be aware of the strong extended family system on Indian reservations. Aunts, uncles, and grandparents often serve as parents to nieces, nephews, and grandchildren. Most play a significant role in the upbringing of these children; others take over completely. Family counseling is an effective approach to use with Native Americans because of their strong family orientation and kinship (Baruth & Manning, 2007; Trimble & Jumper-Thurman, 2007). The traditional healing approaches of shamans and medicine men are also used frequently among the Native American tribes on the reservations, and counselors are urged to cooperate with these healers (Garrett, 2004).

GENDER-BASED COUNSELING

Gender describes the socially constructed masculine and feminine roles that men and women play based on biological sex (Robinson & Watt, 2000). Gender shapes our lives in many primary ways by influencing core beliefs regarding what we and others believe about ourselves (Robinson, 2005). Gender roles for women and men include expectations, behaviors, and attitudes created by society, such as provider, homemaker, caretaker, and soldier. Society also associates the terms *masculinity* and *femininity* with gender. *Masculinity* refers to characteristics traditionally viewed as exhibited by men (e.g., fierce independence, a strong will, emotional restraint), whereas *femininity* is associated with traits exhibited by women (e.g., nurturance, caretaking, not using harsh language) (Robinson & Watt, 2000, p. 590).

Counselors need to be aware of the impact of gender stereotypes and societal gender discrimination on their clients. Stereotypical roles imposed on men lead them to become overzealous in achieving success, requiring them to strive at all times to appear competent, assertive, and invulnerable. Men may be trained to disregard emotions related to tenderness, fear, and grief (Real, 1997, 2002; Robinson, 2005); they may minimize and devalue both their inner self and their relationships. Societal views of women may encourage them to assume responsibility for a disproportionate amount of household and childcare responsibilities, discourage them from entering certain academic pursuits or occupations, or inhibit their ability to be assertive about their needs. In addition, over the past several decades, women have taken on many simultaneous roles—such as employee, parent, caregiver, participant in a committed relationship, and student—each of which requires a great deal of responsibility and commitment (Juliano, 2005; Tang & Tang, 2001). Attempting to balance multiple roles often creates problems for women and affects their overall satisfaction with life, as well as their mental health.

Counseling Women

Research indicates that women generally are the primary consumers of counseling services (Fischer & Farina, 1995; Leong & Zachar, 1999). Among the many reasons that women seek counseling are issues associated with multiple roles. For women, the traditional culture expects their primary function to be that of spouse and parent. Because of society's acceptance of women in the workplace, many women find themselves adding the role of employee to their functions (Keyes, 2000; Simon, 1997). More recently, an additional role of caregiver (one who cares for a family member, usually an older parent) has been added to the list of roles that women play (Martire et al., 2000). These multiple roles may lead to psychological problems or negative life satisfaction; more specifically, problems may involve conflicts in the marital relationship, conflicts between family and work, and personal stress.

Problems in relationships can occur when women choose to change from a traditional role (wife and mother) and begin an educational pursuit or enter the workforce. Husbands may object if their wives plan to return to school or get a job or begin to question the husbands' authority. Even more difficult for women, some husbands may seem to support the changes that their wives are trying to make but subtly undermine them.

For women with multiple roles, many can become overstressed when they try to balance their domestic and job responsibilities. Similar problems occur when husbands want their wives to work to supplement family income, but the wives prefer to remain at home to care for the children. Another stressful role occurs when women suddenly become single parents. Many feel overwhelmed when the breadwinner and dual-parent roles are thrust on them. With issues involving multiple or changing roles, counselors need to help women develop personal strengths, try new activities, and cope with resistance or anger from family members. In many cases, career counseling is necessary.

Counselors need to be aware of the all-too-real existence of domestic violence in our society. In the United States, domestic violence is the leading cause of injury to women, and almost one third of all female murder victims are killed by a boyfriend or husband (U.S. Department of Justice, 2007). Many question the reasons why a woman stays in a violent relationship. In many cases, it is simply dangerous for a woman to leave her abuser. Leaving could realistically mean living in fear, losing child custody, and losing financial support (Riger, Raza, & Camacho, 2002). Counseling domestic violence survivors requires considerable training and supervision specific to treating that population. The goals of therapy include helping to ensure the woman's safety; validating her thoughts, feelings, and choices; helping her to make and trust her own decisions; and helping her to reestablish supportive interpersonal relationships with women and men, family, friends, and intimates.

In addition to problems involving multiple roles and role conflicts, some mental health problems are more common in women than men. For example, nearly twice as many women as men are affected by depression. Depression in women can be associated with a feeling of lack of autonomy and control over one's life, low self-esteem, intimate violence, poverty, lack of social support, loss, and biological factors (e.g., health problems, hormonal changes) (Astbury, 1999; World Health Organization [WHO], 2002). Women also suffer with more anxiety and somatic complaints than men.

Counseling Men

As a result of traditional male socialization, men may be hesitant to seek counseling (Real, 2002; Robinson, 2005; Robinson & Watt, 2000). Men are often socialized to be independent, strong willed, and emotionally restrained. They tend to internalize their feelings and be more aggressive and competitive. Because of their reticence to discuss problems and express feelings, men are often reluctant to seek help. When they do, they tend to resist a close counseling relationship. Counselors working with men need to be aware that many of them will be loners and reluctant to talk (Gladding, 2007). According to Heesacker and Prichard (1992), one aim of traditional counseling—that of trying to help men express themselves emotionally—contributes to men's reluctance to seek counseling.

Men who seek counseling do so for a variety of reasons. They may be experiencing personal dissatisfaction with their jobs, having trouble with intimate relationships, or undergoing life transitions that require role changes that lead to friction with spouses/partners.

Some men who are highly successful in their jobs seek counseling because they are emotionally numb, burdened with responsibilities, and dissatisfied with themselves. They often say that they think that they are frauds and unworthy of their success. Counseling such men can be difficult because of their strong defenses. They have lost touch with their deep emotions because they have developed masks to cover the feelings of vulnerability that underlie their competent behaviors (Real, 1997, 2002). As clients, they tend to intellectualize their problems while resisting a therapist's attempts to make them aware of their emotions.

Male clients of this type are often troubled by the differences in how they deal with problems at work and at home. On the job, they may resolve conflicts in a constructive manner through compromise, arbitration, or consensus. But at home, when conflicts arise, they tend to control relationships either by becoming aggressive or by trying to placate and thus prevent conflict.

Counselors also work with adult male clients who are changing careers or undergoing a major transition in life. Men may experience uncertainty or stress in their work if they are promoted to new and highly demanding jobs, if they lose their jobs and become dependent on their wives, or if their jobs become obsolete and they must seek jobs in fields in which they are untrained. Men who have relentlessly sought success may experience a midlife crisis in which they fear that they have wasted their lives. Retirement may also bring on stress and emotional problems for men. A life based on achievement and power suddenly changes, and they feel useless. At the same time, they are suddenly put into close daily contact with their wives—a situation unfamiliar to them.

Some men who follow male stereotypically aggressive roles excessively may run into trouble with the law. Men commit a high percentage of violent crimes, including homicides, sexual assaults, domestic violence, physical assaults, and child abuse. Aggressive, violent males often come from dysfunctional families in which they routinely experienced emotional neglect, fear of abandonment, or physical abuse. Many of these men have modeled their behavior after their fathers, who themselves were following stereotypical patterns or whose fathers had never bonded with them.

Certain mental health problems are more prevalent in men than women. For example, men have a higher prevalence of substance use disorders and antisocial behaviors than women. Men may use substances or other addictive behaviors to cope with underlying depression (Real, 1997). Addictions can take innumerable forms, such as compulsive drinking, gambling, eating, sex, or spending; workaholism; an obsessive desire to watch football and other sports or to use the computer; and so on. Using substances or engaging in other process addictions enables a man to mask the depression from himself and others around him.

COUNSELING AND SEXUAL ORIENTATION

It is believed that between 5% and 10% of the U.S. population is homosexual (Moursund & Kenny, 2002). This is considered a conservative estimate because some people do not publicly admit that they are lesbian, gay, or bisexual (Baruth & Manning, 2007). Reluctance to acknowledge one's sexual orientation stems from a history of discrimination and abuse. Negative attitudes began to change, however, after the gay liberation movement developed from the civil rights and women's movements. The American Psychiatric Association in 1973, and the American Psychological Association in 1975, both declassified homosexuality as a form of mental illness. Then, in the mid-1980s, after gay communities experienced the spread of the human immunodeficiency virus (HIV), which causes acquired immunodeficiency syndrome (AIDS), former prejudices against gays began to reemerge (Hoffman, 1991). Even though in recent years communities have generally become more accepting of lesbian, gay and bisexual individuals, discrimination and violence against this population remains high (Sue & Sue, 2007).

Transgender is a general construct used to describe people with nontraditional gender identities. Previous labels of *cross-dresser, transvestite,* and *transsexual* were deemed unsuitable to describe this population in favor of the term *transgender,* which Carroll,

Gilroy, and Ryan (2002) defined as "a range of behaviors, expressions, and identifications that challenge the pervasive bipolar gender system in a given culture" (p. 139). Although transgender is not the same as sexual orientation, the two are closely connected: A change of gender has implications for one's sexual orientation. The terms *lesbian, gay, bisexual,* and *transgender* are commonly abbreviated *LGBT.*

Counselors who work with LGBT clients encounter distinct issues and concerns than those of heterosexual clients (Baruth and Manning, 2007; Schaefer & Wheeler, 2004):

- LGBT clients experience different types of discrimination and injustice.
- LGBT clients may encounter career problems caused by *coming out.* They may fear that their career will be jeopardized or that they might be terminated from their job.
- LGBT clients endure family problems caused by coming out. Family members may object to the sexual orientation, resulting in the loss of family support and relationships.
- Transgendered clients often feel guilt in terms of appearing to be one gender, but feeling another, and not fulfilling "expected, acceptable" roles.
- Transgendered clients experience issues involving the transition from one gender to the other.

Adaptation to a positive LGBT identity (coming out) remains a prolonged, complicated process for most LGBT individuals. Coming out can be viewed as the individual's self-acceptance of sexual orientation and identity and/or being open with others about one's sexual orientation and identity (even if the openness is limited to family and friends) (Baruth & Manning, 2007). Coming out is a difficult process because it may raise strong feelings in one's family and friends and rupture relationships (Gladding, 2007). Whereas heterosexual individuals who experience identity or interpersonal problems usually expect support from their families, LGBT individuals often experience parental rejection or withdrawal of support.

Counselors can help LGBT clients work through the coming out process in several ways. Counselors assist clients in managing their fears and anxieties when they first acknowledge, personally or publicly, that they are lesbian, gay, bisexual, or transgender. They can also help them cope with anger or rejection from family and friends, and they can support clients who experience discrimination or violence in social and career interactions.

LGBT clients also have problems common to everyone: problems related to identity, interpersonal, career, and family issues. These problems may be exacerbated for LGBT clients, who often cope with feelings of lack of acceptance and invisibility. Nevertheless, Sue and Sue (2007) caution that counselors should not dwell on issues of sexual orientation or gender identity when clients are not presenting this as a problem; the counselor's responsibility is to attend to the concerns raised by the client.

SUMMARY

Counseling professionals are increasingly aware that they must prepare themselves to work with the complex, diverse needs of growing numbers of individuals whose needs, values, and beliefs differ from those on which traditional counseling theories and techniques have been based. Special attention is now being given in counselor training to increasing counselors' awareness of their potential biases toward clients. The professional literature has been reflecting more understanding of diverse sociocultural characteristics, including the various cultures as well as gender, and sexual orientation.

PROJECTS AND ACTIVITIES

1. Role-play an opening counseling session with a counselor and a client of the opposite sex. The prospective client says that she feels shy and intimidated in her interactions with the opposite sex. Then reverse the roles of counselor and client. Share reactions to the feelings engendered in counselor and client.
2. Invite a panel of speakers who are members of various cultural groups and are community mental health specialists and school counselors to speak to your class about problems in reaching clients from diverse backgrounds. Invite suggestions on how to improve communication with these groups.
3. Explore the traditional healing approaches of a particular cultural group. Invite such a traditional healer (e.g., a Native American shaman or medicine man) to speak to the class about his or her views of mental health and treatment.
4. Invite professionally trained female and male counselors to class to discuss the types of problems that their clients present that are specifically related to gender role conflict. Ask them to discuss how they go about helping these clients.
5. Invite professionally trained counselors from various cultural groups to discuss with your class or group the issues related to multicultural counseling, for example, counseling by non-Hispanic White counselors and the differences and similarities in cultural group values and their influence on counseling.

Part Two
Theories

CHAPTER 5

Human Development Theories

S ince the 1950s, human development theories have influenced and shaped counseling philosophy, training, and practice and have contributed to counselors' unique
professional identity in the counseling field. These theories emphasize helping people of all ages resolve normal conflicts and maintain healthy personal, social, and career
development. The Council for Accrediting Counseling and Related Educational Programs
(CACREP) mandates that counselors, regardless of specialty, study human development
as one of their requirements.

Many theorists have contributed to these human development theories that underlie
today's counseling practice. Jean Piaget's (1926) landmark theory of the cognitive development of children and adolescents emerged in the 1920s and soon had a significant impact
in Europe. Also in Europe were Carl Jung and Charlotte Buehler, who, in the 1930s, expanded theories of development to include adult development. In the United States, because of the prevailing Freudians, trait-factor and maturational theorists, and Skinnerian
behaviorists, it took several more decades before Piaget, Jung, and Beuhler had an impact.

In the 1950s, Erik Erikson offered a more comprehensive, psychodynamic developmental model, which extended from childhood through several stages of adulthood. In
the 1970s and 1980s, theories of moral development and feminist theories influenced the
expansion of theories in human development. More recent theories have focused on
integrated models of human development.

After studying this chapter, you will be able to

- Explain the role of theories in understanding human development.
- Identify the major pioneers of human development theories.
- Convey the key concepts of the contemporary life-span theories.
- Describe the integrated models of life-span development.

PIONEERS IN HUMAN DEVELOPMENT THEORY

Early developmental pioneers in the first decades of the 20th century worked only with children and adolescents, and they focused only on biological drives (Freud) or on genetics and maturational growth processes (Hall and Gesell). G. Stanley Hall (1916) and his student Arnold Gesell (1940, 1948), who based their theory only on heredity and the automatic, maturational growth stages of children, introduced a theory of child development that became an influential system of categorizing development into *normative stages,* which are considered age-related averages computed to represent typical development (Berk, 2006). Jean Piaget and Carl Jung were the first major theorists to break from these earlier biological determinists and maturationists. Other pioneers worth noting as precursors to contemporary psychosocial life-span development were Charlotte Buehler and Robert Havighurst.

Piaget's Theory of Cognitive Development

Generally considered the giant of the 20th-century psychology of human development, Piaget (1926) held that humans have the innate capacity to restructure their cognitive processes based on interactions with their experiences. He proposed a four-stage cognitive development theory, with each stage dependent on, and flowing into, the next stage: *sensorimotor* (ages 0–2), *preoperational* (ages 2–7), *concrete operations* (ages 7–11), and *formal operations* (age 11 and beyond).

Piaget believed that the ability to reason relates to cognitive structures in the mind that become more sophisticated and complex as the individual develops. Cognitive restructuring enables persons to process new experiences and data, and to evolve into higher levels of reasoning, which, in turn, enable them to solve progressively more complex problems. As individuals mature, they move from the infant's preoccupation with sensorimotor interactions with the world, to the capacity to explore concrete objects and specific events in the environment, to the ability to think symbolically, abstractly, systematically, and logically.

Piaget described two types of processes that occur in cognitive learning at all developmental stages. One, *assimilation,* occurs when individuals incorporate new information cognitively into already existing knowledge. The other, *accommodation,* occurs when individuals actively apply this new knowledge to changes in their behavior. Piaget believed that cognitive development involves a move from relative disequilibrium or conflict to equilibrium or resolution of conflict. When problems arise that cause discomfort, individuals try to resolve them—a process that leads to change and growth.

Piaget's theory of cognitive development has been a major influence in counseling theory and practice over the years. His many publications in the 1920s and 1930s include *The Moral Judgment of the Child* (1932), which influenced Lawrence Kohlberg (1969, 1981, 1984), who is discussed later and who extended the stages of moral development through adulthood. Piaget also influenced counseling theorists Albert Ellis, Donald Meichenbaum, and Aaron Beck, who believe that faulty reasoning or distortions in the thinking processes are the major sources of problems. Other theorists influenced by Piaget's theory include constructivists (Neimeyer & Mahoney, 1999). Piaget's work also influenced psychological education activities involving the teaching of cognitive skills, problem solving, and reasoning. Perry (1970) extended Piaget's theory beyond childhood and adolescence to include college students by adding another developmental stage—postformal—and Ivey et al. (2007) followed suit, as discussed later in this chapter.

Carl Jung's Stages of Life

Carl Jung, at age 56, wrote "The Stages of Life" (1933) after experiencing a midlife crisis that included personal and vocational upheavals. In this work, he differed from other developmental theorists not only by extending the scope of developmental study to those in later life, but also by insisting that the period after midlife includes a person's most important years (Jung, 1933; Staude, 1981). Jung conceived of four stages of development: childhood (birth to puberty); youth (puberty to ages 35 to 40); middle age (ages 35 to 60); and old age (age 65 and beyond). He believed that the process of *individuation,* which involves a person's inner search for meaning in life, occurs after midlife rather than during youth or childhood. This theory, though not sharply defined or detailed, was a forerunner of later ideas about stages of life. Jung's conception of life stages foreshadowed Erikson's work in the 1950s and 1960s and is the prime force behind the later adult development theorists, such as Daniel Levinson (1978) and Roger Gould (1978).

Other Pioneers

Charlotte Buehler was probably the first theorist to explore the life cycle systematically (Buehler & Massarik, 1968). She also was probably the first to emphasize the *psychosocial* aspect of human development. In the late 1920s and early 1930s, Beuhler had collected personal documents, letters, and biographies from about 400 people of varying socioeconomic status, national origin, and occupation and had interviewed them. She then identified five psychosocial stages, from early childhood through older adulthood, during which people develop self-realization based on age-related goals.

Buehler is noted for having strongly influenced Donald Super's (1942) career development theory, in which he proposed and, over the years, elaborated on the relationship of personal development to vocational development (see chapters 2 and 12). Equally important, however, is Buehler's systematic attention to stages in life and her integration of self-theory and human development, which underlies current counseling theory and practice.

Robert Havighurst (1953) also developed a psychosocial life-stage model of development after conducting longitudinal studies between 1935 and 1950 of individuals at different stages of life. He coined the term *developmental tasks* to describe necessary actions that individuals must take at each stage of life to move to the higher stage of development. Havighurst emphasized that development is based on the person's relationship to the social world and the person's readiness to perform certain social tasks expected at each stage of life.

CONTEMPORARY LIFE-SPAN DEVELOPMENT THEORIES

As Piaget and Jung were the major pioneers to break from deterministic and maturational theories of development, so were Erikson, Kohlberg, and Gilligan the major figures in the latter part of the 20th century to break from narrow models of child and adolescent development and from narrow cognitive models and male norms of development. Despite Jung's and Buehler's earlier works on life-span development, it wasn't until the last quarter of the 20th century that the counseling and psychotherapeutic profession in the United States acknowledged that human development continues throughout the life span.

Even though Erik Erikson's 1950 theory of life-span development had influenced certain segments of the profession, most continued to adhere to the general assumption that development ceased at adulthood, followed by a gradual decline. William Perry's (1970) work on the cognitive development of college students, which extended development to young adults, gained attention from the profession. But not until the late 1970s, with Daniel Levinson's (1978) and Roger Gould's (1978) works on the midlife period of human development, did the profession acknowledge that human development is a lifelong process. Robert Butler (1975) and others extended developmental studies to include older adults.

As counseling professionals became more aware that adults continue to develop throughout life, counseling services, which initially were only in schools and colleges, expanded into the community. At the same time, the general public became increasingly aware that adults continue to be met with transitional challenges when, for instance, they lose a job, get a divorce, decide to seek a new lifestyle, retire, or face a terminal illness. As a consequence, they continue to make developmental changes.

Kohlberg's (1981, 1984, 1986a) theory of moral development brought about another major breakthrough and generated ongoing debate and research studies. Not only did his work, along with that of emerging cognitivists, help to highlight the work of Piaget, but he brought the fields of philosophy and social science into dialogue with psychology, and he brought the issues of motivation and meaning of life back into the field of psychology (Kegan, 1986).

Carol Gilligan (1982), influenced by Nancy Chodorow (1978), added another missing link to human development studies by providing the women's perspective of connectedness and empathy for others as a fundamental component. Gilligan and Chodorow and those who followed—such as Conarton and Silverman (1988) and Jordan, Kaplan, Miller, Stiver, and Surrey (1991)—proposed alternative developmental theories that emphasize the relational, empathic aspects of human development.

Other major contributions to contemporary development theory came from Fowler's (1995) theory of faith development and Goleman's (1995) theory of emotional development, which indicated the broad, multidimensional nature of human development. Overall, whereas theorists of the past focused on narrow aspects of human development, each ensuing developmentalist took another step in integrating and broadening the various aspects until, by the close of the century, theorists were working toward an integrated, multidimensional theory of human development.

Erik Erikson's Psychosocial Life-Span Development Theory

In 1950, psychoanalyst Erik Erikson published his first book, *Childhood and Society,* in which he proposed eight stages of human development. Erikson's theory influenced counseling theory and practice more than any other developmental theory (Blocher, 2000; Rodgers, 1984). Although he is best known for his attention to identity crises in adolescence and his attention to building one's ego identity, he also had a profound influence on adult development theories throughout the life span. Erikson has since modified his theory, and others have proposed modifications or have rearranged or expanded certain stages. Because Erikson's work over the years has been based predominantly on the healthy psychological and social-growth processes of normal individuals, his theory has undergirded counselors' efforts to establish a unique profession aimed at working with psychologically normal people.

According to Erikson (1950, 1963), human development occurs in eight stages throughout life (see Table 5.1). At each stage, individuals work through transitional conflicts as a necessary means of development by undertaking certain developmental tasks. These stages relate to an individual's struggle to balance inner needs with external cultural forces. Erikson describes the conflicts that arise in this process as opportunities for positive growth and change. He perceived these stages as guidelines, not as rigid steps in development. He believed that many environmental forces affect and complicate an otherwise simple pattern of progressive growth (Coles, 1970). In his definitive biography of

TABLE 5.1
Erikson's Eight Stages of Life Development

Stage	Psychosocial Crisis	Significant Relations	Basic Strengths
1 Infancy	Basic trust versus basic mistrust	Maternal person	Hope
2 Early childhood	Autonomy versus shame and doubt	Parental persons	Will
3 Play age	Initiative versus guilt	Basic family	Purpose
4 School age	Industry versus inferiority	"Neighborhood," school	Competence
5 Adolescence	Identity versus identity confusion	Peer groups and out-groups; models of leadership	Fidelity
6 Young adulthood	Intimacy versus isolation	Partners in friendship, sex, competition, cooperation	Love
7 Adulthood	Generativity versus stagnation	Divided labor and shared household	Care
8 Old age	Integrity versus despair	"Mankind," "my kind"	Wisdom

Note: From *The Life Cycle Completed: A Review,* by Erik H. Erikson. Copyright 1982 by Rikan Enterprises, Ltd. Reprinted by permission of W. W. Norton & Company, Inc.

Erikson, psychiatrist Robert Coles (1970) substantiates Erikson's flexibility: "We do not acquire trust and forever rid ourselves of mistrust or 'achieve' autonomy and thus spare ourselves continuing doubts and hesitations" (p. 76). Coles further says of Erikson's views: "What is won can later be lost—and re-won. The body (and in the case of humans, the mind) is not irrevocably set or determined by any one thing—genes, the mother's 'behavior,' the so-called environment—but by a combination of everything and everyone, both within and outside the flesh" (p. 77).

According to Erikson's theory, the formation and dynamics of each sequential stage are dependent on what occurs in the previous stage. If children develop a basic trust in others and themselves, they can develop the will for self-control and responsibility for their own actions (*autonomy*). This autonomy permits children to develop initiative and purpose in life and encourages attainment of productive skills and competence. If these developmental challenges are met, adolescents can develop a coherent sense of self (*identity*), which will lead to a tendency to be true to oneself and others (*fidelity*). These firm foundations set in childhood and adolescence permit the adult to develop love relationships (*intimacy*) over time, altruistic caring for children and concern for the welfare of the next generation (*generativity*), and wisdom about order and meaning in life (*basic integrity*).

Failure to gain adaptive strength at each sequential stage, however, can lead cumulatively to increased behavioral problems. Children who acquire patterns of withdrawal, for instance, are liable to develop confused identities when they reach adolescence and to have tendencies to repudiate themselves and others. As adults, such individuals tend to isolate themselves or become promiscuous and rejecting of others. In later life, they are apt to be bitter, disdainful, or despairing of life.

Conflicts between the individual and society are central to Erikson's (1968) psychosocial theory; he perceived them as necessary instigators of growth. When conflicts are attended to and resolved in a positive manner, individuals are able to move to a higher stage of development. Says Erikson,

> I shall present human growth from the point of view of the conflicts, inner and outer, which the vital personality weathers, reemerging from each crisis with an increased sense of inner unity, with an increase of good judgment, and an increase in the capacity "to do well" according to his own standards and to the standards of those who are significant to him. (Erikson, 1968, pp. 91–92)

Erikson (1968) believed that conflicts can be either positive or negative. Positive conflicts result from individuals' awareness that they are distressed over an ongoing situation—an awareness that motivates them to change themselves or their circumstances in creative and satisfying ways. Negative conflicts differ: "Neurotic and psychotic conflicts are defined by a certain self-perpetuating propensity, by an increasing waste of defensive energy and by a deepened psychosocial isolation" (p. 163).

Eriksonian belief in working through conflicts as a means of developmental growth influenced many developmental theorists, researchers, and psychotherapists, including Conarton and Silverman (1988), Fowler (1995), Gilligan (1982), Kohlberg (1969, 1981), Lyddon (1999), and Steenbarger (1990). That belief is also shared by others. Polish psychiatrist Kazimierz Dabrowski (1964, 1970), for example, developed a theory called *positive disintegration,* in which tension aroused by conflicts represents a healthy awareness that all is not well in one's interactions with others or with one's feelings about oneself. This awareness motivates the individual to change patterns of behavior or to change environmental circumstances that are inhibiting his or her personal or interpersonal growth. Positive disintegration occurs when individuals are willing and able to face conflicts and break down patterns of behavior that are restricting development so that growth can take place. "For the development of higher needs and higher emotions, it is necessary to have partial frustrations, some inner conflicts, some deficits in basic needs" (1970, p. 35). On the other hand, according to Dabrowski, *negative disintegration* occurs when individuals deny or suppress conflicts and their responses to life's challenges become neurotic or pathological. Passive aggression, chronic depression, destructive behavior, and other debilitating symptoms may arise.

The positive potential of working through conflicts has been a consistent, underlying theme of counseling since the 1940s and 1950s. Carl Rogers (1942), for example, claimed that counseling "can be effective only when there is a conflict of desires or demands which creates tension and calls for some type of solution . . . the tension created by those conflicting desires must be more painful to the individual than the pain and stress of finding a solution to the conflict" (p. 54).

More recently, Steenbarger (1990) reaffirmed and amplified Erikson's earlier developmental views on conflict: "Development proceeds through periods of challenge and crisis, which generate new sources of meaning and identity for individuals. Far from being a sign of maladjustment, distress is perceived as a constructive prod and precursor to healthy growth" (p. 435).

Moral Development: Kohlberg

Among 20th-century psychological theorists, Piaget (1932) was the first major figure to consider moral development as a fundamental component of psychological development. Freudian psychoanalysis and Skinnerian behaviorism—the two schools of psychology that dominated much of the 20th century—had rejected moral issues as a part of psychotherapy. Freudian theory held that moral concerns came from one's superego, determined by authority figures. Behaviorists held that one's behavior is determined by rewards and punishments. Until the appearance of Lawrence Kohlberg's (1969, 1981, 1984, 1986a) publications, Piaget's (1932) work received scant attention from psychologists.

Kohlberg's perspective stemmed from Piaget's premise that moral development is part of one's ability to develop through cognitive structural changes; that is, humans have a self-organizing capacity to restructure their own inner capacities to think and to respond to experiences they encounter in their social environment (Kegan, 1986). Kohlberg expanded Piaget's model by adding more stages, while limiting his study to justice reasoning, or the cognitive capacity of individuals, primarily for research purposes. His theory posited that children, beginning at a very young age, develop morally in a sequence of stages in which they move from a self-centered (preconventional) stage, to a conforming, socially motivated (conventional) stage, and then on to a stage where they employ universal moral principles (postconventional) that consider justice for the good of society. Each stage is hierarchical and must be completed before one can advance to the next stage. Because each structural level "is more comprehensive, differentiated, and equilibrated than the prior structure, each stage is able to do things that prior stages could not" (Kohlberg, 1981, p. 147).

Kohlberg believed that moral development occurs when one is challenged by a moral dilemma in real-life situations: "Moral principles are human constructions arising through human interaction and communication" (Kohlberg, 1986a, p. 542). He developed a series of 11 complex hypothetical stories centering on moral dilemmas; in each story, the main character is faced with a conflict between personal interest and the good of society and acts to resolve the dilemma. After reading a story, subjects are asked to judge the behavior as right or wrong, and then they are asked questions to determine what reasoning they used to arrive at the judgment.

Kohlberg's research and publications, modified and revised several times, culminated in three volumes: *Essays on Moral Development, Vol. 1: The Philosophy of Moral Development* (1981); *Vol. 2: The Psychology of Moral Development* (1984), and *Vol. 3: Education and Moral Development* (1986a). By the late 1980s, the psychological profession could no longer reject morality as an essential component of psychological development.

Kohlberg's work was extraordinary on several counts. It drew international attention from a wide range of academic disciplines, and it drew those schools—the social sciences, theology, philosophy, and the various schools of psychology—into cross-discipline dialogues, despite their notoriety for keeping separate domains (Kegan, 1986; Boyd, 1986; Carter, 1986). Motivation and meaning making, so long ignored by the prevailing schools of psychology, resumed their places as essential parts of psychological development (Kegan, 1986; Boyd, 1986). Kohlberg's controversial work generated critical reviews and streams of research studies expanding, replicating, refuting, or modifying his work; studies broadened and extended his narrow concept of morality into all aspects of human development. Addressing the controversy in the mid-1980s was the text edited by Modgil and Modgil (1986), *Lawrence Kohlberg: Consensus and Controversy,* which included a lengthy response from Kohlberg.

One major weakness of Kohlberg's model was the limiting of morality to justice reasoning. Other researchers proposed broader models of moral development that cover affective, empathic, intuitive, and faith-based components (Berk, 2006; Fowler, 1995; Gilligan, 1982; Haste, 1993; Kohlberg, 1986a; Locke, 1986; Modgil & Modgil, 1986). Arguing from a feminist perspective, Gilligan (1982) pointed out that caring for the welfare of others takes moral precedence over justice in certain circumstances, as in Kohlberg's (1969) well-known case of a man known as Heinz, who needed to steal some prescription medicine in order to save his wife's life. From Kohlberg's moral justice point of view, Heinz's moral dilemma raises questions in judging Heinz's behavior: Which is more ethical—saving his wife's life or not stealing the drug? Is Heinz responsible for saving his wife's life? Does the druggist have a right to protect his interests?

Based on studies she had conducted, Gilligan (1982) noted that girls consider the relationship between Heinz and his wife and between Heinz and the druggist; thus, they propose solutions that go beyond either stealing the drug or letting the wife die. They suggest, for example, that Heinz should get a loan, find other ways of obtaining money, or continue to appeal to the druggist to delay payment. Since such responses do not suit the (male) norms set by Kohlberg, girls generally scored lower than boys, Gilligan claimed, and thus their moral decisions were regarded as inferior to, or less mature than, those of males.

Conceding this weakness, Kohlberg (1986a) modified his model. Recent research studies show that the revised Kohlbergian model is not gender based and that adolescent and adult females display reasoning at the same or higher stages as their male counterparts. Girls are not scored down when they raise interpersonal concern on the modified Kohlberg model (Berk, 2006).

Many others also argued that Kohlberg's use of justice as the universal moral principle was too limited. James Fowler (1995), modeling his faith-based stages after Kohlberg, claimed that moral development has many more dimensions than cognitive reasoning. Kohlberg (1981) conceded that point, saying that the question "Why be moral?" (p. 344) still remains at the sixth stage, but he proposed a seventh stage, which he said is "roughly equivalent" to Fowler's sixth stage of faith (p. 344). Research psychologists, however, rejected his Stages 5 and 6 because they cannot be measured empirically (Rest, Narvaez, Bebeau, & Thoma, 1999).

Many researchers also criticized Kohlberg's claim that young children lack an inherent moral sense. Berk (2006) believes that a key controversy has to do with Kohlberg's belief that moral maturity is not achieved until the postconventional level. Since Kohlberg's time, numerous studies of children's cognitive, social, and emotional levels of development show that moral judgments and actions are prevalent among children. At an early age, children begin to distinguish between a sense of moral fairness for themselves, a sense of moral justice for others, and a sense of conventional social morality (Berk, 2006).

Consistent with Kohlberg's concern that considerations of moral issues must apply to action, Berk (2006) identifies moral issues pervasive in one's personal and social life. Using real-life settings as examples of various moral components, she presents various learning strategies (e.g., strategies for enhancing self-control) that can be applied to individuals, families, and social and cultural settings; discusses how patterns of aggression in early and middle childhood lead to aggression in adolescents and adults; explores negative family, social, cultural, and environmental patterns, especially the family "as training ground for aggressive behavior" (p. 509); and discusses intervention strategies for various age levels and settings.

Although Kohlberg considered moral education essential to moral development, he admitted that it was the weakest component of his proposal. Much of the difficulty, he believed, has been the method of teaching moral education, with many educators being prone to adopt either a doctrinaire or a relativist method, neither of which Kohlberg believed is acceptable. Responding in the 1970s to values clarification, the popular movement among psychological educators, he said, "Value clarification is not a sufficient solution to the relativity problem. Furthermore, the actual teaching of relativism is itself an indoctrination or teaching of a fixed belief" (p. 12). Kohlberg emphasized the importance of professional educators becoming aware of their own moral constructs. Without exception everyone has a moral position, including those who claim to be moral relativists.

Kohlberg (1986a) acknowledged, however, that a relativist perspective is often a phase one goes through on the way to the postconventional Stage 5, especially among college students, who question values held by their own cultural traditions as they listen to values held by students of other cultural backgrounds (see the discussion of Perry later in this chapter). In the Kohlbergian model, however, universal values ultimately supersede sociocultural norms. Numerous cross-cultural studies conducted around the world confirm that different cultures hold similar universal values (Kohlberg, 1981; Boyd, 1986; Berk, 2006). In a review of the literature, Berk (2006) notes that children and adolescents in diverse cultures throughout the world use the same criteria to separate moral concerns from social conventions. For example, when asked about acts that obviously lead to harm or violate rights, such as breaking promises, destroying another's property, or kicking harmless animals, cultural differences diminish.

How then has Kohlberg's work influenced counseling practice? His work directly relates to moral conflicts, a crucial component in counseling. Most theorists, educators, and counselors now believe that moral issues are an essential part of human development. Counselors must be aware of their own values, the values of their clients, and the environmental values surrounding both counselors and clients. Many client concerns are presented as moral dilemmas. How individuals perceive right or wrong behaviors influences their feelings about themselves or others and has an effect on self-esteem, career choice, and the types of relationships they seek. Since the 1990s, critical debates and alternative proposals on moral development have continued, as discussed later in this chapter.

Adult Development Theories

A relatively new field of developmental psychology, adult development, got its major impetus from the work of William Perry (1970), Daniel Levinson (1978), and Roger Gould (1978). Perry studied the intellectual and cognitive development of college-age students. Levinson and Gould each studied men's development in the later years of life, basing their work on Erikson's ideas about adult ego states and on Jung's writings about life's meaning for older people. Levinson (1986) said, "The study of adult development is, one might say, in its infancy. It has been taken seriously in the human sciences for only the past 30 years or so largely under the impact of Erikson's . . . general writings" (p. 3). In another source (1978), Levinson called Jung the father of adult development because he was the first to state unequivocally that the years after midlife are the most important in life. The recent interest in adult development results from counseling professionals' increased awareness that adults continue to develop throughout life.

William Perry: College Student Development

Believing that adult cognitive development went beyond Piaget's final stage of formal thinking in adolescence, William Perry (1970) studied the cognitive development patterns of college students during the late 1950s and early 1960s (Cavanaugh & Blanchard-Fields, 2006). Students were studied during their undergraduate years to determine their patterns of thinking and the range of their views about the nature of knowledge and the degree to which they depended on authorities or on their own independent thinking for informed views about knowledge (Loevinger, 1976). Perry published his results in *Forms of Intellectual and Ethical Development in the College Years* (1968).

Perry found that beginning undergraduate students tended to rely on authorities to give them valid information and correct answers; they relied on knowledge that was derived from and substantiated by rules of logic. As students progressed through their college years, however, they tended to move from fixed thinking to more flexible forms of reasoning. In progressive steps, they moved from the notion that there is one correct view of knowledge, to skepticism about any point of view, to a recognition that there are many different points of view, to ultimately arriving at their own point of view. In the last stage, they recognize that they are their own source of authority, that they must make a commitment to a position, and that others may hold different positions to which they are equally committed (Cavanaugh & Blanchard-Fields, 2006). As students "move through these stages, they integrate their intellects with their identities, resulting in better understanding of their own value systems and related value commitments" (Upcraft & Moore, 1990, p. 47).

Daniel Levinson's Seasons of a Man's Life

Levinson's (1978) interest in adult development was strongly influenced by Jung and Erikson. As mentioned earlier, Levinson called Jung the father of adult development, and he credited Erikson with taking adult development seriously.

Realizing that very little work had been done on adult development, Levinson conducted a study in which he interviewed a diverse sample of adult males over a period of several years. His findings confirmed Jung's and Erikson's view that adulthood is not a plateau, but continues to be dynamic. Adult development is what Levinson calls "the evolution of the life structure during the adult years" (p. 42). That life structure comprises all aspects of the self, unconscious and conscious, its interaction with its sociocultural environment, and its participation in the world. Levinson expanded on Erikson's interest in the sociocultural impact on development by attending to how persons interrelate with their environment. Levinson believed that the self is an active force that builds, maintains, reevaluates, and remodels its life structure throughout life.

According to Levinson, adult development is composed of four major periods—childhood and adolescence, early adult, middle adult, and later adult—each period alternating with transitional phases. Individuals go through seasons, or periods, of stability in which they work at building their life structure, alternating with transitions, during which they reevaluate and reorganize their life structure. Levinson emphasized the transitional periods as crucial times in effecting developmental change: "A transition is a bridge, or a boundary zone, between two states of greater stability. It involves a process of change, a shift from one structure to another" (pp. 49–50). Transitions are conflicting and painful, but they also provide the opportunity for growth into the next stage and are a source of healthy change. For each period, certain developmental tasks must be met that "are crucial to the evolution of the periods" (p. 53).

Although Levinson is best known for describing the midlife crisis, his theory emphasized that changes and transitional periods occur throughout life. Major conflicts experienced by 70% of his sample during midlife led Levinson to believe that a midlife crisis is inevitable for almost everyone. The major task at midlife, he believed, is to begin to look inward for meaning and unity in life. During the last season (age 65 and beyond), adults become caring, compassionate, and attentive to others. Levinson's discussion of the last season is sketchy, however, because no men older than age 47 were interviewed.

After publishing his work on adult male development, Levinson, working collaboratively with his wife Judy, conducted a study of adult women during the 1980s. Their work on women—*The Seasons of a Woman's Life* (Levinson & Levinson, 1996), published 2 years after his death—shows that adult women go through similar stages to those of men, although gender issues within the framework are noticeably different.

Roger Gould: Transformations

As he noticed in his practice and personal life that adults continue to undergo changes, psychiatrist Roger Gould (1978) sensed the limitations of his Freudian training and turned to the Jungian view that adults continue to develop. After conducting several research studies, Gould concluded that "adulthood is not a plateau; rather, it is a dynamic and changing time for all of us" (p. 14). After publishing articles on his results and lecturing to professional and lay audiences, he received such an overwhelming response that he developed his work into a conceptual framework, out of which he published his book *Transformation: Growth and Change in Adult Life* (1978).

Gould described six stages of life: childhood, adolescence, young adult, adult, midlife, and beyond midlife. In each stage, he claimed, certain issues based on false assumptions need to be worked on to help transform the individual into the next developmental stage, with each stage leading to increased maturity. "As we grow and change, we take steps away from childhood and toward adulthood. . . . With each step, the unfinished business of childhood intrudes, disturbing our emotions and requiring psychological work" (p. 14). Like Erikson, Gould accepted emotional crises and conflicts as a normal process of adult life; by confronting them, one goes through a process of transformation. "It is about the evolution of adult consciousness as we release ourselves from the constraints and ties of childhood consciousness" (p. 15).

Of particular significance for adult development theory are his last four stages. From ages 22 to 28, individuals transform into young adults as they become committed to their own careers and to raising children. In doing so, they give up the false assumption that parents have all the answers to life's problems. Between ages 29 and 34, individuals learn to face their own shortcomings and false assumptions about themselves, their relationships, and their careers. Between ages 35 and 45, Gould, like Levinson, says a midlife crisis is apt to occur. Persons at this stage confront the false assumption that there is no evil in the world and in themselves, and they confront moral issues about love and death. They also feel a sense of desperation and urgency in trying to attain something meaningful before time runs out. During the next stage, age 45 and beyond, older adults settle down, accept life as it is, and become less judgmental or demanding of themselves and others.

At about the time of Levinson's and Gould's works, Gail Sheehy (1976) published *Passages,* which became a best seller. Sheehy interviewed 115 women and men and described the unsettling transitions adults must pass through to attain authentic identities. Sheehy has been criticized because she did not give information about the selection of her sample, the method of interviewing, the collection of data, and the basis for generalizing her findings to the general population (Santrock, 2008). Nevertheless, her work made *midlife crisis* a household phrase and its problems a cultural expectancy.

Older Adult Development

Carl Jung (1933) was especially interested in older adult development and emphasized that this was a creative period in one's life. But because of the attention given in the United States to child and adolescent development, his theory on this later stage of life was generally ignored in this country for most of the 20th century. In the 1970s and 1980s, when Levinson and Gould were emphasizing midlife development issues, the prevailing view of older adult development was that of gradual, progressive decline and deterioration.

Robert Butler, a renowned gerontologist, challenged this ageist stereotyping of older adults in his landmark publication *Why Survive?* (1975). He noted that people over age 65, who were the fastest growing segment of the population, were living longer, healthier lives and that they were demonstrating the potential to grow and contribute to society in unique ways. A decade later, Butler, along with Herbert Gleason, published *Productive Aging* (1985), in which they described how older adults individually and as a group can contribute to the betterment of society. These leaders urged that society change its negative attitudes about aging and foster new social roles and opportunities for older adults to continue to be productive.

After Butler, other developmental researchers—Baltes (1987), O'Connor and Vallerand (1994), and Hartley (2006)—investigated development in older adults. They found that older adults do develop capacities in later life quite different from those in their younger days. Tasks involving reflection, judgment, and knowledge related to meaningful and cultural experiences replaced the tasks necessary for younger people, such as abstract reasoning unrelated to experience, timed responses, or rote memorization.

With increased attention being paid to older adults in recent years, the Jungian approach to the later periods of life has gained considerable attention from the general community. Jungian psychiatrist Allan Chinen (1989), for example, proposed three substages of older adult growth: self-confrontation, self-transcendence, and self-transformation.

Feminist Human Development Theories

In the 1970s and 1980s, feminist development theorists pointed out that Piaget, Erikson, and Kohlberg all based their research on male norms of behavior. Feminists contended that women's and men's developmental processes differ: whereas women learn to connect with and care for others, men learn to separate and become autonomous (Chodorow, 1974, 1978; Conarton & Silverman, 1988; Gilligan, 1982; Miller, 1976). Much of the early feminist perspective of human development has since been integrated into mainstream developmental theory.

One of the earliest critics of male-dominated theory was Nancy Chodorow (1974, 1978), who wrote "against the masculine bias of psychoanalytic theory" (Gilligan, 1982, p. 8), a theory that emphasized that persons must separate from others to gain their own identity. Traditional psychology had held that a woman's tendency to relate to and care for others was a sign of inferiority and dependency. However, from research in which she observed small children and their mothers, Chodorow noticed developmental differences between boys and girls emerging early in childhood. Whereas male children break away from their initial bonding with their mothers to find their male identities, young female children maintain connections with their mothers and learn that it is socially acceptable to model their mothers' caretaking patterns (Gilligan, 1982).

Carol Gilligan's landmark book *In a Different Voice* (1982) brought the issue to public attention; she claimed that women, because of their feelings of empathy toward others, speak in a different voice. "Her work on women's development reframes developmental models and brings women's and girls' voices into the center of a new psychology" (Jordan et al., 1991, p. 3). Having taught with Erik Erikson at Harvard and having been strongly influenced by his psychodynamic theory of developmental conflicts (Gilligan, 1982; Wylie, 2002), Gilligan criticized Erikson's theory that humans go through successive stages of separation, an idea influenced by the 19th- and 20th-century American urge for independence and autonomy. She also disagreed with his claim that, after having gained independence and autonomy at midlife, one suddenly acquires a sense of caring and intimacy. Instead, patterns of intimacy and caring develop in a long, extended process; by midlife, women have developed complex ways of caring for others.

Gilligan (1982) also criticized Kohlberg's theory of moral development for basing the hierarchy of moral reasoning on male norms. She asserted that such a narrow perspective about the morality of justice reasoning cannot be generalized to all cases—situations differ. Women tend to view moral decisions from a caring perspective, considering relationships and connections with others; and in certain cases, the moral option of caring for others takes precedence over justice reasoning. Gilligan, who also taught with Kohlberg at Harvard, collaborated with him on studies and publications on moral development and influenced him to modify his proposal to include caring for others.

Conarton and Silverman (1988) present a theory of developmental stages for women that is based on Gilligan's work, Dabrowski's (1964) theory of positive disintegration, and Jungian processes of individuation involving mythic symbolism (see Table 5.2). They emphasize, "The developmental cycle of women must be viewed with the awareness that women's primary striving is for relatedness and connection" (p. 49). Women first bond with their mothers, then expand relationships to others. Of particular note is the adolescent stage of cultural adaptation. During this time, a woman's tendency to develop relatedness is broken because she must imitate male behavior in order to compete, first in high school and higher education and then out in the business world. At midlife, Phase 4, she begins to yearn for a return to her feminine nature and starts the journey of self-exploration.

Conarton and Silverman use symbolism to describe the four stages that follow the midlife period, the stages in which a woman journeys into her deep feminine nature. They compare this journey to the four arduous tasks that Psyche, a figure in Greek mythology, had to carry out. In these last stages, a woman seeks and develops empowerment to claim her right to be feminine, her right to be recognized as a caring person, and her right to apply her feminine ways of "cooperation, consensus, and mediation" (Conarton & Silverman, 1988, p. 58). She moves toward wholeness and integrates her drives to care

TABLE 5.2
Conarton and Silverman's Feminine Development Theory

Stage	Characteristic Tasks
Phase 1. Bonding	Interdependence with mothers
Phase 2. Orientation to Others	Caring and connectedness to others
Phase 3. Cultural Adaptation	Imitation of males
Phase 4. Awakening & Separation	Beginning search for self
Phase 5. Development of the Feminine	Deeper exploration of needs
Phase 6. Empowerment	Exerting power over their own lives
Phase 7. Spiritual Development	Experiencing own interest in life
Phase 8. Integration	Individuation—expanding caring to the world at large

From "Feminine Development Through the Life Cycle," by S. Conarton and L. K. Silverman, in M. A. Dutton-Douglas & L. E. Walker (Eds.), *Feminist Psychotherapies: Integration of Therapeutic and Feminist Systems* (p. 38), 1988, Norwood, NJ: Ablex. Copyright 1988 by Ablex. Adapted with permission.

for herself and others. Then, in the final stage, she turns her caring toward the world, society, and future generations.

Gilligan (2002) also refers to the Psyche myth in her latest book, *The Birth of Pleasure,* which emphasizes again that a woman's perspective differs from the prevailing male-oriented, sociocultural norms. Gilligan uses the Psyche myth to counteract the Oedipal myth, which dominates Western culture and views the human condition as tragic and destructive. Gilligan uses the story of Psyche and Eros to emphasize the striving for and attainment of empathy, love, and regeneration.

Religious and Spiritual Development

For some years now, many counselors and counseling psychologists have indicated that interest in and attention to clients' spiritual concerns have been increasing steadily (Bergin, 1989; Fowler, 1991, 1995; Kelly, 1995; McWhirter, 1989; Worthington, 1989). "The integration of religious perspectives into the professional psychological frame of reference is simply revolutionary" (Bergin, 1989, p. 621).

In his book *Stages of Faith,* James Fowler (1995) proposed a model of faith development that has received considerable attention from counseling professionals and has contributed significantly to the theory of human development. Like many religious leaders of the 20th century, Fowler was concerned about the disenchantment with traditional religious beliefs, the rise of secularism, and the rise of the human desire for material gain, wealth, and power. Concerned religious leaders believed that it was time to reimagine and redefine faith (Fowler, 1995). Drawing upon the work of theologians

Paul Tillich and Reinhold Niebuhr and religious historian Wilfred Cantwell Smith, Fowler defines the meaning of faith, distinguishing it from a fixed religious belief, as a universal feature of human living, recognizably similar everywhere despite the remarkable variety of forms and contents of religious practice and belief. He describes faith not as a separate dimension of life or a compartmentalized specialty, but as an orientation of the total person, giving purpose and goal to one's hopes and strivings, thoughts, and actions.

Combining elements of the Eriksonian psychosocial developmental theory of working through conflicts and Kohlberg's and Piaget's structural theories of cognitive moral development, Fowler (1995) proposed a stage theory of faith development, which he believes is relational, interactive, and part of a dynamic process, rather than a matter of acquiring and adhering to a fixed belief system. He sees faith development as triadic, a relationship between the self, the other (the parent), and one's sociocultural world—the shared central values and power.

Fowler (1995) describes faith as "the search for an overarching, integrating and grounding trust in a center of value and power sufficiently worthy to give our lives unity and meaning" (p. 5). Faith is akin to the imagination, he claims, noting the inherent problem with this theory from a research psychologist's point of view, because it is virtually impossible to fit imagination into an objective, empirical style of research. Rather than being externalized and observable, faith stems from a person's own constructs, a view that is consistent with Piaget's and Kohlberg's cognitive structural theories and constructivist theories. Fowler believes, however, that faith development goes beyond one's cognitive constructs to include affective, intuitive components of human development. One of the early proponents of narrative therapy, Fowler believes in storytelling and telling one's story as a matter of faith development. According to E. W. Kelly (1995), Fowler's discipline of faith "is clearly relevant to the spiritual/religious dimension in counseling because it represents people's inner or psychodynamic orientation to questions of meaning and value, that is, to questions that for many people are associated predominantly with spirituality and religion" (p. 70).

Fowler proposed six stages of faith development that broadened and extended Kohlberg's stages of cognitive moral reasoning to include affective and imaginal components. In the first three stages of faith development, individuals rely on some authority outside themselves for their faith perspective. During the first stage of faith (*intuitive–projective*), young children follow the beliefs of their parents. They tend to imagine or fantasize angels or other religious figures in stories as characters in fairy tales. In the second stage of faith (*mythical–literal*), older children tend to respond to religious stories and rituals literally, rather than symbolically.

Adolescents enter into the third stage of faith (*synthetic–conventional*), during which their faith begins to form on social-conventional belief systems outside themselves—peer and gang loyalties, dress codes, and so on. They go through identity crises as they search for a sense of themselves in relation to how others think of them, and they feel a need to belong to a group. During this period, individuals tend to acquire a conformist acceptance of a faith with little self-reflection or examination of their beliefs. Some critics claim that churches, in general, represent this conformist stage. Most people and church congregations may remain at this level (Fowler, 1995), but many late adolescents and young adults move on to the fourth stage, particularly when struck with a conflict or a crisis of faith and the need to work through difficulties.

Those individuals who move to the fourth stage of faith (*individuative–reflective*) begin a radical shift from dependence on others' spiritual beliefs to development of their own. Fowler (1995) says, "For a genuine move to stage 4 to occur, there must be an interruption of reliance on external sources of authority. . . . There must be . . . a relocation of authority within the self" (p. 179). At this stage, individuals are no longer defined by the groups to which they belong. Instead, they choose beliefs, values, and relationships important to their self-fulfillment.

In the fifth stage of faith (*conjunctive*), persons move from the certainty of their beliefs as expressed in logical, propositional affirmations, to a more intuitive understanding of truth beyond reason. This is the midlife period of development in which, in accord with the Jungian view, life appears paradoxical and divided. Individuals become more tolerant and compassionate toward others' beliefs. But Fowler distinguishes tolerance from relativism:

> The relativity of religious traditions that matters is not their relativity to each other, but their relativity—their *relate*-ivity—to the reality to which they mediate relation. Conjunctive faith, therefore, is ready for significant encounters with other traditions than its own, expecting that truth has disclosed and will disclose itself in those traditions in ways that may complement or correct its own. (p. 186)

Individuals who move to the sixth and last stage of faith (*universalizing*) are rare. In this transcendent state of unconditional love and justice, they sacrifice their own self-interests for the sake of others. It is a subversive form of faith, according to Fowler, because the sense of deep justice and commitment to the welfare of others challenges conventional, cultural beliefs. Mother Theresa and Martin Luther King, Jr., are examples of contemporary people who reached this highest form of spiritual development (Fowler, 1981).

In the field of counseling, Ingersoll (1997), Kelly (1995), Fukuyama and Sevig (1997), and Worthington (1989) have been the most outspoken regarding a counselor's need to attend to the spiritual development of a client. Worthington (1989) claims that religious and spiritual development have received insufficient attention in counseling; he argues that counselors must become aware of how religious faith relates to both normal development and pathological behavior. Research has shown that more than 90% of U.S. citizens believe in a divine being and that approximately 30% consider themselves strong believers (Spilka, Hood, & Gorsuch, 1985). On the basis of these figures, the majority of clients are embodied with some degree of spiritual and religious belief, conscious or unconscious, as they face emotional crises and try to resolve them. Clients who believe that counselors do not sense the significance of religious or spiritual matters will either be reluctant to bring up their beliefs or will decide to drop out of counseling.

In his comprehensive article, "Religious Faith across the Life Span: Implications for Counseling and Research" (1989), Worthington discusses how the views of Erikson, Jung, and Piaget relate to the spiritual development of people at every stage of life. He also points out how an individual's problems—sex, substance abuse, marital conflicts, poverty, retirement—often have overtones of religious or spiritual concerns. Worthington presents five reasons that counselors need to understand how religious faith influences human development:

1. A high percentage of the population identifies itself as religious.
2. Many people who are undergoing emotional crises spontaneously consider religion in their deliberations about their dilemmas, even if they have not recently been active.
3. Despite their private consideration of religion, many clients, especially religious clients, are reluctant to bring up their religious considerations as part of secular therapy.
4. In general, therapists are not as religiously oriented as their clients.
5. As a result of being less religiously oriented than their clientele, many therapists might not be as informed about religion as would be maximally helpful to their more religious clients. (pp. 556–557)

Some years ago, philosopher Harry R. Moody, cofounder and director of the Brookdale Center on Aging at Hunter College, noted that Erikson's developmental stages omitted spiritual growth (Moody & Carroll, 1997). Moody gradually came to realize, however, the correlation between life stages and the stages of spirituality: "Just as there are age-related stages of maturity in each of our lives, I discovered, so there are sequential stages of spiritual opportunity—spiritual passages, as well as social and psychological ones" (pp. 8–9). In *The Five Stages of the Soul: Charting the Spiritual Passages That Shape Our Lives*, Moody and Carroll (1997) note that all of the great religions of the world speak of developmental stages: "The notion of stages of the soul, in short, is a universal one" (p. 9). Moody proposes five stages of the soul that "typically occur during midlife and beyond" (p. 33), after a person has experienced enough setbacks in life to question seriously the meaning of life.

1. *The Call.* This stage is familiar to those who experience a conversion, a change of heart, a deep awakening.
2. *The Search.* During this stage, the person seeks a teacher, a guide, a way.
3. *The Struggle.* During this stage, "the soul's true passage begins" (p. 36). This is the most difficult and longest stage, a period in which the person undergoes many arduous trials and tests and suffers numerous defeats and feelings of despair.
4. *The Breakthrough.* This stage includes illuminating insights. "There are many levels of breakthrough experiences, some small, some great, some lasting, some temporary" (pp. 37–38).
5. *The Return.* "Life goes on as before. There's still work to do. At the same time, we now have special knowledge and experience to give back to the world" (p. 38). Persons now have a compassionate outlook toward others, and many become guides and mentors.

Many counselors find it difficult to work effectively with clients' religious or spiritual concerns because they themselves have not explored their own spiritual needs (Fukuyama & Sevig, 1997). Recognizing the need for counselors to become more aware of the spiritual concerns of their clients, the Association for Counselor Education and Supervision (ACES) has appointed a task force to develop the counselor competencies necessary for effective spiritual counseling. In line with this effort, Ingersoll (1997) and Fukuyama and Sevig (1997) have proposed new courses covering spiritual issues in counseling.

Emotional Intelligence: A Developmental Learning Process

The concept of *emotional intelligence* emerged as a result of dissatisfaction with the intelligence quotient (IQ) and captured public attention in the 1990s through popular books. Critics claim that IQ measures only "a narrow band of linguistic and math skills" (Goleman, 1995, p. 42), which may predict success in school but are unreliable indicators of performance and productivity in the broader field of one's life work. Addressing this deficiency, Howard Gardner (1993) proposed that humans have *multiple intelligences,* one of which is emotional intelligence. In contrast to the idea of an inherently fixed IQ at birth, Gardner proposes that humans, given sufficient learning conditions, are capable of learning various modes of intelligences.

Goleman (1995) took Gardner's emotional intelligence component, which Gardner had described from a cognitive perspective, and developed the concept further, describing it from the perspective of emotions. Goleman's thesis is that human emotions can operate independently, beyond reasoning and thinking capacities. According to Goleman (1995), emotional intelligence results from a learned developmental process that begins in infancy and continues through five sequential stages:

1. Developing awareness of one's emotions
2. Managing one's emotions
3. Becoming self-motivated
4. Recognizing and responding empathically to emotions in others
5. Handling relationships and managing the emotions of others

Goleman (1995, 1998) suggested that emotional intelligence can predict success at numerous life tasks, many of them work or career related. Goleman believes that emotional intelligence influences such abilities as being a team player, accomplishing work-related tasks, and working well with colleagues.

Ivey's Developmental Counseling and Therapy

Allen Ivey (Ivey, 2000; Ivey et al., 2007) modified and expanded Piaget's cognitive theory to include development that continues to occur past childhood and adolescence into adulthood. "We usually think of Piaget's theories as primarily relating to the child, yet they serve as helpful metaphors for the construction of therapeutic theory and method that enables us to examine adult change and development" (Ivey, 2000, p. 78). Ivey combined Piaget's first two stages and then added a new fourth stage: dialectic/systemic. As Ivey (2000) explains, this new stage is needed because "formal operational thinking as usually defined by Piaget 1/4 does not adequately account for the complexity of thinking that starts to occur" (p. 104).

Thus, Ivey added a postformal model, similar to that of his predecessors Kegan (1982), Kohlberg (1969), and Perry (1970). In this fourth stage, individuals develop a propensity for reflection and dialectic within themselves, in their relationships, and in their sociocultural environment. Individuals learn to realize that self-reflection and interactions with family and culture provide for constant change and development. "They can recognize the influence of family and cultural systems and see the complexity and variability of emotions and thoughts, can challenge their own assumptions, can transform their thinking in response to changing circumstances" (Rigazio-DiGilio & Ivey, 1991, p. 6).

During this dialectic/systemic stage, individuals "examine relationships between and among things and objects" (Ivey, 2000, p. 120). Individuals at this stage can be in dialogue with their previously developed structural system of development. Individuals, in effect, conduct an evolving transformational process within their basic self structures.

Ivey's model, which he calls *developmental counseling and therapy (DCT),* emphasizes the importance of the complex, interactive relationship individuals have with others and with their sociocultural environment, that is, "the importance of context" (p. 121). Moreover, this model is particularly valuable for its capacity to encompass both multicultural and older adult developmental issues. Recognizing the dialectical, postformal component in human development and expanding on it, Ivey has contributed a comprehensive, multidimensional, dynamic approach to cognitive development theory.

Sandra Rigazio-DiGilio (2007) expanded Ivey's theory of human development into a therapeutic family systems model called *systemic cognitive–developmental therapy* (SCDT). SCDT emphasizes the importance of families as mediators for the culture and the individual; it works to activate and enhance this role by providing a therapeutic environment for facilitating individual, family, and network interaction and growth (Rigazio-DiGilio, 2007).

TRENDS: TOWARD AN INTEGRATED THEORY OF DEVELOPMENT

Whereas earlier developmental theorists focused on short timespans or only on certain aspects of human development, more recent theorists have been attempting to form integrated models of development that embrace all components of development throughout the life span. Moral development, for example, which was ignored for decades by most psychologists, is now considered an integral part of human development (Berk, 2006; Haste, 1993; Noam & Wren, 1993; Bruner, 1990; Wren, 1990). At the same time, the different schools of developmental thought, such as the cognitive–behaviorists and the postmodern constructivists, are carrying on dialogues and debates about similarities and differences (Watts, 2003). Debates also continue over whether humans are the agents of their own development or whether their development is determined by their sociocultural environment. Bridging this divide are those who argue that human development is based on a synthesis of individual capacities, relationships, and sociocultural influences.

Developmentalists now tend to emphasize a world view, claiming that a contextual approach that recognizes multicultural influences is necessary in understanding human development. Cultural psychologist Jerome Bruner (1990) also emphasizes the cultural, historical context in an attempt to make meaning out of experience. "If the cognitive revolution erupted in 1956, the *contextual* revolution (at least in psychology) is occurring today" (pp. 105–106). Rigazio-DiGilio's (2007) SCDT approach emphasizes a multicultural, systemic, contextual model. And Steenbarger (1991) proposes a comprehensive model, termed a *contextual worldview,* in which human development is affected by individuals' interactions with others, the community, and the world at large.

Many researchers have been challenging or shifting away from the stage theory of human development (Bruner & Haste, 1987; Noam, 1990; Rest et al., 1999; Steenbarger, 1991), with some proposing instead a narrative approach to understanding human development. In light of the overall attempts to integrate theories of development and the ongoing debates over theoretical differences, no single, clear-cut, separate model of human development exists any longer.

Constructivists claim that one's view of the nature of the self has a direct bearing on one's view of human development (Neimeyer & Mahoney, 1999; Neimeyer & Raskin, 2000). They have been strong proponents of exploring the nature of the self and the self's tendency to make meaning out of life's experiences (Kegan, 1982; Kelly, 1995; Lyddon, 1999; Mahoney, 1995; Neimeyer, 1999). Like Piaget, constructivists believe that the self has the self-organizing capacity to make sense of encounters and to reconstruct experiences. This theory of dynamic self-development is opposed to the acquisition of external knowledge (Lyddon, 1999).

Others argue, however, that the self is determined by sociocultural influences. Social constructionists Berger and Luckman (1966) and Gergen (1985) challenged traditional 20th-century psychologists who believed that humans develop as autonomous individuals. They claim instead that human development is determined by one's sociocultural environment. Gilligan (1982), Rigazio-DiGilio (2007), and other leading feminists also advocate that sociocultural influences are a key factor in human development, a perspective that heightens awareness of diversity and multicultural perspectives of human development.

Bridging the gap between these two positions is cultural psychologist Jerome Bruner (1990), who not only supports sociocultural influences, but also believes that humans can act as agents of their own development. Humans find meaning in their experiences, he claims, through a narrative approach to understanding, as opposed to other forms of discourse—logical propositions, conceptualizations, and the use of tests—"as a mode of organizing experience" (Bruner, 1990, p. 43).

Another attempt to bridge the gap is a model proposed by Helen Haste (1993) that synthesizes the two extremes. According to her theory, development is based on a triadic relationship among (a) the autonomous, self-organizing self; (b) the interpersonal self; and (c) the self in relation to the sociocultural milieu. This theory is based on a model proposed decades earlier, in the 1930s, by Russian philosopher Lev Vygotsky (1962, 1978), little known in the United States until recently. Interest in Vygotsky was fueled in the 1980s by sociologists and anthropologists (Bruner & Haste, 1987); he is now highly regarded in professional circles, particularly among child development specialists (Berk, 2006).

Haste's (1993) developmental model, called lay social theory, describes one's sociocultural milieu as a schema with its own complex dimensions—a conceptual framework that humans' do not acquire passively, but gradually grow into, interacting reciprocally in complex ways that affect both the development of the self and the way one interacts with and is affected by the sociocultural milieu. Haste (1993) is among those who believe that moral development is an integral part of human development (Berk, 2006; Noam & Wren, 1993; Bruner, 1990; Wren, 1990). Jerome Bruner (1990), one of the early promoters of narrative therapy, claims that the intention behind telling one's story is to take a moral stand against conventional social mores. "To tell a story is inescapably to take a moral stance" (p. 51).

Although developmental theorists generally have integrated moral development into developmental theory, many are still split over the issue of moral universalism versus moral relativism. Addressing the issue, Haste (1993) proposes a theory of pluralism, "a third option, which goes beyond the dichotomy of relativism and universalism" (p. 179), while at the same time taking into account the many different ways world cultures conceptualize standards of morality. Likewise, Bruner (1990), hoping to move the debate beyond that "dreaded form of relativism where every belief is as good as another" (p. 27), advocates a developmental approach in which one "need not fret about the specter of relativism. It concerns open-mindedness a willingness to construe knowledge and values from multiple perspectives without loss of commitment to one's own values" (p. 30).

A model similar to Haste's is Noam's (1990) integrated model of human development, which regards the self as the organizing core of development in a dynamic relationship with interpersonal interactions and sociocultural influences. Noam's perspective combines constructivist and contemporary psychoanalytic thought, as well as the sociocultural perspectives of Bruner (1986) and Vygotsky (1962). Noam's complicated model of self-development, briefly stated, constitutes a combined system, or two structures, of the self. First, the self develops a biographical structure, or a *thema*, involving one's development as a life story, or living biography, to make meaning out of experience. Second, humans have a self-perspective, which develops a self-complexity, or a *schema,* arising from one's interactions with others and the environment.

Noam (1990) argues that a stage theory is an inadequate model of human development because it breaks the human being into a series of collective categories, in which the self is regarded only as an "'epistemic self,' where a multitude of individual and collective life experiences are condensed into a few ideal developmental types or stages" (p. 362). Noam's model, instead, puts the historical, narrative, thematic self in juxtaposition with the stages of life encountered in the sociocultural world, such as the child growing into adulthood and the graded learning systems in school programs.

SUMMARY

Human development theories have strongly influenced counseling theory and practice. Piaget's cognitive theory of development underlies the use of cognitive theories of counseling with children and adolescents. Kohlberg's theory of moral development has prompted ongoing dialogue in psychology, philosophy, and the social sciences, and has opened up discourse among professionals about the meaning of life and the nature of humankind. It has challenged counselors, therapists, and educators to question their own values, and has made moral issues pertinent to clients and students.

Jung and Erikson expanded developmental theories to include a life-span perspective. Levinson and Gould published theories about human development through midlife. Butler then challenged the view that people over age 65 progressively decline. He and other professionals have demonstrated that older adults have the capacity to continue to develop throughout life.

Feminist developmental theorists Gilligan, Conarton and Silverman, and Miller challenged conventional, male-dominated theories, proposing instead that the developmental processes of women and men differ. A woman's tendency to relate to and care for others is not an inferior or immature state, but rather represents a different developmental process.

Attention to spiritual development continues to expand and deepen in the counseling field after many years of neglect, with increasing interest in Fowler's, Moody's, and Worthington's models of faith or spiritual development. The theory of emotional development proposed by Goleman has also had a considerable impact. Among the first attempts at an integrative developmental proposal have been Ivey's model (DCT) and Sandra Rigazio-DiGilio's systemically oriented model (SCDT).

The trend continues toward forming an integrative theory of development, one that encompasses all aspects of human development throughout life. But debates continue to flourish among postmodern developmental theorists over several issues: (a) the nature of the self (whether the self is the agent of development or whether self-development is determined by sociocultural forces); (b) moral universalism versus moral relativism; and (c) the adequacy of the stage theory, with challengers proposing alternative narrative, contextual models as a means of understanding human development.

PROJECTS AND ACTIVITIES

1. Review the literature on conflict in human behavior, and note how conflict is described. Divide the articles into those that describe conflict as a barrier to growth and those that describe it as a potential for growth.
2. If male, place yourself in the developmental stage of Erikson's theory that most describes your stage of life. If female, do the same for the stages of Conarton and Silverman. Do you find that the crises or conflicts described by Erikson or by Conarton and Silverman are typical of your age and fit your current circumstances? What is similar, and what is different?
3. Interview some retired men and women over age 60. Ask about any changes in attitudes or behaviors that have occurred in

their lives in the last 40 years. Did they experience any midlife crises? Do you notice differences in the men's and the women's responses?

4. Organize a class discussion around Heinz's dilemma. Does the group believe that responses given by contemporary children or adolescents will differ from those of children 20 years ago? How much influence do values presented in the media or in the behaviors of politicians and public figures have on moral judgment and reasoning?
5. Carol Gilligan poses provocative challenges to developmental theories based on men and generalized to women. Do you see evidence in novels, short stories, or the cinema that support or contradict her view?

CHAPTER 6

Counseling Theories and Techniques

A counseling theory is a model that counselors use as a guide for understanding clients' problems and hypothesizing possible solutions. A well-integrated theory can guide a counselor through the therapeutic process and can provide a basis for selecting particular counseling approaches or techniques. Without solid theoretical backing, counselors operate haphazardly in a "trial-and-error manner" and risk being both ineffective and harmful (Gladding, 2007, p. 189). Practicing counselors with a sound theoretical foundation are also able to make evaluations and judgments about new ideas and techniques.

Of the numerous counseling theories in existence today, those chosen for review here have formed the essential foundations of counseling and have generated activity through the years that has contributed to the development of contemporary counseling. Contemporary theories have been selected on the basis of the amount of literature that they are generating, the degree to which the literature crosses disciplines, and the degree to which their ideas are accessible to counselors and the public.

Theories are classified in this chapter into five categories: (a) psychoanalytic and psychodynamic; (b) humanistic; (c) behavioral, cognitive, and cognitive–behavioral; (d) creative and expressive arts and narrative therapies; and (e) brief counseling. The first three categories are based on the differing views theorists have about human nature and human behavior. The fourth and fifth categories demonstrate these perspectives in the context of creative and expressive arts and of brief, time-limited counseling sessions.

After studying this chapter, you will be able to

- Identify the major counseling theories and their diverse views on human nature and human behavior.
- Understand the role of theories in guiding, evaluating, and improving the practice of counseling.
- Describe integrative theoretical approaches in counseling.

PSYCHOANALYTIC AND PSYCHODYNAMIC THEORIES

Psychoanalytic and psychodynamic theorists cover a wide range of beliefs, but all believe that the unconscious is part of the governing process of individuals and that intrapsychic, dynamic forces operate in one's interactions with others. The goal of analysis is to help individuals become aware of and come to terms with these underlying unconscious dynamic forces. As we discuss psychoanalytic and psychodynamic theories in this section, we will use term *patient,* which is usually employed by psychoanalysts. Later, the term *client,* the preferred designation in the counseling profession, will be used throughout the rest of this chapter.

At the turn of the 20th century, Sigmund Freud was developing his theory of psychoanalysis. He believed that a person's unconscious processes are determined by biological, *libidinal,* or *psychosexual* instincts or drives—drives that are potentially destructive unless controlled and channeled. Through psychoanalysis, the analyst helps the patient learn to control these unconscious drives. Carl Jung and Alfred Adler once were followers of Freud, but later broke with him over his deterministic concept of human nature and his belief that behavior is determined by psychosexual drives. They developed their own theories, claiming that other unconscious forces also govern behavior, such as soul and spirit (Jungian) or the drive to socialize (Adlerian).

Psychoanalysts Karen Horney, Erich Fromm, and Harry Stack Sullivan also objected to Freud's psychosexual model of human nature. Following Adler's belief in the individual's fundamental drive to socialize, they emphasized the individual's psychosocial, or interpersonal, development. Contemporary psychoanalysis is based primarily on later significant contributions that came in the name of ego-analytic and object relations theories, which have been countered more recently by feminist psychodynamic theories emphasizing the nature of connections in relationships.

Classical Psychoanalytic Theory

According to Sigmund Freud (1940/1949), human behavior is determined by unconscious, biological, potentially destructive instincts—the *id.* Id impulses (sex and aggression) often clash with a person's need to adapt to society. As children grow, they develop the ego and the superego. The *ego* is the conscious part of the mind that acts as a mediator between an individual's instinctive, uninhibited id impulses and external reality. As their egos develop, children learn to make compromises between their inner urges and parental and societal controls. The *superego* (conscience) helps persons develop a moral code and an ideal of behavior consistent with traditional values in society.

The ego and the superego develop as part of the personality as children go through the psychosexual growth stages—oral, anal, phallic, latent, and genital (Brill, 1938). In the *oral stage* (from birth to about 18 months), gratification centers on feeding. Conflict and anxiety stem from the dependency of the child and the child's demand for immediate gratification. In the *anal stage* (18 months to 3 years), gratification comes from elimination of feces. Toilet training creates conflict and anxiety in child and parent. In the *phallic stage* (3 to 6 years), pleasure centers in the genital area. In this stage, the child experiences sexual impulses toward the parent of the opposite sex and sees the same-sex parent as a rival. In the *latent stage* (6 to 12 years), these impulses are relatively dormant. In the *genital stage* (12 to 18 years), the adolescent begins to develop relationships with members of the opposite sex.

As the child experiences psychosexual conflicts, the ego runs the risk of becoming overwhelmed either by id impulses or by the superego. To protect the ego, children develop unconscious *defense mechanisms,* which help them survive (Freud, 1966). These defenses can become maladaptive if they contribute to the distortion or denial of reality. Examples of defenses are *repression,* or complete denial of impulses; *projection,* in which people ascribe their own unacceptable behavior to others; *displacement,* in which impulses toward something threatening are redirected toward a safe object or person; and *sublimation,* in which unacceptable drives are channeled into socially acceptable or creative activities.

If parent–child relationships are constructive, children express their impulses in acceptable and satisfying ways. If parents are overly strict, rejecting, or neglectful, children will repress impulses and develop defense mechanisms to deny reality. These defense mechanisms may become overly stringent and lead to neurosis or other personality disorders. Psychoanalysts devote more attention to neuroses than to more severe personality disorders because they believe that persons with neurotic symptoms are more responsive to change. The goal of psychoanalysis is to help clients express, in a safe, therapeutic environment, the repressed impulses, fears, and anxieties they experienced as children and to help them learn to channel those energies into socially acceptable behavior.

The therapist assumes an authoritarian position like that of a parent, but is neutral or nonthreatening. The analyst maintains neutrality and distance by sitting behind the client, who lies on a couch. The therapist then encourages the patient to let thoughts come out regardless of their content through *free association* (i.e., saying whatever comes to mind) and by reporting dreams. As patients bring out repressed memories and emotions, they begin to attach or transfer the early unresolved feelings they had toward parents, such as resentment or admiration, onto their therapists. This *transference* is encouraged by therapists as an essential process in therapy. Analysts respond to these distorted feelings in a nonthreatening or nondemanding way, again, unlike parents.

Because of their defenses, patients inevitably begin to resist therapy regardless of how motivated they are. *Resistance* is an unconscious process whereby patients prevent repressed impulses and emotions from coming to awareness. Freud believed that resistance blocked the efforts of client and therapist to gain the patient insights necessary for progress in therapy.

As patients free-associate, report dreams, and experience transference and resistance, the analyst interprets the behavior in a process called *working through.* These interpretations include helping patients see hidden meanings in free associations and dreams, understand the distortions and misperceptions involved in transference toward the analyst, and accept resistance as a sign of progress in therapy. This brings about a nondistorted, real relationship with the analyst and increases client willingness to deal with and resolve unconscious conflicts.

Throughout therapy, therapists must be aware of the possibility of *countertransference,* which is an irrational reaction they may have toward patients that results from the therapists' unresolved needs or conflicts. Therapists may find themselves overprotecting, overidentifying with, or feeling unwarranted irritation toward patients as a result of the therapists' earlier unresolved relationships that may be similar to those of the patients.

Neo-Analytic Theories

Alfred Adler: Individual Psychology

Alfred Adler, a contemporary of Freud, rejected Freud's deterministic, instinct-driven view of human nature and emphasized instead a psychosocial, purposeful perspective of behavior. Moreover, he objected to "Freud's belief that the personality is divided: conscious behavior against unconscious, ego against id and super-ego" (Woodworth & Sheehan, 1964, p. 298). Rather, Adler perceived individuals as unitary, holistic organisms striving to better themselves.

This belief in the unity of personality led Adler to call his theory *individual psychology*—a term that can be misleading, considering his strong advocacy of social forces in human development. The term is clarified, however, in the light of Adler's belief that individuals develop only in the context of their relationship to society.

Adlerian theory is best described as follows: "The nucleus of Adler's personality theory is the concept of a unitary, goal-directed creative self which in the healthy state is in a positive constructive, i.e. ethical, relationship to his fellow man" (Ansbacher & Ansbacher, 1973, p. 6). A person's unifying and organizing life goal shapes his or her orientation to life, strategies for living, and striving for meaningful goals (Corey, 2005). Thus, individuals have the power to develop their own unique lifestyles.

Social interest has been considered Adler's most significant and distinctive concept. This term refers to an individual's awareness of being part of the human community and to the individual's attitudes in dealing with the social world (Corey, 2005). Social interest includes striving for a better future for humanity.

Adler believed that individuals strive to develop themselves in relation to their community throughout their lives. Feelings of inferiority or helplessness that all humans experience are instigators for individuals to seek change. For example, individuals can seek to change a weakness into a strength or strive to excel in one area of concentration to compensate for defects in other areas (Corey, 2005).

Adlerian counseling involves counselors and clients in exploring clients' faulty perceptions about goals. Clients then work toward more constructive goals by developing appropriate social interests, expanding self-awareness, and creatively modifying their lifestyles.

Adler's approach strongly influenced the views of Karen Horney, Erich Fromm, and Harry Stack Sullivan. Each, in turn, elaborated on Adler's psychosocial emphasis:

> Among those who provided psychoanalytic theory with the twentieth century look of social psychology are Alfred Adler, Karen Horney, Erich Fromm and Harry Stack Sullivan. Of these four Alfred Adler may be regarded as the ancestral figure of the "new social psychological look." (Hall, Lindzey, & Campbell, 1998, p. 24)

Adler's belief that individuals develop within a social context led him to focus on family interactions—an emphasis later amplified by Rudolf Dreikurs.

Renewed interest in Adler and the move toward integrating various theoretical approaches prompted several cognitive and constructivist professionals to discuss the degree of compatibility of their theoretical models with Adlerian therapy. Richard Watts, as editor, drew together several professionals to engage in an integrative dialogue, the outcome of which is the book *Adlerian, Cognitive, and Constructivist Therapies* (Watts, 2003). Constructivists claim that their core theoretical concepts are remarkably similar to the Adlerian approach (Neimeyer, 2003). On the other hand, while acknowledging that cognitive behavior therapy (CBT) has some similarities with the Adlerian approach and noting that they have much to offer one another, Dowd (2003) points out that CBT differs significantly from Adlerian therapy:

> Adlerian psychology is a subjective, phenomenological approach, which might be described as long on theory and short on data. By contrast, CBT has long stressed the primacy of observable, objective data and the necessity for phenomena to be observable to external agents, to be of scientific interest and psychologically valid. (p. 97)

Karen Horney

Unlike Freud, and influenced by Adler, Karen Horney emphasized that social–cultural forces are the major influences in human development. She explored how social influences affect the nature or dynamics of a person's character. An example of this process of character development is exemplified in her own experience when she became aware of her difference from Freud's views about feminine psychology:

> Freud's postulations in regard to feminine psychology set me thinking about the role of cultural factors. Their influence on our ideas and what constitutes masculinity or femininity was obvious, and it became just as obvious to me that Freud had arrived at certain conclusions because he failed to take them into account. (Horney, 1945, pp. 11–12)

Likewise, her views about cultural influences on personality were confirmed after she moved from Germany to the United States and noticed that attitudes and neuroses of individuals in Europe differed from those she observed in the United States and that only cultural differences could account for this. Horney believed that the tendency for persons to develop either creatively or neurotically depends on the quality of their interpersonal relationships. Parents thus play a crucial role in the development of their children. When parents are neglectful, indifferent, abusive, or otherwise fail to offer loving guidance, the child develops basic anxiety or, as Horney (1945) puts it, "the feeling a child has of being isolated and helpless in a potentially hostile world" (p. 41). The child, feeling unsafe or insecure, develops a basic hostility toward others, and these feelings further threaten the child.

To assuage this inner conflict, children must develop strategies to repress their impulses in order to maintain a feeling of security. These strategies take the form of three directional interactions with others: *movement toward* others to gain love, *movement away from* others to gain independence, and *movement against* others to gain power (Horney, 1945).

Horney believed that conflicts are an essential and inevitable part of normal human development. She made important distinctions between normal or situational conflicts and conflicts that are neurotic. Normal conflicts arise out of well-defined, stressful problems related to transitions or to everyday problems in work or family relationships. Normal persons are able to resolve these conflicts and learn from them; they may use any or all of the three orientations toward people in a flexible way. Neurotics, in contrast, are unable to resolve their conflicts; they use inflexible and artificial solutions that do not resolve basic anxiety:

> The normal conflict is concerned with an actual choice between two possibilities, both of which the person finds really desirable, or between convictions, both of which he really values . . . The neurotic person engulfed in a conflict is not free to choose. He is driven by equally compelling forces in opposite directions, neither of which he wants to follow. (Horney, 1945, p. 32)

Individuals with either normal or neurotic conflicts can learn to become more adaptive through counseling or therapy. Neurotic persons, because of strong repressed contradictory impulses, find it more difficult to change. The emphasis in therapy is to help neurotic individuals become aware of their inflexible strategies with people and to help prepare them to risk changing these patterns.

Erich Fromm

Erich Fromm believed that social–cultural, political, and economic forces play a dominant role in personality development. Exploitative trends in a culture are major causes of pathology. Personal growth, then, is stifled by economic or political forces that prevent individuals from being productive in society.

In his first book, *Escape from Freedom* (1941), which is based on his experiences in Nazi Germany, Fromm presents his view about the human dilemma: As humans have moved from animal-like dependence on instinctual behavior to beings who can reason, think, and choose, they have developed strong ambivalence about this freedom. The world of choices is less secure:

> He has become free but longs for continued dependency and belonging; he has a biological urge to live but his human reason confronts him with the inescapability of death; unlike animals, he has the capacity to solve problems of his world by thought rather than by instinct, but his brief life span makes fulfillment of his potentialities improbable if not impossible. (Woodworth & Sheehan, 1964, pp. 323–324)

Humans try to escape this freedom of choice and the difficulties of solving problems by preferring the security of submitting to authority and to totalitarian systems. Or they themselves become authoritarian and assume power over others, as occurs in male-dominated societies. Another typical mode of escape is to conform to social norms and to peer groups "in which one renounces selfhood by adopting a 'pseudo self' based on the expectations of others" (Hall, Lindzey, & Campbell, 1998, p. 142). According to Fromm, humans can learn to cope with the challenges that free choice imposes on their existence by understanding and coming to terms with five basic needs: "the need for relatedness, the need for transcendence, the need for rootedness, the need for identity, and the need for a frame of orientation" (Hall, Lindzey, & Campbell, 1998, p. 143).

Harry Stack Sullivan

Harry Stack Sullivan's psychosocial theory is based on the importance of interpersonal relationships in human development. He believed that personality is shaped primarily by social forces, and that because of the powerful human need for interpersonal relationships, personality can only be studied through its interpersonal manifestations (Ewen, 2003).

Sullivan's lasting contribution is his emphasis on the therapeutic interview as a prime example of an interpersonal interaction. The role of the interviewer in therapy sessions, he claimed, is as important as the behavior of the client. "The interviewer becomes the 'participant observer' systematically noting what the patient does, what he says, and how he says it" (Woodworth & Sheehan, 1964, p. 333). Interviewers must also be aware of their own beliefs or attitudes that are incompatible with their clients' (Woodworth & Sheehan, 1964).

Contemporary Psychoanalytic and Psychodynamic Theories

Object Relations Theory

One of the most significant contemporary psychoanalytic approaches is *object relations theory,* which proposes a major restructuring of the classical Freudian instinct-driven theory of human nature. Instead of being governed by id instinctual drives, humans are motivated by their desire to connect or identify with others (i.e., objects).

An early proponent of object relations theory is W. R. D. Fairbairn, who claimed that "the ego's main functions are to seek and to establish relations with objects in the external world" (Hall, Lindzey, & Campbell, 1998, p. 180). Similar to the ego-analytic view of the autonomous nature of the ego, Fairbairn's claim was that

> the ego . . . has its own dynamic structure; and it is the source of its own energy. . . . The ego's main functions are to seek and to establish relations with objects in the external world. . . . The central issue in personality development is not the channeling and rechanneling of instinctual impulses, but the progression from infantile dependence and primary identification with objects to a state of differentiation of self from the object. (Hall, Lindzey, & Campbell, 1998, pp. 180–181)

One of the most influential of the object relations theorists is Heinz Kohut (Hall, Lindzey, & Campbell, 1998). He stressed emphatically the necessity of the nurturing family in the development of self, a family whose primary caretaker can sufficiently serve as the responding object to the infant and child. The primary issue for Kohut is

> the presence or absence of empathic and loving relationships. Healthy mirroring and idealizing afford development of the ideal personality type, the person with an *autonomous* self. . . . Exposure to deficient self-objects produces children who possess a noncohesive, empty, or injured self. (Hall, Lindzey, & Campbell, 1998, p. 182)

Object relations theory has spawned numerous studies and publications. Attention once more has shifted to early childhood relations as a source of a malformed sense of self, but with a significant difference in inquiry from earlier psychoanalytic thinking. Attention now is focused on the deficiencies of relatedness and the repair thereof.

Carl Jung: Analytical Psychology

Like Freudian theories, Jungian ideas fell out of favor in the United States for several decades, primarily because the dominating psychological theories were following the empirical approach to behavior. Unconscious forces were not recognized as influencing behavior because they could not be measured or observed. Moreover, Jungian theory was even less acceptable than Freudian theory because Jungian therapists believed that persons are governed not only by biological forces, but by other forces as well—mind, spirit, and soul—forces foreign to the scientific empirical model of behavior.

Carl Jung began his career as a psychiatrist before becoming a Freudian psychoanalyst. Early on, Jung broke with Freud primarily because he disagreed with the Freudian theory that a person's sexual drive is the primary force determining psychic life. To distinguish himself from Freudian psychoanalysts, Jung called his theory *analytical psychology.* Jung held that the unconscious contains forces that are potentially positive if they are integrated into consciousness. He believed also that the major force in human behavior is an innate purposive drive to attain wholeness and completeness of self, a process he called *individuation* (Bennett, 1983; Jacobi, 1973; Jung, 1933/1970; Samuels, 1985). Individuation is "a process of integration of the world consciousness with the inner world of unconsciousness. Such action and reaction is inherent in development and growth" (Bennett, 1983, p. 172).

Individuation, or the search for wholeness of self, goes on throughout life and is never completed (Bennett, 1983; Samuels, 1985). Individuation falls into two main stages: the first and the second halves of life. Jung is primarily concerned with individuation of adults in the second half of life:

> The task of the first half is "initiation into outward reality" . . . it aims at the adaptation of the individual to the demands of his environment. The task of the second half is a so-called "initiation into the inner reality," a deeper self-knowledge and knowledge of humanity, a "turning back" (*reflectio*) to the traits of one's nature that have hitherto remained unconscious. (Jacobi, 1973, p. 108)

Jung's theory developed out of his observations that the images patients see in their dreams and the symbols drawn from them are similar to those found in ancient folklore, myths, legends, art, and rituals. From this discovery, Jung hypothesized that these images, which he named *archetypes,* come from the collective unconscious, "the storehouse of latent memory traces inherited from man's ancestral past" (Hall, Lindzey, & Campbell, 1998, p. 85).

Among the many archetypes, some significant ones for personality development are the *persona* (mask), which consists of adaptive behaviors that are necessary for social conformity; the *animus* and *anima,* which are, respectively, the woman's masculine side and the man's feminine side; the *shadow,* a person's dark unconscious; and the *self,* a person's inherent tendency to strive for wholeness in life. Therapists help clients bring the unconscious to consciousness and relate unconscious themes to archetypal themes.

Jung (1921/1971) also introduced the idea of two major personality types: the *introvert* (a person oriented toward introspection) and the *extravert* (a person oriented to the outer world). He noted, however, that persons are too complicated simply to be divided into two types, so he hypothesized that these can each be further qualified by four typical styles of functioning: *thinking, sensing, feeling,* and *intuitive.* Considerable work has since been done on what is known as Jungian *typology* (Samuels, 1985). The personality inventory Myers–Briggs Type Indicator is based on these Jungian types (see chapters 7 and 12). It should be noted, however, that Jung objected to classifying people into rigid personality types (Bennett, 1983); he believed that all these character types are inherently in everyone's unconscious and can be drawn into consciousness, a process that is part of individuation. One purpose of therapy is to help the person in this process.

Jung's major procedures were dream analysis and active imagination. Dreams, he believed, are expressions of the unconscious attempting to speak to some situation in the person's conscious life (Samuels, 1985). In *active imagination,* therapist and client plumb the details of a dream, relate the images to ancient myth, and connect them with universal archetypes, as well as with daily events. This process gives meaning to the dream that goes beyond one's ego.

HUMANISTIC AND EXISTENTIAL THEORIES

All humanists believe to some extent that people possess dignity and worth and are purposeful, active, and capable of shaping and directing their own behavior as they work toward self-actualization. Existentialism and humanism are similar in their belief that human nature is basically good and that persons have free choice to grow and develop. Existentialists, however, believe that we are faced with the anxiety of choosing to create an identity in a world that lacks intrinsic meaning (Corey, 2005). In counseling practice, the two also share basic similarities. Both believe that "the client–therapist relationship is at the core of therapy. Both approaches focus on the client's perceptions and call for the therapist to enter the client's subjective world" (Corey, 2005, p. 172).

Rogers's Person-Centered Theory

Carl Rogers (1942, 1951) perceives humans as possessing a basic, innate drive toward growth, wholeness, and fulfillment. People have a basic need for high self-regard. If unhampered, individuals will organize their inner and outer experiences into an integrated self through a self-actualizing process. Unhealthy social or psychological influences, in contrast, tend to inhibit individuals from achieving an integrated, productive self so that they experience conflicts in expressing their basic needs. According to Rogerian theory, humans have the ability to resolve conflicts but are limited mainly by a lack of awareness about themselves. Conflicts arise when there is a disparity between individuals' basic needs and their need to gain approval from others.

Rogers (1939, 1942) was impressed with what was called *relationship therapy,* a method he learned in the 1930s during his work as a clinical psychologist in a child guidance clinic in Rochester, New York. It was based on the psychoanalytic concepts of Otto Rank and was promoted by some of Rank's followers, such as psychiatrist Frederick Allen and social worker Jessie Taft. This mode of therapy differs significantly from traditional psychoanalysis in that the therapist does not make intellectual interpretations or conceptual judgments regarding the client's behavior or expressions, aside from clarifying feelings.

"This is a different sort of interpretation" (Rogers, 1939, p. 346). Rogers's landmark book *Counseling and Psychotherapy* (1942) claimed that the counselor role should be *nondirective,* in reaction against the prevailing authoritarian style of counselors and therapists. "Effective counseling consists of a definitely structured, permissive relationship which allows the client to gain an understanding of himself to a degree which enables him to take positive steps in the light of his new orientation" (p. 18).

Acting on the theory that, in the appropriate environment, individuals self-actualize, the counselor is crucial in providing the right atmosphere to help clients self-correct behaviors that block growth and develop new ways of being that foster growth. Thus, in counseling, the counselor focuses on the individual, not on the problem; acknowledges the feelings of the client; places more importance on the immediate situation than on the client's past; emphasizes the evolving nature of the counseling process; and perceives the emotional relationship that develops between counselor and client as a therapeutic growth experience.

Rogers's insistence that the counselor assume a nonauthoritarian, nonadvisory role was a radical departure from conventional therapeutic practice. Without the counselor acting as adviser, the process itself becomes the essence of counseling, a process that can be delineated in a series of stages that indicate the evolving nature of the process itself. The permissive role of the counselor allows the client to explore feelings and develop insights during the ensuing stages. Gradually during the process, the client develops feelings of confidence, begins changing dissatisfying behaviors, and risks taking action in unfamiliar ways. Although these stages have been modified over the years of counseling practice, they have remained essentially the same (Rogers, 1942).

Rogers's 1942 book on nondirective counseling influenced the immediate postwar years. In his next book, *Client-Centered Therapy* (1951), Rogers virtually eliminated the term *nondirective,* a change that implies that he realized that the term was misleading, a fear he had noted earlier in his 1939 text. Inexperienced practitioners, he worried, would take "nondirective" to mean that counselors "do nothing" (1939, p. 348). Nevertheless, the term *nondirective* stuck for many years.

Rogers's 1951 text describes in more detail his theory that the counseling process itself is the essence. "He focused more explicitly on the actualizing tendency as a basic motivational force that leads to client change" (Corey, 2005, p. 170). Thus, he describes how clients' feelings both emerge and evolve during the counseling process as clients undergo changes and pass through more complex levels of turbulent feelings, including increased feelings of conflict, fear, and anxiety.

By focusing on the evolving experiential nature of the therapeutic process itself, and by delineating the many characteristic changes the client goes through, Rogers emphasized the sense of movement as the essence of the counseling process. The first part of the counseling session involves changes in client feelings, beginning with a movement from feelings of symptoms to self. This is followed by changes of perception about one's feelings of self-worth and of independence, changes in awareness of denial of experience, changes regarding values, changes in the development of an emotional relationship between client and counselor, and changes in client personality structure and organization. The second part of the counseling session involves characteristic changes in client behavior, including increased discussion of plans and behavioral steps to be taken, change from relatively immature behavior to relatively mature behavior, decrease in psychological tension, decrease in defensive behaviors, increased tolerance for frustration as measured in physiological terms, and improved functioning in life tasks (Rogers, 1951).

In 1957, Rogers wrote the article "The Necessary and Sufficient Conditions of Therapeutic Personality Change," in which he elaborated on his earlier views that certain counselor qualities were important in the counselor–client relationship in order to foster client change. These essential counselor characteristics are congruency, unconditional positive regard, and empathy. *Congruency* means that the counselor is an authentic, integrated person. *Unconditional positive regard,* often called warmth, is the nonevaluative, nonjudgmental attitude the counselor has toward the client's thoughts, feelings, and behavior. *Empathy* is the counselor's ability to understand the client's world in the way the client does. When these conditions are present, Rogers claimed, clients can arrive at self-understanding and resolve conflicts.

With the publication of his book *Becoming a Person* (1961), Rogers expanded his theory of the experiential nature of the counseling process to a person's growth experience during the process of life itself. In the late 1960s, Rogers turned his attention to human relationships in all spheres of society and consequently changed from individual to group work. The publication of his *On Encounter Groups* in 1970 promoted a wave of encounter groups throughout the country.

At that same time, Rogers started calling his theory *person-centered* and wrote books and articles on a person-centered approach to teaching and educational administration, on encounter groups, on marriage and other forms of partnership, and on the "quiet revolution" that he believed would emerge with a new type of "self-empowered person" (Raskin & Rogers, 1995, p. 136).

Largely because of Rogers's influence, most counselors today, regardless of their theoretical framework, generally regard the counseling relationship as a crucial part of counseling. Moreover, many counselors also acknowledge the therapeutic value of the experiential nature of the process itself.

Gestalt Therapy

Fredrick ("Fritz") S. Perls (1969) and Laura Perls (1976) were the major developers of Gestalt theories and techniques. After Fritz Perls's death, Walter Kempler (1973) and Gary Yontef (Yontef & Jacobs, 2005) became major proponents of this theory. The purpose of the Gestalt approach is to integrate the person's inner reality (needs, perceptions, and emotions) with his or her outer reality (environment). Human experiences always occur in an interactional field (phenomenal field) in which both inner and outer forces are integrated into a whole (called, in German, *Gestalt*). Thus, any inner behavior is immediately responsive to outer behavior and vice versa (Yontef & Jacobs, 2005). Humans have the potential for functioning in a responsible, genuine way.

Conflict, indecision, or anxiety arises when an inconsistency exists between inner perceptions or needs and demands from the environment. These contradictions can lead to a continual battle between individuals' inherent drive to function authentically, consistent with their inner experiencing self (*self-actualization*), and the need to behave as they believe they should because of expectations of parents and other significant people (*idealized self-actualization*). The goals of counseling are to teach people to become fully aware of themselves and the world and to become mature and responsible for their own lives.

Unlike Rogerians, Gestalt counselors are active teachers who directly confront clients with their inconsistencies. The counselors provoke and persuade clients or manipulate the interview to get clients to correct misperceptions, to express emotions authentically, and to take responsibility for change. The major emphasis is to get clients to respond immediately to experiences. To make clients do so, the counselors confront them with their inconsistencies and with the need to take constructive action regarding unresolved problems related to past experiences (*unfinished business*). This action permits individuals to devote more energy and more awareness to resolving current problems (Corey, 2005).

Besides confrontation, Gestalt counselors use many other techniques, including role playing. In contrast with behaviorists' use of role playing, however, Gestaltists emphasize understanding one's own feelings and the feelings of others, rather than practicing behavior. Another strategy is role reversal, in which clients act out behaviors of individuals with whom they are in conflict. Dialogue games are also used in which clients play out both parts of the conflicting feelings or attitudes they are experiencing. Empty chair dialogues may also be used in which clients act out conflicts with other persons who are imagined to be in the empty chair. In this activity, clients assume both roles and change chairs as they carry out a dialogue. Gestalt counselors encourage their clients to take responsibility for their emotions by using "I" statements, such as "*I* am angry" rather than "*It* makes me angry." Body awareness, massage, visual imagery, and dream analysis are also elements of Gestalt therapy. More complete discussions of this therapy are available in Corey (2005); Ivey, D'Andrea, Ivey, and Simek-Morgan (2007); Levitsky and Perls (1970); and Passons (1975).

Existential Counseling

Existential theories are rooted in the European philosophies of Heidegger, Kierkegaard, and Sartre and in the existential practice of European psychiatrists. In the United States, psychoanalyst Rollo May (1961) and psychiatrists Irvin Yalom (1980, 2002) and Victor Frankl (1963) have applied existentialist ideas to their analytic practice.

For existentialists, humans have the self-awareness and the freedom to make choices that will bring meaning to their lives. This freedom and the responsibility to live with the consequences of these choices lead to existential anxiety—an essential part of living and being. "Existential therapists define anxiety more broadly than other psychotherapeutic groups. *Anxiety arises from our personal need to survive, to preserve our being, and to assert our being*" (May & Yalom, 2000, p. 275).

The well-functioning person is authentically experiencing and expressing needs in a manner not determined by others. People feel guilt and anxiety when they do not take actions they should take or when they do not act responsibly and authentically. Anxieties also arise from an inability to perceive purpose or meaning in life, especially with the realization of death. Existentialists believe that some anxiety is an essential part of life, a condition that encourages people to try to experience life fully and authentically. May (1961) sees awareness of death, for example, as an incentive to live life with zest because people realize that life is only temporary.

Frankl's (1963) views regarding existential philosophy emerged during his terrible experience in Nazi concentration camps in World War II. Through personal experiences and his observations of others in these camps, Frankl came to the conclusion that, under the worst conditions of suffering and torture, humans can maintain spiritual freedom, independent thinking, and opportunities for choice. Meaning and purpose in life are maintained through love and suffering. He says that all things can be taken from individuals except two things—attitude and beliefs.

Frankl's (1963) theory is based on the idea that the unity of an individual has three dimensions—physical, psychological, and spiritual. He emphasizes life's spiritual meaning, including death, love, and suffering. Maladjustment arises when a person has conflicts between various moral or spiritual values. Frankl (1963) developed a technique called *paradoxical intention,* in which clients are encouraged to exaggerate their fears and anxieties, rather than deny them. Paradoxically, this helps dissolve anxiety.

In the post–World War II years, many college students, returning veterans among them, were troubled by existential questions in their search for the meaning of life. At the University of California at Berkeley counseling center, Frank Nugent's early approach to counseling was strongly influenced by Leslie Farber (1966), who was the psychiatric consultant there and who later became known for his work on existentialism.

In 1961, Rollo May published his landmark *Existential Psychology,* and several existential counseling texts were published during the 1960s in which counselors emphasized subjective inner experiencing and a positive outlook on the active, purposeful nature of humans (Arbuckle, 1967; Dreyfus, 1962; Pine, 1969; Van Kaam, 1967). This approach stressed the unique individual who has not only the capacity but also the responsibility to make choices and also emphasized that human beings develop and experience themselves only in relation to other people in the world (Frankl, 1963; Van Kaam, 1967). With the rising popularity of technique-oriented behavior and cognitive behavioral therapies, however, existential counseling faded into the background for a couple of decades until its revival after Irvin Yalom published *Existential Psychotherapy* (1980).

May and Yalom's (2000) existential model draws on psychoanalytic concepts, such as transference and resistance, but they use them in terms of application to current experiencing. In *The Gift of Therapy,* Yalom (2002) describes how he has applied existential theory and techniques over 45 years of clinical practice. His approach is a combination of existential and psychodynamic theories; he emphasizes that existential therapy is not theory or content driven, but instead focuses on the process of the counselor–client relationship. Therapists maintain a nonauthoritative relationship with clients in which they avoid making decisions for clients, but help them work through their anxieties about their responsibilities and help facilitate client decision making. Yalom highlights three significant features in the existential counseling process: (a) Counselors help clients attend to the here-and-now; (b) counselors are open and authentic in their interactions with clients; and (c) counselors judiciously use self-disclosure about the mechanics of therapy, about their feelings toward clients in counseling sessions, and, with particular caution, about experiences in their personal lives.

According to Yalom (2002), "Existential psychotherapy is a dynamic approach that focuses on concerns rooted in existence" (p. xvi). By dynamic, he means that conflicts within the individual, conscious and unconscious, generate and influence the individual's attitudes, thoughts, emotions, and behaviors. Clients must be helped to confront death in order to explore meaning in life. "Keep in mind that therapy is a deep and comprehensive explanation into the course and meaning of one's life; given the centrality of death in our lives, how can we possibly ignore it?" (p. 125).

The goal of existential counseling is to help clients explore and develop meaning in life. The counselor can help clients recognize their choice-making potential and understand and accept the consequences of choice for their lives and for the lives of others. Counseling is essentially an encounter between therapist and client with an emphasis on understanding and being in an authentic partnership with each other. The problem to be faced is that the world is not necessarily meaningful, unless one makes meaning out of experience. Existentialists like May, Yalom, and Frankl believe that confusion and suffering in the world provide opportunity for growth. Existentialist counselors expect clients to commit themselves ultimately to authentic action and to assume responsibility for the consequences of their actions.

BEHAVIORAL, COGNITIVE, AND COGNITIVE–BEHAVIORAL THEORIES

Behavioral, cognitive, and cognitive–behavioral theorists believe that human attitudes and behaviors are learned in response to one's environment. Maladaptive behavior is best corrected by reinforcing appropriate behavior and/or by reshaping or restructuring perceptions and cognitive processes.

Behavioral and cognitive theories originally developed separately and at different times. Following B. F. Skinner's theory, which became prominent in the 1950s and 1960s, *behaviorists* believe that humans are born as a *tabula rasa,* a blank slate, without drives or instincts. All behavior is learned, and behaviors that can be scientifically measured constitute the major concern of behaviorists. In contrast, *cognitive theorists,* who emerged some years later, believe that a person's perceptions are instrumental in processing, selecting, evaluating, and responding to external stimuli. The way a person perceives an event determines her or his response or reaction.

Most behaviorists have since adopted cognitive principles and are now generally known as *cognitive–behaviorists.* Likewise, most cognitive theorists, notably Albert Ellis (2005), have adopted behaviorist principles and techniques; Ellis changed his rational emotive therapy (RET) to rational emotive behavior therapy (REBT). Although all tend now to fall under the term *cognitive–behaviorist,* a few continue to remain primarily cognitive, notably Aaron Beck (1976a, 1976b).

Behavioral Theories

For behaviorists, observable behavior is the main concern in the counseling process. Because people react to events in the environment, counselors focus on rewarding positive behavior and on extinguishing ineffective behavior by eliminating the conditions that reinforce it. New behavior is then introduced and appropriately reinforced. The counselor is essentially a teacher who helps clients learn new and more adaptive responses to old situations.

Operant Conditioning

The first behavioral approach that focused exclusively on observable, overt behavior was developed by B. F. Skinner (1953) and was called *operant conditioning* and *reinforcement theory*. According to Skinner's operant conditioning theory, an individual learns by reacting to observable stimuli. If the response is reinforced through rewards, the behavior will likely be repeated. If the response is ignored or punished, the behavior usually decreases.

This operant approach was popular in the 1960s in working with disruptive children in schools, those with bed-wetting problems, or persons with mental retardation or schizophrenia (Bijou & Baer, 1965; Patterson & Guillion, 1968). Since then, key persons who applied this approach to the normal concerns of people in schools and communities were Hosford and DeVisser (1974) and Krumboltz and Thoresen (1976). Counselors have found this theory to be useful for clients who want to manage or control some undesirable habit or characteristic—such as smoking, overeating, alcohol addiction, or procrastination—or who wish to learn new habits, such as studying effectively, managing time, or improving parenting skills. An important technique is *token economy,* whereby clients gain tokens (positive reinforcement) or lose tokens (penalties), depending on whether they attain a mutually agreed-on target behavior. *Aversive conditioning* may also be used, which pairs an electric shock or some other unpleasant stimulus with thoughts or pictures of undesirable behavior.

Counterconditioning (Desensitization)

Joseph Wolpe (1958, 1969) introduced a behavioral therapeutic approach that reflects the *classical conditioning* work conducted by Ivan Pavlov in the 1920s. Pavlov conditioned dogs to salivate at the sound of a bell. At first he produced the food, which elicited the salivation, at the same time he rang a bell. Later, the bell alone caused the salivation. Using this same learning principle, Wolpe paired anxiety responses with relaxation exercises so that the relaxation exercise gradually extinguished the anxiety response.

Wolpe (1969) demonstrated that emotionally debilitating behavior can be changed by a technique called *systematic desensitization,* a form of classical conditioning called *counterconditioning. Desensitization* refers to a process that gradually decreases the client's sensitivity to an anxiety-provoking emotion by pairing the emotion with relaxation responses. Wolpe assumed that a person cannot physiologically be anxious and relaxed at the same time. For instance, a client might tell a counselor about an unreasonable fear of dentists that is preventing the client from keeping his or her dental appointments. The client would be taught how to relax through a series of relaxation exercises and then would be told to imagine gradually increasing anxiety-provoking images about dentists. In this way, the client would learn to visualize being worked on in a dentist's chair without anxiety and would, it is assumed, ultimately be able to see a dentist without fear.

For persons experiencing unmanageable phobic fears, a desensitization technique is used to encourage them to expose themselves gradually to the feared object in real life under the guidance of the counselor. After progressive exposure, clients learn that the consequences of facing the fear are not disastrous. *Flooding*—a technique that should be used with care—involves having clients fully expose themselves to the feared situation so that they eventually realize that their fear is unfounded. *Biofeedback* has also been used to help clients learn to relax by monitoring their physiological responses: breathing, heartbeat, blood pressure, or muscle tension. Clients are wired to a computerized instrument and are taught to reduce tension by observing feedback about their biological responses. They ultimately learn to relax by becoming aware of feedback from their own physiological responses without the machine.

Behavioral Self-Control and Management

Thoresen and Mahoney (1974) broadened the base of behaviorism by teaching clients to modify or manage their own undesirable behavior by using self-administered reinforcement. For example, a person wishing to lose weight might be taught to implement changes in her or his environment (e.g., keeping records of caloric intake or using smaller plates) and to self-administer a reward (e.g., give oneself a gift) if a certain amount of weight is lost within a specific time or to penalize oneself (e.g., pay a fine) if the weight is not lost.

Cognitive Theories

Cognitive theorists believe that "how one thinks largely determines how one feels and behaves" (Beck & Weishaar, 1995, p. 229). People's thinking, or cognitions, are related to their perceptions about themselves and the world around them. Maladaptive thinking results from faulty perceptions or constructs about oneself and others. Beck (1963) and Ellis (1973) were early pioneers in the development of cognitive theories. In the 1990s, Ellis combined his cognitive rational emotive therapy (RET) with behaviorism and changed its name to rational emotive behavior therapy (REBT), which is discussed in the cognitive–behavioral section of this chapter.

Aaron T. Beck's (1976a, 1976b) cognitive theory, following Ellis's early RET model, is similar to it in that clients are helped to recognize and change self-defeating thoughts and cognitions that occur in inner *self-talk* (Corey, 2005). Beck's approach differs from Ellis's, however, in that Beck's cognitive therapy is less confrontational. Beck works together with clients to help them discover their own misconceptions; he assumes that people live by irrational rules that influence distorted thinking, rather than by irrational beliefs (Beck, 1976a). Beck treats obsessions and phobias, but is best known for his work with depression.

In the treatment of depression, Beck administers the Beck Depression Inventory (BDI), which is based on the typical symptoms and beliefs of depressed persons, to assess the severity of the problem. He then teaches systematic skills in self-observation whereby clients observe their thought-pattern distortions and the faulty inferences, misperceptions, or exaggerations about external events that are not supported by the evidence (Beck, 1976b).

Next, Beck teaches coping skills. If clients are depressed and are withdrawing from activity, he helps them set up a schedule of activities, beginning with nonthreatening tasks that they can complete successfully. In role playing, Beck may play the role of the client and display the client's distorted thinking; with self-critical clients, he may use humor. Beck helps and directs clients to explore and correct misperceptions, list duties and tasks that need to be done, set priorities, and then carry out a realistic plan of action that will reduce depression.

Cognitive–Behavioral Theories

In the 1970s, many behaviorists realized that conditioning procedures were too limited to explain behavior adequately and saw the value of combining them with cognitive theories. Cognitive–behaviorists aim to change clients' inaccurate, subjective perceptions about themselves and their environment by uncovering the faulty assumptions and beliefs that underlie their thinking and are causing them personal or interpersonal problems. The counselors then teach logical reasoning skills to restructure these thinking patterns and correct the problems. This process is called *cognitive restructuring.*

Ellis's Rational Emotive Behavior Therapy

In the 1970s, Albert Ellis (1973, 2005) introduced his theory that most human problems relate to irrational beliefs that arise from illogical reasoning. Believing that thinking and emotion are not separate processes, Ellis claimed that emotional problems result from illogical thought processes. Thus, he coined the term *rational emotive therapy (RET).* In 1995, he changed RET to *rational emotive behavior therapy (REBT)* because he believed that it more accurately describes his approach.

Ellis lists about a dozen irrational beliefs that he believes plague most people in our culture. These beliefs relate to unrealistic ideas or expectations about themselves, about others, and about the world in general. For example, it is irrational to become very upset over other people's problems or to believe that the world is a catastrophic place when things are not as one would like them to be. These ideas form and are reinforced when a child is exposed to parents and others who model irrational thinking. The goal of counseling is to help clients attain logical approaches to solving problems.

Ellis's famous *ABC principle* emphasizes the importance of one's perception of a stimulus. *A* represents the stimulus, *B* is the belief related to *A* (perception of the stimulus), and *C* is the consequence. For example, a male student comes to counseling complaining that he feels worthless *(C)* because he did poorly on a math test *(A)*. The counselor will try to show him that the failure *(A)* is not really what caused these feelings, but rather his perception of the failure *(B)*. Ellis believes that people use illogical internalized sentences, which he calls *self-talk.* In this case, the student thinks *(A)* I failed my math test; *(B)* I should not have failed, for only worthless people fail; and *(C)* I am worthless for failing. The counselor helps the student see that belief *B* is irrational.

After clients go through the *ABC* steps, Ellis helps them change their illogical thinking in a process he calls *disputing (D).* During this stage, counselors teach more rational belief systems; persuasion, cajolery, provocation, and subtle coercion are used where necessary, and homework assignments are given to help clients practice thinking rationally. REBT counselors use other behavioral techniques when appropriate, including self-management, assertiveness training, relaxation exercises, and systematic desensitization (Ellis, 1973, 2005).

Social Learning Theory

Social learning theorists counteracted the behaviorists' conditioning model in the 1960s and 1970s by claiming that learning can occur when individuals imitate the behavior of others, even though the imitation is not directly reinforced. Albert Bandura (1977) has been a major proponent of social learning theory, in which actors, either live or on video, are used to model socially desirable or socially effective behavior. Clients observe and imitate the models' behavior. The modeling of fearless behavior is often effective in treating phobias. For example, children fearful of dentists may be shown films of a friendly dentist interacting pleasantly with cheerful children. Or a client who fears snakes observes a model petting a snake. Video- or audiotape recordings, autobiographies, and typescripts can be used to demonstrate the desired behavior.

The emphasis on external factors makes possible a wide range of techniques. Counselors can demonstrate culturally appropriate behavior by serving as models or by using other persons to model behavior. Problem-solving or logical-reasoning skills can be taught. Another popular approach is role playing, in which counselor and client assume the roles of other persons in the client's life and practice appropriate responses. Clients are given reinforcement, or are taught to reinforce themselves, for desired behavior. Clients can also be trained in specific social skills, such as assertiveness. Homework assignments are considered an essential part of the counseling (Bandura, 1977).

Meichenbaum's Cognitive–Behavioral Therapy

Donald Meichenbaum (1985, 2007) uses a self-instructional technique called *cognitive restructuring*. Like Ellis and Beck, Meichenbaum believes that distorted thought processes are behind stress or emotional problems (Corey, 2005).

Meichenbaum (1985, 2007) also believes that persons are as afflicted by self-talk as they are by the explicit comments of others. The goal of counseling, then, is to teach clients the skills to change their maladaptive ways of talking to themselves. Therapy involves teaching clients first to observe their own behavior and listen to themselves, second to develop a new, more adaptive internal dialogue (self-talk), and finally to learn new coping skills so that they will be able to handle stressful situations in real life (Corey, 2005).

A coping-skills learning program usually starts by exposing clients to an anxiety-provoking situation through role playing or imagery. Clients then evaluate their anxiety level and become aware of their anxious self-statements. Next, they make changes in their self-talk and note the decrease in anxiety after the evaluation (Corey, 2005). This procedure is effective for working with those with social or sexual dysfunctions, test or speech anxieties, phobias, or addictions (Meichenbaum, 1985, 2007).

Meichenbaum (1985) teaches stress management skills by means of what he calls *stress-inoculation therapy (SIT)*. As in desensitization, clients are taught to use a graded system in evaluating stress: They start by imagining low-stress situations and then try progressively to imagine more intensely stressful situations. At each stage, they are taught various problem-solving skills: defining the problem, choosing alternatives, making decisions, and verifying outcomes. Meichenbaum encourages clients to use various kinds of relaxation exercises similar to those used by holistic counselors—meditation, breath control, yoga, jogging, gardening, and walking. He believes that stress management training is useful in assertiveness training, anger control, treatment of depression, improving creativity, and treating health problems.

Coping skills learned in the sessions are practiced in real-life situations through increasingly difficult exercises and homework. These activities prepare clients to apply their new learnings after they terminate counseling.

Lazarus's Multimodal Therapy

Arnold Lazarus (1976, 2005) developed a multimodal therapy in which counseling or therapy is tailored to the individual client's needs by the use of techniques taken from all of the theories—cognitive–behavioral, psychoanalytic, psychodynamic, and humanistic. Lazarus classifies himself as a social and cognitive–learning theorist because his beliefs are based on empirical principles of learning. He makes the point, however, that he is not theoretically eclectic, but rather technically eclectic.

Maladaptive behaviors or problems are assumed to result from deficient or faulty social learning. The goals of counseling are to bring about, in an efficient and humane way, client-desired changes in behavior that will be enduring (Lazarus, 2005).

Using the acronym *BASIC I.D.,* Lazarus describes seven major areas of personality: (a) **b**ehavior (observable action), (b) **a**ffective (emotional), (c) **s**ensation (feelings), (d) **i**mages (imagination), (e) **c**ognitions (thought process), (f) **i**nterpersonal relationships (social), and (g) **d**rugs/biological (physical). A counselor must consider each of these modalities in assessing a person's problem and prognosis. An important feature of this approach is that every individual is considered unique, with her or his own BASIC I.D., so no one theory or set of techniques can work with everyone.

Clients first fill out a life history questionnaire and rate themselves on each modality of the BASIC I.D. profile. The counselor, after making an assessment based on the client's responses and the counselor's observations, uses a procedure called *bridging.* Bridging means that the counselor first focuses on the client's preferred personality mode before exploring the other modalities. If the client functions predominantly from a cognitive mode, for instance, the counselor at first responds in a cognitive way before responding in another modality.

From among the wide variety of techniques used by behavioral and cognitive–behavioral counselors, multimodal counselors may use reinforcement procedures, assertiveness training, desensitization, biofeedback, and cognitive restructuring, especially in behavioral, affective, and cognitive modes. In physical and imagery modes, multimodal counselors may add Gestalt and holistic techniques, such as the empty chair or role-reversal dialogues, confrontation, abdominal breathing, positive visual imagery, and focusing. In the interpersonal mode, they may use self-management, instruction in parenting, and social skills. With drug and biological considerations, they make certain that appropriate medication is available and that inappropriate medication is curtailed. Like holistic counselors, multimodal counselors encourage good nutrition, physical fitness, and exercise.

CREATIVE THERAPIES

Creative and expressive arts therapies are based on the belief that many persons express themselves nonverbally in ways they are unable to do otherwise. Narrative therapy, in which one learns to view one's life as a story, is also a departure from the usual analytical therapeutic approach. Expressive arts and story making, used therapeutically, can reveal one's nature as it evolves over time, also revealing feelings, releasing defenses that block or inhibit growth, and, as symbolic expression, revealing one's inner self or soul.

Creative and Expressive Arts

Creative and expressive arts have rapidly gained favor among counselors and therapists in a wide range of therapeutic settings. Much has been written about creative arts and counseling in which the client works with imagery, drawing, dancing, music, drama, or poetry during counseling sessions (Levine, 1992; McNiff, 1988). Fleshman and Fryrear (1981) comment, "The art therapies, to a very great extent, have grown from the early seed planted by Jung" (p. 33). Carl Jung's theory of active imagination and archetypes, as well as his use of creative arts in his own life and therapy, was a strong influence in the development of art therapies. Dalley et al. (1987) tie Jung's early work to current creative arts practice: "His technique of active imagination which deliberately mobilized the patient's creativity is an approach that many art therapists use today" (p. 9). Jung encouraged art therapy as a conscious way to express elements of the unconscious.

Creative arts therapist Stephen Levine (1992) indicates how archetypal psychology, discussed earlier in this chapter, has given impetus to creative arts therapy:

> Given this conception of psychotherapy and its relation to the imagination, it becomes clear why the arts need to enter into the therapeutic process and why, in recent years, different expressive arts therapies have emerged with such vigor. (p. 3)

Unlike Jung, Freud was ambivalent about the idea of using creative arts in therapy and did little with it in practice (Dalley et al., 1987; Levine, 1992). Even so, some of his followers used creative art techniques, primarily drawing and painting, with children (Robbins, 1980).

Among the humanists, those most closely aligned with the concepts and techniques of art therapies are the Gestaltists, followed by the self theorists (Dalley et al., 1987; Fleshman & Fryrear, 1981). Because of their emphasis on wholeness of body and mind and the connections between feelings and actions, Gestaltists encourage body movement, dance, massage, drama, acting out dreams, and the use of imagery. Self theorists also encourage their clients to express themselves in poetry, drawing, or dance.

Because of their focus on the observable actions of clients and external factors influencing these actions, behaviorists tend to use creative activities as reinforcements or rewards. Cognitive–behaviorists—such as Lazarus, Meichenbaum, and Wolpe—who are concerned about perceptions and distorted thought processes, use imagery as a way of helping clients change behavior (Corey, 2005; Fleshman & Fryrear, 1981; Robbins, 1980).

Personal construct counselors use numerous creative arts therapies to help nonverbal clients become aware of their self-perceptions—the way they construe themselves.

Drawings, including interactive drawings between counselor and client, have been effective for those clients who have difficulty talking. Working with clay, music, and dance is also effective.

Narrative Therapy

Narrative therapy has gained significant attention from counselors and therapists in a wide range of disciplines. Narratives are forms of client self-exploration that offer clients insight into the characteristics of their selfhood and open up ways in which to integrate them. "Clients use these forms of self-exploration to confront important choices in work and in relationships; place past traumas in a more contemporary frame of reference; and give voice to concerns, insights, and new hopes that they may be reluctant to verbalize to another, even to an accepting therapist" (R. A. Neimeyer, 1995, p. 242).

Counselors who use narrative therapy believe that emotional distress or disorder results from a gap or break in an individual's life story (Neimeyer & Stewart, 1998). "Clients come to counselors with stories that are outdated, tragic, and rigidified. As a result, these clients experience their lives as repetitive, negative, and unchangeable" (Presbury et al., 2002, p. 102). "Most narrative therapeutic approaches share the goal of weaving painful, negative or other unexpected events into the client's dominant life narrative" (Neimeyer & Stewart, 1998, p. 556).

Counselors work collaboratively with clients to help them tell their stories and identify major themes or constructs that are inhibiting or limiting their lives. Clients are then encouraged to revise their stories in order to develop new themes and constructs that are more productive to client growth (Seligman, 2001). Narrative therapists emphasize that one's story making is a guide, a map that one can alter and change.

Following George Kelly's (1955) early use of narrative form, counselors encourage clients to see themselves in their stories metaphorically as protagonist and narrator (Neimeyer & Raskin, 2000). Therapists also encourage clients to tell stories from differing points of view or as if they were different characters in the story. Therapists may also help clients project their stories into the future. This process leads clients "to a greater empowerment and the ability to successfully manage their lives" (Seligman, 2001, p. 283).

Another method favored by Kelly (1955), enacting one's story dramatically, is used effectively by many narrative therapists (Efran, 2002; Fransella & Dalton, 2000; Lyddon, 1999). In enactment, the client acts the part of a significant person in his or her life, or client and counselor together act out certain parts and then exchange roles. Therapists can then encourage their clients to relate their roles in dramatic play to real life:

> Similar to drama, narrative psychology treats the narrative as an organizing context for human action. From a narrative psychology perspective, people impose socially constituted narratives (or roles) on the flow of their experience and, as a result, are both the authors of and actors in self-narratives—that is, their own personal dramas. (Lyddon, 1999, p. 77)

Another leading advocate of the narrative approach is cultural psychologist Jerome Bruner (1990), well known for his emphasis on the way humans acquire and use language. Since ancient times, he points out, persons applying language as a means of communication formed and told stories as a way of making meaning out of their lives. This basic folk psychology, he says, has been "a system by which people organize their experience in, knowledge about, and transactions with the social world. Its organizing principle is narrative rather than conceptual" (p. 35). The narrative's "unique sequentiality . . . is indispensable to a story's significance and to the mode of mental organization in terms of which it is grasped" (p. 44). Noting the long-standing fragmented nature of the field of psychology, Bruner (1990) remarks that "naturally a reaction has set in against this fragmentation " (p. xi). According to Bruner (1990),

> What's missing from the field of psychology is the crucial component of the human desire for making meaning of one's life. The central concept of a human psychology is meaning and the processes and transactions involved in the construction of meanings. (p. 33)

Especially important to narrative therapy has been the work of Australian/New Zealand family therapists White and Epston (1990), as described in their seminal book *Narrative Means to Therapeutic Ends* (Presbury et al., 2002; Seligman, 2001). White and Epston introduced a postmodern way of examining how social constructs govern and dominate familial and social patterns (Sharf, 2008). Their narrative therapy enables clients to realize "that our personal realities and self-images are not absolute but are created and maintained by our societies and ourselves" (Seligman, 2001, p. 284). Thus, people are subjected to a *dominant story* (White & Epston, 1990), and client disorders result from this subjection. White and Epston (1990) present ways to help clients restructure and retell their stories so that they become the agents of their narratives, that is, they regain a sense of self.

The therapeutic use of listening to stories and of storytelling has also gained attention among professionals. Especially helpful in describing how stories can be used therapeutically are Clarissa Pinkola Estés's book *Women Who Run with the Wolves* (1992), Michael Meade's book *Men and the Water of Life* (1993), and his Mosaic Foundation (2003), which conducts storytelling workshops with inner-city youth (see chapters 14 and 19).

THEORIES OF BRIEF COUNSELING

Brief counseling has increased rapidly in community mental health practice. As the demand for mental health services in the community increased in the 1980s and funding for these services declined sharply, the idea of planned short-term therapy developed. Health maintenance organizations (HMOs) and employee assistance programs (EAPs) emerged with a deliberate emphasis on "brief, highly-focused therapeutic services" (Wells, 1994, p. 3). Managed care soon followed, and brief counseling became and remains a standard model.

In contrast with traditional counseling practices, therapists using brief counseling set specific goals and specify that the number of sessions will be limited. Clients appropriate for brief counseling have a prior history of adequate adjustment and an adequate ability to relate, but a situational difficulty has arisen that has provoked a dilemma, anxiety, or crisis, such as loss of a job or sudden weight gain. Counselors focus on helping clients to develop coping skills that will enable them to anticipate and manage future problems, as well as resolve immediate concerns.

Psychodynamic Brief Counseling

Lewis Wolberg's (1980) *Handbook of Short-Term Psychotherapy* presents a comprehensive and thorough discussion of how psychodynamic concepts can be adapted to brief counseling. Wolberg indicates that it is important to "focus on what is of immediate concern to the patient, such as incidents in life that have precipitated the symptoms for which he seeks help" (p. 99). Thus, therapists focus on some particular situational problem of the client. Feelings of transference and dream content are related to the client's current concerns and circumstances.

Psychodynamic theories getting the most attention are Strupp and Binder's (1984) time-limited dynamic psychotherapy, Sifneos's (1987) short-term dynamic psychology, Davenloo's (1994) short-term dynamic psychotherapy, and Mann's (1973) time-limited psychotherapy (TLP). Mann's TLP relates particularly well to counselors: "This psychoanalytic approach is compatible with counseling psychology's emphasis on client strengths, is suited to work with intact personalities, and places a premium on brevity" (Gelso & Fretz, 2001, p. 316). Furthermore, this approach is consistent with Erik Erikson's human development theory in that Mann recognizes that conflicts happen during transitions that occur throughout life.

Mann's (1973) approach is limited to 12 sessions. He focuses on a central issue, the crisis of separation and individuation that reoccurs in different forms throughout an individual's life. "There are countless experiences throughout life that revive repeatedly the sense of loss and anxiety related to the separation–individuation phase. Loss of money, of power, of a relationship, of self-esteem, and of a job . . . are obvious examples" (Gelso & Fretz, 2001, p. 317).

The resolution of the client's feelings of loss and anxiety generally focuses on issues regarding the self. In the initial sessions, the therapist looks for the central issue underlying the client's complaint of, say, anxiety or depression. "Mann refers to the central issue as reflecting the client's present and chronically induced pain" (Gelso & Fretz, 2001, p. 318). The central issue involves deeper "underlying self issues that have plagued the client's experience from very early in his or her life" (p. 318). Although the therapist explores the client's past and relates it to the present, this exploration is limited to those experiences that are relevant to the client's central problem.

Therapists employ an empathic approach throughout the 12 sessions, using the counseling process as a positive experience of union and separation. Therapists are understanding of the client's pain, but at the same time are unequivocal in resolving the client's dilemma in 12 sessions:

> The two opening moves by the therapist, setting up an empathic bond for which the patient has yearned and then announcing that it will be terminated, build a structure for the therapy that will continue throughout its course with the oscillation between magical fantasies and harsh reality. (White, Burke, & Havens, 1981, p. 250)

"The time limit in TLP addresses the client's desire and need for independence; the treatment helps such a client mature, separate from childhood in a healthy way, and grow" (Gelso & Fretz, 2001, p. 321).

Strupp and Binder (1984) developed time-limited dynamic psychotherapy (TLDP), which involves 25 to 30 sessions, a system similar to Mann's. Earlier, however, Strupp (1981) had expressed cautions about the limitations of psychodynamic brief therapies:

> We have not gone far enough in this endeavor. I believe there are definite limits to what time-limited dynamic psychotherapy . . . can accomplish, and that outcomes depend importantly on patient selection, the goals to which the therapist (and the patient) aspire, and the nature of the therapeutic changes the therapist is able to engender. (p. 238)

Recent criticism of time-limited brief counseling is discussed later in this section.

Cognitive and Cognitive–Behavioral Brief Counseling

Cognitive and cognitive–behavioral theories generally are easily adapted to brief counseling because they are goal oriented and focus on presenting issues or symptoms of relatively short duration. The major brief cognitive and cognitive–behavioral approaches used in counseling practice today are based on the strategic theories of Jay Haley (1991) and Milton Erickson (1980).

Brief Strategic Therapy

Early strategic counselors used intervention strategies to direct or manipulate changes in clients' repetitive, nonproductive behavior without regard for their emotions or situational factors. Strategic therapists now attend to both client emotions and social context (Cade & O'Hanlon, 1993). They also refrain from using manipulative interventions or interventions that are unethically deceptive or potentially harmful to clients. Cade and O'Hanlon (1993) say, "We have become more concerned with the resourcefulness of our clients and with avoiding approaches that disempower either overtly or covertly" (p. xii).

Genter's Brief Strategic Therapy.   In Genter's (1991) brief strategic model, the counselor defines the problem, establishes goals, designs an intervention, assigns a strategic task, emphasizes positive new behavior changes, and then helps the client learn to incorporate new behaviors into everyday living.

The counselor first asks specific and systematic questions to learn client perceptions of the problem and of social circumstances related to the problem. The counselor also explores attempts the client has made to try to resolve the problem. Goals are specific—only those that can be observed and measured directly. Intervention strategies focus on constructive reframing of the problem and on strategic tasks assigned to encourage the client to make gradual, progressive, positive changes in behavior. The client is then encouraged to try out new behaviors and experiences in everyday life.

Solution-Focused Brief Counseling.   Solution-focused brief counseling has been particularly adaptable to limited therapy as practiced in managed care. Steve de Shazer (1988), one originator of this approach, acknowledges the influence of Weakland, Fisch, Watzlawick, and Bodin (1974); Haley (1991); and Erickson (1980).

Counselors using a solution-focused brief model do not analyze or investigate the presenting problems of clients; talking only about constructing solutions has shortened the time necessary to bring about client change. Counselors "realized that only solution goal talk was necessary, that solution construction was independent of problem processes" (Walter & Peller, 1992, p. 8).

Counselors focus on client strengths and on solutions that are different from the unsuccessful methods that clients have been attempting. They look for exceptions to clients' problem behaviors and aim for small changes. Therapists work with clients who are able to cooperate and who have the ability to solve their problems. They start with changes the clients want, help them select goals that will work for them, and help them choose different tasks when their attempts are not successful (Walter & Peller, 1992).

Traditional Cognitive–Behavioral Models Adapted to Brief Counseling

Burbach, Borduin, and Peake (1988) affirm that cognitive and cognitive–behavioral theories "have much to offer the practitioners of brief psychotherapy" (p. 57) because cognitive approaches have traditionally been based on goal-oriented, short-term procedures. Two cognitive–behavioral theorists described earlier in the chapter—Ellis (REBT) and Lazarus (multimodal therapy)—have adapted their approaches to fit into a brief counseling model. Ellis (1992) perceives little change from his original position that clients learn to reframe or reconstruct and dispute beliefs that are causing emotional or behavioral problems. In a similar vein, Lazarus (1989), who uses a technical eclecticism to help clients solve problems in the modalities (BASIC I.D.) that are causing difficulties, advocates an intermittent short-term approach so that clients, once they solve a certain set of problems, may seek further help as new problems arise.

Limitations of Brief Counseling

Increasing numbers of counselors and therapists, including advocates of brief counseling, are acknowledging that some clients with more severe symptoms or symptoms that are susceptible to relapse require longer counseling. Erica Goode (1998) discusses the importance of distinguishing those clients needing longer term treatment from those who profit best from brief counseling. She recommends that more studies be conducted to determine to what degree the length of counseling depends on the type of client and/or the client problem.

In addition to considering an increase in the number of counseling sessions, more therapists are suggesting intermittent counseling. Psychiatrist Simon Budman, an advocate of brief counseling, is a proponent of this sort of arrangement. Clients, he says, "may benefit from a longer term with a therapist even if they come in for a session every few months, or a few weeks or every few years" (Goode, 1998, p. 10). Budman may see some patients over a period of years, "intermittently dealing with different problems as they come upon the patient's life" (Goode, 1998, p. 10).

TOWARD AN INTEGRATIVE THEORETICAL APPROACH

The 1980s saw a growing trend toward eclecticism among practitioners. At that time, surveys consistently showed that eclectic approaches were the primary theoretical orientation among all counseling professionals (Sharf, 2008). Many professionals in the field have criticized eclecticism, however, charging that inexperienced counselors are apt to adopt eclecticism because they are inadequately trained. Practitioners should not employ various techniques indiscriminately. According to Sharf (2008), unsystematic eclecticism causes problems because "the therapist acts one way at one time and differently at another" (p. 633).

In response to the criticism of eclecticism, increasing numbers of counselors and therapists have moved toward an integrative theoretical approach in which counselors judiciously select and integrate concepts and techniques from two or more theoretical systems (Prochaska & Norcross, 2006; Sharf, 2008). This trend has developed for a number of reasons: (a) Research and experience have demonstrated to counselors that no one therapeutic system has proved to be effective with all clients (Seligman, 2001); (b) clients live in varied cultural and social environments and have varied views about the world and the relative impact of inner and outer influences on their development; (c) clients present a wide range of problems and have differing degrees of support; and (d) a broader theoretical approach encompassing a wide selection of techniques allows counselors different approaches for the different stages of the counseling process.

Sharf (2008) presents three different types of integrative approaches: transtheoretical, theoretical integration, and technical eclecticism. The *transtheoretical* approach tries "to transcend or go beyond specific theoretical constructs" (p. 630) and works toward selecting those concepts and techniques that are compatible. The concepts and techniques used are "based on client readiness for change, the type of problem that needs changing, and processes or techniques to bring about change" (p. 630). In *theoretical integration,* professionals combine personality and theoretical concepts from two or more counseling theories into a systematic theoretical whole. In *technical eclecticism,* the professional uses one theoretical view of personality and selects various techniques from many theoretical orientations. "In contrast to unsystematic eclecticism," Sharf explains, "technical eclecticism is based on a theory of personality" (p. 633). Lazarus's multimodal theory best represents this mode of eclecticism.

SUMMARY

Counseling theories represent rationales about human nature and development that provide counselors with the means to create a framework that guides the way they view the counseling process, their clients and the way they interact with them, and their goals and techniques. Counseling theories are divided in this text into five categories: (a) psychoanalytic and psychodynamic; (b) humanistic and existential; (c) behavioral, cognitive, and cognitive–behavioral; (d) creative and expressive arts; and (e) brief counseling.

Psychoanalytic and psychodynamic theorists believe that unconscious, intrapsychic forces within individuals are central to behavior. Freud proposed that instinctual, psychosexual (id) forces shape behavior; later psychoanalytic theorists Adler, Horney, and Sullivan emphasized instead that behavior developed within a psychosocial context.

Following them, ego-analytic theorists, notably Erikson, proposed that the ego has its own energies that drive individuals to develop the skill necessary to become autonomous and to master their environment. Object relations theorists added that relationships help one grow and become autonomous. Women at the Stone Center, contrary to ego-analytic and object relations theorists, believe that growth develops through mutual connections in relationships.

Jung parted company with the Freudian theory that the unconscious is basically deterministic and destructive, theorizing instead that the unconscious can be positive and productive when it is integrated into one's consciousness, an endeavor that can be accomplished through imaginative activity related to myths and archetypes. Humanists and existentialists believe that humans have potentialities for positive growth. Humanists emphasize that a self-actualizing process moves individuals to increased self-awareness and development. Existentialists assume that individuals' freedom to determine meaning in life creates anxiety, which can potentially become a growth force.

Behavioral theorists believe that behavior is shaped through reinforcement or imitation. Cognitive and cognitive–behavioral theorists assume that perceptions influence one's thinking, feeling, and actions. They both emphasize that learning is central to development.

According to creative arts theorists, individuals' nonverbal expressions through art, dancing, music, or drama, or their narrative storytelling, help them to express the underlying feelings that are blocking their growth.

Brief counseling theories, developed by both psychodynamic and cognitive–behavioral theorists, have become prominent in practice because of the rising costs of mental health care, limited budgets, and an increased demand for counseling in schools, colleges, and the community.

PROJECTS AND ACTIVITIES

1. Compare Rogers's later writings with his original client-centered theory published in 1942. What are the similarities and differences?
2. Interview counselors in a college, in a school, or in the community concerning how they arrived at their current views about counseling theories.
3. Compare a cognitive–behaviorist with a humanist in terms of their views about human nature and their definition of counseling. How do their beliefs and definitions influence their counseling goals and the type of relationship they establish with clients?

4. List techniques used by behaviorists and Gestaltists. Determine the differences in the types and use of the techniques, and indicate how these differences tie in with philosophical views on human nature and reality.
5. Select the theory you like most and the one you like least. Review the current research about the effectiveness of each theory. Does this research change your attitudes or confirm them?

Part Three
Counseling Activities

CHAPTER 7

Assessment, Testing, and Diagnosis

Assessment, testing, and diagnosis are activities that are a critical part of the counseling process (Remley & Herlihy, 2007). Assessment of one kind or another occurs throughout the counseling process. Assessment is a collaborative process whereby both the counselor and client work together to gain a better understanding of the client's problems. Accurate assessment is vital in diagnosing the problem, setting goals for resolving the problem, and determining the best treatment for successful problem resolution.

Although ambiguity exists in the use of the terms *assessment* and *testing,* and some individuals use them interchangeably, most experts make a distinction. *Assessment* is the gathering and integration of client information through the use of tests, interviews, observations, or other measurement procedures for the purpose of making an evaluation. In contrast, a *test* may be defined simply as "a measuring device or procedure" (Cohen, & Swerdlik, 2002, p. 6). It is important to know that the use of tests is only one part of the overall process of assessment.

After studying this chapter, you will

- Understand the history of testing in the counseling profession.
- Be familiar with the types of assessment procedures and instruments that counselors use.
- Have knowledge of the initial interview and the role it plays in the assessment process.

A BRIEF HISTORY OF TESTING IN COUNSELING

The use of tests in the counseling field has a long and controversial history. Psychological tests originated during World War I. As part of the war effort, a group of psychologists developed the first large-scale group test of ability for army applicants. The primary

113

objective of the test was to help identify those who were emotionally unfit for military service (Thorndike, 2005). Tests flourished with the popularity of psychology in the 1920s and 1930s.

In the pre–World War II days of guidance counseling, the primary task for counselors was that of making vocational assessments of clients through the use of standardized tests. The counselors' approach was based on a diagnostic model in which clients were perceived as having fixed personality traits that could be measured through standardized interest and aptitude tests and personality inventories.

Carl Rogers (1942, 1951) objected to this approach because it counteracts the belief that humans are dynamic individuals who are capable of change. The popularity of his client-centered counseling during the 1950s through the 1970s resulted in a sharp decline in counselors' use of tests and assessments. This change from diagnosing traits to facilitating self-exploration dramatically influenced the direction of counseling. Most counselors who used standardized tests and inventories did so only after a counseling relationship was established and then only to enhance client self-exploration.

The 1970s and 1980s brought even greater criticism of testing. Leo Goldman brought about much of this censure through his classic article "Tests and Counseling: The Marriage That Failed" (1972). In a 1994 article, he explains:

> The main problem with tests was that they had been developed in the first place for *selection* purposes, and that the typical level of predictive validity that made tests useful for selecting college students or employees had a very different meaning and value when used in *counseling.* (p. 214)

A dramatic upsurge occurred in the numbers and types of tests used in counseling in the 1980s and continues today. "Nearly ten million counselors each year complete 'tests,' 'inventories,' and other 'assessments'—and that estimate does not include school achievement tests or college entrance exams" (Prediger, 1994, p. 228). One need only observe the huge booths displaying testing and assessment tools at counseling and psychological conventions, or notice the catalogs from more than a dozen testing companies to realize how many thousands of psychological tests are now available and in use. Moreover, these companies offer computerized scoring and standardized interpretations that make tests easy and efficient for anyone to use.

Although tests are easier to administer and score, the vast array of types of tests makes selection and interpretation more confusing than ever—especially for the inexperienced or minimally trained counselor, who may overuse or misuse tests, or misinterpret their results. Goldman (1994) is so dissatisfied with the lack of adequate courses about tests and measurements in counseling programs that he recommends, "Standardized tests would be best used by perhaps 10% of counselors who are well qualified in quantitative methods, whereas the 90% would make better use of qualitative assessment methods" (p. 217).

Testing specialist Dale Prediger (1994) responds to Goldman in the article "Tests and Counseling: The Marriage That Prevailed." A long-time advocate of Goldman's position, Prediger concurs with Goldman's feelings of discouragement about the use of testing in counseling. And he agrees with Goldman that the poor quality of tests and the lack of adequate counselor training in their selection, use, and interpretation persist today: "We are still in the snake-oil era of testing. . . . I invite evidence that professional practice has improved" (p. 229).

Prediger (1994) does not think that all is lost, however, in the alliance between testing and counseling. Although he concurs with Goldman's preference for qualitative testing, he argues that using only qualitative assessment is unrealistic for most counselors because it is too time-consuming. Furthermore, he believes that client self-estimates without confirming data may be inaccurate or incomplete. He suggests instead that test score interpretations be used to help clients make more informed and accurate self-estimates: "Ability test scores should not be used as substitutes for ability self-estimates. Instead, they should be used to inform self-estimates/concepts" (p. 232).

Today, assessment in counseling is a common counselor activity. It is an integral part of the counseling process that is used in all stages of counseling—from referral to follow-up. Assessment activities range from the initial interview to the use of standardized and nonstandardized tests.

TESTS

Virtually all counselors are involved in the use of tests as part of the counseling process. The primary function of tests in counseling is to help clients make better decisions about their futures. Tests may also

- Help clients gain self-understanding.
- Help counselors make an accurate diagnosis.
- Help counselors determine a client's best plan for treatment.
- Help determine a client's suitability for a certain treatment program or modality.
- Help in the development of an educational plan.
- Help assess the effectiveness of an education/counseling program.
- Help carry out research studies.

Counselors may decide that information from tests would help supplement and augment information from interviews. Counselors often differ in the extent and type of tests that they use during counseling or therapy, depending on their theoretical orientation. Humanists, as a rule, depend almost entirely on the interviewing process, with only occasional use of self-exploratory measures. Psychoanalysts or psychodynamic counselors or therapists more readily use projective techniques, drawings, stories, or inventories that tap clients' unconscious. Behaviorists and cognitive-behaviorists tend to use structured interviews and instruments that measure observable behavior; they tend to use behavioral rating scales or checklists to assess client behavior. Cognitive behaviorists may use self-monitoring devices to help clients manage caloric intake or quit smoking.

If testing is agreed to, counselors select appropriate tests of high quality; arrange for administration and scoring of these measures; and then make appropriate, meaningful interpretations. Counselors may administer tests themselves or have psychometrists do them. In public schools, scores from standardized tests, which are administered school-wide, are generally available in student cumulative records. Most test publishers provide computerized test scoring and interpretation. Some tests can be easily scored by counselors or clients; a measure like Holland's Self-Directed Search (SDS) is designed to be self-administered and self-scored.

Learning how to select standardized tests and other assessment methods is only part of the training program in assessment. Learning how to interpret the results of assessments and how to interpret clinical observations is the most crucial part of the assessment process. It is also the most misused and neglected. Interpretation involves integrating results from test scores, interviews, and personal observations into a meaningful, accurate pattern that contributes to a greater understanding of the individual and the individual's problem.

Test results should not be used to label clients in ways that will determine or shape the direction of the counseling process. This caution applies especially to computerized interpretations supplied by testing companies. Assessments of an individual's responses and personality characteristics may change during the counseling process. The counselor makes nonjudgmental, tentative assessments of an exploratory nature and gives feedback to the client that will help clarify the client's feelings and encourage deeper self-exploration. Then counselor and client together make a working hypothesis about the client's problem—a mutual assessment that will help determine a plan of counseling action.

Interpretation of a client's apparent behavioral characteristics often focuses on unraveling and reshaping the client's distorted opinions about his or her behavior. The timing of that interpretation is crucial. Counselors generally withhold making judgments in the initial sessions of counseling, although they are keenly attentive to observing their clients' behavior. These observations provide tentative assessments that will be useful in later interactions during the counseling process.

Classification of Tests

Tests can be classified as nonstandardized or standardized.

Nonstandardized Tests

Nonstandardized tests have no formal procedures for administering and scoring. They include observations about client behavior and clients' self-reports about their feelings, interests, attitudes, and experiences.

Client observation is an important skill that counselors use to assess a client's emotional frame of mind. A client's degree of anxiety, depression, uncertainty, or resentment often can be gauged by his or her body behavior: Does the client sit slumped in a chair? Does the client's hands or voice tremble? Is the client alert or distracted? However, counselors should guard against automatically perceiving a client's body behavior as a sign of emotional distress. A squirming client, for example, may be sitting in an uncomfortable chair or may have a back problem.

Some counselors use client self-reports of various types to encourage client self-observation and self-exploration. These self-reports are as diverse as questionnaires designed to obtain background information, autobiographical or personal essays, or journal keeping. Self-monitoring schedules, in which clients collect and record data of their own behavior, are used frequently. Client self-observation contributes to a counselor's understanding of client needs or conflicts.

Standardized Tests

Standardized tests are based on statistically derived norm groups, with formal and consistent procedures for administering and scoring. Interpretations are based on a comparison of client scores with those of individuals on whom the measure was standardized.

Unlike informal nonstandardized procedures, standardized tests are systematically and statistically designed to give objective information about certain specific client characteristics or behaviors. A client's score on a particular standardized test is compared with the scores of particular groups of people on whom the test was standardized. These comparative representative scores, called *norms,* add meaning to a client's raw scores. A client's score on an intelligence test, for example, can be compared with those of an appropriate norm group to determine whether the client's score is higher, at the same level, or lower than other representative individuals like them. Norms are usually nationally based, but they can also be regionally or even locally based.

Effective counselors are aware of possible problems of norm groups, particularly with diverse groups. Multicultural groups have criticized standardized tests whose item choices and norm groups are based on White, middle-class, male youth populations. Of particular concern are intelligence tests and personality inventories. Sue and Sue (2003) say, "The improper use of such instruments can lead to an exclusion of minorities in jobs and promotion, to discriminatory educational decisions, and to biased determination of what constitutes pathology" (p. 48). Cohen and Swerdlik (2002) further explain:

> Items on tests of intelligence tend to reflect the culture of the society where such tests are employed. To the extent that a score on such a test reflects the degree to which the test takers have been integrated into the society and the culture, it would be expected that members of subcultures . . . would score lower. (p. 247)

To decrease test bias, psychologists attempted to develop culture-fair and culture-specific tests, but they have not proved successful. *Culture-fair tests* include items common to all cultures; a *culture-specific test* contains items expressly related to a specific subculture. Culture-fair tests have had little success as accurate measures of minority groups, and culture-specific tests have low predictive value for the specific cultural group (Cohen & Swerdlik, 2002). According to Cohen and Swerdlik (2002), "Major tests of intelligence have undergone a great deal of scrutiny for bias in many investigations . . . and it has generally been concluded that these tests are relatively free of any systematic bias" (p. 253). Meanwhile, counselors are being alerted to their own biases in selecting and interpreting tests for minorities.

Counselors must also be aware of the reliability and validity of standardized tests. *Reliability* refers to "the degree to which test scores are consistent, dependable, and repeatable" (Drummond & Jones, 2006, p. 65). *Validity* refers to the degree to which a test score measures what it claims to measure. For example, individuals who score high on a measure of mechanical ability should be expected to do well on mechanical jobs or in mechanical training.

Reliability can be assessed in three ways: *retest,* in which one administers the same test twice; *parallel form,* in which one administers an equivalent form; and *split-half,* in which two or more equivalent portions are given to determine the internal consistency of the tests (Thorndike, 1997).

Validity, too, can be assessed in three ways: *Content validity,* often referred to as *face validity,* indicates to what extent a test measures what it is supposed to measure. This form is most often used in achievement and ability testing. *Criterion-related validity* measures how well an individual's scores compare against a particular criterion of success. For example, individuals' scores on a spatial aptitude test may be compared with their success as draftsmen. *Construct validity* indicates whether a test measures the particular construct it is supposed to measure. This form of validity is particularly applicable to unobservable constructs, such as personality and interest variables (Cohen & Swerdlik, 2002; Thorndike, 1997).

TYPES OF STANDARDIZED TESTS

Counselors generally use five types of standardized measures: intelligence tests, aptitude tests, achievement tests, interest inventories, and personality inventories.

Intelligence Tests

Intelligence tests are designed to measure general academic ability or the ability to perform successfully in academic settings. Such tests fall into two categories: (a) intelligence tests that are designed to be administered only to an individual by a specially trained mental health worker and (b) intelligence tests that are designed to be administered to groups, but can also be given to an individual.

The two major intelligence tests that are individually administered are the Stanford–Binet and the Wechsler Intelligence Scales. The Stanford–Binet grew out of an intelligence scale developed by Alfred Binet in France in 1905 to screen mental retardation in children. It was designed only for use with children and adolescents because of its content and because it is standardized on children and adolescents. It relies only on verbal responses. The Wechsler scales are a variety of tests designed for all ages, including the Wechsler Adult Intelligence Scale (WAIS-III) for ages 16 and older, the Wechsler Intelligence Scale for Children (WISC-IV) for ages 6 to 16 years 11 months, and the Wechsler Preschool and Primary Scale of Intelligence–Revised (WPPSI–III) for ages 4 to 6½. The Wechsler scales also differ from the Stanford–Binet in that they include performance tasks as well as verbal responses. For these reasons, the Wechsler scales are widely used for all age levels in measuring intelligence (Walsh & Betz, 2001).

Group intelligence tests are often used when counselors and clients decide it is important to obtain a measure of scholastic aptitude. These tests usually measure a component of intelligence. Verbal and numerical reasoning are most often used in school and college settings. A client may be having academic difficulties in a school setting, or a client may be contemplating college with an academic record that is mediocre. The client or the counselor, or both, may believe that the academic record underestimates the client's true ability, so an intelligence test is used to make comparisons. The most commonly used are the Otis–Lennon School Ability Test, the Henmon–Nelson Tests of Mental Ability (K–12), the California Short Form of Mental Ability, the School and College Ability Tests (SCAT), and the Scholastic Aptitude Test (SAT). A group intelligence test often used in business or in government agencies to help in selecting individuals for job placement is the Wonderlic Personnel Test (Walsh & Betz, 2001).

Aptitude Tests

Aptitude tests, like intelligence tests, measure an individual's ability to learn, but are more specific to given areas of performance. These tests usually include some form of verbal, abstract reasoning, numerical, spatial, mechanical, and clerical ability. Counselors tend to use aptitude tests in career counseling in a variety of settings—schools and colleges, community career centers, employment agencies, and personnel services in business and industry.

Multiple aptitude batteries provide a comparative profile of scores based on the same norm group. The three batteries most often used by counselors are the Differential Aptitude Tests (DAT), the Armed Service Vocational Aptitude Battery (ASVAB), and the General Aptitude Test Battery (GATB). Aptitude batteries are developed to predict how well one will do in specific jobs or training programs. The content of these batteries is determined from analyses of numerous jobs, based on the assumption that different aptitudes relate to different jobs (Thorndike, 1997).

The DAT is specifically designed for high school students exploring career or curricular choices. The ASVAB, originally developed to classify armed services recruits, is now offered by the U.S. Department of Defense to high school students in 15,000 schools at no cost to the students or the school districts. The GATB, used predominantly in state employment services, has for many years been the most widely used battery in career counseling and placement. The GATB also includes performance tests measuring finger dexterity, manual dexterity, and motor coordination—abilities necessary in jobs requiring skills in working with one's hands and with small objects. The GATB currently is administered only in government employment agencies. Counselors in other settings can obtain the results, however, through a written request and with the consent of the client.

Achievement Tests

Counselors use *achievement tests* primarily in educational settings to help clients explore curricular or career options when proficiency in a specific subject is important. Achievement batteries are given to students in most school districts at specified grade levels; all states use some form of statewide standardized achievement tests in public schools (Thorndike, 1997). The same tests are used either for the entire student body or at a specified grade level, and results are placed in students' cumulative files. Counselors and clients can then make use of them in counseling sessions when students want information about their competencies in various subject areas. Examples of these batteries include the Iowa Tests of Basic Skills (ITBS), used in elementary schools, and the Metropolitan Achievement Tests (MAT), the Stanford Achievement Tests, and the Iowa Tests of Educational Development (ITED), used in elementary and secondary schools.

An achievement test often used by community counselors is the Wide Range Achievement Test (WRAT). This battery—which measures reading, spelling, and arithmetic competencies—has norms from kindergarten to 75 years of age. It is individually administered and is used along with individual intelligence tests to determine whether an individual has a learning disability.

Interest Inventories

When clients are concerned about career choices or are seriously dissatisfied with their jobs, counselors often use vocational interest measures to help them identify a more satisfying choice of job or career. The three major interest measures are Holland's Self-Directed Search (SDS) for high school and college students and adults; the Strong Interest Inventory (SII) for high school seniors, college students, and adults; and the Kuder Career Search with Person Match (KCS), for ages from middle school to adult. These inventories, in one form or another, compare client vocational interest scores with those of persons in business, professional, scientific, artistic, technical, and social service occupations.

In recent years, the SDS has become one of the most widely used interest inventories. The SDS was published in 1971 and has been revised several times. This self-administered, self-scored, and self-interpreted inventory measures an individual's self-reported occupational interests and classifies responses into six personality types based on Holland's six themes: realistic, artistic, investigative, social, enterprising, and conventional (RAISEC). These personality types are then correlated to more than 1,000 occupational groups. Although the SDS is designed for individual self-interpretation, it is best used in counseling sessions with a counselor assisting in the interpretation (Thorndike, 1997).

The SII, designed for use with adults, college students, and high school students, is the granddaddy of interest measurement tests. Originally published in 1927, it has gone through innumerable revisions. The SII assesses clients' interests among a broad range of occupations, work and leisure activities, and educational subjects. The inventory compares an individual's profile of scores with more than 200 occupational scales and relates them to Holland's six occupational themes (RAISEC).

Another pioneer interest inventory, KCS, which was introduced in 1934 and revised several times. The current KCS is an Internet-based assessment applicable for ages from middle school to adult. It reports on the test-taker's similarity with groups of employed people in six career clusters: Outdoor/Mechanical, Science/Technical, Arts/Communication, Social/Personal Services, Sales/Management, and Business Operations. In addition, it offers the job titles and first-person job descriptions of the people from the two clusters whose preference patterns are most similar to those of the test-taker.

Personality Measures

Counselors use personality measures to (a) assess client personality traits or characteristics, (b) compare client characteristics with those of individuals in various occupations or careers, and (c) assess a client's degree of emotional trauma or pathology. Personality measures are of two forms: objective inventories and projective techniques.

Objective Inventories.

Objective inventories are self-reports in which clients respond to a series of statements related to their personality characteristics. Examples of objective personality inventories are the Myers–Briggs Type Indicator (MBTI), the Minnesota Multiphasic Personality Inventory (MMPI-2), the California Psychological Inventory (CPI), and the Edwards Personal Preference Schedule (EPPS). Effective counselors use scores on these measures as indicators of client predispositions capable of change, rather than as fixed, static traits. For example, clients who have low sociability scores and are concerned about their ineffective relationships can be helped to develop social skills, or clients showing obsessive-compulsive behavior can learn to modify their behavior through counseling and therapy.

The MBTI was developed by a mother–daughter team, Katherine C. Briggs and Isabel Briggs Myers and is based on Carl Jung's theory of typology. The instrument is used for measuring a person's preferences using four scales with opposite poles: extraversion/introversion, sensing/intuitive, thinking/feeling, and judging/perceiving. The combinations of these preferences result in 16 personality types. Many counselors in colleges and in the community use the inventory to help their clients gain some understanding of how their typology relates to career choices or to personal and social functioning.

The MMPI-2 is one of the most widely used personality measures in clinical mental health practice. The inventory consists of eight clinical scales based on psychiatric-psychological symptoms of neurosis or psychosis: hypochondriasis (Hs), depression (D), conversion hysteria (Hy), psychopathic deviate (Pd), paranoia (Pa), psychasthenia (Pt), schizophrenia (Sc), and hypomania (Ma). Scales also measure masculinity and femininity (MF) and social introversion (SI). Four validity scales are scored to detect faking and distorted responses. The MMPI-2 is used in a variety of counseling and therapeutic settings to assess the degree and nature of an individual's emotional distress. Counselors and other mental health practitioners in private practice, as well as those who work in mental health clinics or mental hospitals, most often use the MMPI.

The CPI is used with clients 13 years of age and older. Personal characteristics in the inventory focus on social interactions and feelings of adequacy. Scales presented of desirable characteristics, including such areas as sociability, social presence, self-acceptance, sense of well-being, and self-control.

The EPPS, with norms for college students and adults, is used when the counselor wants to help clients explore unfulfilled needs that are interfering with their personal, interpersonal, or career functioning. Based on Henry Murray's need theory of personality, it has 28 scales tapping such areas as need for achievement, need for dominance, and need for autonomy.

Projective Tests.

Projective tests are used to tap a person's unconscious reactions to ambiguous pictures or images or through storytelling or drawing. Projective tests are based on psychoanalytic or psychodynamic views about the importance of assessing a person's unconscious motives. In these tests, clients react unconsciously to ambiguous pictures, images, or incomplete sentences, or they may draw human figures or objects that are projections of their self-image. The most commonly used projectives in counseling practice are the Thematic Apperception Test (TAT), the Rorschach, the Rotter Incomplete Sentences Blank, the House–Tree–Person (HTP), and the Draw a Person (DAP). These projective techniques are most apt to be used by doctorate-level mental health practitioners trained in psychodynamic theory and practice.

The TAT consists of picture cards that show one or more individuals in ambiguous settings. The client tells a story about each picture that is assumed to reveal something about the client's conflicts or social constraints. The Rorschach is a set of cards with inkblot images; clients are asked what they see in each image.

Counselors using the Rotter Incomplete Sentences Blank ask individuals to respond to sentence stems, such as "I like . . ." and "I want to know. . . ." The Rotter gives an overall adjustment rating and is used for assessing both how well an individual is functioning and what psychiatric disturbances might exist.

The HTP and the DAP ask clients to draw pictures to indicate unconscious projections of their self-image. These tests are sometimes used by elementary school counselors and community counselors in their work with children. Counselors using these tests need special training in psychodynamic theory, as well as the use of projective tests.

Another drawing test, the Bender Visual–Motor Gestalt Test, commonly called the Bender–Gestalt, is used to assess whether personality disturbances are a result of brain damage. Individuals copy nine abstract designs consisting of dots, curves, and lines; the protocols of individuals being assessed are compared with those of individuals with brain damage. Clinical mental health counselors in the community or in private practice are most apt to use the Bender–Gestalt for this type of diagnostic evaluation.

THE INITIAL INTERVIEW

The cornerstone of assessment and the beginning of every counseling relationship is the intial interview. In mental health and community counseling settings, the *initial interview* (also called the *clinical interview*) remains the primary assessment tool for gathering client information and diagnosing mental disorders (Craig, 2003; Miller, 2003; Sadock & Sadock, 2000; Shear et al., 2000; Sommers-Flanagan & Sommers-Flanagan, 2003). The purposes of the initial interview are to (a) determine the suitability of the client for counseling, (b) assess and respond to a client's crises, (c) familiarize the client with the counseling process, and (d) gather sufficient client information to help formulate a diagnosis and treatment plan (Seligman, 1996).

Most initial interviews are unstructured and consist of counselor-made questions with client responses and counselor observations recorded by the counselor. It is considered unstructured because there is no standardization of questioning or recording of client responses; it is the counselor who is "entirely responsible for deciding what questions to ask and how the resulting information is used in arriving at a diagnosis" (Summerfeldt & Antony, 2002, p. 3). Interviewing involves an unstructured exploration to gain information about a client's presenting problem. Counselors follow a general format consisting of the following content areas:

- Presenting problem
- Family history
- Relationship history
- Education
- Work history
- Medical history

- Substance use
- Legal history
- Previous counseling

Counselors may use other assessment instruments to supplement the information obtained during the interview. If the initial interview is the only means used for gathering client information, counselors need to know what information is necessary to obtain during the interview and how that information is relevant to a making an accurate diagnosis.

DIAGNOSTIC AND STATISTICAL MANUAL OF MENTAL DISORDERS

Today, all counselors should be knowledgeable about the *DSM-IV-TR* and able to converse with other mental health professionals regarding its contents (Remley & Herlihy, 2007). The *Diagnostic and Statistical Manual of Mental Disorders (DSM-IV-TR)* is the official classification system of mental disorders in the United States and is used by psychiatrists, other physicians, psychologists, social workers, nurses, occupational and rehabilitation therapists, counselors, and other health and mental health professionals (American Psychiatric Association, 2000). It is used across settings—inpatient, outpatient, partial hospital, private practice, and primary care, and with community populations. A manual in book form, it classifies mental disorders into 17 categories, including childhood disorders, dementia, substance abuse, schizophrenia, mood disorders, anxiety disorders, physical symptoms rooted in psychological problems, intentional faking of disorders, dissociative disorders, sexual and gender disorders, eating disorders, sleep disorders, impulse-control disorders, adjustment disorders, and personality disorders. Normally functioning individuals experiencing stress are classified as having adjustment disorders.

A unique feature of the *DSM-IV-TR* is the therapeutic use of five axes to classify client problems in a comprehensive and informative way; the axes assume a biophysical-social etiology. The therapist assesses the client's condition according to the axes:

Axis I:	Clinical Disorders
Axis II:	Personality Disorder or Mental Retardation
Axis III:	General Medical Condition
Axis IV:	Psychosocial or Environmental Problems
Axis V:	Global Assessment of Functioning (GAF)

The following is an example of a *DSM-IV-TR* diagnostic assessment of a particular depressed client suffering from diabetes, recent loss of job, and divorce:

Axis I	296.23	Major Depressive Disorder, Single Episode, Severe Without Psychotic Features
Axis II	V71.09	No Diagnosis
Axis III		Diabetes
Axis IV		Divorce, loss of job
Axis V	GAF = 55 (current)	

The advantages of using the *DSM-IV-TR* in mental health practice are numerous: (a) it offers a universal system of diagnosis that permits dialogue among mental health specialists; (b) it includes attention to cultural, age, and gender features (Sue, Sue, & Sue, 2005); (c) the multiaxial system requires that practitioners consider various physical, psychosocial, and environmental circumstances influencing the client's dysfunction; and (d) research and expert opinions were used to construct the classifications.

Diagnosis using the *DSM-IV-TR* has been criticized for a variety of reasons: (a) it emphasizes pathological symptoms; (b) managed care organizations tend to use categories to deny authorization of client treatment for normal conflicts or for longer term care; and (c) it has a strong medical orientation that runs counter to the wellness philosophy that counselors espouse (Remley & Herlihy, 2007).

In addition, some managed care companies decline to authorize treatment for some of the diagnostic categories. Counselors may be tempted to assign clients a more severe diagnosis (i.e., up-coding) or a less severe diagnosis (i.e., down-coding) than is clinically accurate so that clients will qualify for health insurance reimbursement. Unfortunately, an inaccurate diagnosis on a client's record can be harmful to the client, and the counselors are "on shaky ground both ethically and legally" (Remley & Herlihy, 2007, p. 260).

SUMMARY

Assessment involves the use of tests, interviews, observations, or other measurement procedures for the purpose of gathering information about a client and gaining a better understanding of the client's issues. The process of assessment is important to help clients clarify their problems and to enhance their self-exploration. Tests are one part of the overall process of assessment.

Appropriately interpreting test results is a key part in the assessment process. It requires the skill and wise judgment of a trained counselor, one who can integrate information gathered from client test scores, interviews, and personal observations into meaningful patterns and use those appraisals to enhance client self-exploration.

Counselors use both nonstandardized and standardized tests in assessment. Nonstandardized tests include informal observations of client behavior and self-reports of clients about themselves. Standardized tests involve formal and consistent procedures for administering and scoring. The five types of standardized measures include intelligence tests, aptitude tests, achievement tests, interest inventories, and personality inventories.

Counselors use the *DSM-IV-TR* for diagnostic classification of mental disorders. The *DSM-IV-TR* provides a universal system of diagnosis that facilitates communication among mental health and other health care professionals, helps counselors make decisions about effective treatment, and provides a framework for research.

PROJECTS AND ACTIVITIES

1. Visit your university counseling center and determine the type of assessment procedures the staff uses most often.
2. Talk with a counselor whose major responsibility is crisis intervention. Discuss with her or him procedures used and referral sources available.
3. Use an anonymous questionnaire to survey your class about the types of tests they have taken and their opinions about the value of these measures.

CHAPTER 8

Individual Counseling

Individual counseling is a process in which a professional counselor and a client develop an interactive relationship that fosters client self-awareness and empowers that person to resolve her or his particular situational problems effectively. Many complex variables influence the nature, intensity, and duration of the individual counseling process: the counselor's effectiveness, the counselor's particular theoretical point of view, the setting in which the counseling takes place, the client's characteristics, and the nature of the client's problem. Personal and professional characteristics are also essential for effective counseling. Because effective counselors vary in their theoretical approaches, clients need to be aware of a counselor's particular approach to determine whether it is suitable to their needs. One of the most important concepts related to individual counseling is the therapeutic relationship between client and counselor. Counselors have long recognized the importance of a strong working relationship in effecting change. In fact, the quality of a therapeutic relationship appears to be a better predictor of success than the therapeutic approach of the counselor (Nuttall, 2002).

After studying this chapter, you should be able to

- Identify client characteristics that influence how clients will respond to counseling.
- Describe the stages in the process of individual counseling.
- Understand the importance of counselors establishing a safe, trusting therapeutic relationship with clients.

CLIENT CHARACTERISTICS

Research about client characteristics that contribute to effective counseling outcomes has proved inconclusive. This finding is not surprising because the criteria that have typically been used to describe effective clients are those that generally apply to optimally functioning individuals: willingness to admit problems, verbal fluency, ability to cope, and flexibility (Brammer, Abrego, & Shostrom, 1993; Heilbrun, 1982; Rogers, 1942). Researchers have overlooked the fact that clients who seek help tend to be anxious, doubtful, uncertain, or defensive, especially in an initial therapeutic encounter.

Clients differ considerably in their attitudes about starting counseling. Many clients these days have had previous counseling: Older clients and those who have attended college may have had a series of counseling experiences and may have been exposed to a variety of counseling approaches; some may have had counseling for specific needs, such as career counseling or weight-loss counseling; some may be "therapy wise," cynical, and wary; some may have formed certain opinions about therapy and about themselves from reading self-help books or taking self-administered personality surveys; and even those who have never had counseling may have heard varying reports from friends. Despite the individual circumstances, clients generally approach an initial counseling session with apprehension.

Client apprehension is compounded by the anxieties that compelled them to seek counseling in the first place, symptoms that typically surface when individuals feel particularly vulnerable. One significant characteristic can generally be assumed for all clients, at least for those who voluntarily seek counseling: They recognize that they have difficulties and have the insight, strength, and motivation to seek help.

While developing relationships with clients and planning effective counseling sessions, counselors should consider basic client characteristics that might influence the counseling process: values, view of human nature, and worldview. Are they shy or outgoing, articulate or glib, or inarticulate? Do they have positive or negative views about human nature, about themselves, and about the world in general?

Other client characteristics that might influence counseling include whether clients believe they have ultimate control of their lives, whether they tend to blame others for their problems, or whether they tend to blame themselves. Attitudes such as these are apt to influence the degree to which clients can bring about changes within themselves or in their environment. Still other client characteristics—the degree of insight they have about their problems, their stated goals, the strength of their defenses—give clues as to the degree to which they are able to confront and explore their problems.

These factors are all apt to influence how clients will respond to counseling—how they will interact with counselors, what they will expect to happen in the counseling sessions, and how motivated or capable they will be to make changes for growth. In turn, these characteristics will help counselors decide what goals are realistic for clients and what types of strategies will best help the clients attain those goals.

THE COUNSELING PROCESS

In the counseling process, counselor and client develop a trusting, dynamic, interactive relationship that helps empower the client to resolve his or her problem. Counselors and therapists generally agree that a successful counseling outcome occurs when an effective relationship is established between counselor and client (Gelso & Carter, 1985). Moreover, most counselors recognize that an essential role of the counselor is to enable clients to self-explore and develop self-awareness as a way to resolve their problems.

The counseling process evolves through several stages, from the first interview through termination; the process is generally similar regardless of counselor orientation (Brammer et al., 1993; Egan, 2007; Sexton & Whiston, 1994). The counseling process can generally be divided into three overlapping stages: initial, middle and last. In the *initial* stage, counselor and client develop a relationship that will foster client self-exploration, they clarify the nature of the problem, and they set goals and treatment plans. In the *middle* stage, the counselor helps the client self-explore more deeply to increase insight and understanding of the problem. In the *last* stage, the counselor and client work together in helping the client take action to change behaviors or attitudes in everyday living; they then proceed toward terminating the counseling sessions.

Tracey (1988) points out that the dynamics of the counselor–client relationship change during each of the three stages: In the initial stage, counselors relate to clients on client terms, developing rapport, listening, and attending to client needs; in the middle stage, counselors challenge clients to explore deeper emotions; in the last stage, counselors relate to clients collaboratively as peers.

Initial Stage: Developing a Relationship and Clarifying the Presenting Problem

In the early sessions, counselor and client begin to develop the mutual relationship necessary to carry them along on a journey together to resolve the client's problem. Right from the start, counselors must convey through their overall manner that they are accepting and understanding. They must also assure their clients that they will maintain confidentiality throughout the counseling sessions. Furthermore, counselors must create an ambience that assures the clients that their welfare is the primary concern during this time. No telephone calls or interruptions are allowed during sessions; counselors are on time for appointments; and counselors' offices are inviting, comfortable but not fancy, and soundproof.

Setting the Tone and Defining Parameters

In the crucial first interview, counselors lay the foundation and set a climate for an effective working relationship. In doing so, they have a somewhat paradoxical task.

They must immediately convey an aura of understanding and warmth that assures the clients of trust. At the same time, they must clarify the parameters of counseling, as well as gather information about the clients in order to make an initial assessment of the problem.

Clients arrive at the first interview feeling uncertain and ambivalent about talking intimately to a counselor. They may wonder whether they have sufficient strength to undertake the often painful experience of self-exploration. Along with their fears, they come with certain expectations about counselors and counseling (Moursund and Kenny, 2002). They hope the counselor will not make negative judgments about them, they wonder whether the counselor will hold what they say in confidence, they sense the potential power of the counselor and the possible abuse of that power, and they hope the counselor will have the personal characteristics and expertise to help them.

The first interview can be awkward, particularly when a client is shy or reserved. Making social chitchat to set a client at ease is not recommended; the delay in getting to the reason for counseling can increase anxiety. Usually, a simple statement will suffice: "Tell me what brings you here for counseling." If the counselor has already talked on the telephone with the client, it would be helpful to review that conversation: "Last week, you called and said you had split up with your wife," or "The other day when you phoned, you said you were feeling depressed." If the person has been referred, it is usually helpful to go over how the referral occurred and what the client's expectations are.

During the first interview, the counselor generally relies on *open questions* (to bring out general information) and *closed questions* (to obtain more specific information). In the following interchange, for example, the counselor obtains information from the client while also responding to the client's feelings.

COUNSELOR: Have you ever had counseling before? [closed question]
CLIENT: Yes, I saw a counselor about a year ago.
COUNSELOR: What do you think you gained from that experience? [open question]
CLIENT: Nothing much. I was disappointed. My counselor didn't hear what I was saying.
COUNSELOR: You didn't get what you had hoped for, an understanding counselor. [paraphrase]

Besides setting a climate of acceptance and warmth and determining the appropriateness of service, counselors explain to clients what they can expect in counseling. Counselors also describe their qualifications and the policies of the agency they work for. They may ask clients what they are hoping for. Confidentiality, rights of privacy, and other ethical and legal considerations also need to be clarified.

The counselor must make time at the end of the first session to discuss whether the client's concerns are within the counselor's expertise or whether the client believes that the counselor can best serve her or his needs. For example, if the client's main concern is alcohol addiction and the counselor does not work with this problem, then it is necessary to refer the client to someone who does. Or if the client needs more intensive help than the counselor or agency is prepared to provide or the agency limits intensive therapy, then the counselor can suggest an appropriate referral.

Clients, at this time, may also decide that the counselor's theoretical orientation or approach is not what they were expecting. If so, the counselor can suggest someone more in line with the client's preferences. In states where counselors are licensed for private practice, it is mandatory that counselors disclose their educational background, theoretical orientation, and the types of techniques they may use. Even when not mandated, this disclosure is a sound idea because counselor and client then have a better idea about their potential compatibility.

Counselors also need to discuss the length of sessions, fees, and the arrangement of regular meeting times. Those counselors in private practice who are eligible for third-party insurance payments also need to explain the expected diagnosis, because a diagnosis is required by the insurance company.

Developing a Therapeutic Relationship

A strong therapeutic relationship between client and counselor is a key factor in potentiating client change (Nuttall, 2002). A therapeutic relationship occurs when trust develops between a counselor and a client and is maintained throughout the counseling process. Trust develops when clients believe that their counselors accept them as worthy persons with dignity and value regardless of what they disclose about themselves. Bordin (1975), who calls the counselor–client relationship a *working alliance,* divides the process of forming that alliance into three parts: (a) establishment of an emotional bond, (b) mutual agreement about goals, and (c) mutual agreement about tasks.

In the early stage of counseling, while client and counselor are getting to know each other and are beginning to establish mutual trust, the counselor listens to the client's concerns and encourages him or her to express the feelings and thoughts that are bothersome; moreover, the counselor fully accepts what the client has to say. This client-centered approach encourages clients to talk more freely and also gives counselors important information to use later when they explore problems more deeply.

A counselor's accepting, nonjudgmental attitude helps clients reveal more about the hurt, pain, or anxiety they are experiencing. In a warm, accepting atmosphere, counselors demonstrate understanding and genuineness and attention to client feelings even as they focus on the cognitive processes involved in what is happening or how clients perceive what is happening in their lives.

A counselor might respond to a client's concerns with a reflection of feeling intended to encourage the client to express more feelings.

> CLIENT: My whole life collapsed when my husband left me and the children without warning. I'm not sleeping well. I don't have job skills to take care of myself and my two children.
>
> COUNSELOR: You're feeling overwhelmed by it all.
>
> CLIENT: Yes, I am, and I see no way out unless I get some training.

Counselors may also rephrase a client statement to show they are listening and to help the client focus on the concern.

CLIENT: I know it doesn't help my grades when I procrastinate and start projects the night before they are due, but I keep doing it.

COUNSELOR: You know your grades won't improve if you wait until the last minute to begin your project, but up to now you feel unable to change that behavior.

CLIENT: Yes, that's why I decided I need help. I see the problem but not the solution.

To help a client elaborate on the problem, the counselor might ask for clarification.

CLIENT: Sometimes I get a peculiar feeling about myself and my life.

COUNSELOR: Can you tell me more about what you mean by "peculiar feeling"?

CLIENT: Yes, I sometimes feel as though nothing in my life is real, as though I'm in a dream.

Understanding the Client's Problem

Counselors consider several factors about clients and their situational concerns: the severity and complexity of the problem, the length and persistence of symptoms, and the past stability of the client. Counselors also consider the context in which clients are experiencing the problem: social and cultural factors, degree of environmental support, and family relationships. These and the other client characteristics described earlier help determine the way counseling will proceed.

Counselors need to consider the functionality of the client's families of origin, the nature of client's current familial relationships, the way the client functions in his or her career or schoolwork, and the types of environmental support available to the client. Counselors must also assess how a client's changes in attitudes and behavior will be received by persons close to him or her. In other words, what will be the consequences of the client's change?

Counselors must also consider the cultural backgrounds of their clients, particularly those from ethnic groups or from numerous cultural subgroups. Asians, for example, are made up of distinct ethnic groups—Chinese, Japanese, Thai, Korean, Vietnamese, and so on. Moreover, for recent immigrants, ethnic identity also depends on whether one is first, second, or third generation in the United States. Where one lives also influences one's cultural identity: Growing up in California is considerably different from growing up in New York City or Alabama. And for Native Americans, growing up on a reservation as a semisovereign tribal nation is a significantly different experience from that of all of the other cultural groups. Furthermore, growing up on the Sioux reservation is culturally different from growing up on the Swinomish reservation.

Forming a Working Hypothesis and Making a Tentative Diagnosis

An important step begins in the first interview and continues during the initial stage of counseling—forming a hypothesis of the client's problem. Using information gained by observing and interviewing the client, the counselor assesses the nature and complexity of the problem to make a tentative hypothesis, or diagnosis of the problem.

For those clients covered by mental health insurance, counselors and therapists must make diagnoses quickly because diagnoses are required in order for clients to qualify for services. In many college counseling centers and community agencies, determining whether clients qualify for services is accomplished in intake interviews.

Counselors must also determine whether clients require a considerable number of sessions or only a few. If symptoms are mild and of short duration, motivation is high, environmental disruption is at a minimum, and the problem is specific and can be resolved in a reasonable amount of time, the counselor can assume that short-term counseling is sufficient. However, if a client has long-term symptoms, complicated or vague problems, strong defenses, confused values, or complex, immobilizing social–cultural conditions, the counselor can assume that deeper, more intensive work is needed before change will occur. To help in these decisions, many counselors use assessment devices such as tests, inventories, behavioral surveys, or schedules.

During the first stages of exploration, a self-inventory may be helpful for clients who have difficulty expressing their needs or talking about their feelings. Nonthreatening personality inventories can measure normal personality characteristics. Cognitive–behaviorists tend to use behavioral observations and self-monitoring scales, rather than standardized or nonstandardized tests or inventories, to help them assess clients' problems. Many counselors prefer to make a tentative assessment of a client's difficulty over several sessions in the early phase of counseling.

The *DSM-IV-TR* has become a prominent instrument used by counselors. Mental health counselors use the *DSM-IV-TR* to assess the nature and severity of the emotional disorder and to determine the appropriate treatment or referral.

Setting Goals and Designing a Plan of Action

Once a client's presenting problem has been discussed and conceptualized, counselor and client work together to set goals and develop a plan of action. Goals need to be as clear and specific as possible, consistent with the complexity of the problem. They must be realistic, flexible, in line with client resources and capabilities, stated in a way that permits continual evaluation of progress, and possible to accomplish in a realistic amount of time (Egan, 2007). Consideration must be given to whether any external circumstances are hindering a client's goal. For example, a client who desires a particular type of training that is only available 3,000 miles away but who cannot leave his family will have to come to terms with his conflicting goals.

Some counselors, particularly behaviorists and cognitive–behaviorists, find it productive to develop contracts with clients. In such cases, a contract that includes a statement of goals, the techniques to be followed, and the length of time to accomplish the goals can serve as a useful working model for both counselor and client. Goals and treatment plans, however, must be flexible enough to be modified if circumstances warrant a change.

Middle Stage: Exploring More Deeply

In the middle stage of counseling, a shift occurs in the counseling process. Once counselor and client have discussed preliminaries, reached an initial understanding of each other and the client's problem, and agreed on the purpose for working together, they then move into deeper explorations.

For brief, solution-focused, or time-limited counseling, the middle stage is fairly short. Likewise, for those clients who are seeking counseling to solve a particular problem, who have a fairly well developed sense of themselves, and who don't need to go through the complicated process of self-exploration at this time or for this particular purpose, counseling with a brief middle stage is all that is necessary. Counselors and clients can then proceed to the last stage, where they focus on turning new client attitudes and insights into effective behavioral changes in everyday life.

For counseling needs that take more time, however, the process in the middle stage becomes complicated and unpredictable and thus is difficult to describe. As Moursund and Kenny (2002) points out, in contrast with the fairly predictable first and last stages, the middle stage can go in any number of directions; the counselor needs to allow clients to explore the numerous avenues under their own volition and at their own pace. "There will be occasions when you literally will not know what the client is moving into, or when you will think you know, only to discover later that you were mistaken. Ambiguity comes with the territory" (Moursund and Kenny, 2002, p. 86).

Noting Movement and Gaining Emotional Insights

A major characteristic of the counseling process is the sense of movement, accelerating especially in the middle stage of the counseling process (Miller & Stiver, 1997; Rogers, 1942, 1951). Rogers was one of the first to note this aspect (1942), describing, in particular, the client's gaining of new insights, as well as feelings of increasing emotional intensity and turbulence. Expanding on this sense of movement, in his 1951 text, Rogers alerted counselors to watch for the various aspects of movement or change that occur in the client during the counseling process. Counselors should watch for changes in perception and changes in feelings, increasing feelings of self-worth and independence, less denial of experience, and changes in values. Rogers also noted the changing emotional relationship between client and counselor.

Over the years, counselors and therapists have confirmed this movement or evolving process that counselor and client experience, particularly the shift from client concerns about external problems to client exploration of inner feelings and emotions:

> The shift from early- to middle-phase work, then, is marked by a shift from primarily cognitive concerns to an emphasis on emotional work, from focusing on external to focusing on internal events, from talking about relationships outside of therapy to experiencing relationships within the therapy session itself. (Moursund and Kenny, 2002, p. 76)

In this move from cognitions to emotions, clients begin to take more risks in disclosing their feelings and actions to themselves and others, and the process shifts to the client–counselor relationship: "Emotional issues begin to take precedence over cognitive ones, and the therapeutic relationship itself is frequently the arena in which these issues are worked through" (Moursund and Kenny, 2002, p. 76). Therapists and counselors are recognizing that, in the evolving client–counselor relationship, the counselor experiences feelings and new insights as well. These are discussed later in the chapter.

Miller and Stiver (1997), who emphasize developing and maintaining mutual connections in relationships, also note movement as a primary indicator in the therapeutic process. They believe that commencement of movement begins with the awareness of a mutual empathic relationship between client and counselor. This bonding elicits motion itself, which commences precisely when the client notices that the feelings she is sharing have an impact on the therapist. The therapist, feeling moved by the client's experience, responds. Because the client's dysfunction is based on the denial of feelings by others, therapist responsiveness is a new experience for the client and is precisely what moves them both. With a focus on developing mutual empathic connections, the counseling process begins:

> Participating together . . . is very different from struggling alone without a sense of impact or response, or, alternatively, feeling that you have to hold back parts of yourself because you don't know "where the other person is" psychologically. This is what we mean by building increasing mutual empathy and mutual empowerment in therapy. (Miller & Stiver, 1997, p. 133)

Personal construct theorists also recognize motion or movement, similar to taking a journey: After the client ascertains his or her current constructs and those parts that are dissatisfactory, client and counselor embark on the path of reconstruing the client's personal constructs in ways that are compatible with the client's circumstances (Fransella & Dalton, 2000). Personal construct counselors note that an increase of emotional reactions is inevitable during therapeutic transitional phases, which they call the *cycles of change.* These counselors watch for increased feelings of anxiety, threat, guilt, hostility, and aggression—signs that the client is experiencing changes. These feelings occur in increasing and decreasing cycles of intensity during the cycles of change (Fransella & Dalton, 2000).

During the cycles of change, clients alternate between loosening and tightening their constructs. They loosen constructs when they lower cognitive awareness, give into experience, and participate without judgment or without holding back. As they use relaxation techniques or engage in free association or dream work, the counselor uncritically accepts the client's trial behaviors. In tightening their constructs, clients raise cognitive processes to a high level by keeping logs of their new experiences, summarizing what happens, evaluating and comparing them to other experiences, and putting them into historical context. Counselors may challenge what the clients mean, but are careful not to impose their own differing point of view or their own constructs on the clients (Fransella & Dalton, 2000).

The counselor's primary role is to help guide the client between the alternating loosening and tightening of constructs because of the hazards inherent in going too far either way. Becoming too loose brings on strong anxieties as the client tries unfamiliar ways and experiences chaotic reactions. With premature tightening of constructs, on the other hand, the client is apt to conclude that the new experience was bad and thus will revert back to the safety of familiar old constructs.

Transference.   As clients increase their self-disclosure and self-awareness, counselors and clients begin to develop emotional interactions that need to be acknowledged and worked through for counseling to proceed. These interactions—called *transference* and *countertransference*—are the cornerstones of psychoanalysis. Even though these concepts are well known in psychoanalysis, many counseling professionals believe that they are universal in all relationships (Brammer et al., 1993; Gelso & Carter, 1985). Although most counselors, in their focus on short-term situational problems, have not historically dealt with these issues, recently, both counselors and therapists have been attending to problematic transference and countertransference issues that emerge during this stage.

Transference refers to clients transferring onto the counselor emotions developed from an early age toward significant others in their lives. When clients trust a counselor and are encouraged to become aware of their emotions, they begin to express transference feelings—anger, dependency, admiration, love, or hate—toward their counselor. "To varying degrees, transference occurs in probably all relationships. The therapeutic situation, however, with its emphasis on a kind of controlled help-giving, magnifies and intensifies this natural reaction" (Gelso & Carter, 1985, p. 169).

Counselors generally recognize the value of transference as a natural process. In a therapeutic situation, clients who have been projecting feelings and attitudes onto parents and other authority figures start transferring their feelings onto the counselor; with therapeutic help, they become aware of those and similar transference feelings toward other significant persons in their lives. Counselors and therapists help clients express strong feelings by not reacting negatively or making judgments—in contrast to how parents might respond. This accepting attitude reduces client defensiveness and the anxiety related to expressing forbidden feelings.

Brammer et al. (1993) offer suggestions on working through feelings of transference. The counselor might ask a clarifying question, such as, "You seem to be angry with me today. Why is that?" A counselor could also reflect a client's feelings if the client denies them: "You think these feelings might upset me?" Or the counselor may interpret the transference, demonstrating that the client's earlier interpersonal interactions relate to current behavior, while reassuring the client that these feelings are normal: "Perhaps you become anxious when you show anger toward people. Perhaps you are afraid that you are showing too much anger toward me."

Countertransference.   It is equally important for counselors to recognize their own irrational feelings that they have projected onto clients. When counselors feel uncomfortable with clients or experience irritation or resentment toward them, or when they foster client dependence or become too emotionally involved, they must ask themselves why these feelings exist. And if these feelings persist, counselors should consult with another professional. If feelings of countertransference persist with more than one client, the counselor may need counseling or therapy.

Attention has been given to how counselors can use their irrational feelings toward clients to enrich the counseling relationship. In his article "In Praise of Countertransference: Harvesting Our Errors," Taffel (1993) notes that when counselors become aware of and accept their seemingly irrational or inappropriate feelings about clients, they can perceive their projected feelings as "enlightening mistakes and fruitful errors and can make them part of a richer and more realistic vision of the therapeutic experience" (p. 57).

Miller and Stiver (1997) view therapists' countertransference or emotional reactions as positive signs, signals for them to come to terms with their own unresolved emotional issues. "Especially when a particular therapy relationship is difficult or confusing, the therapist needs to make certain she has a growthful relational context of herself" (Surrey, 1997, p. 45). They also urge the therapist who experiences countertransference reactions to share them with other professionals, "not as signs of failure but often as necessary arenas for growth and relationship movement" (Surrey, 1997, p. 45).

Coping with Impasse

During the middle stage, clients begin to make significant changes in their attitudes and outlooks and gain new insights into their problems. They have bonded well with their counselors and have developed trust. Counselors or therapists feel good about the progress. Then, suddenly, right after positive improvements have occurred, clients react, and there's a breakdown. They revert back to old ways, and an impasse develops in the client–counselor relationship that is very frustrating to the counselor (Miller & Stiver, 1997). Some therapists and counselors have recently been dwelling on this period at length because they acknowledge it as the most difficult stage. They have been reconsidering the traditional assessment of impasse and resistance.

Resistance.   Impasses as a sign of client defenses have long been known in psychoanalysis and have been considered typical of the therapeutic process. Over the years, therapists have developed strategies to work with client defenses and resistances, which they have perceived historically as a negative factor impeding progress in counseling. More recently, resistance has been recognized as an expected part of therapy that can be used to produce more effective counseling (Brammer et al., 1993; Cormier & Cormier, 2003).

Assuming that the client comes to counseling voluntarily, counselors can recognize that a client's resistance may be signaling that important sensitive feelings are being tapped; defenses arise to prevent feelings of anxiety or pain. Similarly, when a physician pokes a sensitive spot in the anatomy, the patient winces, withdraws, or cries out in pain. Clients naturally will be ambivalent about change, uncomfortable about the need to disclose painful or shameful things about themselves, and afraid to face what the therapist is trying to help them explore.

Client resistance can range from open hostility or antagonism to more subtle, passively resistant behavior, such as being late for appointments or skipping them, misinterpreting what the counselor says, or agreeing with everything the counselor suggests. These manifestations may be perplexing to new counselors, particularly because the client has initiated counseling and is paying a fee for the sessions. But such behaviors make sense when counselors recognize that these behaviors are a means of preventing disturbing feelings from coming into awareness.

Strategies.   Many counselors use *social influencing skills* suitable for this stage—such as *interpretation, self-disclosure,* and *confrontation*—to help clients in their self-exploration (Ivey & Ivey, 2006). With this approach, they attempt to increase the depth of client understanding or encourage clients to comment on the causes of their behavior, the amount of control they have over their circumstances, or the meaning behind their remarks.

Counselors may offer *interpretations* of the clients' defensive attitudes and behaviors that are keeping the clients from becoming aware of painful experiences (Brammer et al., 1993). Interpretations should be offered, however, only after clients are at least aware of the particular emotions they are experiencing and the context in which the feelings arose. Brammer et al. (1993) suggest that it is wise to focus on attitudes or behaviors that are subject to clients' control, rather than to point out difficulties they are experiencing that they cannot change. Brammer et al. also recommend tentative positive interpretations, rather than a dogmatic negative approach.

Counselors may also use *self-disclosure* to encourage clients to explore feelings. But self-disclosure must be appropriate to client goals, must not burden clients, must not be done too frequently, and must be adapted to a particular client's feelings or circumstances (Egan, 2007).

CLIENT: I'm in a new job, have a new exciting relationship, am moving to a bigger and better apartment. Things are going great, but I feel sick to my stomach.

COUNSELOR: So many major transitions going on in your life all at once can be unsettling and stressful even when they're positive. I recall having butterflies in my stomach when I started my first job in counseling in a new city right after I married.

Other examples of social influencing skills include *encouragement,* in which counselors praise clients' efforts in disclosing more about themselves, and giving *directives* or *information* or *advice* when clients' apparent lack of movement seems related to a lack of appropriate information or experience.

Both psychodynamic feminist therapists Miller and Stiver (1997) and personal construct therapists and counselors such as Fransella and Dalton (2000) object to traditional therapeutic approaches to resistance, in which therapists or counselors blame the clients for not cooperating. They also object to the various strategies that are then employed to break down client resistances, from outright confrontation to subtle and not-so-subtle manipulative strategies.

Miller and Stiver (1997) are emphatic about the necessity for therapists to be aware of patients' needs to hold on to their defenses. The aim of therapists is to be aware of patients' strategies of disconnection. Miller and Stiver emphasize the importance of "respecting these strategies of disconnection rather than viewing them as what therapists typically call defenses—something the therapist hopes to get rid of as quickly as possible" (p. 149). It is so crucial that therapists remain empathic with patients when they shift away and disconnect that Miller and Stiver call their approach the *therapy of honoring the client's disconnecting strategies:*

> Indeed, one way to describe therapy is to say that it is a special place designed for working on disconnections (that's why it can be so hard) and for learning to move on through the pain of disconnection to new connections, that's why it can be so fulfilling and enlarging for both people involved. (p. 149)

Personal construct practitioners believe that when a client gets defensive or shows signs of resistance, counselors should back off and reevaluate their strategies:

> A client may sometimes appear to "resist" attempts to persuade her to loosen her construing. . . . It means that the counsellor has not got a clear enough view of what the client is being asked to do. There is a failure of communication between the client and counsellor. There may be too much threat. The client may be having too great a struggle to keep anchors firmly embedded in reality readily to countenance loosening their hold. (Fransella & Dalton, 2000, p. 97)

Although increasingly intense feelings of fear, threat, anxiety, and guilt are signs of movement in transitions, if the feelings are too intense, clients will revert back, resist, and raise defenses. Such signs of resistance alert counselors to pause and try to better understand where clients are coming from.

Counselors have a particularly difficult time working with clients' hostile feelings. Although these feelings can be recognized as part of the transitional process, they may also be signs of clients' feelings of threat and chaos. After venturing out aggressively when they have been passive most of their lives, clients may react adversely, feel guilty, and retreat back into old patterns. In such cases, counselors can ask clients to describe areas in their lives where they feel secure, where they most feel a sense of themselves. Fransella and Dalton (2000) cite the case of a client who enjoys stamp collecting and who reacts defensively in most situations. However, because the client feels very secure collecting stamps, he can risk trying new possibilities in this domain.

Last Stage: Integrating Client Changes Into Daily Life

As a result of deeper self-exploration and development of a positive relationship with counselors, clients become more self-confident, more assertive, and more authentic in counseling sessions. A "real" counseling relationship emerges in which clients perceive counselors without distortion. This new relationship permits clients to express feelings more authentically, assert their needs, continue to be insightful, and gain understanding of themselves and others (Gelso & Carter, 1985).

In the last stage, the counseling relationship becomes collaborative; counselors and clients are peers working together to help the clients reach agreed-on goals (Tracey, 1988). In addition, counselors become more real; they feel free now to offer their own opinions, give advice, and instruct clients in coping or adopting social and self-management skills.

As counselors and clients focus on reaching the goals laid out in the initial stage, the social contexts in which clients will apply their new attitudes and behaviors become a primary counselor–client consideration. With the counselor's help, the client's major task now is to apply to relationships and circumstances in everyday life the changes in perception, feelings, and behavior generated during counseling sessions.

Clients should be alerted that spouses, other family members, and colleagues, rather than welcoming the client changes, may be puzzled, resistant, resentful, or hostile to them. The counselor has provided an accepting atmosphere to foster and nurture client changes, but these same accepting conditions generally do not exist in the typical client's world. Clients may also be asserting their new feelings in ways that offend others.

Counselors can help their clients consider more effective and less aggressive ways to relate to significant others who are resisting client changes. Counselors can, for example, rehearse with clients effective ways of asserting themselves. And after clients make trial attempts, counselors can give them feedback about the effectiveness of their actions. At the same time, counselors can keep their clients from reverting back to their former ways.

Hansen, Rossberg, and Cramer (1994) point out that this is an important stage, a "working through" stage in which the client's new insights and self-understanding are put into constructive action. "The client gains little in the long run from an intellectual understanding of the problem unless she or he is able to try out new methods of behaving" (p. 239).

Counselors differ in the degree of action-oriented strategies and techniques that they use in this last stage, depending on their theoretical orientation. Client-centered counselors, for instance, tend not to use techniques. Psychodynamic counselors tend to focus only on changes taking place within counseling or therapy sessions. Gestaltists use dramatic enactments—role playing, visual imagery, empty chair techniques—as ways for clients to practice changing behavior, but these practices also are confined to counseling sessions.

Cognitive–behavioral and personal construct counselors, in contrast, use many instructional and directive techniques to help clients apply new learning to their everyday actions and relationships. Some even begin earlier, in the middle stage. Personal construct counselors, for example, integrate restructuring strategies into behavioral action in the middle stage because they emphasize the importance of clients applying new insights and attitudes to behavior as they go along in the therapeutic process. "It is in action, in the person's experiments with ways of *behaving* differently that new constructions of events are tried and tested" (Fransella & Dalton, 2000, p. 114).

Cognitive–behaviorists have taken the lead in developing strategies to help clients take action in their everyday lives; Egan (2007) discusses at length how strategies can be worked out effectively. Briefly, they must be specific and realistic—powerful enough to lead to client changes and move clients toward stated goals with a clear, workable plan of action. They must also be actions that clients decide are best for them and are consistent with their values. It is also important to consider the context in which changes in behavior and attitude are practiced. For example, those who have just stopped drinking alcohol should avoid social interactions that center on drinking alcohol. And clients should try out new behaviors in gradual steps.

Counselors can motivate clients to take action by using the social influencing skills described in the previous stage. They would first use strategies that encourage clients to be willing to take appropriate actions; once the clients are willing, the counselors can teach them certain skills to carry out the actions effectively. The numerous social influencing strategies include confronting, probing, offering information, providing feedback about specific behaviors and attitudes, and considering the logical consequences of one's actions. In the following case, the counselor raises the question of *logical consequences* when a client impulsively decides to make a major life change.

CLIENT: I'm fed up. I'm going in tomorrow to let them know I quit.
COUNSELOR: This is the first time you've mentioned this, and you've not explored alternative jobs. How will you support yourself and your wife?

If a client takes no initiative to change after expressing a strong desire to change, the counselor might *confront* the client.

COUNSELOR: You've expressed dissatisfaction with your work, and you've mentioned some alternative jobs. Yet you've said nothing about changing. What's going on?
CLIENT: I've just been too busy to think about it.
COUNSELOR: Are you feeling ambivalent about leaving your job?

Once the client is ready and willing to take appropriate action, the counselor can instruct the client in various skills or strategies to help him or her make changes in daily life. These strategies include conducting behavioral rehearsals in which clients rehearse new behaviors with the counselor; using coping or adaptive skills, such as self-management or self-monitoring skills; modeling the behaviors of others; keeping journals; engaging in relaxation exercises; completing homework assignments; and getting feedback from counselors.

Self-management and self-monitoring strategies help clients direct and control their own behavioral change. "Self-management methods involve a combination of behavioral and cognitive–behavioral strategies to increase a client's self-control and ability to change his or her behavior" (Brammer et al., 1993, p. 194). These methods are particularly useful for clients with concerns such as weight loss, anxiety, insomnia, poor interpersonal and communication skills, and nicotine addiction (Miltenberger, 2007). Self-management strategies for addictive persons, for example, involve overcoming barriers that arise when clients try to replace negative behaviors that are immediately gratifying with behaviors that lead to better health but have delayed rewards (Miltenberger, 2007). Obese clients who wish to follow a weight-loss diet might make a self-contract that includes reinforcing themselves with desirable and positive nonfood rewards for sticking to the contract. They also might eliminate easy access to immediately gratifying junk food and increase easy access to nutritious and tasty low-calorie foods and to pleasurable, nonfood activities. Meichenbaum's (1985) stress-inoculation therapy is a well-known self-management strategy in which clients learn and practice coping skills to replace nonadaptive self-statements that accompany stress with more adaptive ones (Miltenberger, 2007).

Counselors can also help clients explore community facilities that offer training in the skills they may need—assertiveness training, time management, nutrition counseling, and so on. And counselors can help clients search for and evaluate social support systems in the community, such as single-parenting or eating disorder groups.

Close collaboration between counselors and clients is crucial to the success of these programs. Not only are clients expected to initiate changes, but they are expected to monitor their progress as well.

Termination of Counseling Sessions

Effective termination of counseling sessions is a key factor in how successful counseling outcome will be. An otherwise productive client–counselor interaction can be marred if the process is terminated before the client is ready or if sessions continue beyond the client's needs. Successful counseling outcomes are more likely to occur when counselors and clients jointly decide when termination is appropriate, prepare to end the sessions, and attend to the emotional responses that go along with termination.

During the termination stage, counselors help clients review major themes that have emerged during counseling and help them assess their progress in attaining their goals. Counselors also consider how clients can apply and generalize their new learnings and insights to problems that may arise in the future. And counselors can encourage clients to express their feelings regarding the ending of the counseling relationship (Moursund and Kenny, 2002).

Determining the Appropriate Time

Counselors and clients can determine whether the clients are ready to end the sessions by assessing whether the original symptoms or presenting problems have been resolved. In what specific ways has client stress been reduced? What skills have been developed to help clients cope with concerns? In what ways are clients relating more effectively with others or functioning more constructively in their jobs, academics, or home life? Do clients feel more positive about and more comfortable with themselves?

Fransella and Dalton (2000) list several aspects of client changes or "sufficient psychological movement" to look for: changes in the nature of construing; ability to loosen and tighten construing appropriately; ability to cope with transitional periods of increased anxiety, threat, guilt, and hostility; and the tendency to "move away from the client's 'problems' and his immediate personal concerns into a more dilated field of interest" (pp. 144–145).

If the counselor believes that the client's problem has been resolved, the counselor may raise the issue directly: "I have observed some positive changes in your attitudes, behavior, and relationships. You've made a decision about school, your relationship with your wife has improved, and your work is going well. I wonder if you need any further counseling at this time." If the client agrees, then a termination process can be worked out.

The client may also bring up the idea of termination: "I seem to be doing well on my job and in my relationships. I am sleeping better, and I don't have as many headaches. Maybe I no longer need to see you." If the counselor thinks the client is not quite ready for termination, together they can discuss whether it is advisable to terminate at this time.

Terminating Too Soon

At times, the counselor or client initiates termination before the client has attained counseling goals. A counselor may end a relationship prematurely because the counselor feels resentful toward the client or anxious about whether he or she can help the client—difficulties related to countertransference issues discussed earlier. The client's desire to terminate prematurely may arise from feelings of a lack of progress in the counseling sessions. It may also signal that a client's resistances have not been completely worked through and that a client is not ready for the last stage.

Resisting Appropriate Termination

When they have been in a close and satisfactory relationship, counselor or client or both may resist ending counseling even though all indications show that the client is ready to go. Clients may resist leaving the safety of the relationship because they are anxious about being on their own. Clients with unstable relationships may especially want to hold onto the counselor. In such cases, clients' symptoms may flare up, or they may bring in other problems. Counselors need to attend to clients' feelings and reassure clients if termination still seems advisable (Moursund and Kenny, 2002).

Counselors may also resist termination because they are reluctant to end a satisfactory relationship, are particularly attached to the client, or are overly anxious about the client's ability to function adequately on her or his own. In such cases, counselors must assess their own countertransference feelings.

Leading Up to the Last Session

Sudden termination can be disruptive to client progress even when it is appropriate. A few sessions should be devoted to termination issues before counselor and client say their good-byes in the final session. Personal construct counselors emphasize the importance of the preparation for termination:

> The ending of a period of counseling needs as much, if not more, careful preparation. As at all stages, we need to make predictions about this important part of the process, to ensure that clients are aware of the implications of moving on and able to take into the future the changes in construing which have helped them to overcome current difficulties. (Fransella & Dalton, 2000, p. 142)

Fransella and Dalton (2000) also recommend that sessions not end abruptly but be gradually phased out, with meeting times stretching to every 3 weeks, and then more infrequently, depending on the case.

Moursund and Kenny (2002) emphasizes that the material brought up during the review of progress and feelings about therapy must be considered in the context of separation. Communication must focus on what it means to the client "who is ending a supportive/confrontive [sic] growth-producing relationship" (p. 107). Moreover, counselors should acknowledge and honor client expressions of positive feelings about the counseling relationship, the counseling experience, and the progress made in gaining new insights and resolving problems.

The end of counseling will mean a transition to a new phase, and transition means some loss, which is usually accompanied by feelings of anger, fear, guilt, or sadness. Moursund and Kenny (2002) discusses the various client emotions that might emerge as counseling comes to an end. If anger occurs, it may be a defense against feelings of anxiety or a substitute for the more difficult expression of sadness. At this point, Moursund and Kenny notes, counselors need to help clients see the positive and energizing aspects of their anger. Fear may also emerge prior to termination; counselor acceptance can help reassure clients of their ability to manage their lives.

Sadness often occurs at this time. Not only is there sadness about parting from the counselor, but the experience may also evoke the sadness of earlier partings (Moursund and Kenny, 2002). As Moursund and Kenny (2002) points out, however, there is a difference between therapeutic grief and grief over other losses. Here is an opportunity for clients to talk about and work through their feelings of loss with the person they are losing.

Feelings of poignancy may more aptly describe what may be felt during this period, for poignancy does not imply the sense of finality that grief does. And although counseling sessions do end, the possibility of the client's returning is left open, as in intermittent counseling. In personal construct counseling, clients are encouraged to report back 2 years hence and give a progress report. They are also encouraged to renew contact, if necessary, at any time. So the loss is not a final one, but rather a part of the ongoing life cycle of loss and renewal (Fransella & Dalton, 2000).

Many therapists today, including Dr. Simon Budman, assistant professor of psychiatry at Harvard Medical School, view therapy as intermittent and ongoing. With brief counseling, clients work with different problems as they arise in their lives, much as one sees the family doctor (Goode, 1998).

SUMMARY

In the process of individual counseling, counselors and clients develop a therapeutic relationship to help clients gain self-awareness that will enable them to resolve problems effectively. Factors that influence the counseling process are the counselor's professional and personal characteristics; the client's personal attributes, including age, social–cultural background, and views about gender role; and the overall context in which the client is experiencing problems.

The individual counseling process generally goes through three stages. In the initial stage, a counselor–client relationship is established that focuses on understanding client problems; problems are assessed, tentative working hypotheses are developed, and goals are set. In the middle stage, a shift occurs in which the client turns inward, exploring feelings and developing insights. Client and counselor experience a sense of movement as they work through the client's emotional turbulence, client and counselor transference and countertransference, and client resistance.

In the last stage, counselors help clients apply their new insights and attitudes to their behavior in everyday life. As clients and counselors focus on attaining client goals, the relationship becomes more authentic, collaborative, and instructive. Counselors and clients then work toward effective termination by reviewing what they have accomplished and sharing their feelings about ending the relationship.

PROJECTS AND ACTIVITIES

1. Compare the resistance of a client who has been persuaded to seek counseling against her will with the resistance of a client who volunteers for and comes regularly to counseling. How would you handle them differently?

2. What client characteristics do you think would make it difficult for you to develop a therapeutic relationship—for example, a dominant male, a militant feminist, a person with fundamentalist religious views, an atheist, a

spouse abuser, a spouse having an extramarital affair, an obnoxious client, a very passive client? Play the role of a client who has one of these characteristics.

3. Interview a male counselor and a female counselor with similar backgrounds and experience. Ask each of them to describe the major gender issues. Ask them in what way, if any, male and female clients differ. Compare responses. Do you see any evidence of cultural biases?

4. Read this case study and answer the questions that follow: Sarah is a counselor providing individual counseling for Joe, a 31-year-old man, who is also under the care of a psychiatrist. Although severely depressed, Joe refuses to take the medication his psychiatrist has prescribed him for depression. Sarah begins to feel angry toward Joe for his decision not to take medication.

a. What current personal issues of Sarah's may be contributing to her anger toward Joe?

b. What past experiences may contribute to Sarah's anger?

c. What should Sarah do with her feelings?

CHAPTER 9

Group Counseling

Group counseling became popular in the 1970s when counselors began to realize that individuals who were having problems in their relationships could benefit from sharing their concerns and resolving their problems with others having similar problems. Organized groups make use of people's natural tendency to gather and share thoughts and feelings, as well as find support for change (Gladding, 2007, p. 246). The definition of group counseling by George Gazda (1978), a pioneer in group counseling, remains one of the clearest explanations of the process:

> Group work refers to the dynamic interaction between collections of individuals for prevention or remediation of difficulties or for the enhancement of personal growth/enrichment through the interaction of those who meet together for a commonly agreed-on purpose and at pre-arranged times. (p. 260)

After studying this chapter, you will be able to

- Understand and describe the purpose of group counseling and populations who are best served by this counseling modality.
- Explain the ethical guidelines specific to group counseling.
- Convey the key concepts of group counseling theories.
- List and describe the stages of group counseling.

OVERVIEW OF GROUP COUNSELING

The purpose of group counseling is to increase clients' knowledge of themselves and others, help clients clarify the changes they most want to make in their life, and provide members with the tools they need to make these changes (Corey & Corey, 2006). Group counseling is useful to persons who are either shy or aggressive in their interpersonal interactions, anxious or uncomfortable in groups, or resistant or conforming to social expectations. Individuals may be having difficulty making or keeping friends, or they may be experiencing friction with peers, parents, faculty, or bosses. Groups can be geared to age-related issues—for children, adolescents, young adults, older adults, and for intergenerational groups, such as mothers/teenage daughters or older adults/young children. Group counseling can be effective for a wide variety of special needs—children of divorced parents, teenage substance abusers, young parents, parents with teenagers, those suffering from grief, abused women, adult children of alcoholics, and men who need to learn to control their anger (Corey & Corey, 2006).

Group counseling is inappropriate and inadvisable for individuals experiencing personal or interpersonal conflicts too private to share in a group; it is also unsuitable for those with strong fears about social interactions, for those who might find a group experience traumatic, or for those with low impulse control who might constantly disrupt group interactions (Burlingame & Fuhriman, 1990; Gladding, 2008; Nystul, 1993). In these cases, individual counseling may be more suitable until the individuals feel more confident or more in control of themselves.

When clients' problems relate to interpersonal awkwardness, insecurities, or conflicts, group counseling has the advantage of giving members an opportunity to work out their problems in a structured social setting. In this setting, they can experiment with and practice new behaviors and receive support for their efforts and feedback from other group members and the counselor. Each member becomes aware of the feelings and experiences of other persons (Nystul, 1993), and each has a chance to help others in the group improve social interactions. Counselors can observe clients interacting with other group members and can interact themselves with each group member (Corey, 2007).

Another value unique to group therapy and counseling is that individuals often experience feelings of isolation as they suffer pain, despair, and/or guilt, even if they share with an understanding counselor or therapist. Expressing painful emotions in a supportive group among those who have experienced similar pain and traumas removes those feelings of isolation and, moreover, validates one's trauma as a communal experience, thus relieving the overwhelming emotional burden carried by lone individuals.

Groups do have some disadvantages, though. A client receives less direct attention from the counselor, who must focus on group concerns and group interactions. And some clients may find it difficult to develop the trust in other group members that is necessary for constructive self-disclosure. They may also experience direct or subtle pressure to conform to group norms. In addition, if the leadership is weak, group members may experience psychological distress when they reveal more than they are ready to or when they are confronted inappropriately by other group members.

Groups differ in their purposes, goals, and intensity, depending on the severity of the clients' problems or the degree of the clients' dysfunctions. In group counseling literature, these various types of group work are described as falling along a continuum (Gazda, 1989). Growth groups, designed for persons who feel fairly functional but want more meaning in life, are at one end of the continuum. Group counseling, in the middle of the continuum, serves persons who are not living as effectively as they could, who have learned maladaptive ways of interacting with others, or who have negative views of themselves but are able to manage their lives adequately. Group psychotherapy, at the other end of the continuum, includes persons who are more emotionally disturbed and who require intensive remedial work. The goals of growth groups are to educate and train persons in skills and attitudes; the goals of group counseling are to help persons solve problems, develop self-awareness, and improve interpersonal relations; the goal of group psychotherapy is remedial work. In a similar way, Corey (2007) differentiates between group counseling and group therapy: "Whereas counseling groups focus on growth, development, enhancement, prevention, self-awareness and releasing blocks to growth, therapy groups typically focus on remediation, treatment, and personality reconstruction" (p. 10).

As with individual counseling and psychotherapy, some overlap exists between group counseling and psychotherapy. Thus, at times, the terms *group counseling* and *group psychotherapy* are used interchangeably by theorists and practitioners.

ETHICAL GUIDELINES WITH GROUPS

Ethical guidelines specific to group counseling have been developed by the Association for Specialists in Group Work (ASGW, 1998). These guidelines are consistent with the American Counseling Association (ACA) Code of Ethics for individual and group counseling (2005).

Counselors face different ethical considerations with groups than with individuals. Some of the more important ethical considerations are discussed here: (a) screening for appropriateness for group counseling, (b) allowing the freedom to leave the group, (c) monitoring confidentiality among group members, and (d) guarding against group members manipulating or abusing each other (Corey, Corey, & Callanan, 2007).

First of all, group counselors have an ethical responsibility to screen clients for their suitability for the group. If an individual is not psychologically ready for the group or has purposes different from those of the group, the counselor should let the individual know and refer her or him to individual counseling or to a more appropriate group.

Furthermore, group counseling is most effective and ethical when members voluntarily enter a group and have the freedom to leave it. According to the ASGW Best Practice Guidelines (1998), group participation is voluntary. The Code recommends that group leaders inform prospective members about policies related to entering and exiting the group.

Some recommend that before members leave a group, they explain to the other group members their reason for leaving. Clearly, a leader has no way of forcing a member to explain why he or she wants to leave the group. And for a member who has never asserted him- or herself before, leaving without explanation may be a sign of newly found strength. Furthermore, such a disruption allows the group to tussle with an actual problem that has occurred within the group.

One example of just such an experience occurred in a university group. The members contemplated sending angry letters to the young man who had abandoned the group. But after working through their feelings and discussing group and individual rights, group members decided to send him cards thanking him for his contributions, telling him that they missed him, and letting him know he was welcome to return if he so chose. Although he did not return, he did send the group a letter thanking them for understanding him and explaining that he had learned to assert his needs for the first time in this group, which gave him the courage to break away.

Concerns exist about whether group members will hold in confidence self-disclosures and group interactions (Corey, 2007; Gladding, 2008). In accordance with the ACA Code of Ethics (2005), Corey and Corey (2006) state that group counselors have an ethical and legal responsibility to inform group members of the potential consequences of breaching confidentiality. Because members tend to unwittingly share their group experiences with close friends or loved ones outside the group, counselors should emphasize that members must not share who is in the group or what other members have said. Corey and Corey suggest that group leaders emphasize the importance of maintaining confidentiality, have members sign contracts agreeing to it, and even impose some form of sanction on those who break confidentiality. If counselors clarify the group's responsibilities regarding confidentiality and give reasons for its importance, problems do not often arise. Confidentiality poses more problems in those educational institutions or agencies in which members know one another and share mutual associates and friends. If group sessions are to be recorded or if research based on the group experience is being conducted, confidentiality and the right of privacy require that counselors get written consent from each member (Gazda, 1989).

Attempts by a group counselor or group members to persuade an individual member to behave in a manner that the group thinks is desirable is a greater potential problem in groups than is confidentiality. Consistent with professional ethical guidelines (ASGW, 1998), each member in group counseling has the right and obligation to decide how and when she or he wants to participate. Similarly, counselors have an ethical responsibility not to indoctrinate groups with their own values.

In addition, group counselors must always be alert to the psychological risks inherent in group counseling and must conduct groups in a way that minimizes client trauma. Counselors must monitor groups, intervening whenever someone puts pressure on another to self-disclose more than that person is ready to share. Counselor intervention is also necessary when one member makes hostile attacks on another in the guise of confrontation or makes fun of or scapegoats another person.

GROUP COUNSELING THEORIES

Group counseling theories are classified in a manner similar to that of individual and family theories: psychodynamic (transactional analysis and psychodrama), humanistic (group centered and Gestalt), cognitive–behavioral, and developmental.

Psychodynamic Group Counseling

In psychodynamic group counseling, exploration and analysis of members' unconscious intrapsychic dynamics are emphasized (Hershenson, Power, & Waldo, 2003). Feelings generated by unresolved childhood conflicts are reexperienced, reenacted, and related appropriately to present-day relationships. A counselor must resolve feelings of transference, countertransference, and resistance that arise with each member of the group, as well as with the total group (i.e., group transference). These feelings need to be acknowledged and worked through (Brammer, Abrego, & Shostrom, 1993).

In psychodynamic groups, counselors share their interpretations of individual and group emotional reactions with the members of the group. As counseling progresses, members—with guidance from the counselor—share insights about their own behavior and emotional expressions. Insights and understandings lead to more realistic perceptions of early relationships, as well as of themselves, of other group members, and of the counselor. These new and more accurate perceptions help each group member learn more appropriate ways to express and satisfy authentic, legitimate needs in group sessions. In the final stage of counseling, members are encouraged to apply these new insights and learnings to everyday living (Gazda, 1989).

Transactional Analysis

Eric Berne (1961), a psychoanalyst, developed transactional analysis (TA) specifically for groups; TA is based on analysis and understanding of social communication. A *transaction* refers to the way two people communicate or exchange ideas or feelings, and *analysis* refers to the interpretation of how adaptive or maladaptive these social exchanges are and how to make them more constructive.

In TA, personality structure is seen as consisting of three ego states: parent, adult, and child. The *parent* is the conscience, or a group of dos and don'ts learned as a child; the *adult* is the commonsense, reality-oriented portion of the personality; and the *child* is composed of spontaneous, impulsive feelings—the creative part of the personality. Individuals tend to move from one state to another in their transactions with others.

In 1964, Berne published a best-selling book called *Games People Play,* in which he describes how people behave to get attention, recognition, and physical contact (strokes) in order to flourish and survive. Positive strokes from parents (e.g., warmth and acceptance) lead to healthy functioning; negative strokes (e.g., rejection or severe criticism) lead to dysfunction; and indifference often results in pathology or severe dysfunction. Healthy persons give and receive positive strokes in authentic, open, social transactions; maladjusted persons use repetitive sets of social manipulations called *games* to elicit the strokes they received as children. Through reinforcement with strokes similar to those learned from, and further reinforced by, the games they play, persons develop life scripts that control or shape their lives (Berne, 1972).

Counselors use four progressive stages of analysis to help clients: structural, transactional, game, and life script. Most people complete the first three; few go on to life script analysis, in which they desire to change their personality (Berne, 1966). In structural analysis, individuals are taught to understand their own personality structures and to be aware when one ego state is excluding another or when one state is intruding on or contaminating another. The adult who always denies the child may become computerlike or develop into a workaholic; the child who always intrudes on the adult may lead the adult to expect immediate gratification all the time.

In TA, what people say to each other (i.e., transactions) is analyzed in the group—thus, transactional analysis. Transactions may be either complementary or crossed. In complementary transactions, comments, questions, or requests from one person elicit appropriate and healthy responses from another. Crossed transactions inhibit communication; for example, a request from an adult is responded to as if the initiator were a parent and the responder a child. In TA, crossed transactions are converted to complementary ones (Patterson, 1986).

In game analysis, people are made aware of the games they play to get strokes (Berne, 1964); game playing is exposed and more authentic relationships are taught (Dusay & Dusay, 1989). The final stage, life script analysis, helps group members first recall and reenact childhood experiences, and then discover how they acquired and maintained the dysfunctional life script (Steiner, 1974).

Psychodrama

Jacob Moreno (1946) was one of the most influential figures in the development of group work. He coined the terms *group therapy* and *group psychotherapy*. In 1946, he introduced psychodrama, which has had a considerable impact on group counseling and therapy in hospitals, community settings, and schools (Blatner, 2005). Psychodrama was the forerunner of several current group theories, including Gestalt, encounter, and some behavioral groups that emphasize action–insight and immediate experiencing.

The purpose of psychodrama is to build a therapeutic setting using life itself as a model. Clients act out conflicts instead of talking about them. Ideally, it is carried out on a psychodrama stage, but more often it takes place in an informal room where staging can occur. The client–actor is aided by a director (the counselor or therapist) and by one or more auxiliary egos (other group members) who act out either persons in the client's life who are not present or the client's imagination, fantasies, or dreams (Gazda, 1989).

Psychodrama consists of three parts, or stages: the warm-up, the action, and the postaction, or sharing and discussion stage (Moreno, 1983). In the warm-up stage, the director describes the procedure, interviews each member briefly, and asks whether the members have present, past, or future situations or relationships they would like to explore. The group may break out into smaller groups and practice sharing a conflict. In the action stage, a member volunteers to present and act out her problem, with the help of the counselor and one or more persons chosen from the group.

Blatner (2005) describes certain principles of psychodrama. The client must act out conflict rather than talk about it. The actor acts in the immediate present, regardless of when the incident happened in the past or might happen in the future. The client acts out how she feels, regardless of how distorted her perceptions may seem to anybody else.

Clients are encouraged to play the roles of other persons in their lives, as well as their own. In addition, a double, played by an auxiliary ego, may act out the client's feelings, or multiple doubles may portray ambivalent feelings that are hindering free expression by the client–actor. Sometimes an auxiliary ego mirrors the actor's behavior, with the actor observing offstage. The client–actor may also use soliloquy with side comments to group members. Dream work, as in Gestalt groups, involves persons enacting, rather than analyzing, their dreams. The director interprets or suggests changes in scripts or the use of auxiliary egos when necessary. Afterward, the performance group members share observations and reactions to the psychodrama in a supportive manner. The actor is encouraged to practice new behaviors.

Humanistic Group Counseling

Person-Centered or Group-Centered Counseling

As they do in individual counseling, Rogerian counselors develop warm, accepting, and authentic relationships with each group member to facilitate positive personal growth. Rogerian counselors accomplish this personal growth by modeling warm, empathic, and congruent attitudes and behaviors toward not only the group, but also each member. Thus, an atmosphere is created that fosters these same facilitative characteristics in the interactions of group members with both the counselor and one another. The group works toward building trust and nonjudgmental support for one another, which permits members to drop protective masks and defenses and to face the anxiety of bringing up painful thoughts or shameful acts.

As trust deepens, the counselor helps group members let others know when they are not being genuine, authentic, understanding, or supportive. Misperceptions about self and others are thus corrected, enabling each person to express appropriate needs and relate authentically with others (Corey, 2007; Gazda, 1989). Rogerian counselors believe that substantial personal growth occurs if unconditional positive regard is established.

The counselor expects group members to decide on their individual and mutual group goals; the only direction is that group members ask each other to decide what they want to accomplish. Techniques and games are used sparingly. Trust exercises may be tried, but only if the group decides to do so.

Gestalt Group Counseling

Gestalt is an unusual form of group work in that it is a combination of both individual and group counseling, with the counselor emphasizing one-to-one interactions with group members as well as facilitating group dynamics (Corey, 2007; Perls, 1969).

In the sessions, the typical procedure has been the use of the hot seat, whereby a volunteer agrees to take a seat alongside the counselor in the center of the group circle. The group then observes the counselor/client interactions as the counselor confronts the client's contradictions or inconsistencies or asks the client to describe and act out a recent dream or to role-play with the counselor. The counselor may also initiate group interactions by asking the volunteer to interact with other group members. The counselor allows spontaneous interactions among group members (Vander Kolk, 1985).

As in individual Gestalt counseling, counselors expect group members to attend to immediate experiencing in these sessions, and they expect members to be responsible for themselves. Confrontation and games and gimmicks designed to encourage or goad members to give up dependency and to assume self-responsibility have typically been used (Corey, 2007). By developing awareness in themselves and in others, group members correct distortions in self-perception and in their perceptions of others.

Critics of Gestalt's method of abrasive confrontation have led practitioners to tone down sessions and be more respectful and supportive of client resistance, as well as helping clients learn to manage their emotions. With this in mind, Corey (2007) describes a post-Perls Gestalt therapy, in which the hot seat technique is no longer the primary means of raising awareness.

Cognitive–Behavioral Group Counseling

Cognitive–behavioral group counseling is task oriented. To start off a group session, the counselor first clarifies group procedure, establishes a working relationship, and then assesses each client's problem with input from the other group members. The counselor sets up specific goals with each member for behavioral changes. At the same time, group goals consistent with individual goals are determined. As counseling progresses, the counselor teaches and models effective behavior, helps members clarify cognitive misperceptions about themselves and others, and helps change faulty habit patterns. Group members experiment with new behaviors in the sessions and help one another by modeling effective behavior and giving appropriate feedback and reinforcement to one another. Through these interactions, members learn new attitudes, ideas, behaviors, and skills to help them cope and adapt. In the final stages, group members learn to generalize the new attitudes and skills developed in group sessions to real life through role-playing, behavior rehearsal, and assignments to apply specific new skills at home.

Albert Ellis, a cognitive–behavioral theorist, has been active in group work for many years (Ellis, 2008; Ellis & Grieger, 1977). Ellis attempts to have group members work together under his direction to pick out one another's irrational beliefs, encourage one another to stop self-defeating self-talk, and teach one another to think rationally. He encourages them to practice newly learned behaviors outside the sessions.

Arnold Lazarus (1976, 2008), another cognitive–behaviorist, believes that his multimodal BASIC I.D. pattern works particularly well with groups. He argues that a nonpunitive, nonthreatening group atmosphere enhances the opportunity for group members to correct maladaptive responses across the seven modalities (behavior, affect, sensation, imagery, cognition, interpersonal, and drugs/biological). Under his direction, group members can practice new attitudes and behaviors and receive support, feedback, and reinforcement from one another. As in individual work, the counselor is active, uses and teaches numerous techniques that reinforce positive behavior and increase realization, and models appropriate emotional expression and logical thinking.

Developmental Group Counseling

The developmental group counseling approach is based on concepts similar to those discussed in chapter 5. Theorists assume that persons must complete developmental tasks by learning coping skills and playing social roles at different stages in their lives. These tasks arise from individual biological and psychological needs and from society's expectations of certain behaviors at certain ages. If persons fail to perform expected tasks adequately, maladjustment occurs.

Gazda (1989), the major proponent of this approach, attempts to provide a group counseling system applicable to clients at all age levels. Gazda describes the application of developmental group counseling for four groups of different ages: children, preadolescents, high-school-age persons, and adults. Groups are formed around problems related to particular developmental tasks expected for the age group.

Since developmental theorists have subdivided the adult level into several stages, effective groups have also been forming around the needs of young adults, adults at midlife, and older adults. The demand for group counseling with older adults has been increasing, but services have not kept up with demand.

Because of their age, older adults are good candidates for group work. They have a lot of experience on which to draw, and many have developed extraordinary capacities for introspection, deep thinking, and compassion. Group counseling with older adults can be an effective way to help them confront the myths of ageism. In addition, it can offer the elderly the encouragement necessary to find meaning in their lives (Corey, 2007).

THE GROUP EXPERIENCE

Forming a Group

In university counseling centers, public schools, and community agencies where group counseling has already been established, counselors form groups by announcing that a group will be starting at a particular time with a particular purpose. Potential clients then sign up for the group, and other counselors working with individual clients who could profit from group counseling refer them to the group.

If the center, school, or agency has not yet developed a group counseling program, an interested counselor can make a proposal indicating a need for the group, the anticipated goal, the leader's background, and the procedures that will be used. In public schools in particular, the proposal should indicate which topics will or will not be explored and the risks to the clients.

The recommended number of group members varies with the type of group and the group's age range. For college students or adults, the size is about eight persons. A smaller number (three or four) is recommended for groups with elementary-school-age children because of their shorter attention span (Corey & Corey, 2006). Some experienced counselors and therapists working with special groups are able to work effectively with large numbers of people. Real (1997), for example, describes working with 40 depressed male clients in a group that meets weekly.

Screening of Group Members

As discussed earlier, careful screening of candidates is necessary for ethical and professional reasons. Screening avoids including group members who would be jeopardized by the experience; who might, because of their personality or behavior, inhibit progress in the group; or who have different purposes from the group's purpose (Corey, 2007).

Prescreening prospective group members in individual sessions is the optimal procedure. When the setting does not permit individual screening, however, potential group members can complete questionnaires and be interviewed in small groups. If neither of these options is feasible, a pregroup session can be used as both a screening and an informational procedure (Corey, 2007).

Composition of Groups

Grouping clients with similar concerns and purposes facilitates a working bond and a more cohesive group relationship (Hershenson et al., 2003). Special groups are effective for those with specific problems, such as alcoholism. Grouping in a similar age range permits a group to focus on developmental concerns appropriate for all members (Gazda, 1989). Groups exclusive to men or women are effective ways of exploring gender issues. Special groupings are also effective for abused spouses or spousal abusers.

Frequency and Duration of Sessions

The setting in which group counseling occurs determines the frequency and duration of the sessions. In a community agency or college or in private practice, 2-hour weekly sessions are optimal. In school settings, shorter times twice a week may be more suitable because students have a shorter attention span and they will miss less class time.

In colleges and universities, groups usually run about 10 or 14 weeks—the length of a quarter or a semester—because this is a reasonable amount of time for a group to attain goals and it is a convenient time frame for students and counselors. In communities, 10 to 20 sessions seem reasonable.

Coleaders

Some group counselors prefer to work with coleaders for several reasons. First, there is apt to be less leader burnout, as well as closer attention to group interaction. Second, coleaders can benefit from each other's perceptions of group dynamics and from each other's observations and comments on group members' emotional responses. Third, coleaders can use the way they relate to each other as a model for the group. And fourth, male and female coleaders can, in some cases, better deal with gender concerns (Corey, 2007).

However, one disadvantage of coleaders is the possibility that the group may suffer if coleaders act as rivals, do not trust each other, or try to work out their own relationship struggles in the sessions (Corey, 2007). As in families, triangulation can occur if a leader sides with a group member against the coleader or if group members work one leader against the other in a power struggle (Vander Kolk, 1985).

Group Stages

Corey (2007) divides the group counseling process into four stages: initial stage (orientation and exploration), transition stage (dealing with resistance), working stage (cohesion and productivity), and final stage (consolidation and termination). Gazda (1989) outlines exploratory, transition, action, and termination stages; and Vander Kolk (1985) describes a beginning and building stage, a conflict and dominance stage, and a cohesive and productive stage. The stages used here are a composite of those models: (a) initial exploratory stage, (b) transition stage marked by resistance and conflicts, (c) working stage marked by cohesiveness and productivity, and (d) consolidation and termination.

Initial Exploratory Stage

In the beginning sessions, group members are often strangers to one another. They may be ambivalent about groups; they want help, but may be fearful of sounding stupid or disclosing too much about themselves. Thus, the leader often finds many in the group reluctant to talk or able to bring up only superficial topics in an intellectual manner. In addition, members may expect leaders to have authoritative answers to their problems, and some may focus on only themselves and not on other members of the group.

In the early sessions, counselors generally respond to the group as a whole to foster group feeling; they also allow time for group members to get to know one another (Vander Kolk, 1985). Group members might be paired off to learn something about one another and then introduce each other to the group. Group members can also be asked to share their feelings about being in a group.

It is important to discuss and set goals in the first session. Group members can help one another clarify goals. For example, a member who says, "I'd like to be less aggressive," can be asked to explain what he or she means by being aggressive.

In the beginning stage, counselors facilitate the development of trust, just as they do in individual and family counseling. As in family counseling, group counselors must engender trust between themselves and group members and among all the members as well. Counselors accomplish this by modeling genuineness, warmth, and nonjudgmental attitudes toward all group members and by listening carefully.

Counselors also work on developing those communicative attitudes and skills among group members that will contribute to group cohesiveness, such as self-disclosure and constructive feedback. The leader who discloses immediate feelings and reactions occurring in the group helps the group focus on the immediate experience. When leaders react with positive and negative feedback to concrete, specific, and observable behaviors in a nonjudgmental way, group members more readily accept the feedback (Morran, Robison, & Stockton, 1985).

Transition Stage

As the group moves into the second stage, members begin to realize or are confronted with the need to explore more deeply, to self-disclose more intensively, and to interact more with other group members. Although some trust has been established, the feeling is still tentative, and group members are ambivalent, anxious, and defensive as they realize that they are expected to explore painful emotions and feelings even more deeply. Some wonder whether the group will reject them if they reveal too much, some are afraid that they may lose control and reveal more than they intend, and some are afraid that they'll be ridiculed and shamed.

Group counseling professionals describe this stage as being characterized by conflict or rebellion resulting from a struggle for power, control, or dominance among the members and with the counselor (Brammer et al., 1993; Corey, 2007; Gladding, 2008). Members may test whether they can trust the leader and other group members.

At this time, verbal attacks on the leader may occur, with some members expressing doubts about her or his leadership ability, and others reacting negatively to the counselor's attempts to help them explore their problems. Counselors must recognize that these behaviors represent the resistance to exploring painful feelings that is expected in any form of therapy. Resistance is a sign that members are getting closer to the core of their problems. On the other hand, conflicts should be resolved. If conflict is not addressed, it then becomes a hidden agenda, which blocks open group interaction (Corey, 2007).

Client resistance is a symptom of fears and anxieties and needs to be acknowledged and respected. But the counselor must not ignore the opportunity to help resistive clients become aware of and accept their fears, as well as learn to manage anger and to be respectful of others. Clients should be encouraged to explore their own fears and hostilities rather than projecting them onto others. Clients can be taught the importance of talking about themselves and how they are affected by the behaviors of another group member, rather than telling a member how he or she is or by judging that person (Corey, 2007).

Gladding (2008) views the transition stage as divided into two phases: storming and norming. The time when members become resistant and vent their hostilities and resentments is aptly called the *storming* phase. During this phase, the counselor helps members learn conflict management skills and identify different kinds of power plays and different forms of resistance, such as intellectualization, advice giving, dependency behaviors, monopolizing, band-aiding (i.e., being too quick to step in to ease another's pain), and attacks on the group leader, which is "probably the most direct form of resistance that causes groups difficulty" (p. 139).

Norming describes the second phase, when members begin to emerge from struggles for personal identity and move into feelings of group identity. According to Gladding (2008), some of the goals for counselors during this phase are to promote member feelings of cooperation with the group and a sense of collaborative spirit with one another. Skills that can be introduced at this time include supporting, in which members are encouraged to support one another; empathizing, in which members learn to understand another's difficulties in a nonjudgmental way; facilitating, in which the counselor helps members communicate clearly with one another; and self-disclosing, in which members feel safe enough to share their painful feelings (Gladding, 2008).

Working Stage

In the third stage, group members develop intimacy and cohesiveness. Group identity is high, and members feel close to one another, more aware of one another's problems. Trust has increased, so members are more willing to take risks in sharing the feelings and thoughts that occur within the group and to give constructive feedback to one another.

However, group intimacy may lead to a false cohesiveness in which members protect one another (Vander Kolk, 1985). An overly supportive group may not encourage members to confront one another authentically, express negative emotions in the group, or challenge one another to make changes in their everyday living. Many groups become stuck in this loving, nonproductive lethargy and never move on.

When a group attains cohesiveness and stability but does not allow itself to remain in a comfortable, secure state, the lengthy working process of the third stage can begin to help group members change. When the group becomes productive, group members are more committed to delving into significant problems and giving attention to interchanges in the group. At this stage, group members should challenge one another to convert insights they have gained into action. For example, a group member can confront another who says that she recognizes the need to assert herself, but remains passive in the group and in her interactions outside the group.

Group members now depend less on the leader, and the group begins to focus on working toward specified individual and group goals. Group members feel free to confront one another and are more willing to accept confrontations as a constructive challenge to change. They are more willing to risk experimenting with new behaviors and giving honest, spontaneous feedback without passing judgment. Conflict among members is effectively dealt with in sessions. As group interactions bring about attitudinal and behavioral changes in the group, members accept challenges to make changes in everyday life.

Group leaders use a variety of techniques to help group members explore their problems, confront one another, and make behavioral changes. Eclectic counselors might use Gestalt techniques such as confrontation, the empty chair, the hot seat, psychodrama role-playing, or role reversal to get clients more in touch with their feelings. They might use cognitive–behavioral techniques, as Ellis does, to help persons concentrate on changing self-defeating self-talk or focus on clarifying thoughts through cognitive restructuring. Transactional analysis might be used to improve group members' communication skills. To help members apply new insights to real-life situations, behavioral rehearsal or assertiveness exercises might be tried in anticipation of an encounter outside the sessions or a homework assignment given to carry out a specific new learning.

Consolidation and Termination

In the early years of group counseling, little attention was given to termination of group sessions (Gladding, 2008), but now termination is considered an essential part of group counseling. For effective closure, this period of time cannot be minimized. According to Corey (2007), the final stage is one of the most decisive times for the group. It is a time for summarizing, pulling together loose ends, and integrating and interpreting the group experience.

Most groups have a termination date fixed in advance of the actual sessions, particularly in educational settings and clinics. It is wise to start discussions about separation approximately three sessions before the final one to allow time for members to handle psychological or emotional feelings, to work toward transferring new group experiences to the outside world, to work through any unfinished problems in group relationships, and to review what has happened in the group to each member and how each can build on these changes after the group ends.

Feelings of anxiety, loss, sadness, or anger at losing those with whom group members feel close, safe, and supported must be discussed; it is, after all, the death of the group. The psychological or emotional reactions of significant persons outside the group need to be discussed also, with suggestions about how to deal with those feelings. Family or close friends may resist or be disturbed by changes. In addition, suggestions for further therapy can be made when necessary. Sometimes specific activities—such as joining a support group or a more advanced counseling group, reading, or attending workshops— can increase the chance that learning will continue.

Not all groups will run smoothly through all stages and reach a clear-cut, successful termination. Some groups never pass the comfortable stage. Other groups, because of the personality mix of group members or the leader, or both, may not succeed in becoming cohesive. Like individuals, groups have different capacities for growth.

FUTURE TRENDS

Group work is often used now in business and industry to reduce conflict, increase cooperation among coworkers, and improve satisfaction and productivity among employees. One type of group that is effective with coworkers is the quality circle. Its members are employees in the same work area who meet weekly to try to solve problems related to their joint work efforts (Hershenson et al., 2003). Quality circles are described as follows: "Leaders function in a caring capacity, offering members support as they examine conflicts and detriments to effective coworker relations and explore solutions" (Hershenson et al., 2003, p. 220).

Other trends are the increasing numbers of groups that focus on special needs, such as groups for victims of domestic violence, those with posttraumatic stress disorder (PTSD), those with spiritual needs, male depression, grief work, and debriefing witnesses of public violence.

Research on groups has lagged behind research on individual counseling, a lag attributable to the complexity of studying groups, the lack of effective instruments to measure group process, and the lack of ongoing research into group processes (Gladding, 2008). Although research has indicated that group work is effective, studies haven't yet revealed why this is so (Corey, 2007).

SUMMARY

Group counseling is helpful to persons having difficulties with interpersonal relationships and social skills. The group counseling environment, which is generally safe and accepting, gives members the opportunity to self-disclose, interact with others, and receive constructive feedback. Group counseling theories are adaptations of theories described in chapter 6—psychodynamic, humanistic, cognitive–behavioral, and developmental, approaches.

Ethically, group participation should be voluntary, and group disclosures must be kept in confidence by the group leader. The group leader must also alert group members about the need to maintain confidentiality about group interchanges. Group leaders screen group candidates and generally exclude persons who are highly vulnerable emotionally, overly aggressive, or antisocial. It is unethical for a group leader or group members to persuade or coerce individuals to participate when they are reluctant to do so.

Groups go through stages. The initial stage is exploratory, in which group trust is developed so that clients feel safe enough to participate. This is followed by a transition stage, in which resistance develops among members that must be worked through. A cohesive working stage follows, in which trust is high, self-disclosure is authentic, and feedback is productive. This is followed by the final stage of consolidation and termination of the group sessions.

Trends show increased activity in group work in business to improve worker morale and productivity. Increasing numbers of groups are focusing on persons with special problems—for example, victims of domestic violence, those with PTSD, women's issues, grief, and those with spiritual needs.

PROJECTS AND ACTIVITIES

1. Check with a university counseling center and a community clinic about the types of groups offered. Do they distinguish among group counseling, group therapy, and personal growth groups?
2. Assume that you are a leader of a group of college students. One member tells you he thinks another member has been talking about group revelations outside the group. He thinks he knows who the person is, but isn't sure. How would you handle this complaint?
3. A husband and wife, both counselors, are coleading a group. Some group members ask very personal questions about the husband–wife relationship. The coleaders think they have some right to privacy. How do you think the coleaders should respond to the request for intimate self-disclosures in the group? Role-play a group with coleaders with this type of problem.
4. Trace the history of group counseling. What social, cultural, and psychological factors have contributed to the movement?
5. Select a group population with which you would like to conduct a group experience, such as the elderly, children, adolescents, or battered spouses. Search the literature for group counseling research findings for this population. Find two studies that you think

are statistically sound and two that you think are poorly designed.

6. Debate the merits of having one group leader versus using coleaders. Would the type of group problem, age group, or work setting make a difference?

7. Contact an elementary and a secondary school counselor, and ask whether they han-

dle groups and, if so, what types of groups. What do they see as advantages or disadvantages of group counseling at these age levels?

8. Role-play a group in which a member says that she has decided to leave the group because it is a waste of time, the group leader isn't directive enough, and group members are not leveling with one another.

CHAPTER 10

Consultation

Consultation is a service performed by counselors and other helping professionals through which they assist another person who has responsibility for a client or program (Dougherty, 2004). Counselors provide consultation to individuals, groups, and organizations in various settings (including schools, mental health agencies, organizational settings, and the community) for a variety of reasons. The following are a few examples:

- A school counselor assists a teacher in classroom management techniques for a particular student.
- A mental health counselor attends an Individualized Education Program (IEP) meeting to help a student at risk.
- An experienced counselor assists a new counselor in brainstorming counseling interventions for the new counselor's client.
- A marriage and family therapist meets with parents to discuss parenting strategies for their child.
- A corporation consults a mental health counselor to help find ways to increase employee morale.

After studying this chapter, you will be able to

- Understand a general framework for practicing consultation.
- Describe the process and stages of consultation.
- Discuss the differences in consultation in schools, mental health agencies, and organizational settings.

CONSULTATION DEFINED

What is *consultation?* An easy question, yet there is no widespread agreement on the definition of the term (Brown, Pryzwansky, & Schulte, 2006; Dougherty, 2004). The problem comes from the ambiguity of the process and the similarity between consultation and other services such as counseling and collaboration. In addition, the definition of consultation may depend on the setting in which it takes place.

In its most basic form, *consultation* is "a process whereby the first party (consultant) assists a second party (consultee) in finding a solution to a problem that concerns the third party (client)" (Harrison, 2000, p. 183). In general, the goal of consultation is to solve problems, although what constitutes a problem can vary widely.

Gerald Caplan (1970), considered the originator of mental health consultation, provided one of the most integrated definitions of consultation. He defined consultation as a process of interaction between two professional persons—the consultant, who is a specialist, and the consultee, who seeks the consultant's help with regard to a current work problem, which the consultee has decided is within the consultant's area of specialized expertise. The work problem involves the management or treatment of one or more clients of the consultee, or the planning or implementation of a program to cater to such clients (p. 19). Caplan further described consultation as a voluntary, nonhierarchical relationship between two professionals who are often of different occupational groups and is initiated by the consultee for the purpose of solving a work-related problem (Brown, Pryzwansky, & Schulte, 2006). The goals of consultation are to help consultees deal with their current work problems, as well as to give information or teach skills that help them to deal effectively with similar problems in the future.

Don Dinkmeyer, Sr., Don Dinkmeyer, Jr., and Jon Carlson, leading researchers on consultation in the schools, promoted a skills-based, goal-directed, Alderian approach to consultation (Dinkmeyer, 2006; Dinkmeyer & Carlson, 2006). They described consultation in the schools as a process in which teachers, parents, and administrators are assisted by the school counselor (or other professionals) in resolving problems involving persons or situations. Consultation involves sharing information, observing, providing a sounding board, and developing tentative hypotheses for action. The focus of consultation is commonly on students (although problems can also exist with teachers and other individuals). Effective consultants work with teachers, parents, administrators, curriculum, and the classroom rather than directly with the student. In fact, the student is rarely seen directly by the consultant, but is directly affected by the consultation (Dinkmeyer, 2006; Dinkmeyer & Carlson, 2006).

Historical Overview

Historically, consultation as a practice has its roots in medicine. Consultation in medicine began as early as the 13th century and was widely practiced by the middle part of the 19th century (Brown, Pryzwansky, & Schulte, 2006). As medicine became more specialized, physicians needed to consult with specialists for assistance in diagnosing and treating medical problems. The consultant, a fellow physician, helped the original physician gain insight into the precise nature of the patient's concerns. Sometimes the consultant would leave the original physician to carry out the treatment; other times, the consultant saw and treated the patient. For example, a general physician could consult with a dermatologist when unable to diagnose a patient's skin condition. Through the consultation process, the diagnosis is determined and the general physician would proceed with treatment.

In the 1940s and 1950s, psychologists entered organizational settings using consultation. As consultants, they were involved in such organizational issues as lines of authority, types of leadership, and the distribution of labor (Dougherty, 2005, p. 203). Gerald Caplan is credited with founding the mental health consultation movement in 1949 when, as a child psychiatrist working in Israel, he and a small staff of social workers and psychologists were charged with caring for the mental health needs of 16,000 immigrant adolescents located at more than 100 residential institutions (Caplan, Caplan, & Erchul, 1995, p. 23). Given the large number of children, Caplan realized that providing direct service to each child was not feasible. This led to the development of an indirect service model in which Caplan and his staff traveled to the individual institutions and met with the adolescents and their caregivers to discuss the latter's perceptions of the adolescents. From these meetings, caregivers were often found to have stereotyped, inaccurate perceptions of an adolescent that hindered resolution of the adolescent's mental health problems. Caplan found that after their meeting, the caregiver (i.e., consultee) often returned to his or her duties with a new perspective and ideas on how to work with the adolescent (i.e., client). Although this practice developed by Caplan was originally termed *counseling the counselors*, it was renamed *mental health consultation* to reflect that the clients remained the ultimate professional concern, and the consultees were not undergoing psychotherapy (Caplan, Caplan, & Erchul, 1994, p. 2). Caplan went on to develop mental health consultation techniques during his tenure at the Harvard School of Public Health (1952–63) and Harvard Medical School (1964–77), as well as to refine consultation methods for different populations of consultees (e.g., nurses, clergy).

In the 1960s, consultation was identified as an essential service in the mental health field. In 1963, the Mental Retardation Facilities and Community Mental Health Centers Construction Act (PL 88–164) was passed, which assigned consultation/education as one of the mental health services (along with inpatient services, outpatient services, partial hospitalization, and 24-hour emergency services) that had to be provided by community mental health centers in order to receive funding.

In the early 1960s, consultation was emphasized as an essential element of the school counselor's role and function (Wrenn, 1962). The first formal recognition of consulting in the counseling field occurred in 1966 when the American School Counseling Association identified consultation as one of the school counselor's three primary responsibilities (along with counseling and coordination) (Association for Counselor Education and Supervision, Joint Committee on the Elementary School Counselor, 1966). In 1967, Don Dinkmeyer, Sr., published one of the first articles on the practice of consulting in the schools (Dinkmeyer, 1967). Don Dinkmeyer, Sr., Don Dinkmeyer, Jr., and Jon Carlson have written extensively on consultation in the schools for the last 30 years and have greatly influenced school counselors to adopt consultation models that remain in use today.

Basic Concepts in Consultation

The consultation process involves a *tripartite* relationship consisting of the consultant, the consultee, and the client (Dougherty, 2004). The *consultant*—typically a counselor, psychologist, social worker, or other helping professional—possesses expertise, knowledge, or skill in a specific field and is able to bring new ideas to the consultee. The consultant's primary purpose is to help the consultee work more effectively with his or her client. Although the consultant is not required to have contact with the client, the consultant may choose to observe or interview the client or review client data (e.g., testing results, notes) to gain more information about the case. The consultant then provides recommendations on intervention strategies to the consultee. Thereafter, the consultee has the choice and responsibility to carry out any interventions.

The *consultee* is the individual with whom the consultant works directly. The consultee is generally the party who initiates services with the consultant. The consultee could be a counselor or other helping professional, a parent, a teacher (other school personnel), or even organizations, groups, or a community who are seeking assistance in working with a client or problem situation (Dougherty, 2004). The consultee ultimately has responsibility for the client's outcome.

The *client* is the individual or group with whom the consultee works. The focus of the consultation is typically on the management or treatment of the client or the planning or implementation of a program that provides services to the client. The consultee maintains responsibility for managing the problem and implementing any interventions suggested by the consultant.

Although the consultant provides his or her expertise to the consultee, professional responsibility for the client always remains with the consultee (Caplan, 1963; Dinkmeyer & Carlson, 2006; Dougherty, 2004). Participation in consultation is voluntary, and the consultee has the right to accept or reject all or part of the help provided by the consultant. Caplan believed that the purpose of consultation was not only to aid the consultee with the current problem, but also to add to the consultee's knowledge so that he or she could deal effectively with similar problems in the future.

Consultation is very similar to collaboration. *Collaboration* in the counseling profession involves two or more professionals working together to determine what actions to take with a client. The relationship among parties is reciprocal in nature, and all are considered to have unique expertise to bring to the table. The consultation process consists of collaboration between parties and joint planning to determine the best intervention for the client. The primary difference between consultation and collaboration is that in consultation, the consultee alone has responsibility for direct services to the client; whereas, with a collaborative relationship, collaborators share responsibility for the direct services provided to the client.

The importance of counselors being skilled in consultation has been formally acknowledged for the last 40 years (Dinkmeyer & Carlson, 2006). The Council for Accreditation of Counseling and Related Educational Programs (CACREP) standards recognize consultation as a practice in the helping relationship that is important in counselor training (2001). According to the standards, training programs should introduce students to the historical development of consultation, as well as the stages and major models of

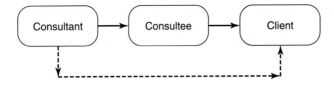

FIGURE 10.1

The Consultation Process

From *Psychological consultation and collaboration in school and community settings* (4th ed.), by A. Michael Dougherty. Copyright 2004 by Wadsworth.

consultation. In addition, the American School Counseling Association (ASCA, 2004) has included consultation in its national model for school counseling programs. Despite the importance of consultation in the counseling profession, many students graduate without proper preparation in consultation.

The Consultation Process

Because the consultant does not provide intervention directly to clients, consultation is deemed an "indirect" service to clients. This means that the consultant's work with the consultee may benefit the client, but only through the direct contact between consultee and client. The consultant delivers direct service to a consultee, who then delivers direct service to a client. Figure 10.1 displays the consultation process and the relationship among the parties. The solid arrows show that direct service is provided by the consultant to the consultee, then from the consultee to the client. The broken line represents indirect service provided by the consultant to the client.

In the consultation process, the consultant listens to the concerns that consultees have about their interactions with their clients. For example, a consultee (a fellow counselor) may wonder whether he has sufficient background to work with a client with a severe eating disorder; he may be perplexed about the lack of client response in the counseling sessions; or he may be experiencing feelings of countertransference that he does not recognize. The consultant helps the consultee gain insight into the situation and suggests ways to work through it. In some cases, consultant and consultee may agree that the client's problem goes beyond the consultee's particular expertise. In these instances, the consultee refers the client to another professional.

Difference between Consultation and Counseling

Comparisons are often made between consultation and counseling, and some believe that the two practices are basically the same process (Schmidt & Osborne, 1981). Similarities between consultation and counseling do exist; specifically, skills important to developing the counseling relationship are also important to the consulting relationship (e.g., active listening, reflecting feelings, paraphrasing, and information gathering) (Davis, 2003). In addition, the importance of a respectful, trusting relationship between consultants and consultees has been emphasized (Cutler & Huffine, 2004).

The founder of mental health consultation, Gerald Caplan (1970), strongly believed that therapy should never occur in a consulting relationship. Although this stance is still generally accepted, the boundary between counseling and consultation is sometimes blurred, and it is sometimes difficult to avoid therapeutic issues when working closely with a consultee (Sears, Rudisill, & Mason-Sears, 2006). Still, consultation, even when taking a consultee-focused approach (described later in the chapter), emphasizes problem solving around issues of the client's performance, as opposed to therapeutic personal insight and growth for the consultee (Parsons & Kahn, 2005).

Although the focus during consultation is on the client's problem and not the consultee's personal issues, consultants need to be concerned about their relationship with their consultee. In order for information to be heard and accepted by a consultee, the information needs to be presented in a manner that acknowledges the consultee's feelings and attitudes in addition to cognitive acceptance (Dinkmeyer & Carlson, 2006).

The fundamental difference between consulting and counseling is the focus of the service. The focus of counseling is directly on the client; whereas the focus of consultation is on how the counselor can better help the client. Dinkmeyer and Carlson (2006, p. 60) offer guidelines to help distinguish consultation and counseling:

It is consultation when

- The main focus of the relationship is on the third person (the client).
- The relationship is characterized by collaboration on ways to help the client.

It is counseling when

- The main focus of the relationship is on the person seeking help.
- The relationship is characterized by collaboration on ways to help the person seeking the help. While the third person may be discussed, the goal of the relationship is focused on the help seeker.

TYPES OF CONSULTATION

Client-Focused Consultation

All consultation could be considered client focused, since the client is the ultimate focus of the consultation. The term *client-focused consultation* is used specifically to describe a form of consultation in which the immediate goal is to find the most effective treatment for the client, by working through the consultee. (Caplan, 1995; Parsons, 1996; Parsons & Kahn, 2005). Because the primary goal is to improve the client, the consultant makes an assessment of the client's condition before recommending appropriate treatment strategies to be undertaken by the consultee. During the assessment process, the consultant may interact directly with the client, implement assessment strategies, and obtain client information (from client records, professional staff, family members) to make an accurate diagnosis of the client's difficulty. The consultant then recommends and implements intervention strategies indirectly, using the consultee as the agent for such activities (Parsons & Kahn, 2005).

Client-focused consultation most resembles the familiar process of referral to an expert (Mendoza, 1993). In contrast to referral, however, the consultee retains the responsibility for either making use of or rejecting the consultant's recommendations and the actual treatment of the client.

Consultee-Focused Consultation

In consultee-focused consultation, the consultant attempts to improve the functioning of the client by targeting changes in the professional functioning of the consultee (Parsons & Kahn, 2005, p. 218). In contrast to client-focused consultation, the primary focus of consultee-focused consultation shifts from improving the client (although desirable) to helping the consultee (Caplan, 1970). The presenting case brought to consultation is used by the consultant as a means for examining and correcting the professional work problems of the consultee, who is the focus of intervention (Mendoza, 1993).

The goal of the consultee-focused consultation is to identify and correct the consultee's professional limitations that have had a detrimental effect on his or her functioning with the client. Caplan (1970) identified several factors that reduce consultees' effectiveness with their clients, including lack of knowledge, skill, confidence, and/or professional objectivity (these are discussed further in the section on Consultation in Mental Health Settings later in the chapter).

A CONSULTATION MODEL

In broadest terms, consultation is a process by which a consultant and a consultee seek to solve a problem situation (the problem situation involves the functioning of a client). Therefore, most models of consultation portray it as a problem-solving procedure that includes the stages common to problem-solving models in many disciplines (Brown, Pryzwansky, & Schulte, 1998; Dougherty, 2004; Erchul & Martens, 1997; Sears, Rudisill, & Mason-Sears, 2006). A classic problem-solving model consists of five stages:

1. *Define the problem.* The first step may sound easy, but problems can be vague and ill defined. Consultees may not be clear exactly what the problem is. Consultants can help with problem definition through a thorough assessment, as well as clarifying what the consultee would like to change.
2. *Brainstorm alternative solutions.* After the problem is defined, the consultant and consultee work together to brainstorm solutions to solve the problem. During this stage, all solutions are discussed without filtering the possibilities.
3. *Discuss the pros and cons of each alternative solution.* During this stage, the implications of each alternative are discussed. Consultant and consultee weigh the pros and cons and discuss the feasibility of each alternative.
4. *Select and implement an alternative solution.* This step involves deciding which alternative to implement. It is important that the consultant be supportive of the consultee during the decision making, but the consultee is always allowed to make the final decision.
5. *Evaluate the impact of the decision.* Once the decision has been implemented, the results should be monitored and evaluated. If the results indicate that the actions taken did not achieve the desired goal, or if new problems develop, then the consultant and consultee can restart the problem-solving model.

Dougherty (2004) presented a generic model of consultation that provides counselors and other helping professionals with an understanding of how to go about the procedure of conducting a consultation. The model, consisting of four stages, provides a framework describing the complete consultation process. Although the stages are labeled differently, the model has some characteristics of a basic problem-solving model.

1. *Stage One: Entry Stage.* The entry stage involves the initial communication between consultant and consultee. During this stage, the consultant *explores the purpose* for the consultation and *determines the needs* of the consultee. All parties involved discuss their expectations about the consultation, agree upon the terms of the consultation (e.g., services rendered, payment, length of consultation), and develop a *contract* (either written or verbal) that reflects their shared understanding and guides the consultation process. The consultant then *physically enters the system* by coming into contact with the members of the organization and the consultee. Finally, the consultant *psychologically enters the system* by gaining acceptance as a temporary member of the organization.

2. *Stage Two: Diagnosis Stage.* During this stage, the consultant *gathers information* about the client and the problem from a variety of sources, including interviews, observations, and records. Next, the consultant and the consultee analyze the information to *define the problem, set goals* to solve or improve the problem, and *generate a list of possible interventions.*

3. *Stage Three: Implementation Stage.* The implementation stage begins with the consultant and the consultee *choosing a specific intervention* from the list of possible interventions that they generated during the last stage. Next, they *formulate a plan* that incorporates the intervention, and then they *implement the plan* and monitor its progress. Finally, once implementation is completed, the *plan is evaluated.* Evaluating the plan is part of the larger evaluation of the entire consultation process.

4. *Stage Four: Disengagement Stage.* The disengagement stage involves the ending of the consultation process. During this stage, the parties *evaluate the consultation process*—this includes evaluating the plan carried out in the implementation stage, the overall effectiveness of the consultation process, and the consultant's behavior. Next, the parties *plan postconsultation matters* and decide how the effects of consultation will be maintained by the consultee. As the consultee is able to assume more responsibility for the maintenance of the results of the consultation, the consultant *reduces involvement* with the consultee and the organization. Finally, the consultation process is formally *terminated.*

AREAS OF CONSULTATION

Consultation in Schools

Consultation is an activity long embraced by school counselors (Parsons & Kahn, 2005). The primary goal of school-based consultation is to change students' behavior or the behavior of the adults involved with the students (Dougherty, 2004). Information concerning student behavior, classroom management, parenting skills, group dynamics, teachers' beliefs, discipline procedures, and motivation techniques are all part of the consultant's repertoire in the school.

Traditionally, consultation has been recognized as one of the four "C's" of school counseling: counseling, coordination, collaboration, and consultation (Baker, 2004). The American School Counseling Association (ASCA), in its national model on school counseling programs (ASCA, 2003), clarified the role of the school counselor and identified consulting as a responsive service that school counselors engage in to meet the needs of students.

Consultation remains a key function of school counselors for a number of reasons, the primary one being the sheer numbers of students who need counseling services. When school counselors only provide direct services such as individual and group counseling, their impact is limited, since it's virtually impossible to reach all of the children in the school. Consultation provides a means to affect larger numbers of students and the school climate. "Whereas a school counselor who works with one student may impact only that student's life, the consultant working with one teacher may indirectly affect the lives of 30 or more children" (Dinkmeyer & Carlson, 2006, p. 11).

Consultees in the school setting are typically teachers, administrators, or parents, each of whom have their own particular concerns or issues involving students.

Consultation with Teachers

Teachers may have problems with individual students or with overall classroom interaction. A student may not he handing in work and may look depressed or agitated, or a student may be disclosing personal concerns beyond a teacher's expertise. Teachers may have personal or marital concerns that are interfering with their class performance, or they may be depressed or anxious about their lives in general.

For problems with students, the process of clarifying the difficulties and determining alternative action follows the consulting procedure previously discussed. If the issue is too difficult to be worked out within the classroom, the counselor may suggest that the teacher refer the student directly to the counselor. If the need is for disciplinary action or a formal evaluation of a student's abilities, the teacher should be directed to the school psychologist. At the college level, faculty should be referred to the dean of students or to the chairs of their departments.

When a faculty member wants to consult about a student, it is wise ethical policy for the member to maintain the student's right to privacy and not identify the student. Thus, if the student under discussion is referred to counseling or comes in independently, the counselor will not have prior knowledge about the student. Also, the teacher will be more likely to generalize suggestions about one student's particular behavior to similar behaviors of others. This approach is feasible in college counseling and in larger high schools because anonymity is fairly easy to maintain. In small schools, however, anonymity becomes more difficult. Nevertheless, it is good policy that students' names are of secondary importance, unless it is determined that a student's behavior is injurious to her- or himself or to others.

Teachers who have personal problems may find it valuable to consult with a counselor for a few sessions. Together, they can evaluate the severity of the problem and decide whether counseling is needed. Most often, consultees are apprehensive about whether they need counseling and where to go for the kind of help they need. If counseling is agreed to, the counselor can refer the teacher to an outside professional. It is not considered wise professional practice for counselors to involve themselves in counseling relationships with colleagues. The counselor and the teacher might find it difficult to disengage social and/or business interactions from the counseling relationship or to establish the kind of relationship necessary for effective counseling (Corey, Corey, & Callanan, 1998).

Consultation with Administrators

Administrators are often faced with conflicting demands and pressures from students, parents, and teachers about student behavior and school policy, student rights and responsibilities, and teacher or parent rights and responsibilities. Administrators may, for example, have difficult interactions with parents or with individual teachers or groups of teachers, or they may face a gap between curricular offerings and student needs. Testing programs, the appropriate use of school records, and changes in laws about administrator–student interactions are other areas in which school administrators may want consultation.

The counseling staff can offer information and guidelines about the potential consequences of certain administrative actions. Counselors can also use their expertise to ensure that testing and record-keeping policies are in line with the rights and responsibilities of students and adults. And guidelines for an administrator's interactions with parents and teachers can be discussed.

It is not wise professional practice, however, for counselors and administrators to discuss a specific teacher's interactions with students or the teacher's proficiency in teaching. This sort of evaluative interview can raise ethical dilemmas for counselors who are inviting referrals from teachers. On the other hand, if a teacher and an administrator request a joint consultation with a counselor about their interaction, such a consultation may he useful as long as it has no evaluative overtones. And when an administrator is concerned about a teacher who is suffering an emotional breakdown or about the safety of others, a consultation with a counselor is in order.

Consultation with Parents

Consultations with parents can be very effective. Parents may request a consultation with a school counselor when they are concerned about their child's poor academic work, lack of friends, poor motivation in school, or unmanageable behavior at home. In these instances, it is most effective for the parents or counselor to let the child know that a consultation has been requested and why. If the child objects, the parents may need to resolve the objections before seeing the counselor. The counselor might also talk with the child about the objections, and that discussion in itself might help communication between parents and child. By establishing, at the outset, effective communication processes based on the right to privacy and confidentiality, the counselor and the parents reduce the possibility that the child will perceive intrigue among the adults. This approach is particularly important because a counseling relationship with the child or the family often arises out of effective consultation (Baker, 2000). After the consultation, if more intensive work with the family is needed, a referral to a family counselor is in order.

If a psychological evaluation of the child or an evaluation of home conditions seems warranted, a referral to the school psychologist or social worker can be made.

Consultation in Mental Health Settings

The use of consultation in mental health settings is for the promotion of mental health and for the prevention, treatment, and rehabilitation of mental disorders (Caplan, 1963; Sears, Rudisill, & Mason-Sears, 2006). Mental health consultation is based on the idea that society's mental health can be promoted through the efforts of consultants who work with human services personnel (counselors) or with administrators of human services programs.

Goals of mental health consultation are to help consultees cope with their specific work-related problems, as well as improve their general level of functioning so that they can be even more effective in the future (Dougherty, 2004). Caplan (1970) conceptualized the role of the mental health consultant as one who helps other professionals work more effectively with their clients in four key areas:

1. *Lack of knowledge.* The consultee may not have the knowledge base to understand the client's problems. The consultant would then serve in the role of teacher, providing education and information resources to the consultee.
2. *Lack of skill.* The consultee may not have the professional skills to deal with the client's presenting issues. The consultant serves in the role of teacher and clinical supervisor, focusing on skill development.
3. *Lack of confidence.* Often, the consultee may be performing very well, but may not be fully effective because of a lack of confidence due to inexperience or youth. The consultant may simply need to provide support and reassurance that the consultee is doing well, and then offer some minor suggestions for improvement.
4. *Lack of objectivity.* The consultee looses a sense of professional objectivity when the consultee's personal issues are triggered by a client, distorting perceptions and clouding judgment, so that the consultee behaves less effectively than usual. The consultant employs techniques to help the consultee resolve the issues and correct the loss of objectivity.

Consultation in Organizational Settings

Organizations are groups of people put together for a particular purpose. When they have difficulty meeting their goals and objectives or are functioning ineffectively, organizations frequently seek the help of consultants. Dougherty (2004, p. 205) provided the following definition: "Organizational consultation is the process in which a professional, functioning either internally or externally to an organization, provides assistance of a technical, diagnostic/prescriptive, or facilitative nature to an individual or group from that organization to enhance the organization's ability to deal with change and maintain or enhance its effectiveness in some designated way."

Consulting with organizations has many similarities to consulting with individuals (Brown, Pryzwansky, & Schulte, 1998), including the triadic nature of the process, the stages of consultation, the goals of the process, and some of the interventions used. However, there are some important differences. One of the major factors that distinguish organizational consultation from consulting with individuals is the complexity of the client. Organizational consultation usually involves one or more consultees (e.g., persons charged with the management of the organization) focusing on the client system, which is the organization or some part of it. The more complex the organization, the more complex the client system becomes. Thus, the client system may comprise dozens of people in the organization who may be formed into subgroups that have their own norms and culture.

The basic assumptions in organizational consultation is that the process is as important as the content (that is, *how* something is done can be as important as *what* is done); the behavior of individuals, groups, and organizations is cyclical in nature; and satisfied personnel make for effective organizations (Dougherty, 2004). Consultation with organizations can focus on any number of problems or issues. Sears, Rudisill, and Mason-Sears (2006) outlined five major areas of operational functioning where problems can arise:

1. *Power/authority.* This focuses on whether power and authority are used effectively in both formal and informal matters within an organization.
2. *Morale/cohesion.* This concerns how members perceive the organization and its direction, as well as the degree to which members see themselves as part of the team.
3. *Norms/standards.* This focuses on the norms of behavior in the organization and the criteria for measuring quality. Issues of norms/standards are raised when an organization is faced with change, either internally or externally.
4. *Goals/objectives.* Issues arise when goals and objectives are either poorly defined or have not been achieved.
5. *Roles/communication.* Understanding the roles in the organization, as well as communication, is important in achieving the organization's tasks and goals. Issues arise as roles become less clear and boundaries blur.

SUMMARY

Consultation as a practice began in the medical field, but has been a common practice in the counseling profession since the early 1960s. Consultation is a service performed by counselors and other helping professionals in which they help another person who has responsibility for a client. Consultation is triadic in nature: two professionals interact for the benefit of the client. The consultant has expertise, knowledge, or skill in a specific field and is able to bring new ideas to the consultee. The consultee is the individual with whom the consultant works directly. The client is the individual or group with whom the consultee works.

Consultation is an indirect service because the consultant does not provide interventions directly to clients. Consultation affects the client through the consultant's direct work with the consultee. The stages of the consultation process are similar to the stages in basic problem-solving models.

Consultation can be client-centered or consultee-centered. In consultant-centered consultation, the consultant attempts to improve the functioning of the client by focusing on the professional functioning of the consultee. Client-centered consultation involves the consultant working more closely with the client to develop recommendations for the consultee.

Consultation in the counseling field occurs in three primary settings: schools, mental health settings, and organizational settings. The consultation approach varies slightly among settings, with the primary difference being the goal of the consultation.

PROJECTS AND ACTIVITIES

1. Interview a school counselor at an elementary, middle, or high school in your area. Ask about his or her role as a consultant in the schools. Here are some sample questions:
   - Do you use consultation in your role as a school counselor?
   - When and where do you employ a consultative approach?
   - What, if any, are the benefits of using consultation as an approach?
2. Tommy is a 3rd-grade student who exhibits "temper tantrums" (screaming, hitting other students, crying) during the morning reading lesson. He has been suspended four times for this behavior. Tommy's teacher contacts the school counselor for help with managing Tommy's behavior in class. Identify the consultant, consultee, and client in this case.
3. Alana, a new student to the school, was referred to the school counselor's office by her 4th-grade teacher, Ms. Dieker. Ms. Dieker reported that since Alana arrived in her class, she constantly leaves her seat, talks excessively to other children, and is almost never focused on the work she is supposed to be doing. Ms. Dieker stated that she believes that Alana has Attention Deficit Hyperactivity Disorder (ADHD) and doesn't know how to help the child. In observing the classroom, the school counselor observed Alana's behaviors, which coincided with what was reported by Ms. Dieker. In looking at Alana's records, the school counselor finds out that Alana has indeed been diagnosed as having ADHD.
   - Question: What type of consultation should the school counselor use in this case? Client-focused consultation or consultee-focused consultation?
   - Question: What should be the focus of the consultation?
4. Karen, a mental health consultant, is working with Jo, a family counselor who provides home-based counseling with primarily indigent families. Jo describes a particular family in her caseload as "just plain lazy" and becoming more so because of the welfare benefits they are receiving. Jo goes on to state that it's just not fair that the taxpayers have to pay for this family's laziness.
   - Question: What type of consultation should the mental health consultant use in this case? Client-focused consultation or consultee-focused consultation?
   - Question: What should be the focus of the consultation?

Part Four
Counseling Specialties

CHAPTER 11

Marriage and Family Counseling

M arriage and family counseling is aimed at improving not only relationship problems but also mental and emotional disorders within the context of family and larger social systems. Marriage and family counseling has its beginnings in the 1940s and 1950s, but it proliferated as a profession in the late 1970s and 1980s (Gladding, 2007). Marriage and family counselors believe that since family influences often contribute to or are affected by an individual's problems, working with the family can contribute to the resolution of the individual's problems. In addition, marriage and family counselors believe in the value and positive impact of stable, long-term, and emotionally enriching relationships and families.

After studying this chapter, you will be able to

- Identify and understand the major theoretical models of marital and family approaches to counseling.
- Describe the variety of interventions that the major marriage and family therapy approaches use.
- Understand diverse family forms and various patterns of family interaction.

FAMILY SYSTEMS THEORIES

The family systems model is based on the general systems theory developed by biologist Ludvig von Bertalanffy (1974), who believed that humans are living systems composed of subsystems that are connected together and are dependent on one another; any change in one subsystem produces change in the others. In this model, the whole system is greater than the sum of its parts. Family subsystems include smaller units of individual family members who interact and affect the total system. Examples of these subsystems

176

are the interactions between parents, various interactions among siblings, and interactions between a parent and each child.

In equating family systems with general systems theory, Foley (1989) describes three important characteristics: wholeness, relationship, and equifinality. He says, "*Wholeness* means the system is not just the sum of its parts taken separately, but it also includes their interaction" (p. 456). Thus, a family does not consist simply of separate individuals, but rather includes the complex interactions occurring among them. *Relationship* describes the types and quality of interactions going on among family members who are in different subsystems in the family. *Equifinality* is based on the idea that any problem a family member or family is experiencing results from numerous causes, rather than from one particular cause. If an adolescent girl is experiencing an eating disorder, for example, one cannot simply say that it is caused by a rejecting mother. Complex interactions between parents, between parents and daughter, and among the girl and her siblings all contribute. For this reason, family systems therapists believe that they can intervene at any time to resolve the family problem. "Regardless of the origin of a problem, any difficulty can be removed if a change is made at any point in time in the system" (Foley, 1989, p. 456). Because of this belief, family therapists do not search for underlying causes of family dysfunction, but instead focus on the current interactions in the family that are perpetuating the problem.

Murray Bowen (Papero, 2000), who began his work in the 1950s, was the first family therapist to apply systems theory to family therapy. He originally called his theory *family systems,* but in the 1970s he changed the name to the *Bowen theory* because the term *family systems* had become widely used to describe numerous family theories.

Marriage and family counselors, regardless of theoretical orientation, follow the general principles of systems theory. They attend to current problems in family dynamics. They explore relationships, alliances, and conflicts within the family and their effects on each member of the family and on the family as a whole. In applying these principles, family therapists tend to be active in the sessions, often acting as instructors, directors, or guides in reorganizing family patterns of interaction. Family therapists differ, however, in the way they work with a family because of differing theoretical positions they have about human behavior.

Because family classification systems are numerous and complex, this text discusses eight family systems theories that represent the basic theoretical approaches: (a) object relations, (b) Bowen's family systems, (c) Adlerian family therapy, (d) Satir's process model, (e) Minuchin's structural family therapy, (f) strategic therapy, (g) social learning family therapy, and (h) cognitive–behavioral family therapy. Also discussed under Trends in Family Therapy are several family counseling models from a social–cultural contextual approach.

Object Relations Theory

Object relations has its psychoanalytic roots in ego psychology. Unlike Freud, who specified that instinctual gratification of sexual drives residing in the id is a person's primary drive, object relations theorists believe that humans relate primarily to others. Children develop strong attachments to significant people (called *objects*) to fulfill this need (Atwood, 1992b). Citing Fairbairn (1954) and Klein (1948), Gladding (2007) explained that human beings have a fundamental motivation to seek objects, that is, people in relationships, starting at birth. Gladding goes on to describe an *object* as a significant other (e.g., a mother) with whom children form an emotional bond. As they grow, children will often internalize good and bad characteristics of this significant other within themselves. Thus, early psychosocial rather than psychosexual relationships influence the development of the child and, later, the adult (Thomas, 1992).

James Framo (1982) is a well-known advocate of this theory. He believes that the emotional responses of each family member and the effects these various emotional expressions have on family interactions are the crux of family dynamics and family functioning. Any unresolved conflicts that exist in either parent's family of origin result in conflicts in relationships in the current nuclear family.

Another important proponent of object relations, Robin Skynner (1981), believes that the family as a unit fosters individual development to the degree that both parents have worked through their own development in their families of origin. When parents request counseling for a problem child, the child's unresolved behavioral problems represent the parents' failure to develop emotional maturity. Skynner believes that when two people marry, each partner brings to the marriage fears and distorted expectations related to blocked developmental processes. Moreover, each partner tries to re-create circumstances in which the undeveloped experience can be reencountered and worked through. He sees these attempts as having a great potential for growth in the marriage relationship. But also, he warns, these undeveloped experiences can lead partners to resist individual changes, resulting in unresolved family tensions and dysfunctions.

Object relations practitioners tend to combine treatment of the whole family with treatment of subgroups and individual members of the family. A man and a woman often work together as cotherapists. First, the therapist assesses the whole family to determine the nature and severity of the problem. One family member, usually a child, is designated as the *identified patient*. After the initial assessment, the therapist decides whether to work with the whole family, a subgroup, or the parents alone. If assessment shows that serious marital conflict exists that would impede progress in family counseling, the therapist may first do marital counseling with the parents and bring in the rest of the family later.

The family and the therapist agree on goals, which are usually quite specific. Therapy consists of attending both to the personal problems of each family member and to family dysfunctional patterns. Both parents' unresolved conflicts with their families of origin are included as well.

Therapists recognize that transference and resistance will occur among family members because they are expressing unresolved feelings of anxiety or anger blocked by either the nuclear family or the parents' families of origin. At the same time, therapists are observing and interpreting family rules and transactions that are causing family breakdown. Skynner (1981) attempts to let family members express their concerns as spontaneously as possible with a minimum of direct guidance or prompting.

Bowen's Family Systems

Murray Bowen (1978) originated the term *family systems* in the 1950s when he developed his theory of family therapy. He believes that an emotional system exists within a family and that this system influences the degree of separateness (*differentiation of self*) and togetherness (*fusion*) of family members. Bowen's major goal is to develop differentiation, or independence, among family members (Atwood, 1992b).

Differentiation of self, according to Bowen, is crucial for the effective functioning of each family member and the family as a whole. Members of a dysfunctional family fuse identities, become emotionally dependent on one another, and lose their individual selves. Thus, growth, maturity, and emotions are stifled. He believes that in an emotionally mature family, an effective balance of differentiation and togetherness is maintained. Members attain sufficient individuality to make their own decisions without becoming fused, while at the same time showing consideration for others. Bowen claims that it is a mistake for a person to try to resolve fusion problems by isolating from the family through emotional withdrawal, denial of problems, or running away. People who use these escape mechanisms behave immaturely and impulsively and fuse with others (Papero, 2000).

Bowen believes that fusion between members of a family leads to the development of triangles. When two members of a family who are fused enter into conflict with each other, one or the other tries to move out of this locked-in relationship by involving a vulnerable third party, who inevitably takes sides with one of the fused partners (Becvar & Becvar, 2006). In a triangle, two members of the family align, while the third becomes an outsider and a scapegoat. When tension becomes really unbearable, a fourth person may be drawn in, forcing realignment of the triangle.

When a family first comes in for therapy, members usually blame the family discord on one of the following: (a) one spouse has a problem (e.g., drinking, gambling, or adultery), (b) serious marital discord exists, or (c) a child's behavior is disrupting the marriage and family harmony (Bowen, 1978). Bowen believes that marital conflict in itself does not cause problem children but that problems arise when parents project their anxieties onto their children. This is called *family projection process.*

Bowen believes that patterns of differentiation, fusing, triangulation, and projection are passed from generation to generation in a *multigenerational transmission* process. Problems in a nuclear family can be understood and resolved only if therapy includes exploration of relationships in the families of origin for three generations. Consequently, in therapy, Bowen traces dysfunctional patterns through the use of a *genogram,* which demonstrates three generations of family structure, triangulations, and alignments. A genogram is a structural chart showing the relationships of family members, including dates of birth and death, marriages and divorces, and number and gender of siblings.

Once family members understand this pervasive fusing and triangulation, Bowen's main goal is to help all involved differentiate themselves from one another and break the tendency to triangulate. Because the triangles are interlocking, a change in one triangle will cause a change in all triangles.

On the basis of his assessment of the family, Bowen may work with the whole family, with individual family members, or with various combinations of family members representing a family subsystem. If he thinks that the conflict between husband and wife is the major factor contributing to a child's symptoms, he may work with the marital discord first before seeing the whole family. If the conflict between spouses is severe, he may see each one separately until they are able to work together.

Bowen does not give the identified patient special attention; he believes that the so-called stronger members of the family play a part in fostering and maintaining the sickness in a weaker member. He helps all members become aware of their roles in the family dynamics.

Adlerian Family Therapy

Alfred Adler, originally a follower of Freud, broke with him because Adler believed that a social drive to belong and to relate to others, rather than biological instincts, directed human behavior. He contended that all behavior is purposeful and that the goal is to attain social status in the family and the community (see chapter 6). In the 1920s, Adler applied his principles of psychotherapy to work with families in schools and in the community. He emphasized the importance of family dynamics, sibling rivalry, and the birth order of children. He also used consultations with nonpathological families struggling with practical problems in rearing and relating to children. Parents were taught appropriate ways of disciplining their children (Dinkmeyer & Dinkmeyer, 1991).

Because Adler started working with families in the early 1920s, he can rightfully be considered the originator of family counseling and therapy. Nonetheless, he was ignored for many years, overshadowed by Freudian psychoanalysts, humanists, and behaviorists among counselors and therapists. However, a resurgence of Adlerian thought has profoundly influenced psychology in the United States (Mosak, 2000), with credit due largely to Rudolf Dreikurs and then Don Dinkmeyer for carrying on Adlerian thought. The worth and viability of Adlerian psychology can be measured by the amount of research and development it continues to generate and the many Adlerian institutes, professional societies, journals, family education centers, and study groups that exist. Counselors and therapists have come to recognize the value of Adler because they have become more socially conscious, have moved beyond treating the family in isolation, and are now treating families in the context of their social–cultural environment.

In the 1940s, Dreikurs updated Adler's pragmatic theory and style and his focus on nonpathological families struggling to bring up children effectively. A manual for Adlerian family counseling centers—published in 1959 by Dreikurs, Lowe, Sonstegard, and Corsini—became "the bible of Adlerian family counseling" (Dinkmeyer & Dinkmeyer, 1991, p. 385). According to Dreikurs (1968), children are motivated for growth most effectively in groups. They try to attain a place in the group, and if they don't, they develop feelings of inferiority. In severe cases, they become discouraged and withdraw from efforts to cooperate.

Even discouraged children, however, try to use creative powers to attain social status. Dreikurs (1968) claims that discouraged children take one of four goal-directed behaviors. They may try to (a) get attention, (b) prove their power, (c) get revenge, or (d) display deficiencies to get special service or exemptions. He does not advocate punishment for misbehavior; instead, he proposes that children experience either the natural or the logical consequences of their actions. *Natural consequences* apply when the activity involves only the child—when the child spends all of her or his weekly allowance on the first day, for example, and has no money for the rest of the week. *Logical consequences* occur when two or more people are involved; for instance, children who are frequently late for dinner may not be served dinner whenever they are late.

Dreikurs (1968) points out that when parents, after World War II, began following a permissive style of raising their children, they were at a loss about how to guide or discipline them. Children in such cases believe that they can make any demand they please, thus becoming irresponsible tyrants, and adults adopt the children's roles. Because they lack methods of disciplining children in a democratic way, parents need help in establishing order. Counseling is meant to give them these methods.

Adlerian theory has also been used as the basis for a system of parenting skills called Systematic Training for Effective Parenting (STEP) (Dinkmeyer & McKay, 1976; see Website at http://www.steppublishers.com). In addition, Dinkmeyer and Dinkmeyer (1991) applied Adlerian principles to school settings and to parenting groups. Dinkmeyer and Dinkmeyer (1991), Sherman and Dinkmeyer (1987), and Sweeney (1998) published articles and texts describing Adlerian family therapy as a systems approach in both educational institutions and community practice.

Dinkmeyer and Dinkmeyer (1991) emphasize the social aspect of Adlerian therapy. Individuals, they say, strive to gain significance by belonging to a social system, beginning with the family. Family members develop feelings of inferiority when they believe that other family members reject them or deem them unworthy. "All behavior attempts to overcome feelings of inferiority. We seek superiority in part because our earliest experiences surrounded us with superiors" (p. 388). Power struggles then emerge in the family as each member tries to gain social status.

Adlerian counselors and therapists act as teachers, advisers, and facilitators. They help families understand the dynamics of family transactions and the ways each member contributes to the family problems. They help family members recognize their mutual interdependence by directing them to attend to one another's needs and cooperate in constructive give-and-take relationships.

With renewed interest in Adler and with efforts to integrate therapeutic approaches in more comprehensive therapeutic models, both cognitive–behaviorists and constructivists have been in dialogue about the degree of their compatibility with Adlerian family therapy (Watts, 2003).

Satir's Process Model

Virginia Satir's model holds that family dysfunction results from faulty communication, a condition directly related to each individual's feelings of low self-esteem. She originally called her theory *conjoint therapy* (1967) to describe the idea that the therapist works with the total nuclear family in counseling sessions.

After completing her work on conjoint therapy, Satir spent time at the Esalen Institute, a humanistic growth center in California. Her exposure to Gestalt therapy, altered states of consciousness, body therapies, and sensory awareness had a profound influence on her, both personally and professionally. From this rich combination of experiences, she developed the *process model* of family therapy (Satir & Bitter, 2000). Satir moved away from her earlier emphasis on pathology, to an emphasis on maintaining the healthiness of normally functioning individuals and wholeness in the family. She used the process model to describe her methods of interacting with individual and family members to help them improve communication styles and feelings of worth. Satir (1982) wrote, "I feel the name 'Process Model' fits how I see what I do. The model is one in which the therapist and family join forces to promote wellness" (p. 12).

Communication and self-esteem are the cornerstones of process therapy (Satir, 1982). Any symptoms displayed by family members result from problems that have blocked their emotional growth, and all members of the family and the family itself have within them the resources necessary to overcome these emotional blocks. Satir's theory emphasizes that the absence of ill health is not the same as the presence of good health. Thus, removing a symptom-producing sickness is not sufficient to ensure positive growth; well-being is directly related to a sense of vitality and to the development of self-esteem.

Because improving communication among family members is the key factor in Satir's approach, congruency between an event and a person's perception of the event is crucial. Dysfunctional family members continually misperceive the behaviors of other family members, resulting in considerable distortions in family communication. Poor communication can also result from family members finding it difficult to accept differences in another member of the family.

When symptoms are observed in families, Satir's model looks for family rules governing the communication in the family system. These rules form the patterns by which children develop their own self-esteem; the system is maintained to preserve all members' sense of self-esteem. Thus, these symptoms have a survival function.

During therapy sessions, therapists become models of communication and growth and act as facilitators for each family member and for the family as a whole. They observe interactions, transactions, communication, and responses. They intervene to ask whether messages are clear and correct and how family members feel about a particular comment made by another family member. Therapists interrupt dialogue to check whether each person thinks the communication is correct. They see themselves as guides, companions, and nourishing educators, rather than as authoritative changers or manipulators. They help families see their nonproductive or destructive patterns and help them engage in health-producing processes.

The goals of Satir's process model are to help each of the family members develop self-esteem and to enable them to grow. Therapists work to change or correct four elements in a family: (a) feelings of self-worth, (b) communication skills, (c) the system of alliances and coalitions, and (d) rules governing the family (Satir, 1982). No one is blamed for the family disturbance; the focus is on the multiple interactions in families. When parents are in conflict, a child often becomes the third angle in a family triangle, and the child must take sides with one parent or another to avoid unbearable conflict.

A major contribution to family therapy is Satir's (1972) classification of styles of communication (see Figure 11.1) and their use in her therapy or counseling. She believes that each individual in a dysfunctional family communicates with the others in one of four ways:

- *The Placater.* Tries to smooth things over, takes blame, apologizes, and tries to please so that other persons do not get angry.
- *The Blamer.* Accuses others and finds fault in order to appear strong.
- *The Computer.* Gives intellectual reasons, is super-reasonable in order to be immune to threats.
- *The Leveler.* Tries to be genuine and straightforward in communicating with others, helps resolve conflict.

FIGURE 11.1
Satir's Communication Stances

Note: From *Peoplemaking* (p. 83), by
V. Satir, 1972, Palo Alto, CA: Science
and Behavior Books. Copyright 1972
by Science and Behavior Books.
Adapted with permission.

Satir also developed a technique called *sculpting,* in which family members take physical postures that indicate how they are relating and communicating in the family system. As family members exaggerate the postures to represent the four communication styles, the sensory responses help them become visibly and tactilely aware of their communication styles. Family members can also switch roles to experience other persons' styles, and the communication styles of close friends, employers, household help, lovers, and former spouses may be role-played, too.

Another strategy has the family enact a current conflict occurring at home and then use communication games to help members see how family rules or patterns are contributing to the conflict. In these activities, Satir used props such as blindfolds and ropes. For example, Satir might literally tie ends of a rope around all members' waists and selectively ask them to move. In this way, the entire family could feel how the movement of one family member influences the rest of the family and thus become aware of the complexity and dissonance in their relationships (Gladding, 2007).

The family might also role-play a system in which all members are either blamers or distracters and then change to a more productive way of communicating.

Minuchin's Structural Family Therapy

Structural family therapy, one of the most influential theories in the 1970s, originated in the work of Salvador Minuchin at the Philadelphia Child Guidance Clinic. Minuchin was trained as a psychoanalytic psychiatrist and became interested in families in the 1950s, when he was working with juvenile delinquents and lower-socioeconomic minority groups (Atwood, 1992b).

When analyzing faulty family patterns, Minuchin (1974) explores how members of families interact and how faulty communication—repetitive and highly rigid patterns and habits—contributes to family dysfunction. He is also interested in how families under stress use these ineffective behaviors as a means of survival.

According to Minuchin, the family is a social system that develops *transactional patterns,* or family rules, which determine how each member relates to other family members and under what conditions or at what times certain transactional patterns occur (Minuchin, 1974; Minuchin, Lee, & Simon, 2006). In transactions occurring in family subsystems, three factors are involved: boundaries, alignments, and power. *Boundaries* are the rules determining who will participate in a family interaction or transaction and what role each member will play. *Alignments* refer to how various family members form coalitions or alliances to join or oppose another member of a subsystem. *Power* relates to the degree of influence each person has on the family system. A healthy, functioning family has clearly defined generational boundaries; parents are the executives in the family, ensuring that children will not take over parental functions and that grandparents will not interfere (Goldenberg & Goldenberg, 2007). In a healthy family, boundaries and alliances are flexible, and the family can adapt to inevitable changes, such as births, deaths, marriages, or job changes. Alignments are also clear between parents on crucial issues such as discipline; and rules about power are defined so that children know that parents' orders will be enforced.

Minuchin, like Bowen, believes that family dysfunctions occur when family members are either enmeshed or disengaged. In the *enmeshed* family, whose boundaries are diffused, members are tightly interlocked, and any change brought about by one member causes quick resistance from another; in such cases, family members become fused and lose personal identity. In the *disengaged* family, boundaries are rigid, and family ties are weak. Members are isolated or disconnected from each other, seldom communicating or making contact with one another. In these cases, children run the risk of developing antisocial behavior. In both enmeshed and disengaged families, the power of family members is unclear or inappropriate. Consequently, children may either have insufficient opportunity to express themselves or may tyrannize the family.

Dysfunctional families are resistant to change; when stress arises because of changes in the family, conflict avoidance occurs. In enmeshed families, disagreements are rare because conflicts are seen as a sign of disloyalty and as a refutation of love and closeness. In disengaged families, the distance that prevents confrontations between members gives a false impression of independence and harmony (Colapinto, 2000). Minuchin believes that whenever conflicts arise, such families use repetitive, stereotyped reactions without modification to preserve family equilibrium at all costs. Thus, instead of resolving conflicts, these rigid responses solidify the dysfunctional family patterns.

A family usually asks for help because of concern about a particular family member (the identified patient). Minuchin's therapeutic goal is to restructure the transactional rules of the family so that members can communicate and relate in a way that is growth producing for the family and for each of its members. He either tightens or loosens boundaries and helps families make changes in their stereotyped, rigid positions or roles so that they become more flexible in their ways of relating, resolving conflicts, and managing stress related to change. He works on current symptoms and does not involve himself in patterns from the families of origin or in multigenerational transmission of family patterns.

Minuchin is very active in therapy. He uses two basic strategies and a variety of techniques. In the first strategy, he joins with the family patterns existing at the beginning of therapy. For example, he may ask the family to enact a conflict that is occurring at home. Using a tactic called *mimesis,* he imitates or models how family members interact with each other. Then, in the second strategy, he begins to restructure the family. He may use the technique of *reframing* by putting a positive interpretation on a person's negative behavior. For example, the attempts of a child to run away may be reframed as an attempt to pull the family together in a crisis. Minuchin may also use manipulative intervention if he believes it will alter rigid, unworkable family structures. He may encourage conflicts and actively join alliances or coalitions against other family members to try to induce the family to interact in healthier ways (Minuchin, Lee, & Simon, 2006). Therapy is completed when both the therapist and the family think that a new and more effective structure exists, which the family can use in coping with future transactions and stress.

Strategic Therapy

Strategic therapy is defined as "a family therapy in which the therapist devises and initiates strategies for solving the family's presenting problem." The therapist gives family members directives or orders to carry out certain strategic tasks that the therapist believes will eliminate the presenting problem. Strategic therapy is best represented in the work of Jay Haley (1987), a pioneer in family therapy. Haley describes his approach as problem-solving therapy; the goal is to solve the family's presenting problem by using specific techniques and skills within the family structure.

Haley believes that changes in families come not through family members gaining their own insights, but from directives given by the therapist. Symptoms are the problem to be treated; current interactions of the family are paramount. No attention is given to historical antecedents in nuclear families or families of origin or to multigenerational patterns. Haley accepts that family symptoms are attempts at survival by family members (Atwood, 1992a). He also agrees with most other family systems theorists that symptoms arise and are maintained because a family cannot deal with changes, such as death, marriage, divorce, illness, or loss of a job. Families cannot solve problems because they are locked into repetitive and nonproductive communication patterns.

The problems, or symptoms, of one family member, the identified patient, may lead the family to seek help. In confronting the problem behavior, however, Haley focuses on power struggles in the family, assuming that maneuvering for power is inherent in families. He defines *power* as a struggle to determine who is in charge of the relationship. All forms of symptoms—depression, drinking, agoraphobia, work addiction—influence a person's behavior. Thus, the problem of the identified patient controls family social activities, as well as interfamily interactions.

Rules governing family functioning come under close scrutiny. In a healthy family, rules are clear. If parents become angry with each other, family survival is not threatened, and children do not become involved in their parents' arguments. In a dysfunctional family with ambiguous or unclear relationships, clear-cut rules about who is in power do not exist. Alliances cross generational lines, so triangulations may occur between a parent and a child that prevent resolution of parental conflict. Parents' fights may become violent; children may feel threatened and develop symptoms of anxiety and rebelliousness or depression.

Haley (1987) contends that the family and the therapist are in a power struggle, just as family members are. As such, some strategic family therapists believe in the importance of the therapist being active and intervening during the session. The therapist works to restructure the family system by reestablishing boundaries, changing hierarchies of power and family triangulations, and improving family communication. The therapist does this by using two forms of directives: straightforward and paradoxical. *Straightforward directives* are called *positive cooperative tasks* because they are based on what the therapist has learned about the family, with the expectation that the family members will carry out the tasks and profit from completing them. For example, the therapist tells a husband and wife that they each need more privacy and directs them to spend specific time by themselves. *Paradoxical directives* are called *negative cooperative tasks* and are used on families highly resistant to following the therapist's directives. "The directives are paradoxical because the therapist has told the family that he wants to help them change but at the same time he is asking them not to change" (Madanes, 1981, p. 26).

Three paradoxical interventions have been recommended for use in family therapy by Weeks and L'Abate (1982): (a) reframing the symptom, (b) escalating or inducing a crisis, and (c) redirecting the occurrence of the symptom. *Reframing* refers to relabeling the problem behavior in a positive way. For example, the therapist may describe a child who refuses to do his assigned household chores as someone who may be expressing an urge for independence, a desire that has not been sufficiently recognized. If the child's needs are recognized, then he will probably be willing to do the chores. *Escalating* refers to a strategy called *prescribing the symptom,* in which the client is told to increase the behavior that is presented as a problem. If a child is lying, the child is told to continue lying at every opportunity, to make up bigger and better lies, and to keep a chart indicating success. In *redirection,* the client is encouraged to continue the symptom, but under altered circumstances. If spouses are continually bickering, for example, they are directed to bicker only at a certain time of day, every day, and to continue bickering without stopping for, say, 2 hours. Clients find it impossible to carry out these directives and end up reducing or giving up the problem behavior.

Weeks and L'Abate (1982) believe that these approaches are best with very resistant families who have severe or chronic problems. They caution, however, against using these techniques in acute crisis situations or with dangerous persons—those who are suicidal, homicidal, sociopathic, or paranoid. For moderately resistive families with less severe or chronic problems, they suggest modifying the procedures and using them with care. For example, the therapist might tell the family what is intended to be accomplished with such a paradoxical intervention.

Social Learning Family Therapy

Social learning theory focuses on learning that occurs within a social context. People learn by observing others' behaviors, particularly through behaviors of family members.

One of the most prominent researchers in social learning family therapy was Gerald R. Patterson, who studied family influences on youth behavior. In his research on social learning and families, Patterson (1971) described two types of parent–child interactions that he observed most frequently: reciprocity and coercion. *Reciprocity* describes one person's behavior that is followed by a similar behavior from another person. A positive move elicits a positive response; a negative action is followed by a negative response. The other type of parent–child interaction, *coercion,* describes situations that involve either punishment or negative reinforcement. For example, a parent spanks a child who later hits a younger or weaker sibling. The aggressive behavior of the parent serves as a model for the child, and the child imitates it.

With the social learning approach, counselors meet with the family and make a behavioral assessment in which they identify the problem as precisely as they can, determining with the family the specific behavior that needs to be changed. They consider it essential to establish a therapeutic environment and a relationship in which the family will feel safe and comfortable while discussing family problems.

After counselors determine the problem and establish baseline data, they begin a program of intervention, or change, in which all positive or desirable behavior is reinforced. Goals are specific and are limited to changing precise behavior or eliminating presenting symptoms. The counselors use behavioral techniques—such as time-out, modeling, and reward systems—to extinguish undesirable behavior. Contracts between family members and the problem child may be made that detail expected decreases and increases in certain behaviors. After the initial interview, counselors help parents learn parenting skills without having the child present.

Behaviorist counselors are basically teachers; they teach skills to parents and train them in reinforcement techniques. Parents are taught to be trainers of child behavior (Goldenberg & Goldenberg, 2007); the counselor helps them make decisions about changing the behaviors of a problem child. Parents and child negotiate a contract specifying behaviors to be changed and rewards or punishments to be given when the child complies or fails to comply (Thomas, 1992). Behaviors to be targeted are specific—lying, stealing, or bullying siblings, for example. Parents monitor the child and give out rewards and punishments. The counselor does a follow-up after therapy is completed.

Cognitive–Behavioral Family Therapy

As discussed in chapter 6, cognitive–behavioral theorists like Beck (1976), Ellis (2000), and Meichenbaum (1985) expanded behavioral counseling approaches to include the influences that cognitive processes—thoughts, beliefs, and attitudes—have on client behavior. These ideas have since been applied to family counseling.

In his theory of family therapy, Ellis (2000) uses principles and techniques similar to those of his individual rational emotive behavior therapy (REBT). Ellis is active, persuasive, and directive; he emphasizes correcting illogical or irrational thoughts. Thus, he assesses family members' illogical ways of relating to one another and explores destructive or irrational inner talk that family members direct toward themselves or others. Without becoming over- or underinvolved, he teaches them how to relate reasonably, logically, and constructively. He assigns homework when necessary.

Alexander and Parsons (1982) developed a cognitive–behavioral family system called *functional family therapy (FFT)*. In this approach, therapists help family members understand and change thought processes and emotional states that are causing problems in the family system (Fenell & Weinhold, 2003).

Cognitive–behavioral therapists follow three stages in the family counseling process: (a) assessing, (b) facilitating change in the family, and (c) maintaining changes. During the assessment period, therapists observe how each family member perceives the problem and how everyone relates to one another. To facilitate change, therapists interpret and clarify family dynamics, reduce blaming, and encourage listening to one another. To maintain changes, families are taught communication skills, ways of monitoring their behaviors, and methods of positive interactions (Alexander & Parsons, 1982; Fenell & Weinhold, 2003).

THE FAMILY LIFE CYCLE

Human development theorists assume that individuals go through stages of development throughout their life spans. At each stage, individuals usually experience disequilibrium or conflict. In family counseling, these stages are called the *family life cycle* (Carter & McGoldrick, 1999; L'Abate, Ganahl, & Hansen, 1986; Thomas, 1992). Families go through stages or transitions, as do individuals; and individual, family, or environmental changes occur periodically that require adjustment or realignment among family members. This realignment often involves changes in attitudes and behaviors, which, in turn, increase family stress and upset family equilibrium.

Carter and McGoldrick (1999) believe that, at each developmental stage in the family life cycle, each family member and the family as a whole experience changes in status that involve emotional and behavioral consequences. For example, the first stage occurs when the newly married couple must learn to commit to a new relationship together, as well as to the extended families of both partners. In the next stage, when children come along, the married couple must learn to make space for their children and assume joint responsibility for child rearing and for housekeeping tasks. When children become adolescents, the couple must adjust to the next stage—one that requires increased flexibility in family boundaries to give adolescents more independence. When adult children leave home, the family must adjust yet again. In later years, grandchildren enter the family, involving new relationships between the older adults and their children and grandchildren. Everyone must learn to adjust to each other's new lifestyles, losses, illnesses, and social roles.

This model readily fits the family systems concept of the family as a social unit; it also fits the multigenerational concepts of psychoanalytic family therapists. It is also suitable for cognitive–behaviorist family counselors, who can use the model to assess target tasks for their clients.

FAMILY COUNSELING AND THERAPY IN PRACTICE

Family counseling relationships follow predictable stages. Although family specialists may not agree on what specifically should occur in each stage, they describe the following similar processes:

Stage I: Initial stage—developing a relationship and assessing the family problem
Stage II: Middle stage—developing emotional awareness and acceptance of dysfunctional family patterns
Stage III: Last stage—learning how to change the family system
Stage IV: Termination—separating from therapy

Initial Stage: Developing a Relationship and Assessing the Family Problem

Family counseling or therapy usually begins with one family member making the initial contact by telephone. The person may be calling about a family member, the identified patient, whose ongoing misbehavior is disrupting the family—an unruly or despondent adolescent, a hyperactive child, an alcoholic spouse. Or a person may call on her or his own behalf because of problems with her or his family. These are common examples of the problems presented: "My husband is depressed, and I am worried about him"; "I feel depressed, and my family is upset about my condition"; "My husband is threatening to divorce me"; "The children are completely out of hand, and my wife and I disagree on how to discipline them."

Family counselors generally try to have all family members who live in the home come together at the initial interview. Later, decisions can be made about whether to see only certain family members, whether to involve children, or whether to have separate sessions at times for some family members. At this stage, counselors explain the purpose and process of therapy, the counselor's role, and the family members' responsibilities in the session. A counselor might say,

> You are all here because you believe your family is not working together well, and you want to change that. My role is to help you. First, I must learn more about you as a family, hear some history, and find out how you work together. I also want to learn what each of you sees as the major problems in your family. Then we can discuss what changes you'd like to make and work together to make those changes.

In the beginning sessions, family counselors or therapists establish rapport, confidence, and trust. They also assess family dynamics or interactions and clarify the central problem. The development of rapport is complex because counselors must build trust relationships between themselves and each member of the family while at the same time helping family members trust one another. As in individual counseling, a warm, empathic, and genuine relationship is essential in family counseling. Counselors must treat each family member as important, insisting that members speak for themselves and listen to one another respectfully. For this reason, counselors ask family members to tell, individually, what they think is the major problem and what they expect of the family.

Counselors also observe family dynamics, conflicts, and the quality of relationships. They determine who is allied with whom, what the power structure is, what triangles are present, and what boundaries and rules implicitly function in the family. How enmeshed or disengaged are family members? Faulty communication patterns arising from and contributing to relationship problems are of particular interest. In their assessment, counselors must also look for positive resources and strengths in the family (Satir, 1982).

In addition to assessing family dynamics, counselors may explore family history and the reactions of family members to significant earlier family events. During this time, it is also important to assess the family's interaction with the extended family, including grandparents and other relatives.

As the family explores itself, counselors begin to reframe the problem as a total family problem and not just the problem of the identified patient. Resistance to this reevaluation must be met with firmness, patience, and tact. Counselors should point out faulty interactions in current relationships and help the family shift to more constructive patterns.

Once the problem has been refocused successfully, counselors help the family set goals for change, clarify the commitment of each family member, and determine whether family members will be seen together or whether separate sessions for individual members are necessary.

Middle Stage: Developing Emotional Awareness and Acceptance of Dysfunctional Family Patterns

In the middle stage, the counselor or therapist helps family members explore and analyze their dynamics to get an understanding of what is causing the problem. The counselor is usually more confrontational, and family members may experience and acknowledge hurt, pain, shame, frustration, and loss. Anxiety increases with emotionally charged self-disclosures, and resistance arises in this middle stage.

In family counseling, as in individual counseling, resistance is generally seen as a positive sign, one that either indicates the family is closer to confronting its problems or alerts counselors that they are moving too quickly. Fear of change contributes to this resistance. Family members may resist counseling or therapy by remaining silent or by discussing only superficial matters. They may also question the counselor's ability to understand the problem, may come late to sessions, or may complain about the counseling fees. Other types of resistance common at this stage occur when one family member refuses to speak to another or when one family member interrupts another who is beginning to reveal something meaningful. At times, the whole family might resist by withholding a family secret pertinent to the problem or by denying that the identified patient is improving. Transference may also arise as family members project unresolved emotions onto the counselor. The counselor can help family members work through resistance and transference by being patient with them and by being sensitive to and empathic with the anxiety or fear generated by disclosures.

Therapists with a psychodynamic orientation, like Framo (1982) and Bowen (1978), help parents see that some of their problems stem from unresolved conflicts in their families of origin. Role-playing or psychodrama may be used; in psychodrama, a parent may reenact an experience when, as a child, she was ridiculed by her parents. Expression of grief is encouraged in this stage of therapy when families have unresolved feelings about losses, such as the death of a loved one, divorce, failure in school, loss of a job, or realization of a childhood loss (Brock & Barnard, 1999).

In this middle stage, the family begins to accept that relationships can change and that destructive alliances can be broken without undue loss of security. These acknowledgments lead to changes in family structure: Roles are less rigid, communication becomes more direct and constructive, and feedback to one another about new behaviors within the family is more authentic.

Last Stage: Learning How to Change the Family System

As family members understand and accept how they each have contributed to the origin and perpetuation of problems, they begin to see alternative ways of behaving and communicating. Needing less prompting from the therapist, they begin to intervene, to confront one another constructively, and to give one another feedback on more effective ways of interacting.

Counselors encourage family members to generalize these changes to interactions at home and may assign homework to practice the new behaviors. For example, a mother who has learned to declare in a session her need for boundaries and her own space may be directed to take time off and go on a weekend retreat. Satir (1982) developed communication exercises to help families compare ineffective and effective ways of communicating. For example, two members may sit back to back and try, without success, to communicate authentically and then, in gradual stages, move to looking into each other's eyes and touching hands while communicating fully.

At this point, counselors can help the family become aware of resources in the community that can support their efforts to continue new patterns of behavior. For example, a single parent can be encouraged to join a group working on parenting skills. Counselors can also help the family look ahead to upcoming transitions and changes that are likely to occur. They can then help family members consider how to make use of their new attitudes and skills to cope with the anticipated changes.

Termination: Separating from Therapy

Termination in family counseling is considered less difficult than in individual counseling. In successful family counseling, the family has learned to work as a unit to solve its own problems and to give members support. In addition, family members have practiced working on communication skills and relationship issues during the sessions. Thus, feeling less dependent on the counselor, they have fewer problems with termination than do individual clients.

In successful treatment, family members show signs that they are ready to terminate when they begin to solve family conflicts at home and when presenting complaints or symptoms are no longer present. Counselor and family members will notice more independent activities, more constructive conflict, and better ways of resolving problems among family members.

Even so, the counselor needs to prepare the family for separation by allowing the last two sessions for the process of termination. A review of what has happened during counseling is helpful. The counselor can also arrange for a follow-up session with the family and convey that the members can return at any time if they feel the need for additional help.

MARRIAGE AND COUPLES COUNSELING THEORIES

Family counseling and marriage or couples counseling overlap considerably, and most practitioners who identify themselves primarily as family counselors thus include marriage and couples counseling with family therapy. Some of them indicate that they will work with the marriage problem first if they think the marital discord is so severe that it would be impossible to work with the whole family. Some counselors also work with spouses first if they think the identified patient's problems are primarily a result of marital discord.

Those who specialize only in marriage and couples counseling, however, make certain distinctions between their type of counseling and family counseling. Many couples seeking help do not have children, are undecided about whether to have them, or have decided to remain childless. Other couples have older children who are not living at home and are not available for family counseling even if it seems advisable. These couples seek help because they are not happy with their relationship, not because they are having trouble with problem children. These couples may be having conflicts over gender roles, finances, infidelity, religious values, sexual disharmony, in-laws, retirement, alcoholism, careers, or other problems not related to children. Some marriage and couples counselors also work with premarital couples, cohabiting unmarried couples, and/or lesbian and gay couples. Some specialize in sex therapy.

Theories designed especially for marital and couples counseling had, for many years, come from the social learning school, which emphasized learning skills and educational information. More recently, other theoretical marital counseling models have been developed and now include family therapy approaches such as structural therapy (Minuchin), strategic therapy (Haley), and transgenerational therapy (Bowen).

Terence Real (2002) became involved in marital counseling after his book on male depression titled *I Don't Want to Talk About It* (1997) was published. The book triggered numerous phone calls from women who were at the end of their rope, "having already dragged their partners to therapy, veterans of at least one, most often several, failed courses of couples work" (Real, 2002, p. 36). Also impressed by his book was Carol Gilligan (1982; Wylie, 2002), who joined forces with him. Together, they developed a marital therapy model called *relational recovery therapy (RRT),* in which couples attend a 3-day intensive workshop (Real, 2002; Wylie, 2002). Couples attending the workshop understand that they will decide after the workshop to either stay with the marriage or divorce.

According to Real (2002), empowered women have been demanding emotional intimacy in marriage, but men are not prepared to change. "We don't raise . . . boys and men to be intimate partners, but to be strong, competitive performers" (p. 38). Because conventional marriage therapy doesn't work in such cases, Real breaks a major rule during the workshop: He takes sides. He sides with the woman's concerns and focuses first on the man's inadequacies and fears. He confronts him with the truth: that he is avoiding intimacy and connectedness by becoming grandiose, withdrawn, or abusive. Through these confrontations, Real helps men take responsibility for their actions, explore and work through shame, express remorse and guilt, and learn steps to maintain intimacy. He then helps women avoid behaviors that reinforce men's tendencies to withdraw while cultivating those that will encourage men to embrace intimacy.

Real (2002) claims that couples counseling, as practiced in traditional psychotherapy, is ineffective with most couples. Women are aware of difficulties in the marriage and seek help, whereas most men claim to be happy with their marriages and thus go to therapy only because wives demand it. Yet therapists are traditionally trained to assume that both partners are motivated to go to counseling and that both desire change. "Pretending that both partners approach therapy equally disturbed is simply a fairy tale. Why do we therapists participate in it? Because, like women, we've been taught to protect men from the truth about themselves" (p. 39). He goes on to say that "the field of psychotherapy has allowed itself to be intimidated. . . . Men's entitlement to withdrawal or attack when confronted" is commonly expected and accepted (p. 39). Therapists reinforce the male's typical reactions to conflict at home—avoid, deny, or flee. The subtext is that men, if pushed too hard, will explode, fall apart, or bolt, so it's best to soothe them, win them over, and *then* tell them the difficult truth. (p. 39)

CHANGING FAMILY AND MARRIAGE PATTERNS

Counselors and therapists need to be aware that family counseling theories and practices are generally based on the traditional American (i.e., White, middle-class) nuclear family. Such a model is no longer typical for most American families. In the traditional, idealized model, a married couple rears its own biologically related children, the father acts as head of the household and provider, and the mother is the family's homemaker and nurturer. Today, the majority of children grow up in families where both parents work outside the home; one third of American children are reared by single parents, usually women; and many families are blended together from remarriages.

Dual-Career Families

In 2006, nearly 60% of women were working or looking for work (U.S. Department of Labor, 2006). As a result, women are spending less time with their children, and men are expected to spend more time with them (Atwood, 1992c). In addition to job stress for both parents, stress occurs at home. Although both men and women experience stress in dual-career families, women's stress is greater because of expectations that women should continue to handle more domestic responsibilities than men (Basow, 1992). Conflicts in managing the dual role of homemaker and out-of-home worker have made it especially difficult for women to meet their own needs.

With the increase in dual-career families, more than 7 million schoolchildren are regularly left unsupervised while their parents are at work or away for other reasons (U.S. Department of Commerce, 2000). The professional literature indicates that those children whose parents work outside the home do not, as a rule, become emotionally disturbed as long as they have had adequate day care and parents who are caring and responsive when they and their children are together (Shaffer & Kipp, 2006).

Family counselors must be alert to parents' changing gender roles and to the stresses resulting from a lack of adequate and affordable child care. They must also be aware that family conflicts are exacerbated because the marketplace and communities have not made allowances for dual-career families.

Single-Parent Families

Single parents head about just under one third of all families (U.S. Department of Commerce, 2000). Divorce is by far the leading reason for single-parent families (70%), followed by death of a spouse (14%) and never-married women (10%) (Atwood, 1992c). Of all single-parent families, 90% are headed by women. Major sources of stress for single mothers include low income, societal disapproval, and lack of another parent to help with domestic chores, discipline, and child welfare in general (Basow, 1992). Single parents try to assume the roles of both parents, financial worries are usually worse, children may be expected to assume more responsibilities, and child care services are increasingly necessary (Baruth & Burggraf, 1991).

Atwood (1992c) proposes using a cognitive–behavioral family systems approach to help single parents resolve problems with their children. In this approach, the counselor teaches behavior management skills to single parents whereby children are rewarded for completing tasks and taking care of some of their own needs. Single parents are also helped to schedule time in ways that provide nurturing to their children while still maintaining appropriate roles and boundaries. "Part of the family counselor role is to teach the family good child-rearing practices and to help them learn age-appropriate behaviors" (Atwood, 1992c, p. 204).

Attention is given as well to helping single parents work through feelings of abandonment, develop social support groups, and, when possible, work toward and maintain civil and respectful contact with former spouses for the benefit of the child or children.

Stepfamilies

Stepfamilies are formed when two previously married individuals with children marry each other. Between 40% and 50% of recent marriages will end in divorce, with 80% of men and 75% of women remarrying within a few years. These figures show that many families will be reconstituted into ones in which multiple parents, stepparents, grandparents, and stepsiblings interact (Shaffer & Kipp, 2006). Because mothers usually gain custody of their children, the stepfamily in which the children live with their mother and her second husband is most common.

Betty Carter (1988), a well-known family therapist, notes the family patterns that arise from complex relationships and roles in remarried families. Role conflicts often occur between the realigned members: Confusion arises over a stepparent's role as disciplinarian, for instance, or remarried families may exclude a biological parent or children not living in the new household. In her counseling model for remarried families, Carter (1988) recommends helping the family develop a flexible system in which it forms permeable boundaries among all family members, including those who do not live together.

CHILD ABUSE AND NEGLECT

The four major types of child abuse are (a) physical abuse, (b) psychological maltreatment (emotional abuse), (c) sexual abuse, and (d) neglect. In 2005, approximately 3.3 million cases of child abuse and neglect were reported to child protective services

(U.S. Department of Health and Human Services, 2005). Approximately 62% involved neglect, 16% physical abuse, 9% sexual abuse, and 7% psychological maltreatment. Children in the age group from birth to 3 years had the highest victimization rates.

In all 50 states, family counselors, mental health workers, teachers, principals, medical professionals, and any other professional person working with children must report evidence of child abuse to child protection agencies. If clients reveal that child abuse is happening to them or to others, the counselor has a legal responsibility to inform child protection services, which can take steps to prevent further abuse.

The Characteristics and Effects of Abuse

The majority of abused children are under 3 years of age. Both male and female parents may abuse children physically, emotionally, and through neglect. Sexual abuse occurs more frequently in father–daughter or stepfather–stepdaughter relationships than in any other family relationship.

Families in which abuse take place are often isolated and have poor relationships with extended family and others in the community (Crosson-Tower, 2005). Relationships within the family may be strained, negative, or in conflict. Abusers in a family are often substance abusers as well; in fact, nearly half of all cases of child abuse and neglect are associated with parental alcohol or drug abuse.

Families in which abuse occurs usually have a multitude of stressors: financial problems, unemployment, illness, family breakups (Crosson-Tower, 2005). In addition, boundaries are unclear or unspecified, and communication is woefully inadequate, with secrecy predominating.

If counseling interventions for abused children and their families are not provided, the children can develop serious emotional disorders that carry into adulthood. These disorders include depression and anxiety, eating disorders, learning disorders, multiple personalities, and substance abuse (Shaffer & Kipp, 2006). Abused children tend to be either aggressive or overly withdrawn with other children, often resulting in their being rejected by their peers. Posttraumatic stress disorder, including nightmares and flashbacks, may develop and continue into adulthood. The risk increases that abused children, when they grow up, will abuse their children. Emotionally abused children also maintain a low self-image and gravitate to those who confirm their feelings of worthlessness.

Counseling Families in Which Abuse Has Occurred

With families in which parents have been shown to be abusive, treatment often focuses initially on individual family members. Physically abusive or neglectful parents are frequently referred to anger management or parenting classes in addition to individual counseling. Parents who sexually abuse their child(ren) are viewed as criminal offenders and may be convicted of a sex crime and sentenced to prison and/or probation. Treatment for sex offenders is specialized and usually occurs in outpatient programs after the offender is released from prison.

Abused children who are moved from the home should receive counseling to help process the traumatic experiences and work through the shame, guilt, anger, or grief.

Shaffer and Kipp (2006) point out that many abused or neglected children develop a great deal of resiliency, especially if a supportive, secure relationship is established with a nonabusive parent, grandparent, or other adult in the family. When working with abused children, counselors should look for and cultivate the children's positive strengths.

Rencken's (2000) comments regarding family dynamics and intervention strategies for sexually abused children, abusers, and their families can be generalized to victims of all kinds of abuse. He describes three patterns of boundary breakdowns in families in which sexual abuse occurs. The first is the possessive father who considers his spouse and children to be possessions and does not differentiate among them. He views his daughter in the same way that he views a wife. Second is the immature, irresponsible father who becomes like one of the children. Third is the child who is pushed into becoming a pseudoadult; the child is described as "parentified" (Rencken, 2000, p. 25) when she assumes a substitute mother role, for example, which the mother has abdicated. In treating families in which abuse occurs, Rencken works with three dyads in the following order: mother–child, husband–wife, and father–child. He then works to shift the dyad into a triad of child–mother–father. Finally, he helps clients view their family unit as a whole.

SUMMARY

Marriage and family counseling has flourished in the counseling field since its inception in the 1940s. Marriage and family counselors focus on the family as a whole, rather than on an individually identified patient. Marriage and family counselors work with married or unmarried couples with or without children, lesbian or gay couples, and those wanting premarital counseling.

Because the family is a social unit, when one family member develops problems, the symptoms represent dysfunctions among all family members. Dysfunctional families are enmeshed with or disengaged from one another, cannot communicate directly and authentically, and form alliances among themselves when conflicts arise. Counselors help family members learn to communicate directly and respect one another's boundaries and privacy.

Changing family patterns have brought about new considerations for marriage and family counselors. The traditional family pattern, with father as breadwinner and mother as caregiver of their biologically related children, is no longer predominant. In the majority of homes now, both parents work, and about one third of American families are led by a single parent (mostly women). Many are remarried families with multiple parents, stepparents, and stepsiblings.

Child abuse includes neglect and physical, emotional, and sexual abuse. Family counselors tend to treat the abused child first and then the member of the family who committed the abuse separately before they treat the family together as a unit. Family sessions include issues about boundaries, assuming responsibility for changing behavior, developing support systems, and working to reunify the family.

PROJECTS AND ACTIVITIES

1. Interview some counselors who specialize in family counseling. Compare their theoretical backgrounds and the techniques each prefers to use.
2. Practice the technique called sculpting, as used by Virginia Satir. Using other classmates to enact the roles of family members, pose the family to demonstrate its pattern of relating (see Figure 11.1).
3. Interview counselors in nearby school districts. Find out what family services are offered to parents and students. If none exist, ask how families with problems receive help.
4. Role-play a telephone conversation in which a parent calls to get counseling for an adolescent daughter with "problems." During the conversation, it becomes obvious to you that the whole family needs counseling. How would you make this clear to the parent?

CHAPTER 12

Career Counseling

Career counseling is the oldest identified counseling service, with its roots dating back to the early 1900s and Frank Parsons. Career counseling involves helping individuals or groups explore career options, make career plans, prepare for appropriate training, and resolve career-related problems. Common client concerns include career indecision and uncertainty, dissatisfaction on the job, unsatisfactory integration of life roles, and conflicts with others about career choice or development. Career counselors provide a wide array of services, including career counseling with individuals and groups, consultations, job placement, testing, and resume development, as well as the development of other employment skills, retirement planning, program evaluation, and work adjustment counseling.

After studying this chapter, you will

- Have knowledge of the historical perspective of career counseling.
- Be able to identify the major theoretical approaches to career counseling.
- Have knowledge of assessment instruments and occupational information useful for career counseling and career exploration.

HISTORICAL PERSPECTIVE

Historically, career counseling has been called by a number of different names, including *vocational guidance, occupational counseling,* and *vocational counseling.* By whatever name, career counseling was influential in the development of the counseling profession and is considered the oldest type of counseling service. counseling was originally initiated in colleges and schools to help students with vocational and career concerns (see chapter 2). Early vocational counseling in the 1930s and 1940s was primarily influenced by the prevailing emphasis on measuring individual differences. The basic assumption underlying this was that individuals have unique inherent abilities, interests, and personality traits that can be assessed through standardized tests and matched with certain types of occupations. In 1942, Donald Super introduced the idea that persons develop vocationally throughout life, an amplification of Charlotte Buehler's theory of human development. Then Carl Rogers introduced a client-centered approach with an emphasis on personal growth.

Leading vocational counseling professionals at the time—Super (1951, 1955), Ginzberg and his associates (Ginzberg, Ginsburg, Axelrad, & Herma, 1951), Holland (1959), and Roe (1957)—believed that vocational counseling should be integrated with personal and interpersonal counseling. Vocational choice and development, they emphasized, are influenced by and related to personality development. Super (1955), in particular, proposed a theory that integrated vocational development with self-development and related personality factors to vocational concerns. Nugent's personal experiences supported this approach.

> As a counselor in college and high school counseling centers, a supervisor of counseling interns, and a private practitioner, I, and those with whom I worked, found this integrated approach worked well. We were able to distinguish when a client's concerns were specific to career exploration and when the client's personal conflicts or emotional disequilibrium might be interfering with career exploration. This practice was compatible with the counseling services in the 1950s and 1960s, which existed almost exclusively in school and college settings and encompassed the normal population with its typical conflicts and concerns related to school and thus to vocational issues.

Even so, during the 1970s many college counselors began to focus only on a client's personal growth issues and tended to ignore the client's vocational or career concerns. Humanistic and behavioral theories of psychology prevailed, which did not address problems related to career development. Moreover, counseling expanded to address such issues as family and substance abuse, in which career concerns were generally not the issue. Consequently, at many colleges and universities, placement centers developed into career centers to assist students who needed help in making career choices. Today, the majority of career counseling at universities is conducted in a separate career development or placement office (Gallagher, 2006).

This primary emphasis on a client's personal and interpersonal concerns was solidified in the late 1970s when the American Mental Health Counselors Association was formed and the master's degree in counseling emerged as a terminal degree. Most counselors who work in community agencies or private practice settings now tend to focus on clients' personal and interpersonal concerns. In addition, managed care generally does not allow insurance coverage for career counseling.

THE CURRENT SCENE

The American Counseling Association has consistently specified that the counseling profession take a holistic approach and consider career concerns as part of the counseling process. Many professionals view general counseling and career counseling as inseparable, rather than independent, processes (Betz & Corning, 1993; Krumboltz, 1993). Many adults in career counseling cope with concerns related to uncertainty, ambiguity, self-efficacy, and personal, as well as occupational, issues. Thus, many researchers conclude that there are few things more personal than career choice and that the overlap between career and general concerns is substantial (Niles & Harris-Bowlsbey, 2005).

Super (1993) affirmed that career counseling and personal counseling are related, but proposed that the two entail distinct approaches, which can be treated as a continuum ranging from career counseling with its focus on situational concerns to personal counseling with its focus on inner self-exploration.

> There are in fact two fields: situational counseling, which has subspecialties that focus on differing types of situations (career, family, etc.), and personal counseling, in which the focus is on individuals whose problems are based primarily in their own approach to and coping with situations, not on factors in the situations they encounter. In accepting this dichotomy one should not actually treat it as a dichotomy, but as a continuum of which these are the extremes. (p. 135)

Career development practitioners in the 21st century seek to empower people as they make meaning of their life experiences and translate that meaning into appropriate occupational and other life role choices (Niles & Harris-Bowlsbey, 2005). Because translating experiences into career choices requires people to have a high level of self-awareness, career counseling involves an extensive set of skills to help clients resolve their career dilemmas. Career counseling involves much more than showing clients occupational information books or administering and interpreting tests to advise clients on what occupations they should choose. Indeed, the skills and techniques required for providing career assistance encompass and extend beyond those required in more general counseling.

Specialized Training in Career Counseling

Presently, career counseling in the United States is provided by many persons in many settings (Herr, 2003). School counselors, college counselors, academic advisers, employment counselors, rehabilitation counselors, mental health counselors, psychologists, and other helping professionals all provide career counseling, although with different purposes and intensity. Career counselors have graduate degrees in counseling with a specialization in career counseling (including career development, assessment, and planning). These professionals are trained to be alert to signs that a client's vocational concerns might relate to personal or interpersonal conflicts; they are prepared to help the client explore personal concerns as she or he works toward career decisions or, in more serious cases, to refer the client for personal counseling.

Specific credentials in career counseling are offered through the National Career Development Association (NCDA), a division of the ACA. These include the Master Career Counselor and the Master Career Development Professional. The *Master Career Counselor (MCC)* is an NCDA member who holds a master's degree in counseling or a related field and has been active as an NCDA member for a minimum of 2 years. In addition, an MCC has at least 3 years of post-master's experience in career counseling and is a national certified counselor (NCC) who either has a state license in professional counseling or is a licensed psychologist. MCCs must also have successfully completed course work in specific educational areas and a supervised career counseling practicum or 2 years of supervised career counseling experience under a certified supervisor or licensed counseling professional. The *Master Career Development Professional (MCDP)* is an NCDA member who holds a master's degree or higher in counseling or a related field and also has been active as an NCDA member for a minimum of 2 years. The MCDP has at least 3 years of post-master's career development experience in training, teaching, program development, or materials development.

THEORETICAL APPROACHES TO CAREER COUNSELING

Career counseling theories are based on the idea that personal development influences one's choice of and satisfaction in a career.

Developmental Theories

The two most widely known developmental theories are those associated with Donald Super and Eli Ginzberg. As stated earlier, Super (1942) was one of the first to relate personality factors and developmental stages to career development. In 1951, using Buehler's concept of developmental life stages, he described vocational adjustment as the implementation of a person's self-concept. He then outlined (1953) a series of developmental stages throughout life that relate to occupational development. Super (1961) continued to develop his vocational theory, extending it to include *vocational maturity*. Ultimately, through choices that are considered mature at each life stage, adults find and establish themselves in appropriate vocations. In 1980, Super expanded his theory further, in what he called a life-span, life-space approach. He proposed that people play numerous roles throughout their life spans that help shape their careers in a broad sense. And he described how various roles interrelate to contribute to career development over the life span.

Ginzberg et al. (1951) published one of the earliest theories of vocational choice based on developmental stages. They described the process of career choice as following three stages: (a) the *fantasy period* in early childhood, composed of unrealistic ideas; (b) the *tentative period,* when children begin to sort out activities they like and can do well; and (c) the *realistic period,* when individuals explore realistically and make a specific choice. In 1972, Ginzberg revised his ideas and concluded that vocational choice is lifelong and always open to change.

Trait-and-Factor Approach

The origin of trait-and-factor theory can be traced back to Frank Parsons (1909). It stresses that the traits of clients should first be identified and then matched with factors inherent in various occupations. In 1959, John Holland extended the trait-and-factor model and developed Holland's typology (Holland, 1997). Published in 1973 and revised in 1985 and 1997, Holland's typology is considered the most widely used and most influential theory in career counseling practice today (Brown, 2002). His approach assumes that we can classify

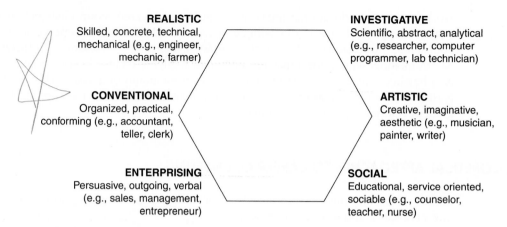

FIGURE 12.1

Holland's Six Categories of Personality and Occupation

Note. From *Making vocational choices: A theory of careers* (3rd ed.), by J. L. Holland, 1973, Englewood Cliffs, NJ: Prentice Hall. Copyright 1973, 1985, 1992, 1997 by Prentice Hall. Reprinted with permission.

individuals into the following six personality types: realistic, investigative, artistic, social, enterprising, and conventional (Holland, 1997). Further, he believes that individuals in each personality type will select jobs or careers that fit their interests, thus forming six matching work environments composed of members who enjoy similar activities and respond to tasks and people in similar ways. Vocational success, satisfaction, and stability, he assumes, depend on how well the individual's personality, as described by interest inventories, matches the work environments selected by the individual.

Figure 12.1 shows Holland's categories of personality and occupation. From the initial letters of the six personality types, Holland coined the acronym RIASEC to portray the total interest pattern. Because few people are only one type, Holland says, he combines the three most dominant types that a person shows on an interest inventory and classifies accordingly. For example, IAE would show investigative interests most strongly, followed by artistic and enterprising. He also classifies working environments by using the same three-letter combinations, which he has listed in a pamphlet called the "Occupations Finder." Holland has conducted extensive longitudinal studies, and results show that personal types and occupational environments do differentiate people. He has used this research to revise his theory over the years.

Postmodern Approaches

Recently, attention has been given to career development theories and interventions that depart from the traditional approaches to career development (Niles & Harris-Bowlsbey, 2005). Referred to as postmodern, these approaches emphasize the importance of understanding the plurality of perspectives, contextual impacts, social constructions of reality, and the meaning individuals give to their experiences. Proponents of postmodern career interventions focus on exploring the meaning clients place on their careers, rather than simply identifying specific traits of individuals and then placing those individuals in corresponding career categories. Peavy (1997) calls for revisions in the practice of career counseling to reflect the more relevant and postmodern philosophy; specifically, career counseling should acknowledge the multiplicity of realities and contextual influences involved in career development.

Constructivists theorize that people form constructs to make meaning and order out of their lives on an ongoing basis throughout life. Applying this theory to career counseling, counselors help clients identify and evaluate the constructions and meanings in their career decisions; then they can assist clients in reconstructing those meanings (Peavy, 1993). From the constructivist perspective, career counseling outcomes are considered in terms of ability to change an individual's outlook or perspective on some aspect of life (Niles & Harris-Bowlsbey, 2005). Career development interventions are framed as experiments conducted both in session and out of session that help clients think, feel, and act more productively in relation to their career concerns. Interventions/experiments can be conducted by using the client's imagination (e.g., guided imagery), or by engaging the client in self-evaluation, simulation (e.g., role-playing), and real-world experiences (e.g., job shadowing, job interviewing).

The narrative approach to career counseling emphasizes clients' understanding of their lives by having them form stories and articulate the main character to be lived out in a specific career plot (Cochran, 1997). Stories can help individuals make meaning out of their life experiences by integrating the beginning, middle, and end of the story into a whole. However, stories are never complete, so it is in exploring what is missing in or not told by the story that alternative ways of thinking and acting often appear (Peavy, 1993). In career counseling, stories of self and career can be used by the counselor and client to bring together the client's present knowledge and to help guide forward movement into anticipated futures.

Contextual approaches to career counseling identify ways in which contextual factors (e.g., family, culture, environment) can be incorporated into counseling. A fundamental assumption of the contextual model is that change in one context has the potential to stimulate changes in all other contexts of one's life. Thus, individuals' lives and their career development are intertwined. Using a contextual approach, career counselors would help clients explore how other factors in their lives affect their career development.

CAREER COUNSELING PROCESS

Although differences exist between general counseling and career counseling, counselors generally function similarly in both approaches. As with counseling in general, career counseling requires that the counselor establish a therapeutic relationship with clients and be able to respond meaningfully to a client's expressed feelings, behaviors, and attitudes. Counselors must also help the client make use of new insights and understandings to develop more constructive attitudes and behaviors that he or she can use to make decisions and implement them.

Yost and Corbishley (1997) developed a career counseling process in which they emphasize a procedure similar to the individual counseling process described in chapter 8.

First, counselor and client develop rapport, assess client needs, and establish goals. Next, the counselor works to promote client self-understanding through interviews and aptitude and interest inventories. The counselor then helps the client develop appropriate career alternatives, making use of occupational information such as the *Occupational Outlook Handbook (OOH),* which is described later. From these possibilities, the counselor helps the client choose a career. Throughout the sessions, the counselor helps the client work through obstacles that hinder making choices—such as too few alternatives, not enough information, inappropriate options, or interference from family. Once a choice is made, the counselor helps the client develop job search skills, write résumés, and prepare for job interviews.

Types of Problems

Exploration of Careers

When clients seek counseling help in exploring careers in schools, colleges, universities, and communities, their primary goals are to make appropriate occupational choices and to look into related training programs. In high schools, clients are in their formative stages of career exploration; they are exploring types of careers and trying to determine whether to find a job or seek further training. In universities, clients seek assistance in choosing majors or in making plans for life after graduation. In community settings, clients seek help in exploring the possibility of switching to new jobs, finding job opportunities that fit their interests and training, or seeking further schooling or training.

When a client requests help in exploring career choices, the counselor uses a goal-oriented approach. Together, they review occupational history and experience, consider the use of occupational testing, and explore data about occupations or training possibilities as part of client and environmental exploration. As stated earlier, few counselors rely solely on tests and inventories to predict appropriate choices in occupations. Most professional career counselors take into consideration social, cultural, and developmental factors when helping persons make career choices.

Conflicts about Careers

Others' expectations about one's career often contribute to vocational concerns. In high schools, colleges, and communities, parents, spouses, or peers may pressure clients to make choices that are incompatible with their own interests or abilities. In the community, job demands in two-career families or a husband's objection to his wife's desire to start a career may cause marital strife. In addition, conflicts with bosses, supervisors, colleagues, or family members may be interfering with progress or satisfaction on the job.

When clients express strong feelings of anxiety or uncertainty related to work, counselors tend to switch to a client-centered approach in which interviewing skills are used to help clients explore feelings and develop insights. An unemployed woman without work experience might ask for counseling because of marital conflict; her concerns about leaving the marriage may relate to her fears about her ability to support herself and her children. A young man in college might seek career counseling to focus on career goals; he would like to major in music, but is confused because his parents will not give him financial or emotional support unless he enters a computer training program. In family or marriage counseling, a wife's decision to start a career is causing dissension, or a husband's dissatisfaction with his job is contributing to conflicts with his wife and children. In all these cases, both career and personal concerns must be met. However, for clients in acute emotional distress, career exploration is delayed.

To integrate personal and career considerations, counselors must think holistically and skillfully merge a client's career-related concerns with the client's personal concerns. For example, rather than interpreting to the client a whole battery of occupational test results all at once, the counselor might discuss each test result whenever it fits into what the client is working through in the counseling session. Ultimately, a decision about, say, staying in a marriage may include career plans, whether or not a divorce occurs. Or a decision about following one's career interest may include changing one's attitudes toward parents.

Clients may also come to career counselors when they are experiencing their own conflict or confusion about their choice of career. A client with strong interests and abilities in two or more areas may become conflicted about which way to go, especially if one choice appears to exclude the other(s). Clients may also experience discrepancies between their interests and aptitudes and their career choices; they may have an interest in an occupation, but insufficient aptitude, or they may have a strong interest in one field and strong aptitude in a different field. In addition, clients' personal values may be at odds with their career choices. For example, an individual may have a strong leaning toward business, but also may believe strongly that the corporate world discriminates against women and minorities.

Life Transitions

Changes in lifestyle, a family move, or family changes may lead to a request for counseling. A husband who has been the sole provider may suddenly divorce or desert his wife or die. His wife, who has not worked outside the home for years, may need help finding employment to support herself and her family. Moreover, occupations become obsolete, and individuals must find new careers. Or those considering retirement want to explore new possibilities. A stay-at-home mom, after her children are in school, might decide to begin a new career outside the home. Perhaps an employed worker who is dissatisfied with his job wants to explore a more satisfying career. Or a client laid off from her job experiences uncertainty, apprehension, and bewilderment about how to find a new job.

When clients' personal concerns interfere too much with career issues, the counselor refers these clients to an outside agency for personal counseling or therapy before proceeding with career counseling. Brown (1995) points out that although it is possible for counselors to address career and personal problems at the same time, this becomes impossible when clients' emotional or psychological distress prevents them from engaging in career exploration.

SPECIAL TOOLS IN CAREER COUNSELING

Innumerable vocational interest and personality inventories and aptitude tests can help counselors and clients explore client characteristics related to careers. Occupational information resources are also valuable aids to help counselors and clients gather data about occupations, jobs, educational opportunities, or vocational training.

Inventories and Tests

Vocational Interest Inventories

Vocational interest inventories, in which clients compare themselves with groups of people in various occupations, are the most popular measures used in counseling. The Strong Interest Inventory (SII), the Kuder Career Search with Person Match (KCS), and Holland's Self-Directed Search (SDS) are examples of widely used interest inventories.

The *SII* is designed for use with adults, college students, and high school students. The client's profile of interests is compared with those of people employed successfully in a wide variety of occupations. These occupations are grouped according to Holland's personality types and environmental structures (RIASEC).

The *KCS* is an Internet-based assessment that is applicable to ages from middle school to adult. It reports on the test-taker's similarity with groups of employed people in six career clusters: Outdoor/Mechanical, Science/Technical, Arts/Communication, Social/Personal Services, Sales/Management, and Business Operations. In addition, it offers the job titles and first-person job descriptions of the people from the two clusters whose preference patterns are most similar to those of the test-taker.

Holland's *SDS* is a self-administered, self-scored, and self-interpreted instrument that can be completed in less than an hour. Clients then compare their personal responses with occupations on the basis of Holland's RIASEC categories using the "Occupations Finder."

Personality Inventories

Some counselors administer *personality inventories* if they sense that personal conflicts are interfering with a client's career resolution. A commonly used personality inventory in career counseling is the Myers–Briggs Type Indicator (MBTI). The MBTI, based on Jungian personality types (introvert–extravert, sensing–intuition, thinking–feeling, and judgment–perception), is of interest to counselors who relate lifestyles to career development.

Ability Tests

Two aptitude batteries are predominant in vocational counseling: the Differential Aptitude Test (DAT), given widely in high schools, and the General Aptitude Test Battery (GATB), administered most often by state employment offices to the general population.

The Armed Services Vocational Aptitude Battery (ASVAB) was developed for use in career counseling in the military. It is now used in high schools for exploration of both civilian and military careers (Zunker, 2006). When used in high schools, the battery should be administered and interpreted by school counselors and not by armed services recruiters, because recruiters tend to be biased toward selection of military careers.

Occupational Information

Information about occupations can be found on numerous Web sites on the Internet. The Web sites of government agencies—particularly the U.S. Department of Labor—and private companies are the major sources of this information. Educational institutions, professional associations, and commercial companies also provide online information about technical schools, colleges, and continuing education. In addition, national and state Web sites provide information on trends in the labor market, including projections of future job openings.

O*NET OnLine

*O*NET OnLine* (located at http://online.onetcenter.org) is the nation's primary source of occupational information. The O*NET database contains information on hundreds of occupations, with descriptions about the distinguishing characteristics of each occupation. The database is continually updated by surveying a broad range of workers from each occupation. See Figure 12.2 for a list of some of the tasks for educational, vocational, and school counselors from the O*NET summary report (U.S. Department of Labor National Center for O*NET Development, 2007).

FIGURE 12.2
O*NET Tasks for Educational, Vocational, and School Counselors

- Counsel students regarding educational issues such as course and program selection, class scheduling, school adjustment, truancy, study habits, and career planning.
- Counsel individuals to help them understand and overcome personal, social, or behavioral problems affecting their educational or vocational situations.
- Maintain accurate and complete student records as required by laws, district policies, and administrative regulations.
- Confer with parents or guardians, teachers, other counselors, and administrators to resolve students' behavioral, academic, and other problems.
- Provide crisis intervention to students when difficult situations occur at schools.
- Identify cases involving domestic abuse or other family problems affecting students' development.
- Meet with parents and guardians to discuss their children's progress, and to determine their priorities for their children and their resource needs.
- Prepare students for later educational experiences by encouraging them to explore learning opportunities and to persevere with challenging tasks.
- Encourage students and/or parents to seek additional assistance from mental health professionals when necessary.

*Note. O*NET OnLine Summary Report for: 21-1012.00—Educational, Vocational, and School Counselors,* U.S. Department of Labor National Center for O*NET Development, 2007. Retrieved August 1, 2007, from http://online.onetcenter.org/link/summary/21-1012.00

Occupational Outlook Handbook

The *Occupational Outlook Handbook (OOH)* (accessible from the U.S. Department of Labor, Bureau of Labor Statistics, Web site at http://www.bls.gov/oco/home.htm) is a classic reference about occupations from A to Z. This national source of career information is designed to provide assistance to individuals making decisions about their future work lives. Revised every 2 years, the *OOH* describes occupations in detail, including educational and experience prerequisites, places of employment, employment outlook, earnings, working conditions, chances for advancement, and lists of government resources that provide additional information.

Computer-Assisted Career Guidance Systems

The use of *computer-assisted career guidance systems (CACGS)* has proliferated in the last 20 years (Bobek et al., 2005). CACGS provide career information via the computer and help individuals sort through their values and career interests. The best known of these systems are SIGI–Plus and DISCOVER.

SIGI–Plus

SIGI–Plus (System for Interactive Guidance Information) (Katz, 1975, 1993) is a computer-based career planning program that helps users identify career options based on their interests, values, and education. Used with high school students, college students, or job seekers, SIGI–Plus provides the following:

- Helps identify users' skills needed for various occupations.
- Helps identify users' workplace values and helps select occupations that best satisfy those values.
- Helps users explore occupations that match their educational background or work experience.
- Helps users determine what education or training is needed for a new career.

Discover

DISCOVER, available through ACT (2007), is a comprehensive career planning program developed for individuals from high school through adulthood. DISCOVER provides information to help people make career and educational decisions through assessment of career-relevant interests, abilities, and work values. DISCOVER organizes occupations into six clusters, parallel to Holland's hexagon, to help users focus on preparing for the career options that fit them best.

It is important to remember that computer-assisted career guidance systems can provide only limited help to clients in their explorations about themselves and their career choices. Clients generally need a counselor's help in expressing their interests or clarifying perceptions about their own abilities before using a computer. Moreover, material gained from computer-assisted programs is best synthesized and integrated in counseling sessions.

Thus, computers do not replace counselors. Taber and Luzzo's (1999) research found that the most effective means of providing career planning assistance to students or clients is by a combination of computer and counselor. Because technology is used significantly in career counseling, needed counselor competencies include a knowledge of computer-assisted software and Web sites, the ability to determine whether a computer-assisted intervention is appropriate for a client, the ability to motivate the client to use computer-assisted systems or Web sites, the ability to help the client process data, and the ability to help the client develop an action plan.

EMPLOYMENT COUNSELORS

Employment counselors specialize in helping people find jobs. They work in state employment offices and in colleges and private placement agencies. These workers are often called *occupational information specialists* or *career information specialists.*

Most placement agencies accumulate job listings from employers online or through telephone calls or visits. Effective placement counselors spend considerable time cultivating relationships with personnel directors and other hiring officials so that their placement offices will be contacted when firms have job openings.

Employment counselors, particularly those in colleges and private placement offices, also teach clients job search techniques and job interview skills and give them tips on developing résumés. By role-playing with clients before they go on interviews, the counselor helps them reduce their anxiety and teaches them how to respond and assert themselves constructively with the person in charge of hiring.

Employment counselors in state employment agencies work with challenging and difficult groups of clients, particularly those who have been laid off from their jobs. Clients may need urgent help, especially if they have families to support. Those who have suddenly lost jobs may experience shock, denial, grief, and anger. Those who cannot find work over a long period of time may feel defeated, resigned, desperate, or resentful. Another group, the chronically unemployed, are often difficult to place because of alcoholism, marginal intelligence, or borderline personality functioning. Their motivation is low, and their employment histories are erratic, at best.

To meet the special needs of unemployed clients, it is essential that agencies hire certified or licensed career counselors, who can consider clients' emotional conflicts as they try to help the clients find work. When employment counselors find that clients are so distraught that they are not ready for placement, referrals to a mental health counselor or to a counseling psychologist are in order.

VOCATIONAL REHABILITATION COUNSELING

Vocational rehabilitation counselors help clients with disabilities find and maintain high-quality employment. A majority of Americans with disabilities in the working-age population are not employed, despite the fact that most want to work (National Organization on Disability, 2000). In general, the vocational adjustment of people with disabilities has been characterized by limited salable work skills, low income, underemployment, and unemployment (Curnow, 1989; Kosciulek, 2004). Effective vocational rehabilitation counselors can be instrumental in empowering people with disabilities to move toward independence, high-quality employment, and fulfilling careers (Kosciulek, 2004).

Vocational rehabilitation counselors use an empowerment approach in working with clients on agreed-upon goals (Kosciulek, 2004). This approach focuses on (a) the development of a positive counselor–client working alliance, (b) collaboration in exploring and determining career options and goals, (c) client informed choice, and (d) client self-determination.

Besides the typical education and training required of all counselors, rehabilitation counselors need course work in the medical and psychological aspects of disabilities, worker compensation policies, environmental and attitudinal barriers related to disabilities, special considerations in job placement for those with disabilities, and knowledge about the psychological, medical, social, or behavioral services needed by clients with disabilities (Patterson, Bruyere, Szymanski, & Jenkins, 2005).

The majority of rehabilitation counselors work in public rehabilitation agencies for federal and state governments. These include rehabilitation centers, state employment services, Veterans Administration facilities, prisons and correctional agencies, mental health clinics, hospitals, and Social Security and worker compensation agencies. Privately run rehabilitation services may contract their services with public agencies or the government. In addition, private schools for students with disabilities and some colleges employ rehabilitation counselors. Rehabilitation counselors are also hired in employee assistance programs, university-based services for students with disabilities, school-to-work transition programs, and disability management programs in business and industry.

Placement is a major focus of rehabilitation counseling (Patterson et al., 2005). Complications may arise because of the negative attitudes of employers, fellow employees, and the clients themselves regarding the disability (Brown, 2007). Some placement agencies have a rehabilitation counselor who specializes in placing persons with disabilities. Such a specialist places a client in a job after the counselor has helped the client become ready for the job (Parker & Hansen, 1981).

SUMMARY

Career counseling relates to personal and social counseling because the development, choice, and establishment of a career are closely tied to personal needs, social and environmental influences, and personality development. The major theories influencing the career counseling process are those that relate career development to personal development; those that relate personal developmental characteristics to occupational environments compatible with the individual; and those that emphasize the plurality of perspectives, contextual impacts, social constructions of reality, and the importance of the meaning individuals give to their career experiences. Typical client problems related to careers are the need for career exploration, conflict with others regarding career choices, doubts about choosing or remaining in a career, and disruptive conflicts arising from transitions in work and family.

Increasing numbers of counselors are hired by businesses to work with employees whose concerns interfere with their work productivity. Some businesses also hire counselors to help employees find the most suitable career path in the company or find jobs in other companies when their jobs are terminated. Individuals with disabilities benefit from rehabilitation services in career and educational planning. Such services have spread from government agencies to private agencies in the community and to schools and universities.

PROJECTS AND ACTIVITIES

1. Ask one or more people in their 50s who are well established in jobs why they chose their fields, how they entered them, and what steps they took to get to their current jobs.
2. Sigmund Freud once said that work and love are two of the most important experiences in life. Alfred Adler, another psychoanalyst, agreed. How does this view relate to the theories of career development currently popular?
3. Explore your university's Web site for information about careers. Evaluate the quality and quantity of the information obtained.
4. Interview counselors at your local state unemployment and vocational rehabilitation offices. From their comments, indicate how you might make use of these agencies as referral sources if you were a counselor in the community.
5. Select one career theory or one vocational interest measure (e.g., Strong, Kuder, or SDS), and read a review of the research. Select a study considered sound and one the reviewer considers faulty. Analyze the strengths and weaknesses.

CHAPTER 13

Substance Abuse Counseling

S ubstance abuse remains one of the major public health problems in the United States. The use of substances is widespread—almost everyone has either used/abused substances at some point in their lives or knows someone who has. *Substance abuse* occurs when a person misuses, abuses, or is dependent on alcohol, illegal drugs, or prescribed medications over a sustained period of time, resulting in impairment in personal and social functioning (Chamberlain & Jew, 2005). These substances are *psychoactive*—they alter mood, behavior, and perceptions, and affect the nervous system through chemical changes in the brain. All these substances can lead to physical or psychological *dependence* with repeated use; *withdrawal* from them can be devastating to the physical, psychological, and social functioning of the individual (American Psychiatric Association, 2000). Because the addicted person develops a *tolerance* to the effects of the substance, maintaining a certain level of euphoria requires increasing dosages, which can lead to more physical and mental damage and more financial burden (Stevens, 2005c). In addition to dependence, withdrawal, and tolerance, substance abuse increases the risk of violence in the home, suicide, mental illness, and work-related accidents.

After studying this chapter, you will be able to

- Identify and describe the effects of the major substances of abuse.
- Understand a variety of models and theories of addiction and substance abuse.
- Describe a variety of treatment strategies for reducing the negative effects of substance use, abuse, and dependence.
- Recognize the importance of family and social networks in the treatment and recovery process.

THE MAJOR SUBSTANCES OF ABUSE

Psychoactive substances that alter mood and affect the nervous system include depressants, marijuana, stimulants, opiates, and hallucinogens (Comer, 2006; Stevens, 2005c). In addition to illegal drugs, people can abuse prescription drugs used to help individuals relax, sleep, or decrease their pain.

Depressants

Depressants of the central nervous system include alcohol, benzodiazepines, and barbiturates. *Alcohol* is the most commonly abused substance. An estimated 20 million people, including 3 million children and adolescents, suffer from alcohol abuse or dependence. Furthermore, approximately 40% of highway deaths are alcohol related (National Highway Traffic Safety Administration, 2000). More than $100 billion each year is lost in business and to society because of absenteeism or the poor work performance of substance abusers as well as the high cost to law enforcement, the justice system, and social services (Stevens, 2005c). Other sources indicate even higher losses of more than $270 billion (James, 2008). Moreover, many diseases are frequently related to alcohol addiction: cirrhosis of the liver, pancreatic disorders, malnutrition, heart disease, problems of the nervous and musculoskeletal systems, brain damage, and psychiatric reactions such as depression and paranoia (Johnson & Ait-Daoud, 2005; Smith & Capps, 2005). In addition, the serious interpersonal problems that result from alcohol abuse include domestic violence, child abuse, marital conflict, sexual dysfunction, and dysfunctional social relationships (Stevens, 2005d).

Barbiturates, such as Seconal and Nembutal, help persons with insomnia. Barbiturates are addictive and may produce effects similar to those of alcohol—feeling "high," slurred speech, slowed reactions, and loss of inhibition. Accidental overdosage can lead to death. They are particularly lethal because the death-producing dose remains the same even though addicts must take higher and higher dosages to get an effect (Sue, Sue, & Sue, 2005).

Benzodiazepines are the most widely prescribed group of drugs in the treatment of anxiety and insomnia. The most commonly prescribed benzodiazepines are Valium, Xanax, Ativan, and Klonopin. Benzodiazepines can be addictive for persons prone to avoiding problems and emotionally painful situations. In the past, physicians have been criticized for prescribing Valium and Xanax too readily without considering their addictive qualities and monitoring patient's use.

An advance in the development of *sedative–hypnotics* occurred with the discovery of the non-benzodiazepine drugs Ambien (zolpidem), Lunesta (zopiclone), and Sonata (zaleplon). These drugs are short-acting hypnotics that produce fewer side effects than benzodiazepines. However, like benzodiazepines, addiction or dependence can occur, especially when non-benzodiazepine drugs are used regularly for longer than a few weeks or at high dosages.

Marijuana

After alcohol, marijuana is the most widely used drug and is considered by some to be the most socially accepted of the illegal drugs. More than 10% of the U.S. population age

12 and older use marijuana (SAMHSA, 2006). It is well known that chronic marijuana users often suffer from listlessness and lack of motivation. Moreover, persons intoxicated from marijuana can suffer from fragmentary thoughts, disoriented behavior, and psychosis (Smith & Capps, 2005). Regular use of marijuana can damage the body; like heavy alcohol use, extended marijuana use causes bloodshot eyes, increased heart rate and blood pressure, lung damage, and cancer (Comer, 2006; Smith & Capps, 2005). And like cigarette smoking, marijuana causes bronchitis and asthmatic reactions. Furthermore, users are often unaware that marijuana bought on the street can be laced with other, more potent and toxic drugs (Palfai & Jankiewicz, 1996).

Stimulants

Stimulants increase arousal in the nervous system. Commonly abused stimulants include amphetamines, methamphetamines, and cocaine. *Amphetamines*, such as Dexedrine and Benzedrine, are stimulants obtained by prescription and have such street names as "speed," "uppers," or "bennies." Adderall and Ritalin are commonly prescribed amphetamines used to treat individuals with attention-deficit hyperactivity disorder. Because moderate dosages of amphetamines increase alertness and reduce fatigue, some students, truck drivers, and athletes use them to help stay awake or have more energy. Stimulants also curb the appetite and are used in prescribed and over-the-counter drugs to help people lose weight (Comer, 2006; Smith & Capps, 2005). Persons taking amphetamines develop tolerance quickly and need dosage increases as much as 200 times or more to attain a desired effect. When drugs are not available or are withdrawn, users may become irritated and paranoid, which can lead to violence. *Methamphetamine* (crystal meth, glass, ice) is a stimulant that is chemically related to amphetamine, but, at comparable doses, the effects of methamphetamine are much more potent, longer lasting, and more harmful to the central nervous system.

Cocaine, which comes from the coca plant, is an illegal stimulant taken to induce euphoria; about 2.4 million people (1.0%) in the United States have used cocaine within the past month (SAMHSA, 2006). It can be inhaled, injected intravenously, or smoked in a highly dangerous compound called *crack*. In the 1970s and 1980s, cocaine was a glamorous status drug used by many upwardly mobile people who believed it to be safer than heroin (Burnett, 1979). Early in that period, cocaine was thought to be nonaddictive, and the dangers of the drug were minimized. Research has since shown cocaine to be addictive; both tolerance and withdrawal effects occur. As with amphetamines, after an initial euphoric state, restlessness, irritability, and paranoia follow, ending in severe depression (Smith & Capps, 2005). Several prominent athletes have died from brain convulsions or cardiovascular failure after ingesting cocaine. Their deaths dramatically changed public opinion about the danger of cocaine addiction.

Opiates (Narcotics)

Opiates (e.g., opium, morphine, and codeine) are derived from the opium poppy. Opium has been used for centuries to reduce pain and induce relaxation (Smith & Capps, 2005). *Heroin* was developed in the late 1800s as a nonaddictive form of opium; however, after two decades, it was found to be addictive and was declared illegal. Today, it is an illegal street drug ingested by smoking, injecting under the skin, or injecting into the blood-stream (*mainlining*).

It is estimated that about 3.5 million Americans (1.5%) have tried heroin at least once in their lifetime, and approximately 136,000 have used heroin within the past month (SAMHSA, 2006). After feeling euphoric for a few hours, heroin users become lethargic and lose interest in food, health, and personal and sexual relationships (Palfai & Jankiewicz, 1996). All heroin users are highly susceptible to physical dependence on the drug and require high dosages to maintain euphoria. Overdosing on heroin can be fatal (Comer, 2006; Sue, Sue, & Sue, 2005).

The nonmedical use or abuse of prescription narcotic pain relievers remains a serious public health concern. The most commonly abused prescription narcotics are OxyContin and Percocet. According to SAMHSA (2006), approximately 2.2 million people engaged in nonmedical use of prescription pain relievers within the last year.

Hallucinogens (Psychedelics)

Hallucinogens include the drugs lysergic acid diethylamide (LSD) and phencyclidine (PCP, angel dust); mescaline, derived from peyote cactus; and psilocybin, derived from a type of mushroom. They produce major alterations in sensation, emotion, and perception (Smith & Capps, 2005). Although many users have described their experiences as won-derful mind-altering "trips," these drugs have also caused psychotic reactions requiring extended hospitalization (Sue, Sue, & Sue, 2005). In addition, LSD can cause severe panic attacks and flashbacks in which a previous LSD trip is repeated even though the person has not taken the drug for months or years. Flashbacks may occur days or even months after the last LSD experience (Comer, 2006).

THEORIES OF SUBSTANCE ABUSE

Disease Theory

The disease theory of substance abuse began in the 1950s when E. M. Jellinek first de-fined alcoholism as a disease (1960). He developed a theory that alcoholism is a medical disorder, like diabetes, and caused by genetic or physiological factors that render persons susceptible to alcohol dependence (Erickson, 2005; James 2008). When defined as a dis-ease, alcoholism is described as a "chronic, hereditary, and eventually fatal disease that progresses from an early physiological susceptibility into an addiction characterized by tolerance changes, physiological dependence, and loss of control over drinking" (Mueller & Ketcham, 1987, p. 9). As in other diseases, a process of deterioration and destruction is based on specific causes, and specific characteristic symptoms are evident. Under this description, abstinence is essential for recovery.

Psychological Theories

Psychoanalytic and cognitive–behavioral theorists provide several theories about the de-velopment of substance dependence. Freudian theorists assume that substance abuse is re-lated to certain pathological personality traits established in early childhood (James, 2008). Object relations proponents emphasize the substance abuser's need to alleviate and deny underlying personal and interpersonal conflicts (Price & Lynn, 1986). Cognitive–behavioral and social learning theorists believe that addiction occurs because substance abusing habits are learned and maintained by sociological, psychological, and physiological factors (James, 2008). They hypothesize that abusing substances serves the seemingly useful purpose of reducing discomfort, anxiety, and tension; this reduction in tension reinforces drug use and increases the possibility of continued use.

Sociocultural Theories

Increased attention has been given to sociocultural influences on addictive behaviors—family patterns, neighborhood settings, peer groups, and the sociocultural milieu. For example, "attitudes toward alcohol consumption and abuse vary from culture to culture and greatly affect the amount and content of alcohol consumption" (Erickson, 2005, p. 110). Studies show that Jewish people and Italians have low alcoholism rates, whereas the Irish and French are high on the scale of alcoholism (Calahan, Cisin, & Crossley, 1969; Comer, 2006; Valliant & Milofsky, 1982). Alcoholism is the leading cause of health problems, fatal accidents, and homicide among Native Americans (Robinson & Howard-Hamilton, 2005). In addition, the high rates of alcoholism among certain minority groups have been attributed to the oppression and poverty imposed by the dominant culture (Sue & Sue, 2007). In terms of family patterns, some view alcoholism as a "family disease" or "family disorder" caused by parental alcoholism, family tension and parental alienation (Steinglass & Bennett, 1989).

Integrated Theories

It is increasingly accepted that "individuals do not live in a vacuum, and behavior is influenced by both external and internal factors" (Erickson, 2005, p. 116). As such, increasing numbers of professionals now acknowledge that many factors contribute to, or have an effect on, substance abuse: genetics, family environment, sociocultural and biological factors, and certain precipitating events (e.g., trauma). Integrated theories attempt to consolidate the many factors that create the conditions under which an individual will abuse substances. By accepting the influence of many different factors, a multifaceted treatment approach can be developed.

COUNSELING PERSONS WITH SUBSTANCE ABUSE PROBLEMS

Assessment and Diagnosis

Assessment and diagnosis of substance abuse problems involves two primary disorders as listed in the *Diagnostic and Statistical Manual of Mental Disorders (DSM-IV-TR):* substance abuse and substance dependence. The *DSM-IV-TR* groups substances into 11 major classes (see Table 13.1).

Substance dependence is characterized by a problematic pattern of using drugs and/or alcohol leading to distress or problems in family or other relationships, work, or school (American Psychiatric Association, 2000). Three of the following seven symptoms within a 12-month period are needed to diagnose substance dependence:

TABLE 13.1
DSM-IV-TR 11 Major Classes of Substances

- Alcohol
- Amphetamine
- Caffeine
- Cannabis
- Cocaine
- Hallucinogens
- Inhalants
- Nicotine
- Opioids
- Phencyclidine (PCP)
- Sedatives, hypnotics, or anxiolytics

- Tolerance, shown by either increased intake of the substance to achieve the same effect or, with continued use, the same amount of the substance having much less effect
- Withdrawal, shown either by experiencing withdrawal symptoms or by using the substance (or a closely related one) to avoid or relieve withdrawal symptoms
- Use of more of the substance than was planned
- Unsuccessful attempts to control or reduce substance use
- Substantial time is spent in obtaining, using, and recovering from the substance
- Reduced or abandoned work, social, or leisure activities due to the substance use
- Continued use of the substance despite awareness of its negative impact

Substance abuse is a residual category for those who do not meet the full criteria for substance dependence. However, their substance use also causes harm or distress to themselves or others in their environment. The criteria for substance abuse *do not* include tolerance, withdrawal, or a pattern of compulsive use. Instead, it focuses on the harmful consequences of repeated use. A diagnosis of substance abuse is made if at least one of the following occurs within a 12-month period:

- Failure to fulfill important roles (e.g., employee, parent, spouse)
- Repeated use in dangerous situations (e.g., driving a car, operating machinery)
- Recurrent use despite legal problems (e.g., arrests for driving while under the influence)
- Continued use despite social or interpersonal problems (e.g., arguments or physical fights with spouse about substance use)

Typically, a diagnosis of substance abuse is more likely in individuals who have only recently started taking the substance or in those who use the substance sporadically (e.g., weekend use rather than daily use). Substance abuse, however, can be a precursor to substance dependence.

Assessing individuals for substance abuse can be a challenging task. Many individuals who abuse substances give unreliable histories to counselors because they don't want to give up their habit. Denying and lying are common behaviors, in addition to minimizing and rationalizing their problem. Therefore, to accurately assess and diagnose a substance-related problem, counselors need to gather information from both the addicted individual and others who know the individual. Those who are close to the person can give the counselor information that either corroborates or contradicts the addicted person's information.

If an informing family member or friend is not available, counselors need to be alert to some of the common consequences or "red flags" associated with substance abuse, including the following:

- Frequent job loss, unemployment, or underemployment.
- Driving under the influence (DUI) arrest or other legal problems.
- Domestic violence.
- Relationship problems (such as irresponsible behavior, financial and emotional dependency on the partner, breakups).
- A series of moves.
- History of psychological or medical problems that remain unresolved.
- Family history of substance abuse.

Counselors may also ask specific questions about the client's substance use. In questioning the client about alcohol use, it is important that counselors know the recommended drinking limits for men and women. A standard drink is defined as one 12-ounce bottle of beer, one 5-ounce glass of wine, or 1.5 ounces of distilled spirits. For most adults, moderate alcohol use—up to two drinks per day for men and one drink per day for women—causes few if any problems (NIAAA, 2007). However, according to epidemiologic research, men who drink 5 or more standard drinks in a day (or 15 or more per week) and women who drink 4 or more in a day (or 8 or more per week) are at increased risk for alcohol-related problems (Dawson, Grant, & Li, 2005). Assessment questions include asking about the client's substance of choice, how often the client uses (daily, weekly), how much the client uses (e.g., a case of beer, a bottle of wine), and about the consequences of use. Table 13.2 provides a list of sample assessment questions. It is important to realize just how much substance abusers can ingest. A person who is not a substance abuser may think that a 6-pack of beer is a large quantity of alcohol, while an alcoholic might easily consume a case of beer in one evening.

To aid in the assessment process, there are many psychometric instruments available to clinicians. The *Michigan Alcoholism Screening Test (MAST;* Selzer, 1971) is the most

TABLE 13.2
Sample Assessment Questions for Substance Abuse

- How often do you drink alcohol? How much do you drink?
- Have you ever used sleeping pills or prescription drugs?
- Have you ever used marijuana or other drugs?
- Can you stop drinking after one or two drinks?
- How often have you missed work (or school) because of drinking or using? Have you lost a job because of drinking or using?
- Did your substance use ever cause problems in your relationships, family, or friendships?
- Have you ever been arrested for driving under the influence or disorderly conduct?
- Did you ever have to use/drink more in order to get the same high or buzz?
- Have you tried to cut down or stop using? If yes, how did you feel?

researched questionnaire. The 25-item test correctly identifies up to 95% of alcoholics. The *CAGE questionnaire* (Ewing, 1984) is a 4-item questionnaire that counselors can easily administer during the initial interview. The questions address attempts to *cut* down on alcohol intake (C), *annoyance* over criticism about alcohol (A), *guilt* about drinking behavior (G), and needing an *"eye-opener"* or a drink in the morning to relieve withdrawal symptoms (E). Two or more positive answers indicate alcohol dependence. *The Substance Abuse Subtle Screening Inventory* (SASSI-3; Lazowski, Miller, Boye, & Miller, 1998) is a brief and easily administered screening measure that helps identify individuals who have a high probability of having a substance abuse disorder.

The Process of Intervention

Individuals who abuse substances frequently deny that they have a problem, so they most often respond negatively to suggestions or pleas that they seek treatment. If the individual continues to deny the problem, and family members and friends are concerned about the individual in terms of danger to self because of the substance abuse, then a more forceful intervention technique may be necessary. An addictions counselor, family members, and close friends may confront the person with the substance abuse problem about the effects that his or her substance use is having on the individual's health and well-being and the well-being of family members and friends (Mueller & Ketcham, 1987). In the substance abuse counseling field, this is called an *intervention*. It is the formal process of attempting to interrupt the progressive and destructive effects of substance abuse by confronting the addicted individual (Johnson Institute, 1987).

The purpose of the intervention is not just to confront the person about his or her behavior; it is also a time for significant others to express their feelings about the individual's substance abuse and its effects on them (Smith & Garcia, 2005). Family members and friends should decide prior to the intervention what their response will be if the addicted individual refuses treatment. The response may include detachment, refusing to give the individual financial support, filing for divorce, or other consequences. These consequences should not be viewed as punitive or as a means to manipulate the addicted person into accepting treatment; rather, it is an "alternative behavior" for significant others when the abuser rejects treatment (Smith & Garcia, 2005, p. 191).

Treatment Settings

Treatment for substance abuse can occur at various private or non-profit settings. Treatment settings can be viewed as a progressive level of care—from the most restrictive (inpatient treatment) to the least restrictive (outpatient treatment). Commonly available treatment services include medical detoxification, hospitalization, residential treatment, day treatment programs, halfway houses, and outpatient programs.

Medical Detoxification is a process whereby individuals are systematically withdrawn from drugs or alcohol, typically through the use of medications and under the care of a physician. Detoxification is considered a precursor to treatment because it is designed to treat withdrawal (i.e., the acute physiological effects of stopping drug/alcohol use). In some cases, detoxification is a medical necessity since untreated withdrawal can be medically dangerous or even fatal. Detoxification can take place in a hospital, in a specialized inpatient detoxification unit, or on an outpatient basis with close medical supervision. Detoxification may take from 3 to 4 days to a week or more.

Hospitalization is appropriate for individuals who (a) have a substance overdose that cannot be safely treated in an outpatient or residential treatment setting, (b) are at risk for severe withdrawal syndromes, (c) have co-occurring medical conditions that need medical attention, (d) have a documented history of not engaging in or benefiting from treatment in a less intensive setting (e.g., residential, outpatient), or (e) have a co-occurring psychiatric disorder that, by itself, would require hospital-level care (e.g., depression with suicidal thoughts, psychosis). Hospital treatment programs that provide services for individuals with concurrent substance abuse and psychiatric disorders are called *dual diagnosis* programs (Smith & Garcia, 2005). These programs may involve 7-, 14-, or 28-day stays in a protected, restricted environment.

Residential treatment programs are "facilities that allow individuals to live within a residential setting, be employed during the day, and receive comprehensive treatment, including individual, group, and family therapy" (Smith & Garcia, 2005, p. 177). Residential treatment may be long term or short term. *Long-term residential treatment,* lasting 3 months or longer, provides a living environment with treatment services. Long-term treatment is appropriate for individuals who do not have stable living or employment situations, who have limited or no family support, and who have been unable to get and stay sober or drug free with other treatment programs. *Short-term residential programs* provide intensive but relatively brief residential treatment based on a modified 12-step approach with a typical length of stay of 20 to 25 days. Reduced health care coverage for short-term residential programs has resulted in a diminished number of these programs in recent years.

Day treatment programs, or partial hospitalization, involves comprehensive treatment for individuals who live at home, but attend treatment during the day (Smith & Garcia, 2005). Day treatment programs may be appropriate for persons who require intensive care beyond outpatient treatment but have a reasonable probability of refraining from drug/alcohol use outside a restricted setting. In these programs, clients attend treatment for 4 to 8 hours per day but live at home. These programs usually last for at least 3 months and work best for people who have a stable, supportive home environment.

Halfway houses are typically community-based homes or buildings near a residential facility that acts as a transitional, less restrictive living environment (Smith & Garcia, 2005). Halfway houses are appropriate for individuals who are not yet ready to function independently in the community, but do not need the intensive structured environment of a residential treatment program. Stays can range from several weeks to several months, and residents are required to maintain employment, attend 12-step meetings, and remain abstinent.

Outpatient treatment programs are provided in a variety of settings: health clinics, community mental health clinics, counselors' offices, hospital clinics, local health department offices, or residential programs with outpatient clinics. Outpatient treatment programs may require clients to attend individual or group counseling sessions anywhere from once weekly up to daily attendance. *Intensive outpatient treatment programs* require a person to attend 9 to 20 hours of treatment activities per week. Outpatient programs last from about 2 months to 1 year. People appropriate for outpatient treatment are willing to attend counseling sessions regularly, have supportive friends or family members, have a place to live, and have some form of transportation to get to treatment sessions.

Treatment Goals

Most researchers and clinicians still believe that abstinence is the primary and essential goal in substance abuse treatment. Most professionals believe that until the underlying issues of addiction are dealt with, substance abusers will continue to be in danger of relapse (Smith, 2005). Fletcher (2001), who offers new solutions to alcohol treatment in her book *Sober for Good,* cautions that for those individuals who have mastered their alcohol problem, only a very few can start drinking again and maintain control. Those individuals who may be able to drink once in a while or moderately are psychologically stable, maintain a stable lifestyle, and have learned to cope well with stress.

After individuals stop drinking, they and their families need counseling. The term *recovering alcoholic* is often used for individuals who have stopped drinking. Some professionals have claimed that these people will always remain in the recovery stage because they will always be addicted to alcohol.

What is agreed on is that abstinence alone is insufficient to resolve the substance abuser's or the family's problems. Abstinence does not resolve underlying problems, nor does it immediately improve family relationships. Instead, family problems often become exacerbated when the denial patterns surrounding the alcoholism and the sedative effects of the alcohol no longer exist. And because alcohol is no longer used as a cover-up for family dysfunction, the personal problems of family members and family discord may erupt. Moreover, family members often unconsciously or subconsciously resist changes in the recovering individual, who begins to assert needs and display strengths. Continued counseling is needed to help both the individual and the family form new patterns of behavior.

Counseling services and support groups for both substance abusers and family members can help change dysfunctional family patterns. These services not only help recovering persons abstain but also help them and their family members learn to interact with one another in more productive ways. Counseling aids the recovering individual in understanding old behaviors and attitudes, developing coping skills for new experiences in the present, and building a framework for continual future growth, individually and as a family.

Treatment Strategies for Substance Abuse

As mentioned earlier, most professionals believe that the best results occur if counselors insist that clients with an addiction problem abstain from using as soon as counseling begins. In his book on therapy for alcoholism, Forrest (1994) notes that if alcohol abusers continue to drink, the toxic effects of alcohol on their psychological and physical well-being inhibit the development of a counseling relationship and interfere with or distort communication between client and counselor. After assessment of the severity of the individual's substance abuse and after detoxification is completed (if needed), the majority of treatment programs, regardless of setting, provide individual counseling, family counseling, group counseling, auxiliary services, and support groups.

Individual Counseling

In individual counseling, recovering individuals receive help in developing feelings of self-worth and responsibility for their own behavior. Most important, they learn to express their own needs more directly. And through exploration of childhood experiences, they get in touch with unresolved feelings of anger, grief, or shame that are affecting their current behavior. They also learn new ways of dealing with stress.

Recovering individuals learn not to depend on substances during times of stress. A spouse learns not to assume responsibility for the recovering person, the spouse must not feel compelled to control or manage the person, and above all, the spouse must learn not to treat the recovering individual as an inferior person.

Individual counseling approaches vary. Psychodynamic approaches may be used to get at the issues and needs underlying the abuse. Cognitive–behavioral strategies, such as stress management and self-monitoring, may be used to help the abuser develop self-control and prevent relapses (Stevens, 2005d).

Motivational Enhancement Therapy (MET) is a commonly used treatment approach to substance abuse. MET seeks to evoke from clients their own motivation for change and to develop a personal plan for change. Because each client sets his or her own goals, no absolute goal is imposed, although counselors may suggest or encourage specific goals such as complete abstinence as well as other life goals. MET is based on principles of cognitive therapy, whereby the counselor confronts client discrepancies between current behavior and significant personal goals. For example, a therapist may point out the discrepancy between a client's current behavior of smoking marijuana daily and his personal goal of completing a master's degree. Emphasis is placed on a client's self-motivation and commitment to change. The working assumption is that intrinsic motivation is a necessary factor in instigating change.

Family Counseling

Once an individual agrees to substance abuse treatment, family members may also need counseling. The attitudes, structure, and function of the family system may be the most important variables in the outcome of treatment (James, 2008). As discussed in chapter 11, one member of a family with a problem represents a problem in the total family system. In the typical family with alcohol abuse, the spouse and children have been caught up in a family dynamic of intrigue, in which the alcohol problem has been denied and rarely discussed so that feelings of shame permeate the family. Family boundaries are unclear, family members are enmeshed, and authentic communication is infrequent.

Families that hide their secret unwittingly assume the role of an *enabler,* allowing the addicted individual to continue drinking and not suffer the consequences. The spouse covers up for the addict, takes over duties the addicted spouse should handle, makes excuses for the drinking, pretends the spouse is ill (not drunk), and ends up acting like a martyr (Hogg & Frank, 1992; Schaef, 1986). Meanwhile, children assume different roles to help themselves and the family survive the emotional stress while maintaining secrecy and denial. One may play the *hero,* who hopes to redeem the family by being successful. Another may hide the pain by acting like the family *clown, joker,* or *mascot.* Still another may play the role of *scapegoat* and act out the family problems. Others may withdraw from stress and act like *lost children* (Gladding, 2007; James, 2008).

The goals of treatment for spouses and families are to work through their own problems and attitudes and gain sufficient independence so that they can drop the caretaking or enabling roles, such as attempting to control, manage, or manipulate one another or the addicted person (Gladding, 2007). They also need help in overcoming any tendency to continue blaming the recovering person for all drinking-related problems in the past. As the recovering individual regains strength, family members are apt to feel stronger rage and resentment against them; the members may begin to act out or become physically ill (Stevens, 2005a). James (2008) notes that, ironically, if the addicted person stops drinking, the maladaptive family may become threatened enough to try to reinstate the perceived homeostasis of alcoholism. This can be quite a problem for recovering individuals and is one main reason that many take refuge in Alcoholics Anonymous (AA) groups—to protect themselves and get the necessary support to remain sober because little support is available from their families.

Group Counseling

Group counseling has always been a very popular and preferred type of treatment for recovering substance abusers. Group therapy is especially effective with those recovering from substance abuse because groups provide social support, empowerment, encouragement to counteract ongoing social pressures to take drugs, and resistance to falling back into addictive behaviors (Fletcher, 2001; Stevens, 2005b). Group counseling is equally effective for other members of the recovering individual's family. Typically, persons with a substance abuse problem meet in one group, and spouses and/or other family members meet with other spouses and family members in a different group.

In a group setting, all clients get feedback from peers, experiment with new behaviors and social skills, experience emotional closeness to others, learn to assert themselves and confront others, and develop spiritual strength—all of which are helpful in recovery (James, 2008).

Self-Help Groups

AA and related 12-step programs (e.g., Narcotics Anonymous) have been very successful over the years in helping individuals to give up alcohol and maintain sobriety. Many counselors and therapists, in working with recovering individuals, have used AA and NA as an adjunct to their therapy. AA is a spiritually based 12-step program in which individuals acknowledge that they need a power greater than themselves to maintain abstinence (see Table 13.3). They give control to a higher power, acknowledge wrongs, make amends, and continue to admit mistakes. They then help others find this spiritual help.

Many counselors insist that individuals recovering from alcohol addiction join AA, and family members and friends are encouraged to join affiliates—Al-Anon for adult friends and family members and Alateen for children and friends (age 12 to 20). AA helps build the confidence needed to remain sober and the skills necessary to interact with family members. The affiliates help family members and friends relate to and interact with the person recovering from alcohol abuse. Al-Anon and Alateen also help spouses, children, and friends learn how to live with nonrecovering individuals or when and how to confront them.

Although many professionals believe that AA involvement is an important factor in recovery, some criticize or express caution about its effectiveness. According to Stevens (2005d), some complain that AA's success has been based on white, middle-class groups. Others

TABLE 13.3
The Twelve Steps of AA

1. We admitted we were powerless over alcohol—that our lives had become unmanageable.
2. Came to believe that a Power greater than ourselves could restore us to sanity.
3. Made a decision to turn our will and our lives over to the care of God *as we understood Him*.
4. Made a searching and fearless moral inventory of ourselves.
5. Admitted to God, to ourselves, and to another human being the exact nature of our wrongs.
6. Were entirely ready to have God remove all these defects of character.
7. Humbly asked Him to remove our shortcomings.
8. Made a list of all persons we had harmed, and became willing to make amends to them all.
9. Made direct amends to such people wherever possible, except when to do so would injure them or others.
10. Continued to take personal inventory and when we were wrong promptly admitted it.
11. Sought through prayer and meditation to improve our conscious contact with God, *as we understood Him*, praying only for knowledge of His will for us and the power to carry that out.
12. Having had a spiritual awakening as the result of these steps, we tried to carry this message to alcoholics, and to practice these principles in all our affairs.

Note. Reprinted with permission of Alcoholics Anonymous World Services.

criticize the 12-step approach as reinforcing the powerlessness of women. According to Fletcher (2001), the two major criticisms of AA concerned the "difficulty accepting the 'higher power'/spiritual concept" and "dislike for AA's focus on the past and the idea that you're in recovery for life" (p. 114). Other perceived shortcomings noted by Fletcher were that AA doesn't use professional counselors; it is "so strongly male-oriented"; and it emphasizes powerlessness and passivity, with little or no attempt to help persons restructure themselves and regain a sense of empowerment (p. 114). In response to this criticism, some groups have modified the AA steps. But despite the criticisms, AA is still regarded as a significant force in the successful treatment of alcoholism, and many credit AA with saving their lives (Fletcher, 2001).

For decades, beginning in the 1930s, AA was the *only* treatment program for individuals who abused alcohol—a program that dignified the individual's addiction, guaranteed a permanent lifeline of support, and helped the individual in sobriety. Similar treatment programs have recently emerged that provide the positive services of AA without the noted shortcomings. The problem, however, is that alternative treatment programs are difficult to find and are nonexistent in many communities, whereas AA is very well known. There are more than 50,000 AA groups in the United States, but there are only about 1,000 groups that offer alternative programs (Fletcher, 2001).

Even so, more attention is being given to alternative treatment programs as professionals realize that people respond differently to treatment. Many cannot fit the one mold that AA proposes (Fletcher, 2001). And even though all significant treatment programs insist on abstinence, their recovery methods differ widely. SMART Recovery, for example, is a cognitive–behavioral model in which participants practice cognitive restructuring. "They learn how to challenge irrational, self-destructive thoughts—thoughts that often lead to problem drinking—and replace them with more rational ones so they remain sober" (Fletcher, 2001, p. 124).

Relapse Prevention

One of the most difficult problems in substance abuse treatment is preventing those in recovery from relapsing into their former patterns. After clients leave a supportive treatment environment, they may be influenced by social pressures, increased personal stress, or a return to low self-esteem. If their coping skills are not sufficiently developed, if they have a pessimistic attitude about their ability to control themselves, or if family and community are not supportive, they may relapse into substance abuse.

Thus, strategies to prevent relapse are essential components of treatment plans (Annis & Davis, 1991; Peel, 1988; Stevens, 2005d). Noteworthy relapse prevention models are those that take into consideration psychosocial and environmental factors influencing the recovering individual. Persons with few complicating emotional problems tend to avoid a relapse if they have good jobs and adequate living conditions and if they take care of their physical well-being. The availability of counseling to the families of former abusers also reduces the risk of relapse. Recovering abusers in high-risk situations are those faced with "interpersonal conflict, negative emotional state, and social pressure" (Stevens, 2005d, p. 295). The ease with which individuals can return to their former lifestyle—such as frequenting a certain bar or joining old cronies for drinks—also heightens the risk of relapse.

According to Fletcher (2001), occasions when the recovering person falls back into a drinking binge can serve as an opportunity for a recovering client to explore with a substance abuse counselor the precipitating factors that led to the relapse. Social learning and cognitive–behavioral techniques have been used to prevent relapses (Stevens, 2005d). Social learning helps clients build up their own capacities to monitor themselves by keeping logs and journals about their feelings and behaviors. In this way, they are more able to anticipate problems and check with counselors. Exploring the feelings that precipitate compulsive urges to drink—such as anger, moodiness, and depression—helps clients gain control of their lives (Fletcher, 2001). Cognitive–behavioral models focus on helping clients make comprehensive changes in lifestyle—changes that involve exercise, relaxation, diet, and cognitive restructuring that will bring about new coping skills. In this way, positive habits replace negative ones.

Comprehensive Rehabilitation Programs

Many substance abuse rehabilitation programs are free-standing, non-hospital-based facilities that are oriented to the *Minnesota Model* of substance abuse treatment (James, 2008; Smith & Garcia, 2005). Hazelden is probably one of the best known treatment facilities that uses the Minnesota Model. The Minnesota Model approach is typically characterized by multidisciplinary, multimodal therapeutic approaches, including group and individual therapy, family education and support, and self-help.

The Minnesota Model consists of three phases of integrated care: detoxification, rehabilitation, and aftercare (Smith & Garcia, 2005). The *detoxification* phase is the process of safely relieving the symptoms of intoxication and withdrawal; it takes several days to 1 week. After detoxification, clients enter the *rehabilitation* phase—a stage that can be either an inpatient or an outpatient service. Group therapy, interaction with support groups, family counseling, self-help groups, and interaction with community resources are included in treatment. *Aftercare* lasts about a year and may include regularly scheduled weekly or biweekly individual, family, and group counseling. "Aftercare helps clients transition into a sober/clean lifestyle that is lasting and integrated into their everyday lives" (Smith & Garcia, 2005, p. 176).

PROCESS ADDICTIONS

Another area related to substance abuse is process addiction. *Process addiction* refers to any process (or behavior) in which one's behavior is similar to the diagnostic criteria for "dependence" (Stevens, 2005c, p. 30). Examples of process addictions include eating disorders, gambling, sex, shopping, working, exercising, Internet use, and many other others.

The process of engaging in these behaviors compulsively leads to typical addiction symptoms, such as withdrawal, tolerance, euphoria, and continuing the behavior despite consequences. For example, Stevens (2005c) Steve identifies several commonalities between eating disorders and substance dependence, including the compulsive behavior, the sense of powerlessness, the obsessive thoughts about food (the substance), and the learned ability to avoid feeling through the abuse of food (the substance). Pathological gambling also has much in common with substance dependency in that individuals cannot resist the urge to wager money, and, similar to the concept of tolerance in substance abuse, the pathological gambler needs to bet more and more money to receive the same thrill. In addition, like substance dependence, the gambling problem is progressive and chronic, resulting in financial problems.

YOUTHS AND SUBSTANCE ABUSE

Concern about teenage substance abuse began in the late 1960s. At that time, adolescents were following a trend in American society and experimenting with alcohol and drugs. Since that time, teenagers' use of drugs has more than tripled, and in 2005, almost 10% of youths aged 12 to 17 were *current* illicit drug users (SAMHSA, 2006).

Marijuana use has decreased over the last several years, apparently because of drug education programs. According to the Centers for Disease Control and Prevention (CDC) 2005 Youth Risk Behavior Surveillance System (YRBSS), 38.4% of high school students surveyed nationwide have used marijuana at some time during their lifetime. This is down from 40.2% in 2003 and 42.4% in 2001.

Substance abuse, particularly alcohol, is the leading cause of teenage deaths; this clearly points to a crisis in schools and communities—a crisis that is exacerbated now that many youngsters have easy access to automatic weapons. Counselors and health professionals are concerned as well about the effects this abuse has on adolescent development and health. Adolescents who learn patterns of avoidance during formative years will find them difficult to change. In addition, nutritional deficiencies arising from substance abuse are more damaging physically to the growing adolescent than to the mature adult. And adolescents, more than adults, are often away from home when they drink, which means that they probably drive while drunk more often than adults do. Although federal, state, and local agencies have been funded to set up clinics, the directors of these clinics complain that funds that would be better spent on treatment are being used to test people for drug use. Counseling services in public schools and communities have developed educational and therapeutic programs that focus on teenage substance abuse.

Almost all drug use begins in the preadolescent or adolescent years. Oetting and Beauvais (1988) point out that young people, in particular, tend to form *peer clusters*—gangs, church groups, Boy Scouts, best friends, and relatives, for example. Such groups contribute to socialization and identity in positive ways, but some also contribute to initiating and maintaining drug use. Drug prevention programs must consider the influence of peer clusters on the drug abuser: These programs will be successful only if new peers are chosen or if the peer clusters themselves discourage drug use.

SUBSTANCE ABUSE IN OLDER ADULTS

Substance abuse among older adults is an increasing problem in our society, especially as greater numbers of people are living longer. The areas of concern are abuse of alcohol, use and misuse of prescription drugs, and indiscriminate use of over-the-counter drugs to self-medicate (Tait, 2005). Lack of structured activity, separation from family, and loss of spouse and friends can lead to depression, anxiety, and insecurity in older adults, which in turn can lead to substance abuse.

According to the Hazelden Corporation (as cited in Tait, 2005), "20 percent of hospitalized older adults are diagnosed with alcoholism, and nearly 70 percent are hospitalized with alcohol-related problems" (p. 255). Physicians, reinforced by managed care's emphasis on treatment efficiency, are quick to prescribe medication; one third of the 1.5 billion prescriptions each year are for the elderly, with older adults averaging 13 different prescriptions per year. Assuming that most of these prescriptions serve ongoing chronic conditions of older age, the average older person takes many pills every day. And often no one monitors the interaction of various medicines prescribed by different physicians and/or over-the-counter drugs purchased by older adults. This sort of substance abuse can be not only addictive, but also fatal.

Both older adults and their families need to be educated about the risks involved in substance abuse and self-medication. Both the type and the amount of medication require monitoring. And when substance abuse is diagnosed in older adults, it is crucial that they be referred for treatment.

TRAINING OF SUBSTANCE ABUSE COUNSELORS

Although the qualifications of substance abuse counselors traditionally have been their personal experiences as former substance abusers, and even though many have worked effectively in treatment programs, most professionals now realize the necessity of adequate training programs for substance abuse counselors. Substance abuse cases are increasing in alarming numbers, and addiction issues have become more complex. And researchers claim that training programs greatly enhance counselor effectiveness in treating substance abusers (Smith, 2005).

Increasing numbers of universities are offering master's degree programs with a specialty in substance abuse counseling. At the same time, certification standards for substance abuse counselors have been set up by the International Association of Addictions and Offender Counselors (IAAOC) in conjunction with the National Board for Certified Counselors (NBCC). To obtain a Master Addiction Counselor (MAC) certification under these standards, one must complete a master's degree with a specialty in substance abuse counseling that includes a supervised internship (Smith, 2005). Some states have also set up training standards for individuals who want to work as a substance abuse counselor. To qualify as a Certified Addiction Counselor (CAC), the individual must meet certain state standards that often include a master's degree in counseling, social work, or psychology.

SUMMARY

Substance abuse is a major public health problem in the United States. Alcohol is the most commonly abused substance, followed by marijuana. Other psychoactive substances include other depressants, stimulants, opiates, and hallucinogens. Misuse of drugs or alcohol can result in physical or emotional impairment and substance dependence. Substance abuse increases the risk of violence in the home, suicide, mental illness, and work-related accidents.

Assessment of individuals with substance abuse problems involves two primary diagnoses: substance abuse and substance dependence. Substance abuse can be a precursor to substance dependence and more severe symptomology.

Individuals with substance abuse problems can be treated in outpatient programs, partial hospitalization programs, inpatient hospitals, halfway houses, or residential treatment programs. Individual, group, and family counseling are all treatment modalities used to treat substance abuse. Relapse prevention is a vital part of substance abuse treatment. In addition, support groups such as Alcoholics Anonymous (AA), Narcotics Anonymous (NA), Al-Anon, and Alateen are valuable adjunct services to treatment.

PROJECTS AND ACTIVITIES

1. Survey the community in which you live to determine what programs are available for treatment of substance abuse.
2. Interview a school counselor in a junior high or middle school and one in a senior high school. Ask for their impressions about the seriousness of the problem of substance abuse in their school district.
3. Contact a counselor in an outpatient community counseling center to ask how they handle a client who comes in with a drinking problem or whose drinking problem emerges during the counseling sessions.
4. Visit an open meeting of your local Alcoholics Anonymous, Narcotics Anonymous, or Al-Anon. Information about meetings can be found at http://www.alcoholics-anonymous.org. What was the meeting like? How did you feel during the meeting? What did you learn?

CHAPTER 14

_____

Counseling Older Adults

For the first time in history, most people can expect to live well into their 70s and 80s with considerable vigor and self-sufficiency. Trends indicate that increasing numbers of people will live into their 90s and beyond. The increase in life expectancy has been truly remarkable. Whereas early in the 20th century only a small percentage of the population lived past 45, life expectancy now is in the mid-70s. In 2006, those over 65 constituted 12.6% of the total U.S. population; by the year 2030, this age group is expected to increase to more than 20% (U.S. Census Bureau, 2007). In the United States, persons over 85 years of age are the fastest growing age group.

As life expectancy has increased and adults are living longer and healthier lives, the demand for older adult counseling services has increased. Counselors can help older adults adapt to the many changes and transitions they experience in the later part of life.

After studying this chapter, you will be able to

- Explain the developmental theories and characteristics associated with older adults.
- Recognize the counseling needs of older adults.
- Describe the various mental health issues of older adult clients, such as depression, loss, and grief.

STEREOTYPES OF OLDER ADULTS

The overriding stereotype is that as adults age, they automatically start deteriorating and declining physically, psychologically, and socially. They are thus considered an emotional and economic drain on society. Paradoxically, however, another prevalent stereotype is the belief that most older people are well-heeled, wasteful spenders who indulge in frivolous activities, using up the resources of their heirs. Yet another misperception is the belief that older people

229

live in a blissful golden age with few hassles and conflicts, contentedly reclining in rocking chairs or peacefully withdrawing from society as they wait for death. Older adults are also mistakenly perceived as being a homogeneous group, very much alike in characteristics.

Of all these stereotypes, the most devastating to the welfare of older adults is equating aging with decline and deterioration. Most articles and books written by health care professionals about aging deal only with those who are physically incapacitated, chronically emotionally disturbed, or victims of Alzheimer's disease. Publications about older adults generally cover only those living in nursing homes, even though only about 5% of older people live in these facilities (Bjorklund & Bee, 2008; Cavanaugh & Blanchard-Fields, 2006; Myers, 1990; Perlmutter & Hall, 1992) and more than three quarters are self-sufficient. Relatively free of heavy responsibilities such as child rearing and career development, most older adults are able to pursue creative, fulfilling activities in the community. Rather than languishing through a long period of physical and mental decline, increasing numbers of older people are realizing the potentialities and possibilities of living two or three more decades with healthy growth and development.

NEW PERSPECTIVES ON OLDER ADULTS

New perspectives on older adults allow for a positive image of aging. Longitudinal designs by researchers and life-span developmental theories indicate that older adults continue to develop. Studies about cognition and memory also indicate that intellectual capacities continue to develop as one gets older.

Older adults are difficult to categorize because they represent the most heterogeneous and diverse developmental group. Whereas young people are noted for looking, dressing, and acting like their peers, and those in the workplace follow certain dress codes and patterns of living, older adults tend to develop pronounced differences. They tend to go their separate ways. Some, for example, become more deeply involved in specialized hobbies, such as raising orchids or collecting miniature train sets; others become engrossed in skydiving or car racing; and some spend all their time traveling in their camper vans while others stay put in the same home and devote themselves entirely to their grandchildren. And some never retire, particularly self-employed persons and professional artists and musicians.

Developmental theorists have recently been countering the prevailing tendency to lump all older people into one age group–the elderly–which extends over three decades (65 to 90 years of age and beyond), the widest span of all age groups. Those in their 60s, for instance, generally have very different concerns from those in their 80s. And those in their 70s tend to have very different concerns from those in their 90s. Some have suggested three substages within this span: *young-old* (aged 65–75), *old-old* (aged 75–85), and *oldest-old* (aged 85 and older) (Bjorklund & Bee, 2008). Unfortunately, such terms imply little sense of development, but rather a decline.

Change in Research Designs

The stereotype of the declining older adult results largely from gerontologists using cross-sectional research that compares older adult performance with that of younger people (Friedan, 1993). Moreover, the subjects of such studies were primarily older adults living in nursing homes or other institutions—a select group of persons with physical or mental incapacities (Bjorklund & Bee, 2008; Myers, 1990).

Life-span developmental psychologists have since made significant methodological changes in their theoretical and research designs. Using longitudinal instead of cross-sectional approaches, they test the same subjects over a long period of time, or they may use a sequential design that combines cross-sectional and longitudinal methods. These approaches permit researchers to look at changes or consistency among cohort groups—groups of individuals who were all born about the same time and who share similar contextual or historical experiences (Bjorklund & Bee, 2008; Cavanaugh & Blanchard-Fields, 2006; Harrigan & Farmer, 2000; Knight, 2004). Those who were teenagers during the Depression, for instance, grew up with attitudes different from those of teenagers during the upheavals of the 1960s. Longitudinal and sequential research on aging, when carried out with normally functioning older adults, shows that older persons continue to maintain their capacity to learn, instead of going through a steady period of decline and deterioration as they age.

Emergence of Life-Span Developmental Theories

Until the 1950s, developmental psychologists theorized only about child and adolescent stages of development. With the exception of Carl Jung (1933), gerontologists and psychologists believed that people started declining after they reached adulthood. Another exception, Donald Super (1942), followed Charlotte Buehler's life-span developmental theory and introduced a vocational development theory in which he outlined the vocational tasks appropriate at different life stages (see chapter 12). In this early model, however, he followed the prevailing view that individuals over 65 years of age simply decline. In later years, Super (1990) softened his position. Although he no longer described older adults as being in decline, he did see older adults only in nonoccupational roles. Exploration for older adults, he said, consists merely of looking for a suitable retirement home; he saw little need for society to cultivate a pool of occupational talent among older adults.

Psychoanalyst Erik Erikson (1950), influenced by Carl Jung, published an eight-stage life-span developmental model in which he proposed that people continue to develop throughout the life span (see chapter 5). At that time, however, he included only two adult stages: the *generativity* stage from age 30 through midlife and the *integrity* stage for everyone over 65 years of age. Even so, these two stages became classic models for the older adult. During the generativity stage, adults are in their caring, nurturing, reproductive years; during the integrity stage, older adults work through despair and disintegration toward reintegration and a renewed sense of meaning in life. In the 1970s, Gould (1978), Levinson (1978), and Valliant (1977) elaborated on Erikson's life-span developmental theory, but emphasized only the midlife crises of 40- and 50-year-olds.

Robert Butler (1963, 1975) took the lead in focusing on the developmental tasks and concerns of older adults. To challenge prevailing opinion that older adults sink into steady decline, he issued the landmark book *Why Survive?* (1975), declaring that elderly persons serve a vital purpose in society. His book *Productive Aging* (Butler & Gleason, 1985) explores roles for older adults and the means by which they can best serve society.

In the days when Erikson (1950) first proposed his stages of development, he believed that the process of searching for and finding new meaning in life–gaining integrity–was sufficient as the last stage of life: One is then ready to die. Some have since criticized Erikson's integrity stage for being the so-called last stage of development; many older adults in their mid-60s still have 20 to 30 more healthy years to live. Friedan (1993) believes that there must be more to life for older persons after they reach the integrity stage. She suggests that generativity, which Erikson proposed as occurring during the midlife period, should extend for the rest of life, but with a different emphasis. Whereas younger adults in the generativity stage focus on bearing children, parenting, and serving others in the workplace, older adults serve the needs of the community at large in meaningful, generative ways.

Erikson (1978, 1980, 1982) continued to revise and develop his work, but his original theories stuck in the public mind. In his later work, he emphasized that older adults, as they become more reflective, draw on resources developed in earlier stages; generativity, rather than being a stage one leaves behind as one moves into the last stage, is an ongoing process but differently expressed. At the integrity stage, one reviews prior stages on an ongoing basis, drawing on one's resources–a dynamic, regenerative practice that also reaffirms one's sense of self, or integrity.

Joan Erikson (1997), Erik's wife, added a ninth and last stage to Eriksonian theory. In her 90s, she speaks eloquently about this final stage, which describes those in their 80s and 90s, who realize that their feelings of hope and trust–the foundations of development–are constantly being challenged as they start losing what was gained in previous stages. Paradoxically, as one relinquishes these aspects of oneself, the remaining qualities–hope and faith–enable one to transcend material needs, except for what is immediately present (e.g., enjoying a child's laughter, enjoying the scent of roses, searching for one's glasses). The final stage–wisdom, or *gerotranscendence,* as she calls it–is similar to the transcendent states expressed in Jungian and Eastern spiritual practices.

Developmental Characteristics

Physical and Cognitive Capacities

As they age, people generally start losing physical agility and endurance; many cannot hear or see as well as they used to; and many suffer from crippling arthritis and need canes or walkers. Such physical losses, however, have been wrongly perceived as affecting all older adults. As mentioned earlier, part of the problem is society's tendency to lump all seniors together, even though the older population represents more than a 30- to 40-year span. The physical capacities of 65-year-olds are usually very different from those of people in their 80s, and 70-year-olds are usually more agile than 90-year-olds. Indeed, "as much variation exists in the type, rate, quantity and the impact of biological changes for the elderly as for younger age cohorts" (Harrigan & Farmer, 2000, p. 29).

Further misconceptions about the degree of physical deterioration in older adults may arise from misdiagnosis. The lack of mobility or agility in many older adults may result from high dosages of medications, poor nutrition, or lack of exercise. Physicians, nurses, gerontologists, psychologists, and other health care professionals may incorrectly attribute an older person's physical afflictions to the normal aging process.

On the positive side, although adults tend to acquire more physical limitations as they age, they also have more time and leisure to attend to good nutrition and to engage in physical fitness programs. Moreover, loss of some physical or sensory capacities tends to enhance other sensory capacities. Blind persons, for instance, are noted for their acute sense of hearing. Those persons slowed down by walkers or canes tend to observe more keenly everything around them, as is so poignantly portrayed in Terry Kay's book *To Dance With the White Dog* (1990).

Recent studies show that intelligence does not decline with age. Reports in earlier studies that intelligence scores dropped in adulthood were based on the use of intelligence tests standardized to youth-oriented tasks. These tests emphasized speed-based performance and abstract reasoning unrelated to experience. Researchers then began to compare the subscores of the intelligence tests of older adults and youths. They found that older adults outperformed younger adults on meaningful tasks involving knowledge, judgment, and experience (e.g., verbal reasoning, performance tests, information), whereas younger adults did better on speed tests, memory tasks, and abstract reasoning unrelated to meaningful or cultural experiences (Bjorklund & Bee, 2008; Cavanaugh & Blanchard-Fields, 2006).

Older people generally become concerned about losing their memory–an essential component of intelligence and reasoning. Studies have tended to show a slowdown, as one ages, in working memory, which involves the capacity to hold information in mind while at the same time using the information to solve problems or to acquire new learning (Bjorklund & Bee, 2008; Cavanaugh & Blanchard-Fields, 2006; Harrigan & Farmer, 2000).

But research also shows that memory differences between younger and older adults are insignificant when the material to be memorized is relevant and meaningful and when older adults are motivated (Cavanaugh & Blanchard-Fields, 2006; Knight, 2004). Younger people are quicker than older adults in memorizing nonsense syllables and digits, but older people may be insufficiently motivated because they do not sense the relevance of rote memorization tasks. Aside from the idea that older persons may be too wise to bother learning meaningless symbols, the question remains whether they have the cognitive capacity for rote memorization. Researchers have found that normally functioning, motivated older adults can regain skills on speed and memory tests with practice (Cavanaugh & Blanchard-Fields, 2006; Knight, 2004).

In 1993, Friedan challenged the prevailing belief among psychologists and gerontologists that human brain cells automatically deteriorate as the adult grows older. She cites the work of Diamond, Johnson, Protti, Ott, and Kajisa (1985), who studied brain cell deterioration in rats, including very old rats. Placing rats in a large cage in an enriched environment with loving care from attendants and with games and mazes to play with, the researchers compared these rats with other rats who were in an empty cage without loving care or an enriched environment. Those in the enriched environment increased their number of brain cells, whereas the brain cells of isolated rats withered.

The latest research findings run contrary to the traditional view that the brain stops developing after childhood and adolescence. Studies conducted by the brain research team at Princeton, headed by Elizabeth Gould (Gould, Reeves, Graziano, & Cross, 1999), found that in adult macaque primates, the brain continues to generate neurons that migrate to several regions of the neocortex, the area of cognitive functioning, learning, and memory. There, in the neocortex, the immature neurons differentiate and mature. Wylie and Simon (2002) support these findings in a review of the literature on brain research. "That the brain produces brand-new cells in maturity has become generally accepted, as has the idea that the brain is changing and growing continuously throughout life, shaped as much by experience as genetic heritage" (p. 28). Knight (2004) commented on this view by stating that older adults may tend to outperform the young, considering the extensive store of knowledge they have about how things are and how things work, especially in their individual area of expertise.

Psychosocial Development

Prevailing views about the aging process have held that as people get older, they become increasingly inflexible in their attitudes and behavior. Older people are stereotyped as adhering to old patterns of behavior, resisting new experiences, and being unwilling or unable to adapt to change.

In reality, however, older adults have gone through many transitions and varied relationships and upheavals throughout their lives, tasks that require considerable adaptation and flexibility. After they retire and their children leave home, older adults experience loss of status, change in housing, loss of friends and spouses, and loss of physical agility. Coping with these many changes requires fundamental adjustments in attitude and perspective.

Another general misconception has been that older people are expected to withdraw voluntarily from society as an inevitable step toward a new life filled with contentment and peace. This disengagement theory, developed by Cummings and Henry (1961) and considered a significant psychosocial process of aging, dominated the thinking of professionals and the general public for decades. Cummings and Henry declared that older adults who detached themselves from society were following a natural and optimally healthy process.

Recent research, however, indicates the opposite. Those who are least disengaged have higher morale, are healthier, and display more satisfaction (Adelmann, 1994; Bjork-lund & Bee, 2008). Healthy, normally functioning older adults tend to be well informed about current social issues and participate in worthwhile community activities (Cavanaugh & Blanchard-Fields, 2006). Older adults who want to serve the community do face barriers, however. Unlike earlier stages of development in which roles and tasks are laid out (e.g., careers, university degree programs, raising a family), older adults must carve out roles for themselves in untracked, innovative ways and must do so in a manner that allows them to maintain a sense of freedom, independence, and control over their lives.

Optimal Aging

Although humans have the capacity to continue to live meaningful, creative lives throughout their life span, many older adults do not attain this form of optimal aging. Instead, many are apt to spend their later years in humdrum, meaningless activities that lead to stagnation, depression, or immobilization. Professionals have been raising questions concerning why some older adults maintain a high quality of life while others do not.

They've been exploring the characteristics, strategies, habits, and environmental conditions that differentiate optimally aging persons from those who are not.

In 1961, Neugarten, Havighurst, and Tobin made the first major attempt to define successful aging when they developed a measure called the Life Satisfaction Index, which consists of five components: "zest (as opposed to apathy), resolution and fortitude, congruence between desired and achieved goals, positive self-concept, and mood tone" (Nussbaum et al., 2000, p. 330). Following this early work, other research studies were conducted, revealing by the mid-1980s "the multidimensional nature of aging" (Nussbaum et al., 2000). According to Ryff (1986), however, the research had generally failed because of little understanding of the aging process and an overall stereotypical view of the declining older adult. To counteract this approach, she proposed six criteria that represent successful aging based on an integration of life-span developmental and personal growth theories. Called an integrated model of personal development, her criteria are self-acceptance, positive relations with others, autonomy, environmental mastery, purpose in life, and personal growth (Nussbaum et al., 2000). In Ryff's view, successful, creative older adults are independent, willing to question and rebel against stifling societal norms, and proactive in shaping the environment to fit their needs.

Another perspective on successful aging was proposed by Rowe and Kahn (1998), who defined it as the ability to maintain three coordinated and integrated personal characteristics: a low risk of disease and disease-related disability, high mental and physical functioning, and active engagement in life. They emphasized that older adults need to follow a good diet, keep fit, and maintain a social network of friends and family while continuing productive activities that are valuable to society.

In their quest for meaning, older adults tend to focus on spiritual concerns and issues. Many undertake a healthy disengagement–not only the very old (those in their 80s and 90s) as discussed earlier, but also those in their 60s and 70s who are seeking an inner spiritual path. The spiritual quest is generally made in solitude; the older person disengages from the outside world, a tendency often misunderstood in an extraverted, ego-centered, secular-minded society. Older persons who retreat into themselves are judged as fading out, losing their minds, or getting senile, not only by caring loved ones, but also by most health care professionals. Even many religious organizations are unprepared to acknowledge and enhance the spiritual inner journey the older person takes. In his book *To Dance With the White Dog* (1990), Terry Kay eloquently describes such a man in his 80s who has lost his beloved wife of 60 years. When he adopts an imaginary white dog as his preferred companion for his inner journey, his overconcerned adult children believe that he's not in his right mind and consider sending him to an old folks home; he finally convinces them to see things his way.

In many other cultures, elders are honored and revered and are given special recognition as persons of wisdom. Baruth and Manning (2007) comment: "Many Japanese Americans equate old age with prestige and honor. Respect for elders is evident in the language used when addressing the elderly and in behavior such as bowing to them and observing strict rules of etiquette" (p. 216). Similarly, in Native American and Hispanic families, elders are not expected to withdraw, but rather to play the role of mentor to younger generations.

In writing about optimal aging, Friedan (1993) extends and adapts Erikson's concept of generativity to include older adults:

> Older leaders . . . as if driven by some larger generative impulse may move beyond the battles of special interests, the politically correct agenda or ideological imperatives. . . . [T]hey seem almost driven to use their wisdom to reconcile implacable differences that are consuming and wasting our human resources. (p. 617)

As an example of becoming more active and innovative participants in the community, seniors are beginning to develop and run their own programs at some senior centers, rather than merely following programs determined and administered by a younger staff. At the Whitney Senior Center in St. Cloud, Minnesota, for example, octogenarian Willis E. Dugan (1993) developed a remarkable senior activity project for the Retired Senior Volunteer Program (RSVP). This project engages seniors in a meaningful social activity that involves and benefits multiple generations: Senior citizens assist frail, elderly nursing home residents in constructing wood blocks and toys for children.

Another widely used activity for adults aged 55 and older is Elderhostel. Elderhostel is a not-for-profit organization that provides learning adventures to nearly 160,000 older adults each year—evidence that elders are eager for learning, but in ways that differ from those at conventional youth hostels (Elderhostel, 2007). Elderhostel offers nearly 8,000 programs a year in more than 90 countries. The success of these hostels is attributable, in part, to older persons' sense of freedom to choose to learn what they want and need. It fits their personal quest–their inner journey to acquire a renewed sense of meaning in life–a zest for learning that surpasses that of the average college student.

The success of Elderhostels that began in 1975 surprised even the founders. At a symposium on productive aging, Elderhostel founder Marty Knowlton (1996) said in his keynote address that he never expected the unbelievable response and progress in the development of Elderhostels worldwide: "We didn't know with whom we were dealing. They are marvelously responsive, extremely mentally alert, open, friendly, challenging." He pointed out that the key to the success of the experience is how challenging older people can be to their professors: "It hones the college professor to be sharper and sharper" every time he or she engages with an older-adult student.

THE COUNSELING NEEDS OF OLDER ADULTS

Many gerontologists and other professionals have been discussing the paradox of aging in our culture: a rapidly growing group of healthy, vigorous, older adults eager to learn and wanting to carve out new roles for themselves in a society that stereotypes them as no longer competent or as standing in the way of younger people (Cavanaugh & Blanchard-Fields, 2006).

As scholars have become more interested in the developmental aspects of aging, the counseling profession, too, has become more interested in the counseling needs of normally functioning older people (Myers & Schwiebert, 1996). Jane Myers (1989, 1990) has been instrumental in changing the attitudes and practices in mental health counseling with older adults.

> Mental health counseling with older persons is an emerging specialty stimulated by changing demographics and dramatic increases in the number of older persons during this century. Because most mental health counselors can expect to encounter older persons and their families with increasing frequency, an understanding of normative and developmental issues and transitions is imperative. (Myers, 1989, p. 245)

Largely through Myers's efforts, a national gerontological counselor certificate was established in 1990 by the National Board of Certified Counselors. Since then, more than one third of counselor training programs have added or expanded course offerings in counseling older adults (Myers & Schwiebert, 1996).

In a review of the literature on aging and counseling, Myers (1990) notes that counseling services for normally functioning older people do not meet the current need. She claims that considerable numbers of older adults have mental health concerns that could be responsive to treatment. Whereas older persons constitute 21% of the U.S. population, older adult clients represent only 6% of mental health clients in outpatient services. In contrast, the 10% to 15% of older adults who are chronically or severely mentally ill take up the major proportion of inpatient mental health resources. Myers (1990) comments: "Although older persons are under-represented in outpatient care, they are over-represented in inpatient mental health populations. More than 60 percent of public mental hospital beds are occupied by persons over age 65" (p. 251).

The latest viewpoints and research about older adults denote a much more optimistic view about therapeutic work with the elderly than the traditionally held attitudes among professional gerontologists and other health care professionals. Increasing numbers of counseling professionals are exploring their attitudes about counseling older adults. Myers (1990) and Knight (2004) have given attention to the unique counseling needs of older adult clients; Waters and Goodman (1990) have presented counseling strategies that are particularly useful in empowering older adults. Knight (2004), Myers (1990), and Waters (1990b) have discussed how counselor attitudes toward older adults influence the counseling relationship.

Other counseling practitioners have presented special techniques, such as life review and reminiscing, that are appropriate for counseling this age group (Crose, 1990; Knight, 2004; Sweeney, 1990; Waters, 1990a). As mentioned earlier, Jungian psychiatrist Allan Chinen (1989) presents the special technique of using elder fairy tales to guide older persons through a series of developmental tasks that help lead them through various transformational stages.

Characteristics of Older Adult Clients

Older adult clients–programmed by society to feel useless, weak, or incapable of learning–generally feel despair. Many are unaware of their potentialities to learn new skills, grow personally, and adapt to the many transitions in their lives. Nevertheless, older adults are potentially good prospects for counseling: They have had more complex and varied experiences in relationships, transitions, and losses than younger clients. They tend to have deeper insights and give more considered thought to issues. They have a longer timespan of past experiences to process and reflect on. They are apt to be more judicious and more contemplative in selecting a method to resolve their problems because they see more alternatives than do younger clients.

Knight (2004) comments about the rich psychological history that older adults bring into counseling. He notes that if an older adult's issue has been of concern for some time, there are probably examples of many different ways that the client has approached the problem in the past, with various outcomes of success and failure. He perceives that the challenge for counselors and clients is to take as much as possible from these past experiences and help clients see them from a perspective that is relevant to current needs.

Furthermore, postretirement individuals often have more time and energy to explore new behaviors, interests, skills, and relationships than do younger clients. Most are no longer committed to full-time jobs, nor are they involved in raising or supporting families. (However, that is changing. With so many adult children returning home to live with their parents, many older adults are now raising their grandchildren.)

Because older people are far more divergent in their outlook and experience and they span a far broader age range, they are just as diverse as younger persons in their attitudes and reactions to counseling and therapy. Elders in their 60s and 70s are usually more favorable toward counseling than are elders in their 80s and 90s. Those in their 80s and 90s, who grew up at a time when counseling was considered to be only for crazy people, are generally reluctant to seek or accept counseling. On the contrary, many in their 60s probably have had counseling of some sort or another. Some may be quite willing to seek counseling; others may be too therapy-wise and cynical about therapists.

With these considerations in mind, one can make some generalizations about the concerns of older adults that differ from those of younger clients. Adolescents, young adults, and midlifers are concerned by and large with strengthening their egos, developing careers, and raising families. The roles they play are fairly well established and reinforced in society. Older adults must contend with several complex changes that are unique to the later stage of life. The transitions that older people go through require changes in long-standing habits and lifelong patterns of living in a society that offers few prescribed roles to help guide them through the necessary adaptations. Some older people think that their skills are obsolete and are unaware of latent talents they may have that could be developed. Others who are eager and optimistic about applying their skills in new ways and developing latent talents in worthwhile endeavors find resistance from employers, training institutions, family, and peers, who are influenced by prevailing stereotypes about aging.

When they are no longer involved in maintaining careers or responsible for rearing children, many older adults are quite happy to be free from responsibility and enjoy taking trips, vacationing, or following a life of leisure. Many others, however, sensing that they are no longer needed either as parents or as valued employees, feel useless and full of despair. Erikson (1950) believes that these feelings of despair are central to the later stage of life-span development. He proposes that older persons faced with despair and disintegration no longer focus on outward or external connections as a way of finding meaning in life. Typically, their search for meaning turns inward. As discussed earlier, they reassess their past experiences and reintegrate them with the present to achieve new meaning, acquiring a renewed sense of self. Butler (1963) elaborates on this process of integration in which one looks back on life, in what he terms a *life review.*

Coping with Changes in Spousal Relationships

After children leave home and one or both spouses retire, the relationship between spouses often changes. The husband may hang around the house, getting in his wife's way. The wife is unaccustomed to having her husband underfoot; besides, she may be preoccupied with caring for her 90-year-old mother, who lives 50 miles away. In another scenario, described more fully later in the chapter, one spouse may become seriously ill and require constant caretaking by the healthier spouse–a role that the caregiving spouse may find emotionally and physically exhausting.

The death of a spouse also forces changes, new responsibilities, and challenges into the life of the surviving spouse at a time when she or he is in shock and grieving. The remaining spouse may have to take on unfamiliar household tasks previously carried out by the other spouse. The spouse may lose contact with previous friends and be uncertain about his or her new role as a single person.

Changing Intergenerational Relationships

Older adults' relationships with their adult children also go through changes. In many instances, adult children may not know how to respond to their parents' new patterns of living. In other numerous instances, adult children in their 30s are not yet economically established and are returning to live with their parents. Older adults are unaccustomed to such a phenomenon, and many are unprepared for such interruptions in their lives. In earlier days, elder parents passed away soon after adult children set up their own households and started raising families; certain predictable static relationships sufficed in those conventional lifestyles and shorter life spans. Now, however, intergenerational relationships take on complicated twists and are unpredictably fluid. Many older adults and their adult children are in contact with each other every day. At the other extreme, many are no longer in contact with each other at all. As with any dynamic interaction, loved ones experience strain and conflict. Working through the conflicts and resolving the misunderstandings are necessary parts of the developmental process.

New Roles in Grandparenting

In numerous cases, older adults are having to take on full-time care of their grandchildren. According to the U.S. Census Bureau, 3.7 million children (18 years of age or younger) are living in households headed by grandparents (Morrissey, 1997). Grandparents are often called upon to take over caring for grandchildren in situations where one parent has died or has left the family; is incapacitated by mental or physical illness, or alcohol or drug addiction; or is abusive or neglectful of the children. In these situations, the other parent, usually the father, is unwilling or unable to be responsible for parenting (Peterson, 2001). Many grandparents who become caregivers for their grandchildren find the job emotionally and financially taxing. Many who had put parenting behind them are once again faced with the challenges of child rearing, often with children who are emotionally damaged. Further complications arise because of confusion or ambiguity in the legal status of grandparents who want to enroll children in school or who want access to children's school or medical records (Peterson, 2001).

Another problem facing some grandparents involves their legal right to visit their grandchildren. Grandparent visitation may be refused or restricted when the parents divorce and an ex-spouse has full custody or when, less often, there are irreconcilable differences between grandparents and their son or daughter.

Over the past 30 years, grandparents have gained legal visitation rights to grandchildren in all 50 states. More recently, however, because of the concern that parents' rights with their children are being eroded, one third of the states have tightened their laws to reduce grandparents' visitation rights. As a result, more grandparents who have been suing for visitation rights have been losing in court (Gearon, 2003).

Changing Perspectives Toward Siblings

Sibling relationships among older adults often undergo marked changes as well. A brother or sister may suddenly take on added significance in one's later years. Sibling bonds differ from parent–child bonds: Siblings are more than peers; not only have they known each other longer than anyone else, but they are also blood relations, kinfolk who share a significant past. Older adults often seek out siblings whom they have not seen for years. Their high expectations of bonding as they used to may turn out to be a disappointment, or they may develop deep, fond relationships that they never had when they were young.

Coping with Physical Disabilities

Physical afflictions of various kinds are a major area of concern for older adults. Although many elderly individuals are physically fit and are involved in exercise programs, run marathons, and go on long bicycle treks, 75% of older people are physically limited in one way or another (Cavanaugh & Blanchard-Fields, 2006). Many have had hip operations, mastectomies, or heart bypass surgeries; many suffer from such chronic health problems as arthritis or back pain. Although some older adults with physical problems retreat to a sedentary, inactive lifestyle, many others partake in preventive health care programs by joining physical fitness clubs and eating healthful, nutritious meals. Many older adults learn to adapt to their physical limitations and increase activities that use other physical or sensory capacities. A once physically active older person now confined to a wheelchair may, for example, turn inward, develop a vivid imagination, and become a beloved storyteller.

Coping with Diminishing Financial Resources

In most cases, older adults' financial status determines their ability to adapt successfully to the many changes of later life, learn new skills, keep physically fit, and continue to be productive and self-sufficient. Whereas many older people are comfortable financially, many others, trying to survive on Social Security checks, worry about how to make ends meet. Their overriding concerns are about the rising costs of medical and dental care and their diminished income, as well as holding onto adequate housing for themselves.

The Counseling Process

The counseling process for older adult clients follows the stages described in chapter 8. Although this process parallels that used with younger clients, there generally are some differences with older clients, particularly in the types of counseling goals, transference and countertransference relationships, encouragement of client action, and the termination of counseling.

Counseling Goals

A major counseling goal is to help empower older adults to gain control of their lives. When they enter counseling, older clients typically express feelings of helplessness and hopelessness; they generally feel overwhelmed by losses, transitions, and changes in life. Such a goal can help older clients explore previously acquired coping skills and learn to use them in new ways. Older clients feel empowered when counselors help them refute ageist stereotypes, a necessary first step as they strive to carve out new roles and new relationships despite resistance from society or from those close to them.

Spiritual questions and concerns are often raised by older adults when former roles and long-held commitments are no longer existent or satisfying. The older client's goal in these instances is to explore new meanings and purposes in life that transcend immediate personal needs.

Another counseling goal particularly important to older clients, who generally feel isolated or lonely, is that of seeking out community support groups. Persons working through grief over the death of a spouse, spouses heavily burdened with caretaking duties, or individuals cut off from family or career relationships can profit from appropriate support groups.

Transference and Countertransference

In all counseling relationships, counselors and clients develop feelings toward each other based on unconscious attitudes arising from unresolved relationships in the past. Client feelings toward counselors are called *transference;* counselor feelings toward clients are called *countertransference* (see chapter 6). Until recently, therapists, following Sigmund Freud's original views, considered these feelings barriers to successful counseling. Therapists now believe that awareness and acceptance of feelings of transference and countertransference offer opportunities for both client and therapist to work through unresolved feelings, thereby strengthening the counseling relationship and rehearsing a process for developing more effective relationships in everyday life (Corey, 2005).

Successfully working through transference feelings with an effective counselor can help older adults clear up unresolved power issues between themselves and their adult children; work through unrealistic or negative expectations about relationships with grandchildren; or work through unresolved guilt feelings, jealousies, or power struggles with spouses or siblings either living or dead (Knight, 2004).

Genevay and Katz (1990) have explored countertransference with older adults. In their book *Countertransference and Older Clients,* they point out that counselors can be more effective with older clients when counselors recognize and make therapeutic use of these feelings.

> We come face to face with thoughts, memories, feelings and unresolved issues from our own lives. . . . We can connect our feelings and experiences with those of the patients and clients we serve; and we can provide better diagnosis and treatment in the process. Out of our own observations of ourselves and our aging families we can become more effective professionals and more sensitive to the people we help. (p. 13)

Counselor countertransference is a particularly important and complex part of the counseling process with older clients because clients are apt to be older than the counselors. Thus, counselors may overreact to client concerns on the basis of experiences that they, themselves, have had or are having with their own aging parents; they may overreact to their own fears about aging or to society's neglect of elders. At times, these counselor feelings may arise in reaction to the type of problem the older client is confronting–suicidal thoughts, declining physical or mental capacities, or death.

When an older client reminds a counselor of his or her mother or father, the counselor may become oversolicitous if the client seems frail. Or if the client disagrees or takes issue with what the counselor says, the counselor may feel threatened and think that his or her expertise is being challenged. The counselor may become more authoritative, determined to point out the client's faults or the need to change, or the counselor may distance him- or herself from the client and become indifferent to the dynamics of the relationship. When the age differential is large, the counselor may regard the client as a grandparent; countertransference reactions may then evoke protective feelings with the counselor perceiving the older person as one who must be protected from the middle generation's interference (Knight, 2004).

Counselors need to be alert to the pressures of negative countertransference when, for example, they become convinced that a client is too old to profit from therapy, they consistently misdiagnose depression as dementia or Alzheimer's disease, they insist without evidence that medication will be more satisfactory than therapy, or they feel bored, anxious, or unable to help (Genevay & Katz, 1990; Knight, 2004).

Encouraging Client Action

In the final stages of counseling, counselors and clients work jointly to search out new resources or new opportunities for growth and change based on insights gained in earlier sessions. This stage is particularly important for counselors and older clients because society tends to be unprepared for, unresponsive, or even resistant to older adults developing new social and career roles.

Older clients can take action to change their lives by making use of talents and skills in new and innovative ways. Retired history or language teachers, for example, may lead tours to foreign countries; retired biologists may lead nature treks. Others might develop talents that they had put aside early in life, such as playing a musical instrument, renewing their skills by taking lessons, becoming proficient, and/or joining the community orchestra. Someone who has collected antiques over the years might open an antiques shop.

Terminating Counseling

Counselors working with clients considerably older than themselves tend to find terminating sessions the most difficult part of counseling. Knight (2004) believes that it is almost always the therapist rather than the client who experiences termination as very difficult. Older clients, Knight says, often are reassured by termination, seeing it as an indication of having completed something successfully. They often have had more experience with endings and so are more used to them. Therapists, in contrast, tend to be more reluctant to end sessions because they fear that older persons may be too frail to deal with problems on their own or will experience loneliness or feel abandoned. Nevertheless, counselors do need to be alert to any client feelings of sadness, fear, resentment, or anxiety that might occur during the terminating stage of counseling. Counselors need to address these issues to the satisfaction of their clients before counseling is concluded.

Life Review: A Special Technique with Older Adults

In 1963, Robert Butler proposed that *life review* is a natural process experienced by older adults–a process in which a person reviews and reflects on past experiences, achievements, joys, and sorrows as a way of searching for a renewed sense of meaning in life.

Butler's life review is an amplification of Erikson's original view of the major developmental task of older adults. Erikson proposed that when older adults feel despair, they review and reevaluate their past and gain integrity, or a sense of coherence, in their lives. In later writings, Erikson and other developmental theorists expanded the life review concept as a means whereby elders can develop new, productive ways of living (Friedan, 1993; Harrigan & Farmer, 2000; Knight, 2004).

Life reviews are truly meaningful if older adults use them in life-enhancing, generative ways. They have become a popular technique in counseling and therapy with older adults. Crose (1990), Disch (1988), Knight (2004), Sherman (1991), Viney (1993), and Waters (1990a) have all written about life reviews and their appropriate use in counseling and therapy.

Life review activities are also led by those who are not counselors or therapists; writers and biographers often lead such workshops for older adults. The purpose and approach of noncounselors is quite different, however, because they use life review nontherapeutically. In this discussion, life review is used therapeutically by professionally trained counselors and therapists for those clients who express a need for it.

A counselor cannot expect a client to come forth with a complete life review that encompasses many decades of life. Knight (2004) sees the counselor as a directive in helping the client through the life review process. According to Knight, counselors should note any large gaps in client stories to encourage deeper exploration of areas that clients might be avoiding. Counselors act as editors in helping clients make choices about what areas are important to cover. Knight recommends that positive elements be emphasized if the goal of counseling is to help clients improve their sense of well-being. If the aim is to change long-standing behaviors, counselors may have to work on hidden negative experiences that need to be acknowledged and worked through. Consideration of how lifetime stories tie in with clients' future ways of life is essential (Knight, 2004; Waters, 1990a).

In contrast with Knight's directive approach, many counselors prefer to act as guides, rather than as editors, in the life review process. Rather than trying to influence or shape the content of older adult recollection, they encourage clients to talk about memories that are important to them. Furthermore, they encourage clients to do their own interpreting of these remembrances.

Life review should be done by well-trained counselors. Disch (1988) has expressed concern that mental health practitioners who are untrained in adult development might misuse or overuse life review. Waters (1990a) considers it a valuable tool for counselors, but cautions that "life reviews may trigger sadness and depression for people who feel extreme dissatisfaction with their lives" (p. 277).

Knight (2004) also believes that life review should not be used indiscriminately. He suggests that it is not typically appropriate or useful for problem-focused concerns related to specific situational changes that do not unduly disrupt the older adult's life. He recommends using life review when older adults are grieving and need to develop new perspectives about their lives or when they are experiencing new emotions that must be integrated into the self. Furthermore, he sees life review as a useful technique when older adults themselves raise doubtful, despairing questions about how well they have lived their lives and wonder how they can continue to live productively.

Life review techniques have been incorporated into some well-established counseling approaches–for example, Gestalt, Adlerian, personal construct, and Jungian. Gestalt techniques can be used during a life review to help delve into unfinished business (Crose, 1990). Clients are encouraged to reexperience their past stories by enacting them. The older person may be asked to dialogue with someone who is dead or otherwise unavailable in order to resolve conflict with that person (the empty chair technique). Alfred Adler believed that individuals' earliest recollections are essential clues to understanding their unique styles of life. In line with this view, Sweeney (1990) encourages older adult clients to use purposeful reminiscing as a means toward modifying their lifestyles in a positive way.

Personal construct theory (see chapters 6 and 9) can also be effectively applied during the life review process (Viney, 1993). This approach is based on the assumption that elders have acquired complex constructs of meanings from the events they have experienced over the years. These constructs are reconstrued and modified during the therapeutic process, enabling clients to experience change or transformation. Commenting on a personal construct approach to elders, Viney (1993) says,

> They are also seen like all adults, as actively handling their own flaws of experience, being able to reflect on that process and to recognize that they are, themselves, agents of it. They are also able to integrate separate aspects of this experience over time in the stories they construct and to reintegrate it when events make such change appropriate by retelling their stories. (p. 9)

Viney (1993) believes that reconstruing and reintegrating experiences is at the core of psychological development. This integration can best be accomplished by listening to elders tell and retell their stories in therapy. Through this process, elders can "work through grief and guilt, getting in touch with strengths, both personal and interpersonal, and unleashing creativity and enjoyment as well as that most fulfilling sense of integrity" (p. 50).

Jungian psychiatrist Alan Chinen (1989) uses the telling of elder fairy tales as an imaginative way to help older adults review their lives. In working through the messages of the elder fairy tales, Chinen says, "The elder embraces the past, not to regress but to illuminate all of life. The end is the beginning transfigured" (p. 137). Chinen (1989) makes a sharp distinction between youth fairy tales, in which the young hero is the protagonist in search of achievement and glory, and elder fairy tales, in which the older person is the protagonist in search of maturity and wisdom. Youth tales, common in our culture, focus on ego identity and achievement–essential developmental tasks in the first half of life. Heroes and heroines conquer dragons, witches, and evil older people to achieve perfect love and a kingdom. End of story. Elder tales, on the other hand, which begin where the youth-oriented tales end, are concerned with essential developmental tasks in the second half of life: self-confrontation, self-transcendence, and emancipation–tasks that lead to compassion and wisdom.

Life review can be effective in group counseling, as well as in individual counseling. When working with groups, stimuli such as music or memorabilia such as newspaper clippings or old family photographs can be used to trigger recollections (Waters, 1990a). Sharing stories is another way of evoking memories. As in any group counseling, however, counselors need to be certain that neither they nor any group members pressure or try to persuade another group participant to share memories that she or he is not ready or willing to share.

Special Problems of Older Adults

Depression

Depression has become the major mental health problem of older adults. It is estimated that 20% of the elderly have some sort of mild or moderate depression (Myers, 1990). Chronic clinical depression among older adults is relatively uncommon; those suffering from chronic depression tend to have intense and persistent sadness and pessimism not obviously related to anything specific in their lives. These intense feelings interfere with their ability to function adequately socially or physically. Those with mild or moderate depression feel sad or in a down mood because they are suffering from specific losses or transitions that are stressful or unexpected. They are, however, usually able to meet daily responsibilities (Schmall, Lawson, & Stiehl, 1993).

Depression in older adults is often overlooked or misdiagnosed. Health care professionals tend either to misdiagnose depressive symptoms or to overprescribe antidepressant medication and ignore the value of counseling and psychotherapy. Stooped posture, minimal physical activity, sleep disturbances, and reduced appetites, all of which are typical symptoms of depression, are also characteristic of many frail, sickly older people who are not depressed. In addition, misdiagnosis may occur because many older adults who are depressed deny and cover up their feelings because they are afraid they would be diagnosed as crazy. At times, symptoms of depression such as weakness and fatigue may be misdiagnosed as a sign of a particular physical illness. Furthermore, some older depressed people exhibit temporary memory problems and confusion that mimic dementia or Alzheimer's disease. If mental health workers are unaware of this similarity, they may make incorrect diagnoses of dementia (Schmall et al., 1993). Ageism may also contribute to misdiagnosis. Professionals who automatically equate older age with cognitive loss fail to consider other factors, such as feelings of depression, lack of exercise, or malnourishment.

The misuse or overuse of medication for depression has particular ramifications for older adults. Physicians and mental health workers who believe that older adults are not responsive to counseling because of their age tend to prescribe only medication. This occurs despite statistics showing that psychotherapy or counseling, along with medication, has a higher success rate than medication alone (Jakubiak & Callahan, 1996).

Suicide

Adults 65 years of age and older have the highest risk of suicide of any age group (Granello & Granello, 2007). If an older adult's depression goes unrecognized or is misdiagnosed as dementia, the person may become suicidal. Counselors must be particularly attentive to the possibility of suicidal intentions in depressed older adults.

Factors that contribute to the high risk of suicide in older adults include severe losses, such as the death of a loved one; prolonged feelings of hopelessness, helplessness, or isolation; prior attempts at suicide; heavy alcohol or drug use; an expressed desire to kill oneself; and the availability of a lethal weapon (Schmall et al., 1993). Most of these symptoms are similar to those of suicidal younger people. In older adults, however, chronic physical ailments, adverse reactions to multiple prescription drugs, losses, and isolation play a larger part. Moreover, older people are more determined to follow through with the intent to kill themselves, and they are more likely to succeed in their suicide attempts.

Elder Abuse and Neglect

Elder abuse or neglect by caregivers has only recently come to the attention of mental health counselors and other professionals. Elder abuse occurs in various ways–physical and psychological abuse, financial exploitation, and neglect. Caregivers may physically or verbally assault elders, steal or misuse elders' money or property, leave elders in unsanitary or hazardous living environments, or withhold appropriate care.

According to the best estimates, between 1 million and 2 million Americans age 65 or older have been injured, exploited, or otherwise mistreated by someone on whom they depended for care or protection (National Research Council, 2003). Older persons are most likely to be abused by their adult children and by their spouses. But abuse also occurs all too often in nursing homes. Pillemir and Moore (1989) surveyed more than 500 nurses and nurse's aides working with older adults in nursing facilities. Results showed that 10% of the respondents said that they had physically abused a resident, and 40% reported that they had psychologically abused a resident. When they were asked about their observations of how other staff members treated elderly patients, however, the levels of abuse rose dramatically: 36% reported that they had observed other staff members physically abusing elderly patients, and 81% reported witnessing acts of psychological abuse.

Abuse or neglect of the elderly is more likely to be detected and prevented in long-term care (LTC) facilities than in private homes. For those elderly people who live in private homes, abuse rarely gets reported (Sue & Sue, 2007). The elderly often are powerless when spouses or sons or daughters abuse or neglect them. Overcome with shame or fear of abandonment and impaired by physical disability, they are reluctant or unable to report abuse. Shelters are available where abused children or abused spouses can escape for protection, but unfortunately, no such emergency facilities are available for older abused persons who need to be separated from their abusers.

Elder protective services have been mandated in all states to serve older adults who are being neglected or abused. Whenever health care professionals notice signs of elder abuse in clinics or in LTC facilities, they are required to report it to elder protective services. When abuse is reported to protective services and the circumstances are assessed, several actions are possible. Arranging for alternative care is one option; another is determining whether the abuse was precipitated by a caregiver becoming overstressed. Caregivers can be helped to assess the degree of overload and can be taught how and where to seek help when stress levels escalate (Sue & Sue, 2007).

Respite care is available in most communities to give overburdened caregivers assistance, relief, and time-out. Arrangements can also be made for visiting nurses or other health care professionals to come to the home at regular intervals to bathe the patient, check on medication, change bedding, and attend to other similar tasks. These services are particularly helpful when the caregiver is physically unable to lift or move the elder. In addition, caregivers can get help in preparing meals or in doing household chores. These services ease stress and permit caregivers to have some time to themselves, run errands, or engage in their own social activities. Many caregivers could also benefit from counseling, which can help them work through feelings of helplessness, anger, grief, or guilt when strained relationships reach a breaking point (see "Counseling Needs of Caregivers" later in this chapter).

When professionals become aware that an elderly person is being exploited financially, they can assist the elder in getting legal advice and legal protection. Reputable attorneys now specialize in elder law. In these instances, counseling can help the older person work through feelings of anger, depression, or grief at the betrayal of a trusted adviser, loved one, or caregiver.

Loss: Death and Dying

Losses can happen at any time during a person's life–for example, the loss of one's job, loss of a home, loss of a loved one, or, for the terminally ill, the imminent loss of one's own life–but such losses generally occur more often in the later stages of life. Individuals suffering from losses such as these without an opportunity to go through the process of grieving can experience emotional and physical problems (James, 2008; Marino, 1996). Depression, disorientation, and anxiety disorders result from unresolved grief (Marino, 1996). Many therapists claim, however, that those suffering from losses develop new strengths as they work through the grieving process; it enables them to realize new opportunities for growth. Accepting change in life empowers and revitalizes.

Confronting one's own mortality and facing one's own death are the ultimate stages of development (James, 2008; Kübler-Ross, 1974). In her classic book *On Death and Dying* (1969), Elizabeth Kübler-Ross points out the general denial of death among most people in our culture. She explores the need for greater understanding of the emotional problems–the fears and denials–of terminally ill patients and their families.

Through interviews with 200 terminally ill persons, Kübler-Ross found that most people go through five emotional stages: denial, anger, bargaining, depression, and final acceptance. She perceives that *denial* is a normal stage of getting ready to die. After accepting the reality of death, patients then experience *anger* and resentment, which are generally projected onto the family and caregivers. In the next stage, they try *bargaining* to delay or postpone death. When they realize that this is futile, *depression* sets in, followed by *final acceptance* of the inevitability of death and a sense of peace. In a later publication, Kübler-Ross (1974) cautions against considering these steps to be fixed stages that everyone experiences at the same time. The process of emotional response may differ significantly in individuals.

When working with a client who is dying, counselors need to consider the client's degree of physical pain and deterioration, psychological outlook, the number and nature of interpersonal attachments, and the amount of energy and degree of hope (Cavanaugh & Blanchard-Fields, 2006; Corr, 1991–1992). Counselors also need to take into account the setting in which the client is being cared for–at home, in a hospital, or in an LTC facility. Cavanaugh and Blanchard-Fields (2006) recommend using a form of life review in which counselors encourage clients and family members to write narratives about earlier life experiences, which can help them work through emotional blocks to grieving.

The most valuable contribution that counselors and other mental health workers can make is to help dying individuals maintain some semblance of control and independence in their lives. Whenever possible, the dying person should be involved in all end-of-life decisions (Cavanaugh & Blanchard-Fields, 2006; Schulz & Salthouse, 1999). These considerations are especially important to older adults because these people are particularly susceptible to feelings of helplessness.

HOSPICE CARE.   Until the 1940s, most terminally ill older adults spent their last days at home, being cared for by family members and friends. From the 1940s through the 1970s, most dying persons died in impersonal, clinically oriented institutions, isolated from loved ones and family and with little or no attention paid to their emotional and psychological needs (Cavanaugh & Blanchard-Fields, 2006).

In 1967, in reaction to the sterile, isolating institutional approach, St. Christopher Hospice was established. This center emphasized a more humanitarian approach to caring for the terminally ill, a method that combined institutional and home care. This movement spread quickly throughout the United States, and today, there are more than 2,200 hospice programs.

The major focus in hospice care is involving family members in the care of the dying person in a warm, personal atmosphere. Hospice services generally work out of a patient's home or a family home. Cared for in familiar surroundings and in significant contact with family and friends, the patient can attend to her or his impending death with less fear and apprehension. Not only are family and friends more involved in daily caretaking, but they also are able to visit with the patient more often, listen to the patient's stories, and offer comfort and reassurance in the patient's last days. The patient and loved ones have more opportunities to say good-bye and to let go of past conflicts through reconciliation and forgiveness.

Professional assistance is provided by an interdisciplinary team of professionals, which may include physicians, visiting nurses, social workers, and counselors. Assistance is also given at regularly scheduled times with such caretaking tasks as bathing the patient, preparing meals, and doing household chores. A counselor can be particularly helpful when family members experience undue stress from caretaking, express unresolved conflict with the terminally ill patient, or experience debilitating grief over losing their loved one.

THE GRIEVING PROCESS AND GRIEF COUNSELING.   Kübler-Ross (1969) suggests that the family members of the dying person go through similar stages of grieving: denial, anger, guilt, preparatory grief, and the final stage of saying good-bye. Their emotional reactions and behaviors, however, are quite different from those of the dying patient. Family members may shop around from physician to physician, hoping for a different diagnosis, or they may feel guilty that they did not do more for the patient. Counseling family members during the early stages of grief can help them continue to work through the grieving process after their loved one dies. For those patients who are terminally ill, family members have some time to anticipate and begin the grief process. Sudden, unexpected deaths, however, have the additional impact of shock and a lack of opportunity to say good-bye or to resolve unfinished business.

Whether death is expected or unexpected, counselors must consider various factors when assessing the intensity and duration of a client's grief. How central was the deceased in the client's life? How troubled was the client's relationship with the deceased? Has the client recently experienced other deaths or serious losses? Does the client have unresolved grief reactions from earlier stages of life?

More recently, some counselors and other mental health professionals have questioned the value of the stage model of grieving based on Kübler-Ross's work. Grief work specialists Neimeyer and Worden believe that the stage theory implies a passive process that clients go through over a period of time. They propose instead a more active mode in which persons actively resolve grief (Marino, 1996). Worden (2001) has developed a series of grief work stages that he believes allows clients to have that more active role. Termed *emotional tasks,* the stages are (a) accepting the reality of the loss, (b) experiencing the pain of grief, (c) adjusting to an environment in which the deceased is missing, and (d) withdrawing emotional energy from the lost relationship and investing it elsewhere.

Marino (1996) describes how Robert Neimeyer has adapted Worden's approach and has developed what he calls an *active adaptation model* of grieving. Neimeyer has clients face denial by encouraging them to tell the stories of their loss and share their loss with family and friends. He helps clients acknowledge the pain, not only of the initial loss, but also of the suffering afterward from the deprivation. Clients are then helped to adapt to new environments without the loved one. In the case of the loss of a spouse, this adaptation often includes taking on tasks that had been done by the partner. Suddenly faced with unfamiliar responsibilities, the survivor often has to learn quickly to manage finances, prepare meals, repair the house, or learn to drive. In the last stage of grief counseling, clients are encouraged to connect with other people and to develop new interests and activities in life.

Feelings of guilt are the most complex emotional experiences a survivor must work through, especially if the death was sudden and traumatic or the result of suicide, or if the relationship with the loved one had been troublesome. Caregivers are apt to feel guilty when they experience relief after a patient dies. Or a grieving widow may believe that she neglected the dying husband or was unnecessarily difficult with him (Knight, 2004; Worden, 2001). In these cases, Gestalt techniques are recommended, such as role-playing or the empty chair dialogue, in which the client has imaginary discussions with the deceased over unresolved issues (Knight, 2004; Worden, 2001). Psychodrama also works well in a group setting in which the client enacts scripts with other group members, one of whom portrays the deceased person (Worden, 2001).

Grief specialist Gary Price believes that this active adaptation model works best in group counseling (Marino, 1996). The process of having group members share stories of loss helps normalize the grieving process, offers mutual support to group members, and expedites the resolution of conflicts resulting from the loss.

ABNORMAL GRIEF REACTIONS. Sorrow, sadness, loneliness, denial, anger, disbelief, guilt, and depression are all natural and expected emotional reactions to loss. What distinguishes normal from abnormal reactions, however, is not the type of emotion being expressed, but rather the intensity and duration of the response (Cavanaugh & Blanchard-Fields, 2006). Persons suffering from guilt and self-blame that persist over a long time are experiencing abnormal grief reactions. These feelings disrupt the individual's life and turn into long-term depression, which may manifest itself in chronic fatigue or tension or may include obsessional thoughts about the deceased long after the person has died. The grieving individual may refuse to move the deceased's belongings or may resist developing new relationships long after a reasonable time of mourning has passed (Cavanaugh & Blanchard-Fields, 2006; Knight, 2004).

Counseling in Long-Term Care Settings

Increasing numbers of counselors are working with older adults in long-term care (LTC) settings. Counseling may occur in nursing homes, residential centers, adult day care centers, or clients' homes. These older adults may be experiencing emotional distress related to a disability, grief over a loss or conflicts with caregivers or family members, or depression or difficulty in adjusting to the restraints of LTC settings.

For various reasons, the counseling needs of older adults in LTC settings have not been adequately met. Nursing homes have replaced mental hospitals as the major institution caring for older adults with mental illness; as a result, about two thirds of the elderly in these facilities have some form of psychiatric disorder (Jakubiak & Callahan, 1996). Of the remaining elderly residents, those with developmental concerns tend to be ignored. Thus, neither group receives psychiatric help or counseling. Nursing home surveys in the 1980s show that only 2% of nursing home patients received care from a mental health professional (Jakubiak & Callahan, 1996).

In the 1990s, counseling in nursing homes increased following the enactment of the Omnibus Budget Reconciliation Act (OBRA) in 1987 (Jakubiak & Callahan, 1996). Subsection C, entitled Nursing Home Reform, deals with the regulation of activities, services, and certification of nursing homes. This act calls for monitoring of the quality of life in nursing homes and screening of persons with mental illness and mental retardation before admission. The act also specifies that counseling and therapy services must be offered by trained professionals.

Counseling in LTC settings differs in some ways from counseling in most other settings. In long-term care, most of the counselor's work is done outside the office, through a lot of brief, intermittent counseling and response to crises. Counselors must also work closely with physicians because older adult clients usually have medical problems accompanying their psychological issues. It is particularly important that counselors be aware of the various medications that clients are taking and their effects on the clients' physical and emotional well-being.

LTC clients generally show anxiety or depression and feel helpless as a consequence of having lost autonomy and independence. Feelings of loss are central in the lives of LTC elders: the loss of spouses, relatives, and friends, as well as the loss of independence and control. In these instances, counselors help clients work through emotions such as denial and anger–feelings that are a normal part of the grieving process. Working through grief, as discussed earlier, permits clients to explore ways of adapting to life as LTC patients.

Older LTC adults may be referred to counseling because they are striking out at caregivers or other residents or are yelling, swearing at others, or otherwise being disruptive. The counselor's role is to provide a safe place for them to vent their feelings of helpless rage and frustration and to suggest ways they can gain some sense of control over their lives (James, 2008). Counselors can consult with caregivers about allowing clients to have more options and be able to make choices in their daily lives. For example, clients may be involved in menu selection, choice of recreational activities, or decisions about the number of visitors allowed or the timing of the visits. At the same time, counselors can encourage clients to express their feelings about their disability. Counselors can also discuss how clients can approach their daily activities in new ways.

Professional counselors working with LTC clients use relaxation techniques, cognitive restructuring, Gestalt techniques focused on naming and expressing emotions, and life review (Knight, 2004; Waters, 1990a). Relaxation exercises can be effective with older adults who are overly anxious. The exercises can focus on relaxing muscles, deep breathing, or light exercise. Clients generally find it easier to explore their feelings or concerns after therapeutic body work.

Cognitive restructuring can be helpful with clients who are depressed or who have exaggerated feelings of helplessness. A realistic appraisal of their physical and emotional concerns helps them confront their problems directly and reduces their tendency to exaggerate or overgeneralize their symptoms (Knight, 2004). For LTC clients who appear stoic, strained, and tense because of losses, Gestalt techniques can help them identify and express emotions. For example, while clients bring up painful feelings, they are encouraged to notice their bodily sensations and emotional reactions.

Life review can be effective with older LTC clients who express concerns about a lack of meaning in life or who express interest in exploring their past. Gestalt techniques can be helpful in the life review process. Clients can reenact past experiences as if they were in the present or can have an imaginary dialogue about an unresolved conflict with someone who has since died, bringing forth painful past experiences into the present. These activities permit new perspectives and new meanings to reshape the memories of past experiences (Crose, 1990).

Counselors can work closely with caregivers when counseling LTC clients, but as in all other settings, maintaining confidentiality between counselor and client is essential to the integrity of the counselor–client relationship. Only if clients are in danger of harming themselves or others may counselors share information without client consent.

Counseling Needs of Caregivers

It is estimated that about 44.4 million Americans (21% of the adult population) are involved in the caregiving of older adults (National Alliance for Caregiving and AARP, 2004). Family members, especially spouses, are the most common and preferred source of caretaking, followed by friends, volunteer agencies, and, lastly, nursing home and other caretaking agencies (Kropf, 2000). Caregivers often are spouses who themselves may have some degree of physical incapacity. Many middle-age adults also do some form of caretaking of one or more of their parents. According to Bjorklund and Bee (2008), about 37% of middle-age women will do some caretaking. Many of these women will be caught in a generational squeeze, having to care for both their children and their ailing parent(s).

Older adults requiring long-term intensive care generally have higher morale and more peace of mind when family members are the major caregivers. Family members who provide such care out of love and concern give generously of their time and energy. But caretaking can also become taxing financially, physically, and emotionally (Kropf, 2000). When the demands of caretaking become overwhelming, caregivers often become overstressed and depressed (Belsky, 1998; Bjorklund & Bee, 2008). Factors other than the actual duties of care often contribute to that pressure. For instance, if caregivers feel a lack of appreciation or support from other family members, if their relationship with the older person has always been troublesome, or if they have not learned problem-solving strategies, the burden of care may become particularly stressful (Belsky, 1998).

Counselors can help caregivers deal with the ongoing stress of caretaking by helping them explore and work through feelings of resentment and entrapment. These feelings often result from countertransference when the patient makes unrealistic demands on the caregiver or becomes overly dependent or manipulative (Delmaestro, 1990; Katz, 1990). Counselors can also suggest ways to reduce stress, such as making arrangements for respite care. In addition, caregivers can be encouraged to talk with health care professionals about ways to manage caretaking more efficiently. Counselors can also refer them to caregiver support groups, if available in their community, where feelings and suggestions about caretaking are shared.

Counselors should become informed about support networks in the community that specialize in working with older people. Local hospitals often have social workers on staff who can arrange regular visiting nurse and housekeeping services for older people in their homes. Counselors can also help caregivers develop and make use of support services that help with shopping, meals, and housekeeping. In addition, churches and synagogues often provide supplementary caretaking services for older adults (Kropf, 2000).

During counseling, caregivers may come to realize that they are unable to continue giving personal care to loved ones. Counselors can then help clients express and work through the feelings of guilt or ambivalence about giving up caretaking duties and help them make alternative caretaking arrangements for their loved ones.

Because of frustration, caregivers in LTC facilities at times get overly angry at residents when they are disruptive or unmanageable or when they curse or hit staff and other residents. In reaction, some staff members have resorted to subduing residents by applying physical restraints (e.g., tying patients to beds or wheelchairs) or sedating them heavily with drugs. Counselors can help caregivers in LTC facilities acknowledge and work through their feelings of anger and frustration when elderly patients make unrealistic demands or become overly dependent or manipulative (Delmaestro, 1990; Katz, 1990). When caregivers work through their own countertransference feelings with a counselor or therapist, they can better assess and understand elderly patients' feelings of helpless frustration and anger. Caregivers then are more responsive to counselor suggestions regarding ways to prevent the emotional or physical outbursts of their elderly patients.

CONSULTATION WITH FAMILIES OF OLDER ADULTS

In addition to offering counseling services to older adults or to the caregivers of older adults, counselors offer counseling services to family members who have concerns about their aging parents. One example is helping adult children determine whether their parents are capable of living independently or whether they need care. If they need care, then the type of care needs to be explored. Should the older adults live with their children, get full-time or part-time help from visiting nurses, or move to an assisted-living center or a nursing home? A counselor can also help adult children of the elderly recognize when they may be overanxious about their parents' welfare and when they realistically need to intervene on their parents' behalf.

SUMMARY

Healthy older adults have become a significant force in society as life expectancy has increased dramatically since 1900. By the year 2030, older adults will represent more than 20% of the total population. The increased longevity of healthy older adults stimulated human development scholars to explore the unique developmental processes of people 65 years of age and older. Contrary to general belief, they found that most individuals continue to develop and grow throughout their life spans.

Stereotypes about older adults interfere with their growth potential. The most detrimental stereotype is that of equating aging with decline and deterioration. This stereotype is based on society's tendency to idealize and emulate a youth model.

As more and more older adults are living longer and healthier lives, the demand for older adult counseling services has increased. Counselors can help older adults adapt to the many changes and transitions they experience in the later part of life. They can guide older adults in their search for new and productive roles and activities.

The counseling process with older adults is similar to that used with clients at other age levels. Some aspects, however, are unique to counseling older adults: (a) Counseling goals focus on helping clients regain control over their lives; (b) countertransference issues related to ageism and to the fear of getting old are common among counselors working with clients who are much older than the counselor; (c) counselors need to help clients overcome barriers in society that interfere with their carving out new roles in their lives; and (d) life review, in which a person reflects on and reevaluates past experiences to gain new meaning or purpose in life, is particularly suitable for older adult clients.

Gerontological counselors must be aware of problems that are especially troublesome for older adults. Their rates of depression and suicide are the highest of any age group. Elder abuse or the neglect of frail elders, often unreported, occurs frequently in the elders' own homes, as well as in long-term care facilities. Losses of loved ones, careers, and family responsibilities are commonplace in older adults. The numbers of those suffering from terminal illness increase with advancing age. Grief work counseling helps older adults and their loved ones work through suffering and loss. In the case of terminally ill patients, counselors work with hospice services specifically developed to care for dying persons and their families.

Gerontological counselors also offer valuable services to individuals who are long-term caregivers. They can help caregivers work through countertransference, recommend ways of reducing stress, and refer the caregivers to appropriate support groups.

PROJECTS AND ACTIVITIES

1. Interview one of your grandparents or someone old enough to be your grandparent regarding his or her views about the transitions, changes, or conflicts he or she has experienced in the later years. How consistent are these views with the views discussed by developmental theorists?
2. Think of an individual 65 years of age or older who you believe is functioning optimally and another who seems to be having difficulty coping with changes in life. What factors may be contributing to their differences in functioning?
3. Interview two counselors, one male and one female, regarding their views about counseling older adults. Do you notice any differences in their views about the developmental processes of older adults? If so, what are they?
4. Visit a senior center. Notice whether any activities are related to counseling services.
5. Check television, newspapers, and films and note any stereotypes of older adults.

CHAPTER 15

Counseling Programs in Schools

Children's mental health has declined sharply since the mid-1980s as a result of changing family patterns, an unstable society, rapidly changing values, and a deteriorating home life. According to the 2003 National Survey of Children's Health, the most commonly diagnosed problems among children 6–17 years of age were learning disabilities (11.5%), attention-deficit/hyperactivity disorder (8.8%), and behavioral problems (6.3%) (Blanchard, Gurka, & Blackman, 2003). The number of children with "developmental delays" being served in schools under the federal Individuals with Disabilities Education Act (IDEA) has increased 633% between 1997–1998 and 2000–2001, and the number of children with "autism" being served has increased 400% since first reported in 1992–1993 (U.S. Department of Education, 2002).

Children's emotional and behavioral problems are most evident in classrooms, where children generally spend most of their waking hours under adult scrutiny and supervision. Emotional stress interferes with children's academic and social progress and causes children to withdraw from or disrupt classroom activities. Adolescents face developmental and transitional challenges in which they struggle with their identities, make important educational and career decisions, develop intimate peer relationships, and try to become more independent and self-sufficient. School counseling programs can help address students' emotional problems that may affect academic and social performance, as well as benefit parents, teachers, administrators, and the overall community as well (American School Counseling Association [ASCA], 2005).

After studying this chapter, you will

- Have knowledge about the profession of school counseling.
- Be familiar with the ASCA National Model: A Framework for School Counseling Programs.
- Understand the differences in school counseling in elementary, middle, and high schools.

255

- Be acquainted with the types of activities and interventions commonly used by school counselors.

THE PROFESSION OF SCHOOL COUNSELING

At the turn of the 20th century, school counselors did not exist. Instead, teachers used a few minutes of their time to offer vocational guidance to students preparing for work (ASCA, 2005, p. 8). In the late 1950s and early 1960s, the National Defense Education Act provided funds to colleges and universities to develop programs to train school counselors to focus primarily on vocational guidance. Since that time, the profession of school counseling has continued to grow as new legislation and new professional developments were established to refine and further the profession and improve education (Schmidt, 2003). The role of the school counselor has grown from simply a vocational focus to addressing the emotional and developmental needs of students.

Along with growth over the years came confusion about the role of school counselors. This was brought on by differences in opinions about how to train school counselors, what to call school counselors (e.g., vocational counselor, guidance counselor), and questions about appropriate activities of counselors in the schools. In addition, the No Child Left Behind Act of 2001 (NCLB)—which imposed a system of accountability on schools focused almost exclusively on academic achievement—brought about more changes to the functions of school counselors (Akos, 2005).

As a result of the profession evolving, school counseling has gone through, and continues to go through, a period of extensive reform and restructuring. In the 21st century, "school counselors will need to define who they are more definitively as well as deal with external forces that wish to define or confine them" (Gladding, 2007, p. 422). Devising, implementing, and documenting the effectiveness of comprehensive school counseling programs will be essential in this process.

The ASCA National Model: A Framework for School Counseling Programs

In response to the historical and ongoing challenges in school counseling, the American School Counselor Association (ASCA) developed the *ASCA National Model: A Framework for School Counseling Programs* (2005). This model redefined and more fully developed the role of the school counselor. In the ASCA National Model, emphasis is placed on comprehensive counseling programs that are central to the academic mission of the school, are accessible to all students, include the knowledge and skills all students need, and are delivered systematically to all students.

The ASCA National Model defines the role of the professional school counselor as a certified/licensed educator who addresses the needs of students comprehensively through the implementation of a school counseling program (ASCA, 2005). The model consists of the following four interrelated components:

1. Foundation—the beliefs, philosophy, and mission of a school counseling program.
2. Delivery system—the activities, interactions, and methods of delivering a school counseling program.
3. Management system—the organizational processes that ensure that a school counseling program is organized, concrete, clearly delineated, and reflective of the school's needs.

4. Accountability—the collection of data that are used to evaluate and hold accountable the school guidance program.

The second component of a comprehensive school counseling program, the delivery system, specifically addresses how school counseling programs will be implemented by school counselors in terms of guidance curriculum, individual student planning, responsive services, and systems support. *Guidance curriculum* refers to structured developmental lessons designed to help students achieve desired competencies and to provide students with the developmentally appropriate knowledge and skills. *Individual student planning* involves school counselors coordinating activities that help students establish personal goals and future plans. *Responsive services* refers specifically to the primary activities school counselors engage in to meet students' immediate needs (ASCA, 2005, p. 42) (see Table 15.1 for a description of responsive services). *Systems support* involves the school administration establishing, maintaining, and enhancing the school counseling program.

TABLE 15.1
Responsive Services Employed by School Counselors

Consultation	Counselors consult with parents or guardians, teachers, other educators, and community agencies regarding strategies to help students and families.
Individual and small-group counseling	Counseling is provided in a small group or on an individual basis for students expressing difficulties dealing with relationships, personal concerns, or normal developmental tasks. Counseling is typically short term, and, when necessary, referrals are made to community resources.
Crisis counseling	Crisis counseling and support are provided to students and families facing emergency situations. Such counseling is normally short term, and, when necessary, referrals are made to community resources.
Referrals	Counselors use referral sources to deal with such crises as suicidal ideation, violence, abuse, depression, and family problems. Referral sources may include mental health agencies, vocational programs, and other social and community services.
Peer facilitation	Counselors train students as peer mediators, conflict managers, tutors, and mentors.

COUNSELING CHILDREN IN ELEMENTARY SCHOOLS

The elementary school years are a time when students begin to develop their communication and life skills, their physical skills, and their feelings of competence and confidence as learners (ASCA, n.d.). Children beginning elementary school are required to spend considerable time away from their parents or other primary caretakers for the first time, navigate a new social system and peer structure, and learn a new set of rules and expectations (Cobia & Henderson, 2007). They are confronted with expectations of social adjustment and mastering academic competencies, which may lead to anxiety about their abilities in school performance or making friends (Vernon, 2004).

School counseling programs in elementary schools provide education, prevention, and intervention services. Early identification of children's academic and personal/social needs and early intervention are essential in removing barriers to learning and in promoting academic achievement and laying the foundation for future success.

Presenting Problems of Elementary School Children

Learning Difficulties

Referrals for learning difficulties may be associated with learning disabilities. Learning disabilities are disorders that affect the ability to understand and use written or spoken language, do mathematical calculations, or focus attention. Although learning disabilities occur in very young children, a disorder may not be recognized until the child enters school. The most common treatment for learning disabilities is special education.

If not associated with a learning disorder, learning difficulties are often tied in with personal values, attitudes, and interpersonal problems. Teachers tend to refer children who lack the motivation to begin or complete work assignments or who are not working up to their estimated ability. Children may seek out a counselor and complain that they are bored with school or that they find the work too difficult.

The counselor can help children explore the reasons for their difficulty with school-work. Children may be feeling undue pressure from teachers or parents over the quality of their academic performance, or, conversely, teachers or parents may not be paying sufficient attention to the child's work. The counselor can help determine whether a child is being expected to do work above his or her ability; if so, the teacher can be alerted to modify expectations. The counselor can also recommend referral to a school psychologist if the educational difficulty looks severe enough to warrant evaluation for a possible learning disability. If the home situation is contributing to the lack of educational progress, referral to a community counseling agency is in order.

Following are examples of problems students typically present to counselors and some possible approaches counselors can take.

Client 1: Allison is a 4th grader referred to the counselor by her teacher because she is not working at the level her teacher believes she should. Allison has above-average ability and superior scores on reading and standardized achievement tests. She does not hand in assignments on time, is careless in her work, and generally acts bored. Allison is apparently willing to see the counselor, but seems uninterested during the first counseling session.

Response: Allison has been referred by her teacher, so her motivation for counseling may be minimal. The counselor may find it helpful to clarify with the student why the referral was made, whether the student agrees with the teacher's appraisal, and whether the student believes that a problem exists. The counselor could explain to Allison that she does not have to continue with counseling if she prefers not to, but could come back whenever she felt she needed to. If she decides to continue, then counselor and client could discuss her classroom attitude, feelings, and behavior.

If Allison has difficulty expressing herself, the counselor might use play media, such as free drawing or puppets, as a means of helping her relax and start talking. Her drawings or puppet play might give some clues to her feelings about herself and her interactions with others. If she talks freely, instead of using play media, the counselor could rely on client-centered listening to help her explore the reasons for her lack of interest in school.

Emotional Problems

Elementary school age children experience feelings of loneliness, inadequacy, rejection, and self-hate similar to the feelings experienced by adolescents and adults. They have doubts about their intellectual ability and worry about their classroom or playground behavior. Some children express beliefs that they are dumb, unattractive, or worthless. In other cases, anger, disappointment, or bewilderment may be felt, but not recognized or articulated. Counselors need to help children express, understand, and label these feelings and work toward more productive perceptions of themselves.

Client 2: Marcus, a second grader, is referred by his teacher because he has difficulty in his interactions with other children. He is very sensitive to criticism and breaks into tears when students tease him or the teacher corrects his work. The teacher has talked with his parents. The mother is overprotective and blames the teacher and other children for picking on Marcus; the father acts uninterested.

Response: Marcus may readily agree to talk with a counselor because he wants to do what he is asked and not risk disapproval. Because he may have strong feelings of inadequacy, however, he may find it difficult to open up about his negative feelings or impulses. At any rate, Marcus needs a nonevaluative, trusting relationship in which he can express his doubts about himself and his apprehensions about others' opinions. Play media may be useful during the sessions. The counselor should help him explore whether his expectations and/or the expectations of his parents are unrealistic. The counselor should try to help Marcus become aware of and label his feelings when he cries. It is likely that his tears reflect unexpressed feelings of anger and frustration, as well as hurt and shame. If Marcus responds well, the counselor might suggest a conference with his parents.

Attention-Deficit/Hyperactivity Disorder

Counselors in elementary schools are often called on to work with children diagnosed with attention-deficit/hyperactivity disorder (ADHD), one of the most frequently diagnosed psychiatric disorders of childhood. More prevalent in boys than in girls, the prevalence of ADHD is 3% to 7% for school-age children (American Psychiatric Association, 2000). ADHD is characterized by persistent and developmentally inappropriate problems with attention, impulsivity, and hyperactivity. Students with ADHD consistently drift off task, are distractible, act with no forethought to consequences, refuse to obey instructions, are disorganized, experience learning problems, have social skills problems, and have low self-esteem (Erk, 2004).

The hyperactivity component may not always be readily observable in a counseling session, because children with ADHD are able to maintain attention in one-to-one situations that are unique or novel, such as individual counseling sessions (Erk, 2004). Thus, counselors are often apprised of ADHD-related problems in children by their parents. To diagnose ADHD, referral to the school psychologist for a thorough assessment is recommended.

School counselors can implement multidisciplinary interventions for children with ADHD, coordinating the efforts of parents, school staff, and physicians. Counselors can also provide ADHD workshops for parents and school staff and can become advocates of ADHD children in the community. In addition to referral to a psychiatrist or medical doctor, Erk (2004) recommends parent training and counseling, teacher education, individual counseling, group counseling, behavioral interventions, self-esteem education, social skills education, and family counseling for children with ADHD. The treatment of choice for ADHD is pharmacotherapy and behavioral interventions (Wicks-Nelson & Israel, 2000). The most commonly used medications for ADHD are stimulants—for example, Ritalin, Concerta, Dexedrine, and Adderall (Greenhill et al., 2002).

Client 3: Kenny, age 9 years, was not considered a bad child by his parents, but he had always been overly active. Starting at 3 years of age, he was in constant motion, rushing from one activity to the next, leaving a trail of toys behind him. He was reckless and impulsive: He would run into the road without looking for cars, no matter how many times his mother explained the danger or scolded him. He chattered nonstop at mealtimes and frequently did not follow through on his parents' requests, although this seemed not to be deliberate. At recess, his tendency to overreact—such as hitting playmates for simply bumping into him—had already gotten him into trouble several times. He couldn't concentrate on his schoolwork and was in danger of failing his grade. His parents didn't know what to do.

Response: In working with Kenny, the counselor should begin by interviewing his parents and getting information about him and his family's history, the degree of stress the family is experiencing in caring for him, and his behavior problems and strengths. The counselor should also interview teachers to obtain information on learning and academic problems and on peer interaction. The counselor should then refer the parents to their family physician, pediatrician, or psychiatrist for a medical evaluation for potential pharmacotherapy. The counselor should also refer the family to a community mental health counselor to help the parents learn behavioral interventions to use with Kenny at home. The counselor should suggest that teachers implement behavioral interventions in the classroom, too, such as token reinforcement, time-outs, and contingency contracting. A daily report card could be sent to the parents to promote communication between the teacher and the parents and to inform them of Kenny's performance so that he could be rewarded for progress.

Child Maltreatment

In 2005, approximately 899,000 children were found to be victims of child maltreatment— 63% suffered neglect, 17% were physically abused, 9% were sexually abused, and 7% were psychologically maltreated (U.S. Department of Health and Human Services, 2005).

Child abuse is reported more frequently in elementary schools than in other settings because of teachers' close interactions with the children. Physical signs of child abuse include bruises, fractures, and burns; however, many signs of abuse do not have physical indicators. Some behavioral signs of abuse include withdrawal, aggression, hypervigilance, difficulty concentrating, and poor school performance.

School counselors must report incidents of physical abuse, neglect, or sexual abuse. In addition, school counselors are increasingly called upon to coordinate counseling services for abused students and to develop child abuse prevention programs for their schools. School personnel have learned to rely on counselors when confronted with procedural and legal concerns regarding the subject of abuse (White & Flynt, 2000). Although school counselors are mandated to report suspected child abuse, counselors need to work diligently to maintain the relationship with the child so that ongoing counseling services can continue after the crisis is over and/or referral to appropriate community agencies is made. In addition, school counselors can work with nonoffending family members in collaboration with community agencies to help them deal with the trauma.

Client 4: Sarah's 4th-grade teacher, Mrs. Johnson, consulted with the school counselor to discuss Sarah's behavior in class. Mrs. Johnson noticed that Sarah's schoolwork, which usually had been good, had declined significantly in the last few months. Sarah seemed preoccupied in class and unable to concentrate on assignments. One day, Mrs. Johnson noticed Sarah eating alone during lunch and asked her how she was feeling. Sarah was quiet, but she stated that she wasn't feeling well because she hadn't slept the night before. When asked why, Sarah became more withdrawn, but said something about being afraid of her father when he drank beer.

Response: In this case, the student has not disclosed a specific incidence of child abuse. However, approximately half of all cases of abuse happen at the hands of substance-abusing perpetrators, so the counselor should keep in mind that abuse is a possibility. The counselor should initiate individual counseling with Sarah to build a relationship and assess the reasons for her recent poor school performance. The counselor should provide informed consent information to Sarah, describing the limits of confidentiality. The purpose of counseling would be to provide Sarah with an opportunity to express and be validated for her feelings and to teach her coping strategies. If Sarah was relatively nonverbal in the sessions, the counselor could engage her in nondirective play therapy. If she disclosed child abuse, the counselor would remind her of the legal and ethical requirements to report what she had disclosed and would then make a report to the appropriate authorities. The counselor should continue to see Sarah individually to provide support for her in the possibility of an upcoming investigation.

COUNSELING CHILDREN IN MIDDLE SCHOOLS

Middle schools (grades 6–8) came about in the 1960s and have replaced junior high schools (grades 7–9) in many communities across the country (Lounsbury & Vars, 2003). The age range of middle school students is usually between 10 and 13. They are often referred to as *tweens* because they are caught in the difficult developmental stage between childhood and adolescence. In addition to experiencing the normal problems that happen in family, school, and the community, middle school children also have to adjust to changes in their body, pressure from peers, pressure in school, and other problems with establishing self-identity (Gladding, 2007).

Middle school counseling programs focus on the key developmental tasks of 6th-, 7th-, and 8th-grade students, including rapid physical changes, puberty, cognitive development (a shift from concrete thinking to formal operational thought begins), and the beginnings of identity formation (Vernon, 2004). Depression, anger, and mood swings may be common. In addition, middle school children may begin to worry too much about how they look, how they act and whether they belong, and their sexuality.

Middle school counselors perform the same functions as other school counselors in a comprehensive school counseling program. They work with students individually and in groups, consult with teachers and administrators, collaborate with community agencies, and consult with parents to address the specific needs of their children. Because of the unique developmental issues of middle school students, counselors must be developmental advocates for rapidly developing students within a developmentally responsive environment (Galassi & Akos, 2004). Middle school counselors also must intervene in crises, including divorce, the death of a student, the death of a student's family member(s), family violence, child abuse, homelessness, peer conflicts, substance abuse, academic failure, teen pregnancy, incarceration, and medical problems.

Presenting Problems of Middle School Students

Developmental Changes

A key issue for middle school children is developmental changes. This coming-of-age transition for children in this age group is a complex interaction between internal changes (e.g., self-exploration, cognitive development, physical changes) and interaction with a new and changing environment (e.g., elementary to middle to high school, peer interactions) (Akos, 2005). Puberty, identity development, and increasing autonomy are three primary developmental forces experienced in early adolescence, oftentimes affecting school behavior and performance.

Physical changes occur more rapidly during this time than at any other point in the life span, with the exception of infancy (Dusek, 1991). Puberty, and its associated changes, begins at 11 years old for females and 13 years old for males. Following this, a growth spurt occurs, lasting approximately 3 years. The physical developmental changes often result in self-consciousness and anxiety (Vernon, 2004). Both males and females may become clumsy and uncoordinated for a period of time because the size of their hands and feet may be disproportionate to other body parts. Their rate of physical change affects how they see themselves, and they are painfully aware of appearing awkward or different. In addition to physical changes, hormonal changes occurring in the body can cause confusion about sexual thoughts and feelings, accompanied by shame and guilt (Vernon, 2004).

Identity and Increasing Autonomy

During puberty, an emerging identity and increasing autonomy become focal points for early adolescents (Akos, 2005). Middle school students are often, for the first time, making independent and autonomous choices. At this time in their lives, they have more freedom and more responsibility, and they must learn to negotiate multiple teachers and new peer groups. Integrating these experiences is fundamental to identity formation.

While many students are excited about the increase in independence and adapt well, some have difficulty with the change. Although they strive for identity and increased autonomy, they are still immature and lack life experience. As a result, they may be unable to cope effectively with the changes and show increased dependency, which can be very confusing to them and to the adults involved in their lives (Vernon, 2004).

Counselors can watch for signs of a sharp drop in academic achievement, increased behavioral difficulties, or more absences to identify a student who may be struggling (Cobia & Henderson, 2007). Counseling interventions, including coping strategies, parent consultation, and peer mentoring, can be helpful in aiding students through this developmental transition.

Client 5: Christie, a 6th grader, runs up to the counselor in the hallway during lunch and asks to see the counselor sometime during the day. When she comes in, she exclaims that she is both angry with and afraid of her social studies teacher. She says that her teacher expects too much of her and blames her for things she hasn't done. She appears very anxious and admits feeling overwhelmed with the amount of schoolwork expected of her.

Response: Christie presents a type of problem that requires the counselor to be diplomatic. If teachers perceive that a counselor takes the student's side in teacher–student conflicts, the staff might become resentful. If students perceive that a counselor takes the teacher's side, they will probably avoid the counselor. A counselor's goal is to help improve relationships between teachers and students.

Keeping in mind that middle school students are in the midst of the common developmental task of increasing their autonomy, the counselor needs to explore Christie's coping in terms of the increased academic expectations of middle school. If the counselor finds that Christie is having difficulty dealing with the changes in expectations, counseling that focuses on helping Christie adjust to these new experiences may be beneficial. In addition, a peer mentor may help with Christie's managing the increased expectations of middle school. The school counselor may also wish to consult with Christie's teacher to determine whether other issues exist involving Christie's academic ability that could be causing problems.

Social Skills Problems

Middle school students are trying to discover their own identity, while at the same realizing that they are a part of a social group. Students may express feelings of inadequacy about social skills. Counselors may provide training in communication skills or assertiveness. The use of role-playing, either individually or in group counseling, can be helpful to allow students to practice new skills in a safe environment. Middle school counselors may also utilize peer mentors to help students develop social skills and shape positive identities (Akos, 2005).

Client 6: Rosa expresses concern about an inability to make friends or feel part of her own peer group. People do not dislike her, she says. It is worse: They are indifferent. She describes herself as shy. She wants to learn to be more outgoing.

Response: If Rosa's concerns were more complicated than she originally presented, the counselor should first explore personal and social issues. If her problem stemmed mostly from inexperience, the counselor needs to help her develop social skills early in the sessions. Group counseling might be useful for Rosa to practice interacting with others in the group who are experiencing similar concerns. Assigning a peer mentor may also help Rosa in terms of modeling appropriate social skills and practicing social skills between counseling sessions.

Client 7: Carrie, an 8th grader, comes to the counselor's office in tears. She has had a fight with her best friend. Now her friend is giving a party and has not invited her.

Response: Peer friction occurs frequently with children at this age and most often quickly disappears if adults do not complicate matters. If Carrie has good interpersonal relationships and this incident is simply a spat, the counselor should listen sympathetically but not overreact. Carrie will probably figure out a way of resolving the conflict. However, the counselor can help her deal with her feelings of disappointment at not being invited to the party. On the other hand, if Carrie has had persistent problems with her peers, the counselor should explore what is contributing to the ongoing friction. Carrie might benefit from group counseling with students who are having similar problems.

COUNSELING CHILDREN IN HIGH SCHOOLS

High school is the final transition into adulthood as students begin separating from parents and exploring their independence. During these adolescent years, they must deal with academic pressures as they face high-stakes testing, the challenges of college admissions, and entrance into a competitive job market (ASCA, n.d.). In addition, they face increased pressures of potentially risky behavior involving peers, sex, alcohol, and drugs.

The historical role of the high school counselor was that of course scheduling, college placement, and academic record keeping. Although some secondary school counselors may spend a significant amount of time doing quasi-administrative duties, they are still expected to provide the important services of any comprehensive school counseling program: individual counseling, group counseling, peer facilitation, and consultation.

Presenting Problems of High School Students

Career/Educational Exploration and Conflicts

Students in secondary school put top priority on vocational or career exploration and choice. They are approaching the time when they must become financially independent, so they try to find a suitable and satisfying job or decide on and prepare for a challenging career or life's work. In October 2005, 68.6% of high school graduates from the class of 2005 were enrolled in colleges or universities (U.S. Department of Labor, Bureau of Labor Statistics). While in high school, they must decide on the institutions to which they

will apply and the kind of training they wish to begin. Or, if the student is not considering continuing his or her education, vocational issues need to be addressed. Consider the
students' concerns and approaches in the following examples:

Client 8: Gail, a sophomore, pops her head into her counselor's office and asks for an
appointment. She is trying to work out her junior year program. Her grades are very
good, and she likes all subjects. She says that she wants to go to college, but is not sure
what careers to consider. She would like to explore her interests and aptitudes in order to
get some ideas about vocational direction.

Response: Gail appears likely to be highly responsive to tests; she may even ask for them.
Her question relates to a general career exploration, so career testing is appropriate. If the
personal and test data bring up exploratory career patterns, Gail can be given readings
about these occupations.

Client 9: Bob is interested in acting and has demonstrated his talent by performing in
plays. He is thinking of directing and writing, as well as acting. He is verbal, expressive,
and articulate. His father is a successful pipeline contractor who wants Bob, his only
child, to come into the business. He scoffs at drama as an effeminate occupation. Bob's
mother is quiet and unassuming, but subtly supports Bob. His father refuses to support
him in college if he persists in drama. Bob thinks that he is letting his father down. At the
same time, he wonders whether drama is a realistic choice economically.

Response: Sometimes, a student's questions about career concerns may be complicated by
interactions with, or the expectations of, significant people in their lives—in this case,
Bob's father. Conflicts among family members may contribute to confusion or doubts
about vocational planning. The counselor should probably not begin vocational testing or
appraisal with Bob until the counselor explores with him any dependency/independency
conflicts and ambivalences in his relationship with his father.

Through increased knowledge about self, occupations, and relationships with others,
Bob may become convinced that his career planning is correct and successfully change
the minds of the dissenting persons. It is also possible that if both Bob and his father
were to modify their positions regarding Bob's future plans, a reasonable compromise
could be reached. If Bob and his father are willing to meet with the counselor to discuss
their differences, the chances of a compromise are enhanced. For example, Bob might
continue with drama and work during the summers for his father to learn a practical trade
and to explore further his interest in some phase of the business. If an impasse were to
develop between Bob and his father, the counselor needs to refer them to a family counselor at a community agency.

Antisocial Behavior

Antisocial behavior in adolescence includes stealing, cheating, lying, defacing school
property, being truant, aggressive behavior, or drug or alcohol use. When students seek
out counselors to confess that they have been involved in antisocial behavior, the counselors should not necessarily turn them over to the authorities unless the children are a
danger to themselves or others. Instead, counselors can help the students control antisocial
impulses and direct them into constructive avenues before these impulses overwhelm

them. In addition, if disciplinary action is not automatically meted out, other teens with similar impulses will be more likely to see counselors.

However, if students are indeed a danger to themselves or others because of their behavior, the counselor is ethically bound to tell them that their families and other mental health professionals must be contacted so that they can get more intensive help.

Client 10: Gregory has been in a few times to discuss poor study habits. He received an A in a history course. You notice that he is uncomfortable. When you mention this, he stammers that he got the A by cheating on the final. He admits that this was not the only time he has cheated.

Response: The counselor should not involve the parents, other authorities, or professionals in this situation, since the behavior is not chronic and Gregory is serious about seeking help. The counselor should commend him for recognizing the need for help and give him full opportunity to express his anxieties. The counselor needs to make it clear that Gregory cannot be protected from disciplinary action if his behavior continues and is discovered while he is in counseling. Although Gregory's actions should not be condoned, the counselor should try to help him explore the factors contributing to his antisocial behavior. Exploring with Gregory his anxiety about grades would be beneficial in this case.

Suicide

Suicide is the second-leading cause of death for adolescents aged 15–19 years (Granello & Granello, 2007). A study by Eaton et al. (2006) found that, in a 12-month period, 1 in 6 teenagers seriously considered attempting suicide and 1 in 12 actually attempted suicide. Factors that increase the risk of completed suicides in adolescents include gender (male), higher rates of psychological distress (e.g., depression, anxiety), problems with identity (including sexual identity), hopelessness, impulsivity, and substance abuse.

Despite the high risk of suicide among adolescents, suicide prevention programming is virtually absent in schools (Granello & Granello, 2007). In one survey of 1,200 educators, only 20% indicated that their school had a suicide prevention program (Speaker & Petersen, 2000). Schools may avoid implementing suicide prevention programs because of the lack of awareness about the prevalence of teen suicides, the difficulty in talking about the topic, or even the fear that talking about suicide will cause a child to attempt suicide (Granello & Granello, 2007). Interestingly, a study by Gould et al. (2005) found that depressed teens were more likely *not* to consider suicide after it was brought up for discussion.

The reality that adolescents complete suicides at a rate of 11 per day and that suicide is the second-leading cause of death among teens clearly emphasizes the importance of suicide prevention programming in the schools. Suicide prevention programming has two fundamental goals (Granello & Granello, 2007, p. 161):

1. To help students know what to do if they come into contact with a person (primarily a peer) who is suicidal
2. To help students know what to do if they feel suicidal or depressed

School counselors do not have to begin from scratch to start suicide prevention programming in their school. Resources are available to school counselors to help them develop such a program (see Granello & Granello, 2007, p. 162). These authors provide details about the components of programs (e.g., in-service training guidelines, parent education, classroom presentations, and intervention strategies), as well as handouts, bibliographies, and other literature that is helpful for implementing a program.

Violence

Violence in the schools has been a prominent issue for the last two decades. According to a nationwide survey of high school students (Centers for Disease Control [CDC], 2004), 33% reported being in a physical fight one or more times during the last year and 17% reported carrying a weapon (e.g., gun, knife, club) within the last month. In addition, an estimated 30% of 6th through 10th graders in the United States were involved in bullying as a bully, as a target of a bully, or both (Nansel et al., 2001). Although nonfatal acts of violence are relatively common on school property, the number of children and youth homicides that are school-related make up only 1% of the total number of child and youth homicides in the United States (CDC, 2006).

Violence disrupts normal school operations; students do not learn and teachers cannot teach (Speaker & Petersen, 2000). It degrades the quality of life and the education of children, and it forces some schools to allocate many of their already limited resources to security and prevention measures. The causes of violence in our culture are extremely complicated. Factors predictive of violence among adolescents in schools may include a history of violent behavior and/or victimization, the carrying of a weapon, school problems, substance use, emotional and health problems, and a friend's suicide (Resnick et al., 2004). Protective factors that aid in diminishing or buffering against the likelihood of involvement in violent behaviors in teens include the quality of family relationships and parental involvement, grade point average, and a sense of connectedness to adults outside of the family.

Because of the impact that school violence has on students emotionally and academically, the need for prevention programs that address the risk for violent behaviors continues. Based on a comprehensive review of violence prevention activities, the U.S. Department of Health and Human Services (2001) noted that there are numerous effective intervention programs aimed at reducing and preventing youth violence. The most effective youth violence prevention and intervention programs addressed environmental conditions as well as individual student risk factors. School counselors can provide violence prevention activities, assess students' risk of engaging in violent behavior, and provide appropriate interventions when the potential for violence exists (Hermann & Finn, 2002).

SCHOOL COUNSELOR ACTIVITIES AND INTERVENTIONS

Alderian Counseling

One of the most widely used counseling approaches in elementary schools is Adlerian counseling (see chapter 6), which emphasizes that all children's behaviors are goal directed. Sweeney (1998) focused on helping teachers and parents understand that the issues underlying children's misbehavior include attention, power, revenge, and inadequacy. The use of encouragement, as well as natural and logical consequences, is recommended to change inappropriate behavior. For instance, a logical consequence for a child who disrupts others in the classroom might be for the teacher to move the child to an isolated location, thereby preventing further disruption (Baker & Gerler, 2001, p. 295). Adlerian counseling also focuses on birth order, family constellation, feelings of inferiority, and lifestyle assessment.

Play Therapy

Young children under 12 years of age have a relatively limited ability to verbalize their feelings and thoughts and to use abstract reasoning; thus, traditional talk therapy may not be effective. Because play is thought to be the natural language of young children (Landreth, 2002), play therapy may be a more effective means of working with elementary school children in helping them play out their experiences and feelings. *Play therapy* is a counseling approach in which the counselor uses toys and play as the primary vehicle for communication (Kottman, 2004). The goals of play therapy include increasing client self-esteem, helping the client learn about self and others, helping the client explore and express feelings, improving decision-making ability, practicing self-control, and learning social skills.

Although there are many different theoretical approaches to play therapy, the two primary approaches are nondirective and directive. *Nondirective* play therapy emphasizes the client–counselor relationship and the innate ability of children to solve their own problems in their own time. Nondirective play therapists depend on the skills of tracking, paraphrasing, reflecting feelings, returning responsibility to the child, and setting limits (Landreth, 2002; Landreth & Sweeney, 1997). They avoid leading the child in any way— for example, through interpretation, the design of therapeutic metaphors, bibliotherapy, or any other more directive technique. *Directive* play therapy, on the other hand, involves the counselor facilitating or directing the counseling process in a way that he or she believes would be appropriate for the child and the goal of counseling. A variety of play media is used to create the play situation, "attempting to elicit, stimulate, and intrude upon the child's unconscious, hidden processes or overt behavior by challenging the child's defense mechanisms and encouraging or leading the child in directions that are seen as beneficial" (Gil, 1991, p. 36). Nondirective and directive play therapy are two ends on a continuum; other theoretical approaches to play therapy often fall between these two extremes.

Creative and Expressive Arts Therapy

Other nonverbal means of counseling that school counselors can use with children are the creative or expressive arts. These include music, dance or movement, imagery, visual arts, literature and writing, and drama and psychodrama. The use of expressive arts in counseling adds a sense of playfulness to the process, promotes the client–counselor relationship, improves client–counselor communication, promotes client self-understanding, and helps nonverbal clients participate meaningfully in the counseling process (Arnheim, 1990; Gladding, 2005).

Because they take naturally to creative activities, children tend to respond sponta-neously and creatively as long as they have not been unduly inhibited. Music therapy can be very helpful with children, particularly those in elementary school, because they seem to love music and spontaneously sing, listen, or play musical instruments (Gladding, 2005). Dance helps children get in touch with their bodies and with the relationship of their physical beings to the environment, as well as allowing a creative release of energy. Imagery increases divergent thinking and activates the imagination. Painting and drawing are safe ways for children to express suppressed feelings on paper or to "tell" what has been forbidden to talk about (Riley, 1997). Children's literature—for example, storybooks, fairy tales, and nursery rhymes—provides a mythic plane that reveals meaning usually unavailable in ordinary observable events. Puppets help children act out dreams that manifest inner conflicts with their families and others.

Therapists encourage children to act out stories based on Moreno's (1946) psy-chodrama. With younger children, acting out dramas with toys or talking to puppets is usually safe and fun for them and revealing for counselors (Gladding, 2005). Children can make up stories about their family by using puppets, they can use role plays to act out a variety of real-life situations, or they may enjoy writing and producing their own plays or skits.

For culturally diverse students, Cochran (1996) recommends using both play and art therapy. Elementary school children from different cultural groups may have difficulty expressing themselves verbally because of language and/or cultural differences, but they can express themselves more freely through play activities, art, music, dance, and drama.

Choice Theory

Choice theory was introduced in the 1960s as "reality therapy" (which is now considered the "process" of choice theory) by William Glasser. It focuses on two general concepts: the environment necessary for conducting counseling and procedures that lead to change. The approach of choice theory, described as an internal control psychology, is completely opposite from behavioral theory, which is an external control psychology (Glasser, 1998). The basic tenets of choice theory are that all we do is behave, that almost all behavior is chosen, and that we are driven by our genes to satisfy five basic needs: survival, love and belonging, power, freedom, and fun. The most important need is love and belonging, and closeness and connectedness with the people we care about is re-quired for satisfying all of the needs. Glasser believes that disconnectedness (the lack of love and belonging) is the source of almost all human problems, including mental illness, drug addiction, violence, crime, school failure, and spouse and child abuse.

The role of a school counselor who uses choice theory is primarily as a teacher and model, accepting the client in a warm, involved way in creating an environment in which counseling can take place. The counselor immediately seeks to build a relation-ship with the client and focuses on behaviors the client would like to change and ways to go about making these changes occur (without the use of any behavioral techniques such as reinforcement). The process of choice theory encourages the client to self-evaluate his or her own behavior by asking questions such as "What are you doing now?" "Is it working?" and "What are the consequences?" The counselor does not focus on early childhood experiences, insight, blame, or "excuses" for behavior, but rather emphasizes aspects of the client's life that he or she can control. Because of its emphasis on what the client can choose and can control, choice theory is well suited for working with students in the secondary school environment.

Group Counseling

The school counseling literature has encouraged the use of group counseling since the late 1950s. Today, the ASCA National Model identifies group counseling as an important strategy in the services provided by school counselors (ASCA, 2005).

Group counseling provides a setting in which students can share their concerns, learn and practice new behaviors, identify with common issues held by other group members, and develop effective listening skills. It can be useful for children who have conflicts with family or peers or whose shyness or aggressiveness interferes with social development. Group counseling can also be effective for groups of children who are experiencing such problems as anger control, grief, parental divorce or single parenting, or alcohol and drug abuse. Students having academic difficulties can also benefit from group counseling.

Group counseling methods and processes that are used for adults and adolescents apply to children as well; however, counselors must adapt techniques to fit the developmental stages of children. The size of groups in elementary schools is usually no more than five students. In addition, because elementary school children have short attention spans and lack social maturity, group counseling sessions typically last from 20 to 30 minutes.

Part of group counseling for school counselors involves *classroom instruction* of the school guidance curriculum. *School guidance curriculum* refers to structured developmental lessons designed to help students achieve desired competencies and to provide students with the developmentally appropriate knowledge and skills. Classroom instruction of the school guidance curriculum is similar to psychoeducational groups, but differs from traditional group counseling in terms of the depth of interaction. It isn't intended to explore or encourage confidential, personal sharing among group members. Instead, it involves the school counselor presenting instructional material to small groups (10 to 15) or large groups (25 to 30) of students, usually situated in a classroom. School counselors create instructional units around three general content areas: academic achievement, career development, and personal/social growth (ASCA, 2005). In these areas, specific topics can include school success, social skills, dealing with peer pressure, conflict resolution, career planning, safety around strangers, drug education awareness, assertiveness skills, and many others (Wittmer, 2000).

Consultation

Consultation is a major function of school counselors (Dinkmeyer & Carlson, 2006). It involves providing information, presenting instruction, giving suggestions for handling situations, and facilitating planning processes (Schmidt, 2003). Simply stated, *consultation* is "a process whereby the first party (consultant) assists a second party (consultee) in finding a solution to a problem that concerns the third party (client)" (Harrison, 2000, p. 183). In other words, the school counselor in the consultant role helps teachers, parents/guardians, or administrators find a solution to a problem that involves a student. Consultation is considered an indirect service to students through direct involvement with teachers, administrators, and parents/guardians. In the consulting role, school counselors assess problems, determine goals, explore alternatives, and choose appropriate courses of action.

Teachers who trust their counselors often request consultations with them about classroom interactions. Sometimes, the focus centers on children; at other times, the focus is on the teachers themselves. Following are two examples of concerns that teachers might bring to their school counselor, along with suggested responses.

Teacher 1: Mr. Colby, a 6th-grade teacher, complains about two disruptive children in his class. The children talk out loud, answer insolently at times, and in general demonstrate rudeness and disrespect. The class laughs and becomes restless when these children act up. When one or the other, or both, are absent, the class works smoothly. Mr. Colby has had similar difficulties before. He prefers trying to change his behavior, rather than sending the children to the administrator for disciplinary action.

Response 1: The school counselor can show Mr. Colby how to set limits with disruptive students and can give him guidelines on how to stick with those limits. The counselor can also encourage him to confront the students about their behavior and set up an agreement or contract outlining what is acceptable classroom behavior.

Teacher 2: Mr. Fletcher drops into the counselor's office and sits down heavily. He appears to be highly perceptive, but a little unsure of himself. He is being evaluated for tenure. His administrator visited his class and told him afterward that he is well organized, but too distant from his students. The administrator recommended that he be more outgoing and friendly—characteristics of the administrator. Mr. Fletcher senses some need to be more approachable with students, but cannot see himself emulating the effervescent administrator.

Response 2: The counselor should support Mr. Fletcher's reluctance to emulate another personality. The counselor can also discuss with him the reasons for his uncertainty about his professional ability and possible ways that he can capitalize on his sensitivity to his students' needs to make him more approachable with students.

The counselor also can consult with the parents. Parents want their children to succeed in school. They usually want their children to behave well in school at all times, too (Harrison, 2000). The counselor, in a consultant role, can assist parents by teaching them effective ways of promoting positive behaviors in their children.

Crisis Intervention

Due to an increased awareness of crisis situations occurring in schools across the country, there has been a heightened recognition of the need for effective crisis intervention in public schools (Allen et al., 2002). A *crisis situation* creates "a temporary state of upset and disorganization, characterized chiefly by an individual's inability to cope with a particular situation using customary methods of problem solving" (Slaikeu, 1990). In schools, a crisis situation exposes children and staff to a traumatic event that threatens the security and stability of the school community (Brock, Sandoval, & Lewis, 2001; Johnson,

2000). Specific types of crises in schools can include suicide; death, grief, and loss; school shootings; gang activity; natural disasters (earthquakes, hurricanes, floods, and tornadoes); drug abuse; sexual and physical abuse; and medical emergencies. The school counselor is usually the first call when emergencies arise. Counselors are generally expected to take steps to calm persons down and to take immediate action when necessary.

Training School Staff

As part of system support in a comprehensive school counseling program, training school staff to facilitate their personal and professional development is another primary function of today's school counselor. School counselors possess many skills that teachers need— for example, communication skills, conflict resolution skills, and stress management. By conducting regular in-service sessions, counselors can train staff, especially teachers, so that they can master the skills needed to work with students more effectively (Coy & Sears, 2000). For instance, counselors can provide training in interpersonal communication skills, such as active listening, genuineness, acceptance, open-ended questions, paraphrasing, reflecting feelings, and summarizing.

In-service programs can be tailored to provide teachers with information that will enhance their understanding of their students (Dollarhide, 2003). Resiliency, child abuse, at-risk students, working with ADHD children and families, and ethics are just a few of the many topics that would be valuable for teachers. In-service training for teachers and school administrators about the role and contributions of the school counselor is also important (Clark & Amatea, 2004).

Peer Facilitators

Students are often actively involved in a school counseling program, not as clients, but rather as peer facilitators. Peer facilitators can be trained to provide a variety of services, including peer mediation, peer helping, peer tutoring, peer orientation, and peer facilitation of groups (Dollarhide, 2003). Peer facilitators need to be carefully screened for appropriateness, and special training needs to be provided with regard to the helping process, communication skills, the basics of confidentiality, and facilitation of interaction. In addition, peer facilitators have to be well trained about the limits of their involvement so that they know to contact the school counselor immediately if any problems are beyond their helping ability.

The benefits of peer facilitators are numerous. They can provide feedback about the progress of the student being helped, serve as a role model for other students, and assist with some of the logistics of running the school counseling program. The benefits to the peer facilitator include the development of helping and leadership skills, as well as the opportunity to experience what it's like to work in a school or in a helping profession.

ADDRESSING CULTURAL DIVERSITY

It is essential that counselors in schools attend to the developmental, transitional concerns of a rapidly increasing number of diverse students. The U.S. Census Bureau (2004) predicted that by the year 2050, the U.S. population will be 24.4% Hispanic, an increase of

11.6%; 50.1% non-Hispanic White, a decrease of 19.3%; 14.6% non-Hispanic Black, an increase of 1.9%; 8% Asian, an increase of 4.2%; and 5.3% all other races, an increase of 2.8%.

Children from different cultures face many difficulties when attending a school at which the student body and the teachers are predominantly White middle class or most of the other children are from ethnic groups other than theirs. Language barriers and barriers attributed to differing family and cultural values and expectations especially affect young children.

Counselors must develop the resources to bridge the cultural gap between the staff and the schoolchildren and their families. Counselors should have available bilingual interpreters from the community and consult regularly with respected members of neighborhood communities.

SUMMARY

Children's emotional and behavioral problems are most evident in schools and can interfere with children's academic and developmental progress. School counselors are responsible for designing programs and services to meet the needs of students at various growth and developmental stages (ASCA, 2005). School counseling programs are considered an integral component of the academic mission of schools. Programs are accessible to all students for the purpose of helping them attain personal and social growth to progress through school and into adulthood.

School counselors are responsible for developing, implementing, and evaluating the effectiveness of comprehensive school counseling programs. School counselors follow the guidelines of the *ASCA National Model: A Framework for School Counseling Programs* in designing their school counseling programs (ASCA, 2005). Through a cooperative effort, they work with teachers, administrators, parents/guardians, students, and the community to ensure the quality of their school counseling program.

PROJECTS AND ACTIVITIES

1. Interview a school counselor and ask him or her to describe a typical day on the job. What task takes up most of the counselor's time? What activity does the counselor enjoy doing the most?

2. A teacher tells a counselor that she wants to talk to him about a child in her class who is in counseling. The counselor explains that he wants to obtain permission from the child in order to preserve confidentiality. Later, the principal tells the counselor that the teacher is upset because he acted as though she could not be trusted. Consider how this situation could be handled to preserve confidentiality and yet not antagonize the teacher.

3. Assume that a new counselor is meeting with a group of teachers to discuss her role and to suggest guidelines for referrals. A teacher tells the counselor that he is confused about to whom he should refer children with discipline problems. He asks the counselor when he should refer a child to the principal and when he should refer a child to the counselor. How should the counselor respond?

4. You are asked to talk at a Parent Teacher Association (PTA) meeting about your role as a school counselor. Outline what you believe would be important considerations to include.

5. Compose a letter that could be sent to parents at the beginning of the academic year that defines your role and duties as a school counselor.

6. Conduct a survey of the literature or of high school students about adolescents' contemporary concerns. Are the counselor preparation programs with which you are familiar geared toward meeting these needs?

7. With two other students, role-play a three-way interaction using any of the case studies listed in this chapter.

CHAPTER 16

Counseling Programs in Colleges and Universities

Young adults of college age are faced with developmental, transitional challenges related to adjusting to academic life, developing academic skills, and planning a career, as well as struggling with personal identity, developing social relationships, and forming intimate, romantic partnerships. Counseling centers are available to students at most universities and colleges to help with these challenges. The number of students seeking counseling on campus has grown in recent years, and in 2006, college and university counseling centers provided services for approximately 9% of all enrolled students (Gallagher, 2006).

Counselors contribute to the growth and development of college students by providing individual and group counseling, psychoeducational workshops, consultation with faculty and staff, training of peer counselors, and career planning services. After studying this chapter, you will be able to

- Explain the organization and administration of college and university counseling centers.
- Understand the cognitive, emotional, social, and moral development of college students.
- Understand the diverse presenting problems of college students seeking counseling and the variety of counseling services available to them.

BRIEF HISTORY OF COLLEGE AND UNIVERSITY COUNSELING

College counseling centers as we know them today developed after World War II; they were originally intended to meet the needs of returning veterans. These new postwar counseling centers focused on integrating the client's vocational concerns with personal and psychosocial developmental needs. This approach was influenced by Super's (1953) view that vocational development is an intrinsic part of total personality development and by Rogers's (1942, 1951) emphasis on client-centered approaches and on personal growth. Prior to the formation of these new college counseling centers, colleges had generally relied on the faculty to conduct academic and vocational advisement—functions that were not considered counseling according to those professionals who were part of this new movement. Although confusion existed over the nature of college counseling and who was best equipped to deliver it, these early college counseling centers became models for the creation of role definitions and training standards for professional counselors in all settings.

College counseling centers flourished in the 1960s, expanding and spreading to colleges and universities throughout the country. To clarify the counselor's role, Kirk et al. (1971) published the article "Guidelines for University and College Counseling Services," which was based on input from counseling centers throughout the United States. These guidelines affirmed that counseling focused on students' developmental needs is the primary function of counselors.

The 1960s and 1970s witnessed the Civil Rights movement, the women's movement, and the breakdown of social barriers to higher education for minorities and women. In addition, large numbers of older students with families entered colleges and universities, resulting in more diverse and complex campus environments. Concurrently, the student services field expanded to keep pace with the evolving needs of students. Administrative functions traditionally performed by faculty were reassigned to student affairs offices (Hodges, 2001). During this time, counseling for college students emerged on campuses throughout the country as a separate professional service offered only by counseling professionals with specialized training.

During the 1980s, many new, comprehensive therapeutic approaches and techniques were incorporated into counseling practice—psychodynamic family systems approaches, psychosocial life-span developmental models, various cognitive theories and techniques, and new theoretical approaches to gender and multicultural issues. To address the transitioning from late adolescence into early adulthood among college students, counselors in college counseling centers adopted developmental approaches to counseling, emphasizing interpersonal, emotional, physical, and spiritual dimensions. In addition, the career counseling that had emerged after World War II as part of college counseling services was largely taken over by campus career advisement and placement centers.

In 1991, college counselors formed their own professional organization called the American College Counseling Association (ACCA). They had formerly been affiliated with the American College Personnel Association (ACPA), which focused on overall student personnel work. But when ACPA disaffiliated from the American Counseling Association (ACA), college counselors who wanted to continue to identify with ACA formed the ACCA as a new division of ACA. In 1998, ACCA published the first issue of its new journal, *Journal of College Counseling* (Benshoff, 1998).

The number of students with severe psychological problems has increased in recent years (Gallagher, 2006). Even small college counseling centers have seen an increase in psychopathology (i.e., diagnosable mental disorders) among the student population (Hodges, 2001). Issues such as clinical depression, anxiety, suicide risk, and substance abuse, as well as disorders involving psychosis and other severe pathology, are now relatively common among student clients in college counseling centers. Today, approximately 25% of college counseling center clients are on psychiatric medication (Gallagher, 2006). Although career issues are commonly related to or affected by clinical problems, career counseling remains separate from many college counseling centers.

ORGANIZATION AND ADMINISTRATION OF COUNSELING CENTERS

College counseling centers are typically under the jurisdiction of a vice president of student affairs or a dean of students. As a part of student services, counseling centers work together with the student affairs office to facilitate students' general welfare and academic progress. Besides the counseling centers, student services include residence life management, financial aid, health services, student life activities, academic advisement, registration, admissions, and special programs for foreign students, minorities, and disabled students.

Although closely interrelated with other student services, counseling centers maintain their unique role with clients by remaining autonomous and separate from other student services. They differ significantly from other services in that counselors develop a confidential, voluntary, and nonauthoritarian relationship with clients in order to best help them resolve personal doubts and conflicts that are interfering with academic, personal, or social functioning. Although some student services, such as health services and academic advisement, may have some similarities to counseling, those services are primarily diagnostic, prescriptive, advisory, or instructional. Only those counselors trained in mental health counseling or counseling psychology are qualified to work in counseling centers. Counseling centers can prevent confusion with other student services by clearly defining the counselor's unique role and clarifying its distinction from other student services.

The counselor's role in college counseling centers also differs from that of counselors in campus career centers. Career exploration as an integral part of personal development has been the hallmark of college counseling since its inception. Unfortunately, since the 1970s, the number of college counseling centers offering career counseling has declined. On campuses where counseling centers no longer offer career counseling, career placement services respond to student needs by expanding their services, hiring professional counselors who specialize in career counseling, and changing their name to career counseling services.

College counseling services are provided by well-trained counselors, social workers, and psychologists who, for the most part, are available at no fee to help students work through their issues. In addition, most counseling centers serve as resources for the placement of counselor interns from the departments of psychology and counselor education and, less frequently, from the school of social work. These counselor interns are at either the master's or the doctoral level and are supervised by full-time counselors at the center. College counselors may also train resident assistants (RAs) in residence halls about interviewing skills so that they can interact effectively with students and instruct them in referral policies and procedures.

Individual and group counseling is the most common treatment modality; however, college counseling centers continue to address academic problems by offering outreach activities, such as consultation with faculty, psychoeducational groups and workshops (e.g., stress management, time management, study skills, conflict resolution), and crisis intervention. Each center has a director, typically an experienced clinician with a doctoral degree, who hires, oversees, supervises, and consults with staff. The director is also responsible for carrying out center policies, budgeting, setting up counseling loads, and overseeing the supervision and training of new staff members and student interns. Most directors also take on a small caseload of clients. The student records kept by counselors are confidential and unavailable to college administrators and faculty.

Because of the escalating need for counseling services among students and the lack of resources to hire needed counselors, many centers refer clients to off-campus community counseling centers. In a 2006 survey, Gallagher found a ratio of 1 counselor to almost 1700 students in college counseling centers. The ratio generally recommended by counseling center directors is 1 counselor to 1,000 to 1,500 students (International Association for Counseling Services, 2005). This latter ratio is minimally sufficient only if other necessary psychological personnel services are available to students. Adequate on-campus psychiatric services can reduce the number of people with crises or chronic problems who would otherwise need to use counseling centers. Well-staffed minority affairs offices and alcohol or drug information and referral services also reduce the pressure on college counseling centers.

College counseling staffs spend about 78.5% of their time providing personal counseling (Gallagher, 2006). Various outreach programs take up the rest of their time—psychoeducation, crisis prevention and intervention, consultation with faculty and administration, and supervision of interns. Crisis services have expanded to deal with the increasing numbers of students who experience traumatic crises, who abuse substances, and who are suffering from violence, abuse, and sexual assault.

Collaboration with Student Services

As stated earlier, college counseling centers are clearly distinct from other student services. However, students are best served when all student services, while maintaining their separate identities, actively collaborate with one another. Counseling services can effectively collaborate with other student services through cross-referrals. For example, when student clients at the counseling center need to explore career options, they can be referred to the career center. Likewise, when students at the career center express doubts and conflicts that interfere with career choice, they can be referred to the counseling center.

Cross-referrals also work effectively between counseling centers and health services. Counselors refer students to health services when they are experiencing symptoms of physical or mental illness. Likewise, health services refer students to counseling when students are under the type of emotional stress that does not require hospitalization or medication. Counseling centers can also collaborate effectively with other services by offering joint psychoeducational workshops. They can work jointly with career placement in planning a career fair, or they can work jointly with health services in offering educational programs on alcoholism.

Maintaining Referral Networks

Most college campuses are self-contained minicommunities for students, featuring health services, counseling services, financial aid, housing, dining, and recreational facilities, as well as student centers and associations for various religious, cultural, and sociopolitical action groups. Even so, many students feel isolated and out of touch with campus student support groups. A good cross-referral system among all student services and student associations helps reduce students' feelings of isolation.

As mentioned earlier, collaboration is an essential function of campus organizations. Counseling center staffs use a variety of ways to inform the campus community about counseling services—for example, distributing brochures, featuring services in the school newspaper, and having open houses. Excellent sources of referral to counseling centers are the directors of the residence halls and their assistants, student services personnel, and the various student support groups and associations.

Counseling centers can also set up guidelines for faculty and administrators on when and how to refer students. The faculty is in a key position to refer students whose academic difficulties seem related to signs of emotional blocking or distress.

Regarding administrative referrals, counseling centers must continually keep administration officials informed about the center's role. The administrators responsible for students' scholastic standing and discipline may see the counseling center as a place to which they can refer students who are on academic probation or who have broken campus regulations. However, counseling in such cases should still be voluntary; a student whose grade point average has fallen below the university's minimal standards should not be required to get counseling in order to remain in school.

University Testing Services

University testing services are generally under the jurisdiction of academic services, separate from the counseling center and student services. In some universities, however, counseling and testing services are combined. The roles of the two services are very different. The function of campus testing services is to manage a variety of tests for the university: administering and scoring entrance examinations for applicants to various graduate programs, administering and scoring student evaluations of faculty, and scoring and making statistical analyses of classroom exams for professors. These screening and evaluative types of tests are not counseling or counseling-related functions and should not be confused with the psychological testing provided at many college counseling centers. Test scores from the former are not placed in students' confidential records, but belong to the administration and faculty. Testing services such as these should be offered by a separate testing bureau with the sole function of administering tests and evaluations and giving feedback to administrators, department heads, and faculty.

DEVELOPMENTAL NEEDS OF COLLEGE STUDENTS

During their college years, students continue to develop cognitively, socially, emotionally, and morally. College counseling services involve understanding how college students of all ages learn, grow, and develop (Gladding, 2007). Counselors need to distinguish between students who have normal developmental issues, such as autonomy and identity, and students who have more serious psychological problems.

According to Erik Erikson's (1950, 1968) psychosocial developmental theory (see chapter 5), students of college age continue to develop a sense of ego identity as they move into the next stage of developing relationships. As they focus on developing their academic, personal, and social competencies, they are also absorbed in developing and maintaining close relationships. As was true with adolescents, college students who have not adequately worked through Erikson's earlier stages—that is, trust, autonomy, achievement, and initiative—need to confront and work through these challenges so that they can develop an authentic sense of identity and effective interpersonal relationships.

William Perry (1970) came up with nine stages of college student development, focusing primarily on intellectual and moral development. Extending Piaget's cognitive development theory to include late-adolescent college students, Perry listed the steps by which students progress from a simplistic, categorical view of the world to more complex forms of thought about the world, their disciplines or areas of study, and the self. The nine stages, grouped into four categories, are described here:

Dualism: There are right and wrong answers to all problems that only authorities know.

1. *Basic duality:* All problems are solvable; therefore, the student's task is to learn the right solutions.
2. *Full dualism:* Although some authorities may disagree, there are right solutions to problems; therefore, the student's task is to learn the right solutions and ignore the others.

Multiplicity: The right solution, or the truth, remains unknown even to authorities; everyone has a right to his or her own opinion; no one is wrong.

3. *Early multiplicity:* Students learn that there are two kinds of problems: those whose solutions we know and those whose solutions we don't know yet. The student's task is to learn how to find the right solutions.
4. *Late multiplicity:* Most problems have solutions that we don't know yet; therefore, it doesn't matter which (if any) solution the student chooses. At this point, students may become frustrated and either enter an educational program, such as mathematics, that has clear answers or drop out of college.

Relativism: Solutions are relative and dependent on context; there is more than one approach to solving a problem.

5. *Contextual relativism:* All proposed solutions are supported by reasons; the student's task is to learn to evaluate solutions.
6. *Precommitment:* The student sees the necessity of making choices and committing to a solution.

Commitment: Solutions are based on knowledge learned from others, on personal values, and on personal experiences.

7. *Commitment:* The student makes a commitment.
8. *Challenges to commitment:* The student experiences the implications of commitment and explores issues of responsibility.
9. *Ongoing commitment:* The student realizes that commitment is an ongoing, unfolding, evolving activity.

Perhaps the most widely known and applied theory of student development is Arthur Chickering's (1969; Chickering & Reisser, 1993) psychosocial model. On the basis of Erik Erikson's "identity versus identity confusion" stage of development, Chickering proposed seven vectors along which traditional-age college students develop. Chickering and Reisser's revised 1993 model shows some significant changes from Chickering's (1969) earlier model, which had indicated that achieving autonomy is a significant feature of development. The revised model indicates that becoming autonomous is only one step in moving toward forming relationships, a change influenced by the relational theories of the feminist theorists, discussed later.

1. *Developing competence:* Student confidence that they have the ability to cope with any situation and can successfully achieve what they set out to do; this includes intellectual competence, physical and manual skills competence, and interpersonal competence.
2. *Managing emotions:* Finding ways of balancing negative or painful feelings with positive, uplifting emotions and integrating feeling with thought and action; bringing self-control and self-expression into balance; managing two major impulses—aggression and sex.
3. *Moving through autonomy toward interdependence:* Some level of separation from parents and increased reliance on peers, authorities, institutional support systems, and self.
4. *Developing mature interpersonal relationships:* Tolerance and appreciation of differences and the capacity for intimacy.
5. *Establishing identity:* Growing awareness of competencies, emotions, and values; confidence in standing alone and bonding with others; moving beyond intolerance toward openness and self-esteem; comfort with body and appearance; comfort with gender and sexual orientation; and a stronger sense of self.
6. *Developing purpose:* Increasing ability to be intentional, to assess interests and options, to clarify goals, to make plans, and to persist despite obstacles.
7. *Developing integrity:* Clarifying a personally valid set of core beliefs and values and matching those values with socially responsible behavior.

During the critical period of late adolescence, college students question their ethical and moral values and the meaning of life. According to Kohlberg's (1981) theory of cognitive moral development, as discussed in chapter 5, college students raise doubts and become skeptical of their own conventional beliefs as they dialogue on moral issues with other students who come from different sociocultural backgrounds. Kohlberg (1981) acknowledged Perry's theory that, during their college years, students acquire relativistic moral attitudes as they learn to accept their fellow students' differing value systems. However, Kohlberg said that this period of moral relativism is a transitional phase as individuals move on to postconventional Stage 5.

Adolescence has long been a particularly difficult time for women (Chodorow, 1978; Conarton & Silverman, 1988; Gilligan, 1982; Miller, 1976). During adolescence, girls are expected to break away from their developmental inclinations of relating and caring for others if they are to survive the academic system and the business world, which are geared toward male standards of competitiveness, autonomy, and dominance. Girls thus go through what Conarton and Silverton (1988) call *cultural adaptation* (see chap. 5).

Following their predecessors Chodorow (1978) and Gilligan (1982), Jordan et al. (1991) challenge Erikson's developmental model, claiming that, for women, developing relationships is a necessary component of developing a sense of identity and therefore precedes the developmental stage of forming one's identity. Likewise, Gilligan (1982) criticized Kohlberg's (1969) cognitive model of moral development—a model limited to justice reasoning—for excluding the relational, caring considerations of women as crucial components of moral decision making. Kohlberg (1986) consequently modified his model to take into account women's empathic perspective. Further counteracting the male-oriented cultural expectations of women's development, Kaplan and Klein (1991) advocate a model of women's relational developmental patterns, which evolve in ever more complex modes of relationship throughout life. Their core modes of self-development are laid out by adolescence, however. "The late adolescent woman does not develop 'out of' the relational stage, but rather adds on lines of development that enlarge her inner sense as a relational being" (p. 131).

College students are also very interested in exploring spiritual issues—questioning, expanding, and deepening their faith perspectives. According to Fowler's (1981) theory of faith development, students at the college level go through a period of doubt and skepticism, similar to Perry's model of college development, as they exchange ideas with others in the dynamic process of faith development. In their hunger to explore the meaning of life, college students redefine their faith as distinct from doctrinal religious creeds. Fowler considers faith development an ongoing process, "a dynamic existential stance, a way of leaning into and finding or giving meaning to the conditions of our lives" (p. 92).

COLLEGE COUNSELING CENTER SERVICES

Individual Counseling

Individual counseling focuses on college students' personal issues, such as relationship problems, self-esteem, identity, and loss. Many college counseling centers limit the number of counseling sessions available to clients, much as managed care programs have done in the community. College students with specific situational developmental concerns related to academics, careers, and relationships are appropriate for time-limited counseling. Additionally, clients who have mild disturbances and are capable of focusing on specific goals are also generally able to benefit from brief counseling.

Testing

College counselors may use standardized tests and inventories in the counseling process when they and their clients agree that the information gained from these measures can help client self-exploration. These tests and inventories are confidential and are kept separate from the entrance exams or student evaluations of faculty discussed previously. Tests and inventories are often used to augment interviews when client concerns are related to career choice and exploration, but they can also be helpful when clients are exploring interpersonal relationships, are identifying a specific clinical syndrome such as depression or anxiety, or are seeking deeper self-awareness. The use of tests has increased over the last several years because of the need to evaluate the effectiveness of counseling services and to accurately provide a *DSM-IV-TR* diagnosis for the client.

Common clinical tests used for evaluation and diagnosis include the Outcome Questionnaire–45 (OQ-45), the Beck Depression Inventory (BDI), and the Substance Abuse Subtle Screening Inventory (SASSI). For those students requesting career counseling, the following interest and personality inventories are generally used: the Strong Interest Inventory (SII), the Kuder Occupational Interest Survey (KOIS), and the Self-Directed Search (SDS). The Edwards Personal Preference Schedule (EPPS) and the Study of Values (SOV) are also popular for both career and interpersonal and personal concerns. In some centers, the Minnesota Multiphasic Personality Inventory (MMPI) and the Wechsler Adult Intelligence Scale (WAIS) are used with persons experiencing personal problems or academic difficulties.

Group Counseling

Most university counseling centers offer group counseling. The groups tend to focus on difficulties in developing intimate relationships and the consequent feelings of loneliness and isolation. Many young adults who lack the capacity to be open and trusting with others exacerbate the problem by giving up, withdrawing, or overintellectualizing. The opportunities to socialize that are readily available on college campuses may aggravate a student's feelings of isolation and loneliness. With older students, age 36 to 50, groups address anxieties that relate to doubts about being in school, a lack of peer support, conflicts with a spouse or children, the pressure of changing careers, and the stress that results from separation, divorce, or a broken relationship.

Personal growth groups focus on behavioral and skills training that reduces stress and anxiety, develops relationships, and handles transitions related to normal life development (Gazda, 2001). The group leader defines the problem, assesses how participants are functioning, provides a rationale for learning, and uses direct instruction, modeling, role-playing, cognitive restructuring, and more to accomplish goals.

Online Counseling

Internet use for private counseling continues to grow and evolve. Many colleges and universities have tried to decide how to provide counseling services online for the convenience of all students—both on campus and off; such services meet the needs of students with limited time and access to in-person counseling.

The definition of *counseling services* in the college setting is neither clear nor universal and often encompasses both counseling and student services. Thus, online counseling often simply addresses general questions regarding education or academic goals, questions about transcripts, financial aid information, and so on. Some colleges and universities integrate psychological services into online counseling services by providing online screenings and assessments. Although they are not a complete evaluation, these screenings can help students determine whether counseling services with a professional counselor are needed. A typical online screening includes demographic questions about the student and a symptoms checklist, typically assessing depression, eating disorders, anxiety, or substance abuse. Screening results are provided within a few minutes, and students are given recommendations regarding seeking professional consultation.

PRESENTING PROBLEMS OF COLLEGE STUDENTS

The presenting problems of college students generally parallel those of high school students. Both groups are in educational settings with requirements they must fulfill to graduate and policies they must agree to follow in order to remain in school. College students differ from high school students, however, in that most are of legal age, so they are primarily responsible for their own behavior. They also are not legally compelled to attend school. In addition, college students usually have more choice of instructors than do high school students.

Although they are legally adults, most undergraduates remain in a suspended state of semi-immaturity and dependence, compared with persons of the same age who do not go to college but begin a career, have a steady income, get married, and start raising a family. For college students who work, jobs are usually part time and involve menial tasks. If they decide to go on to graduate school, they generally experience further delays in developing a stable economic life and permanent relationships.

Many college students must obtain student loans that put them into considerable debt. They are under constant stress to perform optimally in their academic work; a poor relationship with an instructor may hinder or delay graduation or jeopardize entrance into graduate school. Attending college may also place a strain on intimate relationships, particularly when one partner wants more time and commitment from the other.

Even with the available on-campus special interest support groups, many students feel isolated and lonely. Many come from far away, from places where they are accustomed to close identification with family and community. This description may be particularly apt for international students, whose concerns are addressed later in this chapter.

With the increased numbers of older students on campus and the return to college of women who left to raise children, college counselors are now working with older people and must be aware of the issues and developmental needs of persons in their 30s, 40s, and beyond. Counselors should know theories of family and marital counseling even though they work less directly with families than do counselors in other settings. Problems concerning marriage, career change, aging parents, and child care show up more often in 2-year community colleges than in 4-year colleges because the average age of students in community colleges is higher.

Career/Educational Concerns

During the period of intense student activism and the push for alternative lifestyles in the late 1960s and early 1970s, many students were less interested in exploring traditional career choices or attaining high grade point averages than they were in personal growth and encounter groups. Thus, some counseling centers either neglected career counseling or considered the vocational concerns of students to be secondary. As discussed previously, that trend has continued steadily throughout the years, resulting in a continuous decline in the number of counseling centers offering career counseling. In 2006, a national survey of college counseling center directors showed that 22% of campuses offer career counseling primarily through counseling centers, 67% through career counseling and placement offices, and the remainder through both counseling and career centers (Gallagher, 2006).

The cases presented here are typical of career concerns that clients bring to counseling centers still involved in career counseling. If career counseling is done in a separate career counseling center, the procedures laid out here apply as well. Career concerns and academic success appear to be foremost in students' minds today. Faced with the high-tech revolution and stiff competition, many students react with dismay and even panic. Jobs in some professions are not readily available at graduation, and the entrance requirements of professional schools have become challenging. Many students are concerned about entering graduate school; some have two or more interests that appear to conflict. Other students may have difficulty choosing majors; some parents try to persuade a daughter or son to select a particular major whether or not she or he has any interest or ability in that area. Some women decide to return to school after raising families, but may express doubts about their ability to do academic work. Some are in conflict with husbands who are ambivalent about their wives going back to school. Other college students who made top grades in high school are flunking out of college. Some students may want to discuss the advisability of dropping out of school.

Counselors often see students who may be in the wrong major, may be unsuited for college, may be working too many hours, or may lack motivation because they see no purpose in attending college. In addition, many students experience anxiety reactions and blocks when taking tests, doing mathematics assignments, presenting speeches before a class, or writing English themes or term papers.

Client 1: Janet, age 32, requests counseling because she is concerned about her academic progress and her vocational goals. She has returned to college after 13 years of marriage. Her children are 11 and 9 years old; her husband is a busy executive in a local advertising agency. Janet says that he supports her attending college, but is too busy to give much help at home. She finds schoolwork stimulating but overwhelming, particularly because she must make arrangements for child care and must still assume the major responsibility for the home. She also is not sure what career she wants; law and environmental science are two possibilities. She looks anxious and fatigued.

Response: The counselor first needs to help Janet reassess how she and her husband are sharing household tasks. Counselor and client need to discuss the degree to which her husband is willing to share responsibility for the home and the children, and the degree to which Janet has been able to accept his help. Any residual guilt feelings about leaving the children or any doubts about her academic ability must be worked through. After these factors are clarified, career options can be explored from the standpoint of how her interests, abilities, and values relate to law, environmental science, or other fields. Interest inventories, personality inventories, and other appropriate testing might be used. If Janet appears to need support, the counselor might suggest that she join a group for older women students on campus.

Client 2: Neil, a freshman, is taking a mathematics course that is required for graduation. He was referred to the counseling center by his mathematics teacher. Neil says that he does well in his homework assignments but he blanks out on tests. He studies hard, but as soon as the test is handed out, he becomes immobilized. The teacher is sympathetic and believes that Neil understands his work, but that he has no option but to fail him on tests.

Response: Blocks, or anxiety reactions, are common among students and occur most frequently in mathematics, speech, and English classes. Neil's immobilization on mathematics exams may represent anxiety about the consequences of failing or the need to be perfect, or it may be a fear conditioned by poor teaching in earlier mathematics classes. Ellis's rational emotive techniques, which involve logical reasoning, are often used in these situations (see chap. 6). Some counselors might use Wolpe's (1973) desensitization techniques.

Personal Concerns

College students have continuing questions about traditional social mores, sexual patterns, and lifestyles. Many students are exploring religious, spiritual, and philosophical beliefs. As students move away from the immediate jurisdiction of their parents, their behavior changes as they encounter new experiences.

Self-doubt and uncertainties are as frequent in college as in high school. Homesickness, if severe, may lead some students to drop out of school. Students may also worry about why they are floundering while others their age are doing well. Anxieties may increase as students near graduation. In addition, questions and concerns about homosexuality and bisexuality are more frequently raised by college students than by high school students.

Client 3: Vivian is a 20-year-old junior who feels attracted to some women. She has dated men and has had intimate and pleasant heterosexual relationships. However, in a discussion with members of the campus gay advocacy group, it was suggested that she seek counseling because of her ambivalence.

Response: Vivian is expressing a need to clarify her sexual orientation in a nonjudgmental, neutral atmosphere. A client-centered approach seems appropriate in helping her sort out her feelings, attitudes, values, and concerns. The counselor should help her confront her ambivalent feelings and explore more directly the quality and quantity of her relationships with men and women and any pressure she might be receiving from either lesbians or heterosexuals. No attempt would be made to sway her in one direction or the other.

Client 4: Georgia is a 20-year-old junior who describes herself as lacking motivation and self-discipline. Neither college nor social life is stimulating. She has done well academically, but is beginning to have trouble in some courses. She attended a women's consciousness-raising psychoeducational group, jointly sponsored by the student affairs office and the counseling center. Her apathy prompted leaders of the group to refer her for counseling.

Response: Georgia appears to be depressed. The counselor should notice that she has already taken two proactive steps: attending a women's group session and coming in for counseling. The counselor should help her explore the uncertainties she has about herself academically, personally, and socially. Workshops based on behaviorally oriented theories help clients confront the degree of reality of their concerns. They also help change negative reinforcers to positive ones and use techniques to spur the depressed person into action. Beck's approach to depression (see chap. 6) is also appropriate.

Client 5: Gina is a freshman who was referred by a resident assistant because she is experiencing severe homesickness. She feels nauseous, has periods of crying, and has missed classes. She has been thinking of dropping out of school. She has telephoned her parents, who have tried to convince her to work it out on campus.

Response: A counselor should work closely with Gina to help reassure her and to help her stay in school. Gina might require more than one counseling session a week for a while. The counselor should talk with her about any concerns—ability to do the work, inability to make friends, guilt about leaving her family, and any other sources of unhappiness, such as an uncooperative roommate, an intimidating professor, or an overload of classes. In most cases, when a student is given support and reassurance, homesickness wanes. Cooperation between residence hall personnel and counseling center staff, albeit with due regard for confidentiality, can be a plus for a student's ultimate resolution of the problem. A support group can also be helpful.

Interpersonal Conflicts and Concerns

Students in dormitories often seek counseling because of friction with roommates. To get along with roommates, students must learn to accept different values and different lifestyles. They also must learn appropriate ways of asserting themselves if roommates behave in an inconsiderate way or take unfair advantage of them.

Premarriage, marriage, or couples counseling also occurs fairly often. When couples break up, for instance, problems may be difficult to overcome because both may live on campus, and it may be difficult for them to avoid seeing each other. In addition, they must often contend with roommates or acquaintances on campus who want to know about the breakup and/or help them somehow.

Even though the majority of students at many colleges live away from home, much of college counseling relates to parent–student relationships. Common issues include parents being overly involved in their child's life at college, discouraging independence in their child, and trying to influence their child's decision on academic major or career choice. Many college students also worry about their parents' problems at home, such as divorce, illness, or loss of a job. Counselors can often help students and parents work through the difficult process of confronting their differences, resolving conflicts, and developing more constructive relationships.

Client 6: Carla, a freshman, is having problems with her roommate. Unlike Carla, the roommate is friendly and sociable, but is also untidy and brings in friends at all hours without checking with her. Carla expresses fondness for her roommate and wishes that she could have the dates and social contacts of her friend. However, she dislikes her roommate's inconsiderate behavior but cannot express it directly to her. Her resident director referred her for counseling.

Response: Roommate problems often result from students' inability or reluctance to assert themselves with their roommates. In Carla's case, the counselor can help her confront her roommate constructively. Assertiveness training might be appropriate. Gestaltists might focus on her ambivalence about her roommate. She may need help developing social skills other than assertion. As counseling progresses, if communication between room-mates reaches an impasse, Carla may decide to move. The counselor can refer her to another dorm if that plan seems appropriate.

Client 7: Matt has an excellent grade point average but is having trouble with a professor who teaches a required course in his major field. Matt believes that his midterm grade, which was below average, was unfair. He describes the professor as belligerent. Conse-quently, his motivation to work on assignments is low. The counseling staff has received similar complaints from other students about this professor. However, this professor is the only person teaching the course.

Response: The counselor needs to clarify with Matt what he hopes to gain from counseling. If he wants to develop ways of interacting with the professor, then counseling is in order. The counselor could help him confront the professor in a constructive manner. Role-playing might be used to help Matt practice the proposed interaction. The counselor might explore why the professor has had such a bad effect on Matt's motivation. Ways of coping with similar situations could be discussed. If Matt wants to register an administra-tive complaint, the counselor can suggest that Matt talk with the head of the department. However, the counselor should not intervene; it is not the counseling center's role to report a professor's behavior to the authorities.

Client 8: Bert is a 26-year-old graduate student living with his mother in an apartment off campus. His mother is in her early 60s. She cooks for him, cleans house, and waits up for him when he dates. Bert wants to move out on his own. However, when he mentions this to his mother, she worries about being able to take care of herself; she has felt this way ever since her husband's death 10 years before. Bert feels frustrated and guilty.

Response: The counselor can help Bert confront his mother with the importance of his developing his own life and of her developing her own. Guilt feelings must be explored. If Bert's mother continues to express anxiety about his deserting her and about her inability to take care of herself, counseling for her might be suggested. Bert could also join a men's group. This experience, combined with individual counseling, would help him take constructive action that would be beneficial to both him and his mother.

Gender Issues

Gender issues are generally expressed most intensely on college campuses. Women study gender role concerns in courses and tend to join together to object to discrimination or harass-ment from faculty, administrators, or male students. Women also question the sociocultural stereotyping that contributes to depression, domestic violence, and career discrimination.

A trend that continues to raise implications for college campuses and counseling staffs is the large number of women returning to college after they have fulfilled homemaking responsibilities (Padula, 1994). A comprehensive literature review was conducted by Padula (1994) regarding women who return to college (i.e., *reentry women*) at a nontraditional age after a prolonged absence of as much as 35 years. Studies show that these returning women tend to have significantly higher grade point averages and higher educational aspirations than do traditional students. Studies also indicate, however, that they have less confidence in themselves and in their career planning, suffer from role conflict and emotional distress from family demands, and express significant dissatisfaction with advisement and counseling services. Positive attitudes and support from family, friends, and professors are particularly important (Padula, 1994).

Padula (1994) concluded that career counseling programs need to be improved for these women: Counselors need to become aware of the special needs and concerns of older women and provide counseling, support groups, and psychoeducational programs that address their particular needs. Women reentering educational institutions do have characteristics and needs that are different from those of traditional students. Reentry women are also very concerned about vocational, family, and financial issues, as well as issues of personal development. These concerns underline the necessity of developing counseling, advisement, and educational programs that will meet the needs of these reentry women.

Antisocial Acts and Alcohol Abuse

Some college students come to counseling because of antisocial, aberrant, or illegal acts similar to those of secondary school students and persons in the community. Shoplifting, drug or alcohol abuse, and sexual aberrations occur in all settings where counselors work. Misbehavior and illegal acts occurring primarily on college campuses include cheating on exams, creating havoc in a dormitory or elsewhere on campus, harassing teachers, and stealing exam questions. When students voluntarily seek counseling, confidentiality is upheld. No report goes to the office of the dean of students or the vice president for student affairs unless the students are endangering others or themselves.

Antisocial behaviors generally come to the attention of a dean in the student affairs office who decides whether disciplinary action is necessary. The dean may recommend that the person receive counseling without taking disciplinary action. In these cases, it is important that the counselor let the student know that she or he cannot be protected from legal proceedings or disciplinary action if the illegal or inappropriate behavior continues.

Management of underage consumption of alcohol on college campuses has been and remains an ongoing problem for college counselors. Research suggests that alcohol abuse is widespread among college students, with approximately 20% of all students qualifying as heavy drinkers and more than 40% of students reporting at least one binge-drinking episode in a given 2-week period. This kind of drinking is associated with a number of adverse consequences, including sexual misconduct, damage to property, academic difficulty, drunk driving, unsafe sex, and suicidality (Steenbarger, 1998; Freeman, 2001). Sexual assaults on college campuses are often related to alcohol abuse (Gallagher, 1997).

College counseling centers often receive referrals from school administrators regarding students who have violated the school's alcohol policy. In this situation, the college counseling center may become part of the punitive process of the student affairs office, rather than a neutral territory for students and a haven of assured confidentiality. Freeman (2001) describes a nonpunitive college alcohol education program for first-time alcohol policy violators. The program consists of a 90-minute workshop session that (a) works toward building a positive connection between the facilitator and the participants, (b) emphasizes personal responsibility, and (c) focuses on lifelong goals and personal values. The nonconfrontational, nonpunitive approach results in increased trust and sharing among participants. Freeman recommended that second-time, minor to moderate alcohol policy violators be referred for an individual alcohol assessment session to determine more appropriate intervention.

Crises

Crises arising out of suicides or suicide attempts or threats are fairly frequent among the college student population. Many aspects of college life are stressful: competition for grades, lack of support, indifferent or hostile reactions from professors, jockeying for academic and athletic honors, and increased use of drugs and alcohol. In addition, anxiety attacks or acute psychotic reactions requiring immediate counseling, hospitalization, or drug therapy are also common on college campuses. Students may collapse under academic pressures, the need to make too many decisions, a traumatic break in a relationship, feelings of loneliness and isolation, or the death of a relative or friend.

Cooperative emergency policies and procedures should be developed among the staffs of counseling centers, student personnel offices, student health services, residence halls, and mental health clinics. In residence halls, where emergency situations most often occur, immediate intervention is necessary to determine whether a crisis is of short duration or whether the student appears too incapacitated to continue in school. Further decisions may be necessary about hospitalization, drug therapy, and notification of the student's family. If the crisis is temporary, follow-up counseling may be appropriate. If the student needs hospitalization and the family must be informed, the student affairs officer in charge should take the necessary steps.

Psychiatric services and consultation to help counseling center staff working with clients in crisis are available on two thirds of college campuses. These are offered in the counseling centers, student health services, or both. Counseling centers average about 22 hours of psychiatric consultation per week by staff members (Gallagher, 2006). For students experiencing crises after hours, emergency on-call services are provided by counseling centers at about three fourths of all campuses.

ADDRESSING CULTURAL DIVERSITY

College counselors are in a uniquely favorable position to work with the concerns, transitions, and issues of students from diverse backgrounds. College campuses typically draw a wider variety of multicultural groups than do many public schools or communities; diverse groups may come together to raise issues and discuss multicultural problems. Counseling centers continually explore ways of meeting the needs of students of diverse cultural backgrounds.

Effective counseling with multicultural groups, discussed in chapter 4, also applies on college campuses. Not covered earlier, but especially evident on college campuses and in concentrated numbers, are international students, whose presence raises issues that need to be attended to by college counselors.

Increasing percentages of the college student population are from countries outside of the United States. For international students, the usual stresses encountered in college are compounded. When students come from different political or socioeconomic systems, the cultural or values differences they face become very complex. This may show up in how faculty and students interrelate, how much medical care is expected, how much freedom the individual has to choose a major, and how males and females interact. Feelings of isolation and alienation may overwhelm these students when family support is not available, in addition to culture shock, changes in socioeconomic status, expectations about academic performance, and family-related pressures. Many students also face worry and concern about political unrest in their home countries, fear about deportation, grief over the death of a family member, or anxiety about family problems back home.

Counselors must be aware of any stereotyping of clients and the need to be alert to cultural differences without losing sight of the individual. In a review of the literature on counseling international students, Leong and Chou (2007) emphasize the importance of developing creative alternative modalities for international students, given some of the cultural barriers and inhibitions about seeking professional psychological help. They suggest time management and language skills workshops, precounseling orientation sessions to acquaint the student with Western counseling approaches, and training of residence hall assistants.

SUMMARY

College and university counseling centers closely follow professional counseling association recommendations that well-trained professional counselors provide services geared to persons with normal developmental concerns. Students' flexible schedules and close proximity to campus services make it relatively easy for students to get counseling.

Counseling services include individual and group counseling, various outreach services, supervision of interns, referral networking, and collaborating with health and social services on and off campus. Counselors see clients about concerns related to careers/academics, personal concerns, relationship conflicts, gender issues, antisocial behavior, alcohol abuse, and suicide and violence. Outreach programs includes psychoeducational groups and workshops focusing on stress management, time management, study skills, and conflict resolution.

Although most college students do not live with their parents, many still depend on them for financial support, and many are affected by negative parent–child interactions. College counselors thus need to be familiar with family theories and techniques. Marital, couples, and family counseling is becoming more common on college campuses as older married persons are returning to school.

PROJECTS AND ACTIVITIES

1. A counselor in a college counseling center receives a visit from a roommate of one of her clients. The roommate tells the counselor that he is concerned that the client is not leveling with the counselor about his real problem. He offers to give background information about his friend that he believes will be helpful. How should the counselor respond?

2. The director of a college counseling center notices that the proportion of minority students seeking counseling is significantly lower than their proportion of the student body as a whole. What steps can the director take to be sure that minority students who need help will receive it?

3. Referrals from faculty and other professionals on campus are encouraged by the directors of counseling centers. Some faculty members who have referred students to the center call and ask whether the students have shown up and what has happened. What should a counselor do in these instances?

4. A residence hall director refers a student to a counselor. The student, who is underage, has been drinking in the dorm. The student is willing to receive counseling. After a few sessions, the residence hall director calls and tells the counselor that the student is still drinking and wonders what to do. How should the counselor respond?

5. A student who is a resident assistant calls the counseling center to explain that a student on his floor appears to be in a serious emotional state. The student refuses to leave his room, eat meals, or attend classes; he is incoherent and seems to be hallucinating. The college has no psychiatrist on staff, and the health center offers primarily first-aid treatment. How should the counseling center staff respond?

CHAPTER 17

Mental Health and Community Counseling

M any counselors want to work in the mental health or community counseling field or eventually work in private practice. Mental health and community counselors have opportunities to practice in a myriad of settings, including community mental health agencies, managed behavioral health care organizations, substance abuse treatment centers, career counseling agencies, domestic violence shelters, rehabilitation programs, employee assistance programs, military settings, churches, college counseling centers, hospitals, and even schools.

In these settings, counselors provide services to a variety of populations, including children, adolescents, adults, couples, and families. In addition, the types of problems clients can present with in counseling are vast and can encompass depression, anxiety, suicidal thoughts, eating disorders, substance abuse, relationship problems, parenting, behavior problems, child abuse, and domestic violence, as well as normal, developmental concerns.

After studying this chapter, you will

- Understand the roles and activities of mental health and community counselors.
- Have knowledge about the various work settings of mental health and community counselors.
- Recognize the impact of managed care on the mental health and community counseling profession.
- Be knowledgeable about Internet counseling and the provision of mental health services online.

OVERVIEW OF MENTAL HEALTH COUNSELING
AND COMMUNITY COUNSELING

The profession of mental health counseling and community counseling can be considered relatively young, having begun in the 1960s and 1970s. Historically, mental health counseling and community counseling have been considered two distinct specialties, albeit with much overlap. Gerig (2007), described this best:

> Community counseling was considered a specialization for training counselors whose primary focus was on community interventions and agency work settings. In contrast, mental health counselors, while frequently working in agency settings, had interests in private practice. Thus, the mental health counseling specialization had an increased emphasis on diagnosis, treatment planning, third-party reimbursement, and psychopharmacology. (p.7)

Today, the boundaries between the two professions have blurred considerably, and graduates from either specialty tend to work in similar settings. In fact, the Council for Accreditation of Counseling and Related Educational Programs (CACREP), which currently accredits both community counseling and mental health counseling as two separate programs, is considering merging the two programs into one, entitled clinical mental health counseling.

History of Counseling Services in the Community

Counseling services provided in the community can be traced back to one of the founders of counseling, Frank Parsons, who opened the Vocational Bureau of Boston in 1908 to help youngsters who were leaving the public schools with their career choices. From that time on and during the first half of the 20th century, counseling in community settings generally did not occur before the 1960s. During that time, mental health care for the general population was not considered the responsibility of local communities. Persons with severe mental illness were placed in state-run mental hospitals (asylums) that housed thousands of patients for years, sometimes decades. Those with less severe mental health problems received little or no help. Affluent people could afford to see a psychotherapist or seek care at a private clinic; however, there was very little in the way of mental health care for the vast majority of Americans.

This continued until the U.S. Congress passed the Community Mental Health Centers Act of 1963 (CMHC Act). As a continuation of the deinstitutionalization process that had begun in the 1950s, the CMHC Act authorized federal grants for construction of public or nonprofit community mental health centers (CMHCs), which focused on shifting treatment for people with severe mental illness from state mental hospitals to the "least restrictive environments" within communities (Accordino, Porter, & Morse, 2001; Bachrach & Clark, 1996; Broskowski & Eaddy, 1994). The objectives of the CMHC Act were for community mental health centers to provide services through inpatient treatment, outpatient treatment, partial hospitalization programs, emergency/crisis treatment, and consultation/education (Hadley, Culhane, Mazade, & Manderscheid, 1994).

With the expectation that the CMHCs' facilities would eventually become self-sufficient, Congress built time-limited and declining federal support into the original CMHC Act

In 1965, Frank Nugent served as the chairman of the board of the Whatcom County Mental Health Clinic in Washington State. He recalls the difficulties of opening a new community mental health center:

> The psychiatric director and the board of the Whatcom Community Mental Health Clinic envisioned a comprehensive center in our community, so we applied for and were granted federal funds to start building a community mental health center. Unfortunately, however, the CMHC Act mandated that federal funding for these comprehensive programs would be cut annually, with the stipulation that states gradually take over the funding. As we worked out plans to develop the facility, federal funds dwindled, and the Washington State legislature was unable or unwilling to provide what was needed. As a result, completion of the facility was delayed for almost 10 years, and it ultimately consisted only of an outpatient clinic serving those with severe or chronic mental disorders. No provisions were made for any other needed services. In addition, our nearest state mental hospital was closed even though inpatient facilities were unavailable in the community. The local hospital eventually provided a limited number of beds for temporary inpatient care.

(Dorwart & Epstein, 1993). As a consequence, operating funds were an issue from the inception of the program. Many CMHCs, overwhelmed with the demands for service, developed serious financial difficulties within a few years of opening and could not respond adequately, given their considerable resource limitations (Dowell & Ciarlo, 1983; Hartley et al., 2002).

Despite its limitations, the CMHC Act paved the way for large numbers of counselors to work in community mental health centers. During that time, counselors were not trained in the disciplines of social work, psychology, or medicine (psychiatry). These practitioners were considered paraprofessionals—without a professional organizational home and unqualified for the traditional credentials or licensure (Beck, 1999; Pistole & Roberts, 2002). However, these counselors were soon recognized as being among the primary providers of care in community mental health agencies (Brooks & Gerstein, 1990).

Responding to the demand for counselors to work in the community, counselor education programs devoted greater attention to preparing master's level counselors to work in community counseling settings. Most community counseling programs began after 1970 (Stadler & Stahl, 1979), and the first textbooks on community counseling were published in the 1970s (Amos & Williams, 1972; Lewis & Lewis, 1977). In 1981, the Council for Accreditation of Counseling and Related Educational Programs (CACREP) was established and community counseling was one of the first programs accredited (along with school counseling and college student personnel).

The Emergence of Mental Health Counseling

By the mid-1970s, there were many counselors who were educationally prepared at either the master's or doctoral level; were working in community agency, community mental health, or private practice settings; and were delivering a wide variety of services very similar to the more established mental health care provider groups (psychiatry, psychology, social work, etc.) (Smith & Robinson, 1995). Yet, they felt that they had no professional home by virtue of their uniqueness. In 1976, a group of these new practitioners came together to form the American Mental Health Counselors Association (AMHCA) to provide themselves with a professional organization and identity. These founders of mental health counseling began the political process of differentiating their activities, roles, and identity from other helping professions (Pistole & Roberts, 2002). The organization thrived, and today there are approximately 8,000 members of the association.

By the mid-1980s, mental health counselors felt that new and more rigorous educational standards were needed in order for counselors to be taken seriously as qualified providers (Smith & Robinson, 1995). This meant including issues such as psychopathology, diagnosis, and treatment planning in the educational curriculum. The 1986–1987 AMHCA Board of Directors adopted a set of comprehensive training standards for mental health counselors that required at least 60 semester hours and a minimum of 1,000 clock hours of clinical supervision. These standards were adopted, with some modifications, by CACREP in 1988.

The mental health counseling movement was in full swing in the 1980s and 1990s, establishing itself as a distinct profession. The profession was characterized by role statements, codes of ethics, accreditation guidelines, competency standards, licensure, certification, and other standards of excellence (VanZandt, 1990).

Community Counseling

Although an increasing number of counselors identified themselves as "mental health counselors," many did not and remained "community counselors." Unlike mental health counseling, the term *community counseling* was not considered a specific profession and referred generally to any counselor in a community setting (Hershenson & Berger, 2001). Unfortunately, a clear conception of community counseling as a distinct profession is lacking to this day. Community counseling has never established a professional organization, a professional journal, or a specialized certification procedure. Confusion about the definition of community counseling exists even among counselor educators: A survey of directors of community counseling programs indicated that "respondents were evenly divided between those who seem to see community counseling as generic counseling preparation for nonschool settings and those who seem to see it as a community-oriented specialization in its own right" (Hershenson & Berger, 2001, p. 188).

Despite its lack of clear professional identity, community counseling remains viable as a "CACREP category" of counselor education programs. In fact, the number of CACREP-accredited community counseling programs exceeds mental health counseling programs by more than 3 to 1 and exceeds the combined total of all other recognized specializations. The primary difference between mental health and community counseling programs is academic requirements. According to CACREP standards (CACREP, 2001), community counseling requires 48 semester hours of graduate study, whereas mental health counseling require 60 semester hours.

MENTAL HEALTH AND COMMUNITY COUNSELORS IN PRACTICE

It is important that students entering counselor education programs in community counseling or mental health counseling know what to expect from the profession and to know what counselors do. People often envision counselors simply as providing individual counseling sessions lasting 50 minutes in a private office. Although this does happen, the actual practice of counseling is much more complex.

Approaches to helping clients are many and varied. It is estimated that there are between 100 and 500 different theoretical orientations and approaches to counseling (Corsini, 2001; Herink, 1980, Parloff, 1979). Regardless of which counseling approach is used, the process of counseling remains virtually the same. Young (2005) identified five stages in the counseling process:

1. Relationship building
2. Assessment
3. Goal setting
4. Intervention and action
5. Outcome evaluation and termination

Relationship Building

The heart of the helping process is the therapeutic relationship, which provides the core condition for the use of other therapeutic activities and interventions (Young, 2005). In fact, many see the therapeutic relationship as being the primary curative factor in the treatment process (Gerig, 2007). In building the relationship with the client, the counselor uses listening and attending skills to convey understanding, to allow the client open up, and to create a safe environment. The counselor communicates warmth, empathy, and acceptance of the client as worthwhile and significant.

Assessment

The assessment stage in the counseling process involves collecting and integrating multiple forms of data from multiple sources about the client in order to define the client's problem. The assessment process occurs throughout the counseling relationship, but the initial interview with the client supplies counselors with the majority of the information. Information can also be gathered through tests, observation, and contact with the client's family, friends, previous mental health providers, and other collateral contacts. The following are some of the purposes of the assessment process:

- To determine the client's presenting problem.
- To make an accurate diagnosis.
- To determine the client's goals for counseling.
- To gather information to aid in the development of a treatment plan.
- To gather baseline data to measure the client's progress in counseling.
- To determine a client's suitability for a certain treatment program or modality.

The Clinical Interview

In mental health and community counseling settings, the initial clinical interview remains the primary assessment strategy for gathering client information. During the interview, counselors gather information about the client's presenting problem as well as various types of client history.

Interviews can be unstructured, structured, or semistructured. The most commonly used type of interview, the *unstructured interview,* consists of counselor-designed questions with client responses and counselor observations recorded by the counselor. It is considered unstructured because there is no standardization of questioning or recording of client responses; it is the counselor who is wholly responsible for deciding what questions to ask and how the resulting information will be used in arriving at a diagnosis (Summerfeldt & Antony, 2002).

Structured interviews consist of (a) a standardized list of questions, (b) a standardized sequence of questioning, including follow-up questions, and (c) the systematic rating of client responses (Rogers, 2001). *Semistructured interviews* are less uniform than structured interviews and allow some flexibility for clinicians (Craig, 2003). Although the initial questions regarding diagnostic symptoms are specified and typically asked verbatim to the client, counselors have latitude in how to follow up on responses (Hersen & Turner, 2003). Structured and semistructured interviews are used more frequently in research settings than in practice settings.

Diagnosis

An integral part of the assessment process is diagnosis. Diagnosis involves the process of assessing a client's signs and symptoms to determine whether the client meets the criteria of a certain diagnosable mental disorder.

To diagnose someone with a mental disorder, counselors use the *Diagnostic and Statistical Manual of Mental Disorders, fourth edition, text revision (DSM-IV-TR)* (American Psychiatric Association, 2000). The *DSM-IV-TR* is a manual of classifications of the various mental disorders that is published by the American Psychiatric Association. It is written to be used by psychiatrists, psychologists, mental health counselors, social workers, nurses, and other health and mental health professionals. In addition, it is used across settings, including hospitals, community mental health agencies, and private practices. The *DSM-IV-TR* defines a mental disorder as "a clinically significant behavioral or psychological syndrome or pattern that occurs in an individual and that is associated with present distress (e.g., painful symptom) or disability (i.e., impairment in one or more important areas of functioning) or a significantly increased risk of suffering death, pain, disability, or an important loss of freedom" (American Psychiatric Association, 2000, p. xxxi).

The *DSM-IV-TR* classifies over 300 mental disorders into 17 categories, including childhood disorders, dementia, substance abuse, schizophrenia, mood disorders, anxiety disorders, physical symptoms rooted in psychological problems, intentional faking of disorders, dissociative disorders, sexual and gender disorders, eating disorders, sleep disorders, impulse-control disorders, adjustment disorders, and personality disorders. Each mental disorder includes a list of *diagnostic criteria* that need to be met in order for a diagnosis to be made. The criteria set is a list of symptoms that make up a specific disorder. Typically, a specified number of symptoms must be present before a diagnosis can be made.

A unique feature of the *DSM-IV-TR* is the therapeutic use of five axes to classify client problems in a comprehensive and informative way; the axes assume a biopsychosocial etiology. The therapist assesses the client's condition according to the axes:

Axis I: Clinical Disorders and Other Conditions That May Be a Focus of Clinical Attention
Axis II: Personality Disorders or Mental Retardation
Axis III: General Medical Conditions
Axis IV: Psychosocial or Environmental Problems
Axis V: Global Assessment of Functioning

Whether counselors work at agencies, hospitals, or in private practice, they are required to diagnose a client and complete a treatment plan based on that diagnosis. Any treatment intervention a counselor uses must relate back to the client's treatment plan, which is based on the client's diagnosis. Diagnosing mental disorders becomes an integral part of providing the most effective treatment for the client.

Goal Setting

After gaining an understanding of the client's problem and important background information, the counselor and client work together to determine the client's goals. Some clients come to counseling knowing what they want and clearly stating their goals. Others, though ready to tell their story and talk about their problems, don't really know what outcome they desire. Thus, counselors help clients determine their goals in counseling and what they would like to change.

Clients may word goals vaguely or lack a clear vision of the outcome they are seeking. In addition, they may have difficulty imagining or envisioning success. It is helpful if counselors help clients identify specific goals that are manageable and clearly understood by the client and counselor (Young, 2005). Goals that are stated in positive terms help the client focus on strengths and resources rather than weaknesses and problems. Examples of questions that are useful for helping clients establish goals include the following (Young, 2005):

- "You say you want higher self-esteem. How would you like to see yourself exactly?"
- "I understand you want to be happy, but if you were happy, what would you be doing that you are not doing now?"
- "If the problem were solved, what would you be feeling, doing, or thinking that you are not now?"

Intervention and Action

After the assessment process and determining the clients' goals, the counselor can begin the intervention and action stage. This stage involves the advanced skills or treatment strategies that counselors use to help clients take active steps to reach their goals (Young, 2005). During this stage, the client moves beyond the problem and is encouraged to consider new alternatives, recognize inconsistencies, and try new behaviors. Counselors may employ various treatment modalities during this stage, including individual counseling, group counseling, and marriage and family counseling (see chapters 8, 9, and 11). The treatment strategies chosen during this stage are based on the client's presenting problems, diagnosis, and identified goals.

Treatment Planning

An important activity in the intervention and action stage is treatment planning. *Treating planning* is the process of plotting out a course of action so that both counselor and client have a road map that delineates how they will proceed from their point of origin (the client's presenting problems) to their destination and ultimately achieve their goals. In other words, a treatment plan helps the counselor and the client know where to begin, where to go, and the path for getting there.

A formal, written treatment plan is a concise statement of a client's presenting problem, *DSM-IV-TR* diagnosis, goals, and treatment objectives and interventions. A general format for a treatment plan is shown in Figure 17.1. Overall, written treatment plans are beneficial to the client, the counselor, the counseling process, third-party payers, and the counseling profession as a whole.

The Client.   Treatment planning is important primarily for providing the best treatment for clients. The goal of treatment planning is to provide sound therapeutic decisions so that counselors can help clients reduce their symptoms, feel better about themselves, and achieve their goals. Because both client and counselor share the process of treatment planning, clients don't have to wonder what therapy is trying to accomplish.

Client Name:

Case #:

Date:

Diagnosis: Axis I:

Axis II:

Axis III:

Axis IV:

Axis V:

Problems/Symptoms:

Goals:

Objectives:	**Interventions:**
1.	1.
2.	2.
3.	3.
4.	4.

FIGURE 17.1
Treatment Plan Format

The Counselor.   Counselors are benefited by treatment plans because they are forced to think critically about the techniques and interventions they want to use with a client. Through treatment planning, counselors have a rationale on which to base their counseling interventions. Thorough documentation of treatment using a treatment plan can also provide a measure of protection from possible client litigation.

The Counseling Process.   Because both counselor and client jointly develop the treatment plan, the process of counseling becomes clearer to the client. The counselor and the client determine what problems exist that brought the client to counseling, what goals the client wants to work on, and how those goals will be achieved. Because clients share in the development of the treatment plan, they may feel more comfortable with the counseling process, may be more motivated to work on the issues identified in the treatment plan, and may be more willing to try interventions that will help them meet their counseling goals.

Third-Party Payers.   Treatment planning is critically important to third-party payers. A *third-party payer* is an organization other than the client (the first party) or counselor (the second party) involved in the financing of health care services. Third-party payers for mental health services include Medicaid, state or local government health care plans, managed care companies, private health insurance providers, and workers' compensation programs, among others. Because the cost of mental health care is high, third-party payers want accountability from mental health care providers before funding services. In order to receive third-party payments, mental health care providers must now justify the services they provide through the use of treatment plans. Therefore, treatment planning is essential in order for counselors to receive payment from third-party payers for the services the counselors provide.

The Counseling Profession.   The counseling profession benefits from the use of treatment plans to evaluate the success of the counseling services provided. It is important for the counseling profession to know what treatment is effective for certain mental disorders. Outcome research using the data provided on treatment plans helps provide information on the most effective treatments.

Outcome Evaluation and Termination

The final stage, outcome evaluation and termination, addresses the question of when to end a counseling relationship (i.e., termination) (Young, 2005). The treatment plan plots out a course of action for how the counselor and the client will work together to meet the client's goals. The final stage comes about when the treatment plan is revisited, and the client's goals are compared with the client's present status. If progress has been made and the goals have been met, it may be determined that termination is appropriate.

Assessing client progress is an ongoing activity. Throughout the counseling process, the counselor needs to ask the client how he or she is progressing toward the goals. In addition to discussing progress with the client, a variety of methods and strategies may be used to evaluate outcome, including progress notes, symptom measures of outcome, and client satisfaction surveys (Young, 2005).

Progress notes are entries made in the client's file that document each time the counselor has a session or other significant interaction with the client. Each progress note restates the client's goal(s), summarizes the content of the session, indicates any progress made by the client, and specifies plans for future sessions. Counselors can use progress notes to evaluate the client's progress toward goals from session to session.

Another method of evaluating client progress and outcome is the use of symptom measures. *Symptom measures of outcome* are assessment instruments used to detect client distress and psychopathology and to assess symptom change during the course of counseling. These instruments can be *global* and assess a variety of symptoms and behaviors (e.g., Outcome Questionnaire), or they can be *specific* and assess particular symptoms, such as depression (e.g., Beck Depression Inventory). Symptom measures may be designed for repeated measurement of client progress throughout the course of counseling and following termination.

Client satisfaction surveys are measures of how happy the client is with the counseling services received (Young, 2005). Most surveys are developed by agencies, schools, or the counselors themselves; thus, they usually have not been tested for psychometric validity. In addition, surveys do not address symptom change and are weakly related to symptom measures (Leibert, 2006). However, surveys can provide valuable feedback about how satisfied clients are, particularly in terms of achieving their goals and their relationship with their counselor.

CREDENTIALING OF MENTAL HEALTH AND COMMUNITY COUNSELORS

Credentialing of mental health and community counselors is the process of validating a counselor's training and experience to determine his or her competence to provide particular counseling services. Two types of credentials are commonly used for mental health and community counselors: certification and licensure.

Certification

In the counseling profession, a *certificate* is verification that a counselor has met certain qualifications of education and/or work experience or has earned a certain score on a specified examination (Collison, 2001). Typically, certification is a nongovernmental credentialing process by which a specific professional group or organization seeks to set standards to ensure quality within itself (Gerig, 2007). These professional groups can exist at the local, state, national, or international level. Counselors who are certified have gone through a voluntary process to confirm that they meet or exceed the minimum standards for practice as set by the profession. For example, the Florida Certification Board certifies professionals in Florida who treat individuals suffering from addictions. To become a Certified Addictions Professional (CAP) in the state of Florida, a counselor must have specialized education and supervised work experience in the area of substance abuse counseling.

The premiere certification board for community and mental health counselors is the *National Board for Certified Counselors (NBCC)*. NBCC is an independent not-for-profit credentialing body incorporated in 1982 to establish and monitor a national certification system, identify those counselors who have voluntarily sought and obtained certification, and maintain a register of those counselors. NBCC's flagship credential is the *National Certified Counselor (NCC)* credential. This credential signifies that counselors have met specified requirements in training, experience, and performance. Although the NCC credential isn't required for private practice and is not a substitute for the state licensure, those who hold the credential are viewed as meeting or exceeding the minimum standards for practice as set by NBCC. Requirements include

- an advanced degree (master's level or higher) in counseling;
- at least 3,000 hours of counseling work experience for at least 2 years after graduation;
- at least 100 hours of counseling supervision for at least 2 years after graduation; and
- a passing score on the National Counselor Examination (NCE).

In addition to the NCC designation, NBCC offers other specialty certifications for persons who meet the particular qualifications of each. Counselors may apply for specialty certification in mental health counseling (Certified Clinical Mental Health Counselor [CCMHC]), addictions counseling (Master Addictions Counselor [MAC]), and school counseling (National Certified School Counselor [NCSC]).

Licensure

A goal among many mental health and community counselors is to work in private practice. To do so, states require licensure as a professional counselor. A *license* is permission to either do a particular thing or use a particular title. States pass licensure laws as a way to protect the health, safety, and welfare of its citizens. Licensure as a professional counselor is a governmentally sanctioned credential regulated by the state. Once a state legislature has passed a counseling licensure law, only individuals who have applied for a license and have met the requirements can call themselves licensed counselors. The title of their profession varies by state—for example, Licensed Professional Counselor (LPC), Licensed Professional Clinical Counselor (LPCC), or Licensed Mental Health Counselor (LMHC). Professional counselors are licensed in 48 states (except California and Nevada), the District of Columbia, and Puerto Rico. Licensure requirements for professional counselors are equivalent to those for clinical social workers and marriage and family therapists—two other disciplines that also require a master's degree for independent status. Most states require licensed professional counselors to meet or exceed the following professional qualifications:

- Earned a master's degree in counseling or a closely related mental health discipline;
- Completed a minimum of 2 years of post-master's degree clinical work under the supervision of a licensed or certified mental health professional; and
- Passed a state-developed or national licensure or certification examination.

WORK SETTINGS

Because counselors work in a wide array of agencies and programs, counselors need knowledge of the range of services they may be called upon to provide and the variety of agencies in which they may provide those services. This section will briefly describe a few of the principal settings where mental health and community counselors work.

Agency/Community Mental Health Centers

Community Mental Health Centers (CMHCs) have long played an important role in providing mental health services to a wide range of people. Originally created by the U.S. Congress in 1963 with the passing of the Community Mental Health Centers Act (CMHC Act), federal funding enables CMHCs to serve all members of the community regardless of their ability to pay. While CMHCs are located in both urban and rural settings, centers in rural areas are often the primary source of mental health services in communities across the country.

CMHCs are currently among the primary service providers of services to adults who have severe and persistent mental illness and who are at or near the poverty level (Hartley et al., 2002; Narrow et al., 2000). *Severe and persistent mental illness (SPMI)* refers to such disorders as schizophrenia, major depression, bipolar disorder, or other severely disabling mental disorders that require crisis stabilization or ongoing support and treatment. CMHCs also provide mental health care for children and adolescents under the age of 18 who are *severely emotionally disturbed (SED)*—that is, they have a diagnosable mental disorder and exhibit severe emotional or social disabilities that are life threatening or require prolonged intervention.

CMHCs typically provide these core services:

- *Outpatient counseling* is the most basic service CMHCs provide. Counseling is typically provided on a weekly basis, although more frequent visits may be scheduled (such as intensive outpatient group counseling, which may be held two or three times a week). Services include primarily individual and group therapy, with the focus on helping individuals better understand themselves, coping strategies, and, if necessary, medications.
- *Inpatient services,* or hospitalization, typically involve short-term stays and include medications, therapy, recreation, discussions, and medical treatment when necessary.
- *Day treatment programs,* or partial hospitalization, are intensive, structured mental health programs that provide treatment to individuals who need help with severe psychiatric symptoms that could lead to hospitalization. Day treatment programs are typically open 5 days per week from about 4 to 8 hours per day (although some programs include nights and weekends) and include a full range of therapeutic and rehabilitation activities, such as medication management, psychoeducational groups, therapy groups, family therapy, crisis services, and occupational therapy. Day treatment programs provide clients with the opportunity to receive services while residing at home.
- *Emergency and crisis services* are intended for those individuals who are experiencing an emotional crisis (such as a high suicide risk) and are typically available 24 hours per day, 7 days per week, through telephone crisis lines, walk-in treatment, or involuntary referrals.
- *Consultation and education services* provide and promote knowledge and guidance about behavioral health care issues to community agencies, businesses, industries, schools, individuals, and groups concerned about mental health issues in the community.

In addition to these core services, some CMHCs provide substance abuse treatment services on either an inpatient or an outpatient basis. Individual or group counseling, 12-step programs, community prevention programs aimed at reducing risk factors, and first-offender programs are among the types of services provided. Because research has long demonstrated that many persons with a mental illness have a co-occurring substance abuse disorder, many CMHCs offer *integrated* mental health/substance abuse disorders programs that treat both problems simultaneously.

Mental health and community counselors may engage in a variety of counseling activities in CMHCs. Working in emergency and crisis services, a counselor may spend most of the day assessing and diagnosing clients who have voluntarily or involuntarily sought services. The majority of these clients may be suicidal or have some form of active psychosis. In outpatient services, a counselor may carry a case load of 20 to 25 clients, providing individual or group counseling. In day treatment programs, a counselor may spend the day providing individual and group counseling, case management, and psychoeducational groups such as life-skills training and medication management. It is important that counselors remember that the core clientele for CMHCs are those with severe and persistent mental illness such as schizophrenia, major depression, manic depressive disorder, or other severely disabling mental disorders.

Substance Abuse Treatment Programs

Rehab, drug/alcohol rehabilitation centers, drug treatment programs, recovery centers, and *substance abuse treatment programs* are all terms used to describe basically the same thing: a safe and supportive environment for the treatment of drug addiction and/or alcoholism. The ultimate goal of all drug abuse and alcohol treatment is to enable clients to achieve lasting abstinence, but the immediate goals are to reduce drug use, improve the client's ability to function, and minimize the medical and social complications of drug abuse.

Substance abuse treatment is provided at various settings that can be viewed as a progressive level of care—from the most restrictive (inpatient treatment) to the least restrictive (outpatient treatment). Commonly available treatment services include medical detoxification, hospitalization, residential treatment, intensive day treatment programs, and outpatient programs. A description of substance abuse treatment settings is located in chapter 13.

University and College Counseling Centers

University and college counseling centers provide counseling services to students who are experiencing stress due to academic, career, or personal problems that may interfere with their ability to take full advantage of the educational opportunities before them (Boyd et al., 2003). Students who receive services from university and college counseling centers experience a wide range of emotional and behavioral problems, such as depression, anxiety, eating disorders, relationship problems, self-esteem issues, and even substance abuse problems.

University and college counseling centers are usually centrally located and readily accessible to all students and are physically separate from administrative offices, campus police, and judicial offices. Services are provided by professional counselors, as well as interns and paraprofessionals who receive close supervision by qualified personnel.

University and college counseling centers provide primarily individual and group counseling, with brief counseling as the most commonly used approach. In addition, counselors provide psychoeducational programs, crisis intervention and emergency services, consultation, and referral services (Boyd et al., 2003).

Private Practice

Although the majority of mental health and community counselors work in community agency settings, many move on to private practice after obtaining licensure. Full-time private practice counselors are self-employed and independent, they work in a private office or suite of offices, and their primary source of income comes from clients paying for their services. Some counselors choose to work for an agency while doing part-time private practice. Carney and Granato (2000) identified several factors that influence counselors' decisions to enter private practice:

Autonomy. A leading factor associated with the decision to go into private practice is a desire for autonomy. This involves a need for more independence or the desire to be one's own boss. In agency settings, some counselors might feel frustrated by the lack of input they have into decisions that directly affect their clients or practice. In private practice, counselors are more independent and are solely responsible for decisions related to their practice. They are unburdened by the bureaucratic policies and procedures of agencies.

Scheduling flexibility. In private practice, counselors are able to make client appointments around their own daily schedule. They are not bound by traditional 9 to 5, Monday through Friday office hours. Many reasons go into the desire for the flexibility that private practice provides. The demands of parenthood lead some practitioners to private practice based on a need to have a flexible work schedule. Private practice also provides an opportunity for counselors to have more flexibility in vacation and daily work schedules.

Financial. Some counselors are motivated to go into private practice based on the potential to earn more income. Private practitioners can determine their fees on the basis of the "community standard," that is, what other counselors, social workers, or psychologists in their area charge. Fees for counseling vary from community to community and can range from $60 to $150 or more per individual session.

Client Types. In many community counseling settings, counselors often have little or no input into the type of clients they treat. In private practice, counselors can choose the client population or type of client issues they treat. While many private counselors elect to specialize (e.g., alcohol/drug abuse, pastoral, children/adolescents, marriage and family), others adopt a generalist approach that involves seeing a variety of different client populations and client issues (Ginter, 2000).

Challenge and Creativity.   Many aspects of private practice can bring about many challenges for the private practitioner. These include developing business skills (such as marketing, organizational, and financial skills), in addition to providing effective clinical skills. Promoting a private practice requires a great deal of creativity in terms of marketing oneself and developing referral sources.

Successful private practitioners view the practice of counseling from both a theoretical and a business perspective. In addition to being an effective therapist and following ethical/legal counseling guidelines, they are successful in such entrepreneurial activities as marketing and advertising, gaining client referrals, and managing their office. Unfortunately, the business skills necessary for a successful private practice are often not a standard part of counselor training.

Understanding and dealing with financial issues is a key business skill that is needed by successful private practitioners. Private practice provides the opportunity for professionals to influence their financial situation more directly; however, with greater control comes greater responsibility (Carney & Granato, 2000). The private practice counselor is solely responsible for billing and collecting counseling fees from clients and/or third-party payers (insurance companies, managed care). Although the thought of making $60 to $150 per hour is attractive, it is important to put this amount in perspective. Typically, a counselor does not see 40 clients in a traditional 40-hour work week; more realistically, a full-time private practitioner sees an average of 20 to 25 clients per week. Counselors need time for treatment planning, recording progress notes, billing, communications with third-party payers, marketing, and other non-clinical activities. Private practitioners also understand that the only way they earn money is by seeing clients: Days off and vacation days are days without pay. In addition, how much a counselor earns per client is often determined by the client's insurance company, which could be well below the counselor's per hour fee.

Many expenses associated with private practice affect a counselor's income. Private practitioners are accountable for the overhead expenses of their office, including rent, utilities, telephone, and secretary services, as well as taxes, advertising, and other expenses associated with running a business. They now may be solely responsible for all forms of insurance, including liability, health, life, disability, and business. They also are responsible for all medical and retirement benefits.

Autonomy is clearly a benefit of private practice, yet it has a definite drawback: isolation. Professionals in private practice often report feeling isolated from colleagues (Carney & Granato, 2000). This may entail a lack of companionship, someone to talk or consult with—even simply someone to go out to lunch with. It is important for private practitioners to establish professional contacts, consultation, support networks, and other sources of professional and personal support.

Having a successful private practice is a challenging and formidable goal. Through private practice, counselors have the opportunity to be independent and autonomous professionals with a direct influence on the decisions that shape their professional career and practice. They are able to focus on an area of specialization or to make decisions affecting specific client services and fees. Moreover, private practice may provide the personal and professional challenge they crave and thereby reenergize their practice as a counselor (Carney & Granato, 2000).

MANAGED CARE AND THIRD-PARTY REIMBURSEMENT

Much of the fees for counseling services, whether in an agency setting or in private practice, come from third-party reimbursement. *Third-party reimbursement* is a general term applied to health care benefit payments. It is derived from the fact that with normal market transactions, there are only two parties: the consumer and the supplier. Under a health care benefit plan, a third party (e.g., government, a health insurance company, an employer, etc.) is ultimately responsible for paying the costs of services provided to covered persons (Vogel, 1993).

The majority of mental health care today is funded by a type of third-party reimburser known as managed care. *Managed care* is a general term popularly associated with health insurance organizations (e.g., health maintenance organizations [HMOs] and preferred provider organizations [PPOs]) that arrange for the financing and delivery of health services. It is a form of medical plan that was created to control the spiraling costs of health care in the United States. Originating in the 1980s, managed care organizations (MCOs) caused dramatic changes in the provision and financing of mental health services that greatly affected the way services are provided.

History of Managed Care

Managed care came about as a method to organize and finance health care services in a way that emphasized cost-effectiveness and coordination of care. Until the late 1970s, the delivery of health care in the United States was guided by two underlying assumptions: "The doctor knows best" and "We must spend whatever is necessary" (Chambliss, 2000, p. 26). From the time they were introduced in 1929 until the 1990s, *indemnity insurance* (fee-for-service) plans, such as Blue Cross/Blue Shield, were the most common form of health insurance. Insurance plans would identify the range of services they considered effective for the treatment of all health conditions and then reimburse physicians, hospitals, and other health care providers for the "usual and customary" fees charged by independent practitioners. To prevent the overuse of services, insurance companies would often require patients to pay for some portion of the costs out of pocket (i.e., co-pay), as well as fulfill annual deductibles.

Between 1965 and 1990, U.S. health care expenditures increased from approximately $42 billion to more than $800 billion (Mirin & Sederer, 1994). By the early 1990s, health care expenses were rising at a rate three times greater than the rate of inflation, causing a national crisis in health care costs (Polkinghorne, 2001). Mental health care had increased at a rate that exceeded the cost of overall health care costs.

Many blame the health care cost crisis on the lack of economic incentives associated with traditional indemnity insurance. Because indemnity insurance paid the major portion of the cost, consumers lost their cost-consciousness and were unconcerned about the costs of health care (Miller, 1996). In other words, less out-of-pocket cost to the consumer resulted in increased utilization of services. As a result, consumers overused treatment and allowed providers to provide excessive treatment and to overcharge (Coddington, Keen, Moore, & Clarke, 1990; Consumer Reports, 1992; Kronick, 1991).

MCOs came about during the 1980s in response to this health care crisis. MCOs have continued to grow and today is the dominant form of health insurance in the United States. Most Americans are enrolled in some type of managed care plan.

Managed care in mental health is thought to have been the result of the unprecedented expansion of mental health care in the 1980s (Boyle & Callahan, 1995). During this time, profit-making inpatient drug and alcohol abuse treatment programs (i.e., 28-day programs) and adolescent psychiatric programs grew exponentially. Many suspected, even proved, that there was misuse—if not abuse—of intensive mental health treatments, especially for children and adolescents (Jellinek & Nurcombe, 1993). Many also thought that most outpatient therapy was "a hobby for the self-indulgent," connoting endless, pointless, and often useless therapy provided by their all-too-willing therapists (Boyle & Callahan, 1995, p. 9). To better manage the quality and cost of care and to stem the perceived misuse of mental health services, MCOs reduced the intensity of services, for example, by limiting inpatient treatment. Today, 28-day hospital treatment programs are no more.

MCO Practices

MCOs engage in a variety of practices to control health care costs, including utilization review, capitation, and contracting. *Utilization review* refers to the MCO practice of reviewing patient care (e.g., diagnosis, treatment plan) to determine whether treatment is a "medical necessity" and is appropriate on the basis of the patient's diagnosis before authorizing medical care. *Capitation* involves paying health service providers a fixed amount for each patient regardless of the cost of caring for the patient. *Contracting* involves the process in which MCOs contract with health care providers, who then agree to offer discounts from their usual fees in exchange for providing health care to patients referred from the managed care company. Thus, MCOs receive reduced fees, and health care providers obtain access to more patients.

Mental health professionals who contract with MCOs are required to be more accountable for the diagnoses they give, the treatment they provide, and the fees they charge. In MCOs, mental health care providers must obtain *authorization* before providing direct services to a client. This means that the practitioner is required to complete certain MCO forms designating the identified problem, the *DSM-IV-TR* diagnosis, and the treatment plan in order to gain approval to treat the client. Frequently, only a specified number of counseling sessions is allowed by the MCO. Thus, the counselor must apply for reauthorization (submitting more forms and documentation to the MCO) if he or she believes that the client needs more sessions.

Even though managed care plans are typically less expensive for consumers than traditional insurance plans, managed care companies have been criticized for cutting costs by limiting treatment options and patient choice. Those seeking counseling services are forced to look for services from professionals identified as acceptable by the MCO (i.e., "in-plan" providers) rather than being allowed to choose whoever they want (Palmo, Shosh, & Weikel, 2000). If their managed care plan allows them to use "out-of-plan" providers, it is at an extra cost to the consumer.

In terms of payments for private mental health services, MCOs established fees for counseling services that are below the typical fees charged by independent, private practitioners. Needless to say, this affects the income of private practitioners. Although managed care provides challenges in terms of reimbursement for counseling services, private practice counselors can prosper in the managed care environment by adopting the following knowledge and skills necessary for success (Lawless, Ginter, & Kelly, 1999):

- Use of the *DSM-IV-TR*
- Knowledge of standards of practice for various clinical problems
- Treatment plan writing
- Record-keeping procedures
- Brief-focused and solution-focused counseling skills
- Evidence of formal training in one's stated specialty area (e.g., licensure, certificates)
- Mastery of managed care terms and language
- Procedures for receiving reimbursement for services
- Collection of treatment outcome and effectiveness data
- Basic accounting procedures
- Ability to work with managed care personnel in a cooperative manner

Ethical Issues of Managed Care

Professional counselors who contract with MCOs may face certain ethical issues in delivering quality care. In a survey of over 100 mental health counselors from four regions in the United States, Danzinger and Welfel (2001) found that 75% of respondents reported that managed care presented ethical dilemmas regarding confidential counseling, the right to privacy, free choice of the counselor, and informed consent. In a similar survey of 16,000 psychologists, Phelps, Eisman, and Kohout (1998) found that 4 out of 5 psychologists reported that managed care had a negative impact on their professional practice, primarily because of ethical dilemmas similar to those described here.

MCOs controlling policies may cause numerous ethical dilemmas for mental health providers. The client's freedom of choice in receiving counseling and in selecting a counselor is limited or nonexistent in MCOs. Confidentiality, so important in encouraging constructive self-disclosure and the establishment of a trusting counselor–client relationship, can no longer be ensured because MCOs often require client information for determining reimbursement (Cooper & Gottlieb, 2000; Danzinger & Welfel, 2001). Furthermore, when mental health providers share confidential client information with MCOs, neither the provider nor the client has control over what is done with the information. MCOs also frequently limit the number of counseling sessions, regardless of the nature of the client's problem.

Another ethical concern involves certain *DSM-IV-TR* codes that are not honored by MCOs. MCOs use diagnostic codes to determine whether, and to what extent, insurance reimbursement is granted for mental health services. Managed care plans often deny benefits and insurance reimbursement for adjustment disorders or for "V-Codes" (e.g., relationship problems, problems related to child abuse or neglect, bereavement, and phase-of-life problems, just to name a few). Adjustment disorders and V-Codes are often erroneously construed as mild, although the levels of distress associated with these problems may be as severe as or greater than the distress experienced with other mental disorders (Braun & Cox, 2005). A counselor may be unable to receive reimbursement for services rendered because certain *DSM* codes are not accepted by MCOs, even though the counselor believes that the client needs ongoing treatment. In this circumstance, a counselor may be pressured to choose between an accurate diagnosis that does not provide third-party reimbursement and a deceptive diagnosis (usually more severe) that does offer payment (Danzinger & Welfel, 2001).

INTERNET COUNSELING

Internet counseling, also called *online counseling, e-therapy, e-counseling,* or *cyber counseling,* generally refers to mental health services provided online. The majority of online counseling takes place via e-mail (Stofle, 2001), but services may also be offered by instant messaging and video conferencing.

Fee-based Internet mental health services began to appear in the mid-1990s (Skinner & Zack, 2004). The precursor to Internet counseling was the enduring success of online self-help support groups, which established the potential of computer-mediated communication for discussing sensitive personal issues. Early on, most fee-based Internet counseling services were of the "mental health advice" type, offering to answer one mental health question for a small fee (Skinner & Zack, 2004, p. 436). This expanded into e-therapy practices in which individual private practice counselors worked with clients in an ongoing series of in-depth e-mail or chat sessions.

The phenomenal growth of the Internet led to the appearance of "e-clinics," large group practice Web sites from which many counselors offer services. An e-clinic offers an improved environment for e-therapy by providing resources most independent e-counselors cannot afford (Ainsworth, 2007; Skinner & Zack, 2004):

- State-of-the-art online security to protect the confidentiality of communications between counselor and client
- Online credit card billing capability
- Active marketing

Therapists may join these e-clinics for a modest monthly fee and are offered a generic template Web page through which they may conduct their own e-therapy practice (Skinner & Zack, 2004). Literally hundreds of counselors are available for consumers to choose from, all of whom have been screened to ensure that they are qualified professionals. Other features of e-clinics include the ability to select a therapist according to various criteria, access to self-help information, and support groups for members. Examples of e-clinics include:

- HelpHorizons.com
- MyTherapyNet.com
- Find-A-Therapist.com
- TheCounselors.com

Internet counseling is not meant to replace traditional face-to-face counseling. Internet counseling can be provided as a stand-alone service or as an adjunct to traditional face-to-face clinical work (Rochlen, Zack, & Speyer, 2004). In addition, mental health professionals have turned to the Internet to provide a variety of other services, including online testing (Barak & English, 2002), career counseling (Boer, 2001), and information-resource Web sites for consumers, such as PsychCentral.com.

Because of the growth of Internet counseling and other technology-assisted distance counseling, various certifying bodies and accreditation agencies have developed standards and guidelines for ethical online counseling practice. The National Board for Certified Counselors (NBCC) and the Center for Credentialing and Education (CCE) created a document entitled "The Practice of Internet Counseling" that contains a statement of principles for guiding the evolving practice of Internet counseling (National Board for Certified Counselors & Center for Credentialing and Education, 2001). CCE also offers a credential for counselors practicing various forms of distance counseling, including Internet counseling: the Distance Credentialed Counselor (DCC). CACREP (2001) focused attention on the appropriate use of technology in the *2001 Standards.* In addition, the *2005 ACA Code of Ethics* greatly expanded its codes on technology applications, broadening the ethical use of technology in research, record keeping, and the provision of services to consumers (American Counseling Association [ACA], 2005).

The biggest single obstacle to widespread use of Internet counseling is probably the lack of coverage by third-party providers (Skinner & Zack, 2004). It is believed that Internet counseling's true potential will only be realized if large insurance plans and government health programs begin to cover online work.

Advantages of Internet Counseling

Clients typically seek out Internet counseling services for the same reasons that people seek professional help through traditional, face-to-face counseling. Internet counseling may be especially appealing for individuals who are unable or unwilling to see a counselor in person. Some advantages of Internet counseling over traditional counseling include the following:

- *Confidentiality and privacy.*   Many people are uncomfortable talking about their personal problems while in the physical presence of another, and may be more likely to disclose when they cannot be seen. Researchers have hypothesized that anonymity of the contact is especially appealing for introverted people (Hamburger & Ben-Artzi, 2000); people with anxiety disorders, such as agoraphobia and social phobias (Bouchard et al., 2000); and problems surrounding body image or eating (Rochlen, Zack, & Speyer, 2004). A study by Leibert et al. (2006) found that participants reported experiencing greater ease self-disclosing with their Internet mental health counselors compared with self-disclosing with face-to-face counselors, especially during the beginning stages of counseling.
- *Convenience.*   Convenience is the most-often cited reason why people use Internet counseling services. Internet counseling makes services accessible to clients at any time, on any day of the week; provides services to clients in remote and underserved

regions; and makes services available to clients who are unable or unwilling to leave their homes. It can be convenient for clients and counselors alike to engage in the counseling process from the comfort of their homes or offices, at times which are most convenient for them.

- *Cost.* Internet counseling fees can vary from site to site. In general, the cost of Internet counseling is often 50–60% of in-person counseling because Internet-based counselors may not have the overhead costs normally needed to maintain an office. Online counselors have developed a variety of pricing arrangements, including flat fees for standard message lengths, by-the-minute charges for time spent replying, or package deals for a set number of e-mails. Insurance companies do not pay for Internet counseling.

Challenges of Internet Counseling

As the Internet exploded in the late 1990s and the number of Internet counseling sites grew, many professionals and organizations expressed apprehension about providing counseling services in this way. The challenges of Internet counseling include the following:

- *Confidentiality.* Ensuring the confidentiality of the client through Internet communications is an ongoing concern. The ACA Code of Ethics addresses Internet confidentiality issues by stating that "counselors use encrypted Web sites and e-mail communications when possible. When the use of encryption is not possible, counselors notify clients of this fact and limit electronic transmissions to general communications that are not client specific" (ACA, 2005, p. 7). In addition, counselors need to inform clients about how records are stored; whether verbatim session records or other types of notes are maintained; and if colleagues, supervisors, and employees have authorized or unauthorized access to electronic transmissions.

- *Counselor credentials.* Another issue with Internet counseling is the ability of the client to check the counselor's credentials. Counselors who provide online counseling services must be licensed in the state in which the client lives. Clients can determine whether a counselor is licensed by accessing their state's licensure board Web site. The American Counseling Association provides contact information for all state licensure boards that license counselors in their state, including Web sites (www.counseling.org/Counselors/LicensureAndCert/TP/StateRequirements/CT2.aspx). From these sites, individuals can search counselors' names to verify their licensure status. In addition, counselors should provide clients with the counselor's background, license and certifications, specialties, and availability, as well as links to relevant state licensure and professional certification boards that protect consumer rights and facilitate addressing ethical concerns.

- *Lack of nonverbals.* Many question whether Internet counseling is even a viable form of counseling without in-person contact with clients. The lack of nonverbal information, such as facial expression, eye contact, vocal tone, and body language, is believed to hinder the development of the counseling relationship and the effectiveness of the counseling process (Cook & Doyle, 2002; Rochlen, Zack, & Speyer, 2004). Research investigating the effectiveness of Internet counseling is very limited; yet, a recent study by Leibert et al. (2006) found that participants rated themselves as satisfied with online mental health counseling and as having established a working alliance with their mental health counselors.

- *Time delay.* A technical challenge related to Internet counseling via e-mail is time delay. As an asynchronous form of communication, the practice of e-mailing includes an interval between the sending and receiving of the message. These time delays are inevitable; yet, clients may wonder about the meaning of unexplained delays in a therapist's response.

- *Crisis intervention.* Another challenge relates to how counselors deal with crises online (Rochlen, Zack, & Speyer, 2004). More specifically, concerns involve the Internet counselor's ability to deal with suicidal/homicidal clients. Because of the time delays inherent in e-mail communications, if a client reports suicidal/homicidal ideation, there can be no certainty of an immediate e-mail response from the counselor. Thus, the ability to deal reliably with a crisis is challenging, if not impossible.

- *Misreading.* A concern in text-based communication is the potential for clients to misread counselors' remarks (Rochlen, Zack, & Speyer, 2004). Without reassuring visual and auditory cues, clients may misunderstand counselors' remarks without a means for clarification.

Which Clients Are Appropriate for Internet Counseling?

Because Internet counseling is not appropriate for all people seeking help, counselors need to assess who is appropriate for online services. The ability to benefit from online therapy will be partly determined by the client's computer proficiency, computer access, and amount of Internet usage. A study by Leibert et al. (2006) found that the more hours individuals spent each week on the Internet, the more likely they were to make use of online counseling.

Suler (2001) suggests that clients need other basic skills fundamental to effective Internet counseling, including reading and writing skills, cognitive skills, and typing skills. These skills are necessary in reading, understanding, and responding to text-based communications from the counselor. The online medium appears best suited to those who value written forms of self-expression (Mitchell & Murphy, 1998).

One basic issue is the level of care a client may require. People who have severe psychiatric disorders and need psychiatric hospitalization or even intensive outpatient treatment are not appropriate for Internet counseling (Stofle, 2001). As a rule of thumb, individuals with severe pathology (such as delusions and hallucinations) and risky behaviors (such as a high suicide risk) are not appropriate for online work. Other client issues that are not appropriate for Internet counseling include thought disorders, borderline personality disorder, or unmonitored medical problems (Stofle, 2001). In cases in which an individual is not advised to undergo online care, counselors should have the skills and resources to make appropriate referrals.

SUMMARY

Since its beginnings in the 1960s, the field of mental health and community counseling has changed and grown dramatically. The field remains vast and diverse, and the roles and activities of counselors vary greatly depending on the work setting. Counselors may find themselves providing individual counseling, group counseling, assessment, couples counseling, family therapy, child and adolescent counseling, crisis intervention, consultation, or psychoeducation. In addition, a new and ever-expanding specialization is that of Internet counseling.

Mental health and community counselors have the privilege of helping people work through difficult times or difficult issues in order to attain improved mental health. Counselors may help clients experiencing severe and persistent mental illness, suicidal or homicidal ideation, trauma, or substance abuse problems. Or, counselors may work with individuals experiencing less severe problems, such as parent–child issues, career concerns, or relationship problems.

The multiplicity of settings and clients requires counselors to be knowledgeable about numerous and diverse client issues and effective treatments. Although beginning counselors-in-training may initially feel overwhelmed by this, community and mental health counselors are trained to be well positioned to meet the needs and demands of the people they treat.

PROJECTS AND ACTIVITIES

1. Survey your local community mental health centers to determine what services they offer to the community.
2. Interview counselors working in a community mental health center. What is a typical day like for them? What types of clients do they see and what services do they provide?
3. Develop a list of mental health counseling resources available in your community. Provide information about local counseling centers, the populations they serve, the services they provide, and contact information.
4. Interview a counselor in private practice. Ask questions about credentials, services provided, populations served, area of specialization, fees for services, and managed care. What is his or her opinion about working in private practice versus working in an agency setting?
5. Develop a list of Internet sites for mental health counseling. Include Web site name, address, services provided, and fees for services.

References

Accordino, M. P., Porter, D. F., & Morse, T. (2001). De-institutionalization of persons with severe mental illness: Context and consequences. *Journal of Rehabilitation, 67*(2), 16–21.

Adelmann, P. K. (1994). Multiple roles and physical health among older adults: Gender and ethnic comparisons. *Research on Aging, 16*(2), 142–166.

Ainsworth, M. (2007). *Types of online counseling services.* Retrieved June 15, 2007, from http://www.metanoia.org/imhs/type.htm

Akos, P. (2005). The unique nature of middle school counseling. *Professional School Counseling, 9*(2), 95–103.

Akos, R., Konold, T., & Niles, S. (2004). A career readiness typology and typal membership in middle school. *The Career Development Quarterly, 53,* 53–66.

Alexander, J. F., & Parsons, B. V. (1982). *Functional family therapy.* Pacific Grove, CA: Brooks/Cole.

Allan, J. (1988). *Inscapes of the child's world: Jungian counseling in schools and clinics.* Dallas: Spring.

Allen, M., Burt, K., Bryan, C., Carter, D., Orsi, R., & Durkan, L. (2002). School counselors' preparation for and participation in crisis intervention. *Professional School Counseling, 6*(2), 96–102.

American Association for Marriage and Family Therapy (AAMFT). (2001). *AAMFT Code of Ethics.* Alexandria, VA: Author.

American Counseling Association (ACA) Governing Council. (1997). *Definition of professional counseling.* Alexandria, VA: American Counseling Association.

American Counseling Association (ACA). (2005). *ACA Code of Ethics.* Alexandria, VA: Author.

American Counseling Association. (2007). *Licensure requirements for professional counselors.* Alexandria, VA: Author.

American Educational Research Association (AERA), American Psychological Association (APA), & National Council on Measurement in Education. (1999). *Standards for educational and psychological testing.* Washington, DC: Author.

American Psychiatric Association. (2000). *Diagnostic and statistical manual of mental disorders* (4th ed., text revision). Washington, DC: Author.

American Psychological Association (APA). (1973). Guidelines for psychologists conducting growth groups. *American Psychologist, 28,* 933.

American Psychological Association (APA). (2002). *Ethical principles of psychologists and code of conduct.* Washington, DC: Author.

American School Counseling Association (2004). *Ethical standards for school counselors.* Alexandria, VA: Author.

American School Counseling Association (ASCA). (2005). *The ASCA national model: A framework for school counseling programs* (2nd ed.). Alexandria, VA: Author.

American School Counseling Association (ASCA). (n.d.a). *Why elementary school counselors?* Retrieved April 10, 2007, from http://www.schoolcounselor.org/content.asp?contentid=230

American School Counseling Association (ASCA). (n.d.b). *Why secondary school counselors?* Retrieved April 10, 2007, from http://www.schoolcounselor.org/content.asp?contentid=233

Amos, W. E., & Williams, D. E. (1972). *Community counseling: A comprehensive team model for developmental services.* St. Louis, MO: Warren H. Green.

Anastasi, A. (1996). *Psychological testing* (7th ed.). New York: Macmillan.

Annis, H. M., & Davis, C. S. (1991). Relapse prevention. *Alcohol Health & Research World, 15,* 175–177.

Ansbacher, H. L. (1992). Alfred Adler's concepts of community feeling and social interest and the relevance of community feeling for old age. *Individual Psychology, 48* (4), 402–412.

Ansbacher, H. L., & Ansbacher, R. R. (Eds.). (1973). *Superiority and social interest: A collection of later writings.* New York: Viking.

Arbuckle, D. (Ed.). (1967). *Counseling and psychotherapy: An overview.* New York: McGraw-Hill.

Association for Counselor Education and Supervision (ACES). (1978). ACES guidelines for doctoral preparation in counselor education. *Counselor Education and Supervision, 17,* 163–166.

Association for Counselor Education and Supervision, Joint Committee on the Elementary School Counselor (1966). *Report of the ASCA–ACES joint committee on the elementary school counselor.* Washington, DC: American Personnel and Guidance Association.

Association for Specialists in Group Work (ASGW). (1998). *ASGW best practice guidelines.* Retrieved August 1, 2007, from http://www.asgw.org/PDF/Best_Practices.pdf

Astbury, J. (1999). *Gender and mental health.* Cambridge, MA: Harvard Center for Population and Development Studies.

Atkinson, D. R. (2004). *Counseling American minorities: A cross-cultural perspective* (6th ed.). New York: McGraw-Hill.

Atkinson, D. R., Wampold, B. E., Lowe, S. M., Matthews, L., & Ahn, H. (1998). Asian American preferences for counselor characteristics: Application of the Bradley-Terry-Luce model. *Counseling Psychologist, 26,* 101–123.

Atwood, J. D. (Ed.). (1992a). *Family therapy: A systemic–behavioral approach.* Chicago: Nelson-Hall.

Atwood, J. D. (1992b). The field today. In J. D. Atwood (Ed.), *Family therapy: A systemic-behavioral approach* (pp. 29–58). Chicago: Nelson-Hall.

Atwood, J. D. (1992c). A system–behavioral approach to counseling the single-parent family. In J. D. Atwood (Ed.), *Family therapy: A systemic–behavioral approach* (pp. 191–205). Chicago: Nelson-Hall.

Aubrey, R. F. (1978). Consultation, school interventions, and the elementary counselor. *Personnel and Guidance Journal, 56*(6), 351–354.

Aubrey, R. F. (1982). A house divided: Guidance and counseling in 20th-century America. *Personnel and Guidance Journal, 61,* 1–8.

Bachrach, L. L., & Clark, G. H., Jr. (1996). The first 30 years: A historical overview of community mental health. In J. V. Vaccaro & G. H. Clark, Jr. (Eds.), *Practicing psychiatry in the community: A manual* (pp. 3–26). Washington, DC: American Psychiatric Press.

Baker, S. B. (2000). *School counseling for the 21st century* (3rd ed.). Upper Saddle River, NJ: Merrill/Prentice Hall.

Baker, S. B. (2004) *School Counseling for the twenty-first century* (4th ed.). Upper Saddle River, NJ: Prentice Hall.

Baker, S. B., & Gerler, E. R. (2001). Counseling in schools. In D. C. Locke, J. E. Myers, & E. L. Herr (Eds.), *The handbook of counseling* (pp. 289–318). Thousand Oaks, CA: Sage.

Baltes, P. B. (1987). Theoretical propositions of life-span developmental psychology: On the dynamics, growth, and decline. *Developmental Psychology, 23,* 611–626.

Baltimore, M. L. (2002). Recent trends in advancing technology use in counselor education. *Journal of Technology in Counseling, 2*(2). Retrieved March 15, 2007, from http://jtc.colstate.edu/vol2_2/editor.htm

Bandura, A. (1977). *Social learning theory.* Upper Saddle River, NJ: Prentice Hall.

Barak, A., & English, N. (2002). Prospects and limitations of psychological testing on the Internet. *Journal of Technology in Human Services, 19*(2/3), 65–89.

Barrett, M. S., & Berman, J. S. (2001). Is psychotherapy more effective when therapists disclose information about themselves? *Journal of Consulting and Clinical Psychology, 69,* 597–603.

Baruth, L. G., & Burggraf, M. Z. (1991). Counseling single-parent families. In J. Carlson & J. Lewis (Eds.), *Family counseling: Strategies and issues* (pp. 175–188). Denver: Love.

Baruth, L. G., & Manning, L. M. (2007). *Multicultural counseling and psychotherapy: A lifespan perspective* (4th ed.). Upper Saddle River, NJ: Merrill/Prentice Hall.

Basow, S. (1992). *Gender stereotypes and roles* (3rd ed.). Pacific Grove, CA: Brooks/Cole.

Beattie, M. (1987). *Codependent no more.* New York: Harper & Row.

Beck, A. (1976). *Cognitive therapy and the emotional disorders.* New York: International Universities Press.

Beck, A. T. (1963). Thinking and depression: Idiosyncratic content and cognitive distortions. *Archives of General Psychiatry, 9,* 324–333.

Beck, A. T. (1976a). *Cognitive therapy and emotional disorders.* New York: New American Library.

Beck, A. T. (1976b). *Depression: Clinical, experimental, and theoretical aspects.* New York: Harper & Row.

Beck, A. T., & Weishaar, M. E. (1995). Cognitive therapy. In R. J. Corsini & D. Wedding (Eds.), *Current psychotherapies* (5th ed., pp. 229–261). Itasca, IL: F. E. Peacock.

Beck, E. S. (1999). Mental health counseling: A stakeholder's manifesto. *Journal of Mental Health Counseling, 21*(3), 203–214.

Becvar, D. S., & Becvar, R. J. (2006). *Family therapy: A systemic integration* (6th ed.). Boston: Allyn & Bacon.

Bednar, R. L., Burlingame, G. M., & Masters, K. S. (1988). Systems of family treatment: Substance or semantics? *Annual Review of Psychology, 39,* 401–434.

Belar, C. D. (2000). Ethical issues in managed care: Perspectives in evolution. *The Counseling Psychologist, 28*(2), 237–241.

Belsky, J. K. (1998). *The Psychology of aging: Theory, research, and interventions* (3rd ed.). Pacific Grove, CA: Brooks/Cole.

Bennett, E. A. (1983). *What Jung really said.* New York: Schocken Books.

Benshoff, J. M. (1998). On creating a new journal for college counseling. *Journal of College Counseling, 1,* 3–4.

Berger, P. L., & Luckman, T. (1966). *The social construction of reality.* Garden City, NY: Anchor Press.

Bergin, A. E. (1989). Religious faith and counseling: A commentary on Worthington. *Counseling Psychologist, 17,* 621–624.

Berk, L. E. (2006). *Child development* (7th ed.). Boston: Allyn & Bacon.

Berne, E. (1961). *Transactional analysis in psychotherapy.* New York: Grove Press.

Berne, E. (1964). *Games people play.* New York: Grove Press.

Berne, E. (1966). *Principles of group treatment.* New York: Oxford University Press.

Berne, E. (1972). *What do you say after you say hello?* New York: Grove Press.

Beutler, L. E. (2000). David and Goliath: When empirical and clinical standards of practice meet. *American Psychologist, 55,* 997–1007.

Bijou, S. W., & Baer, D. M. (1965). *Child's development* (Vol. 2). New York: Appleton-Century-Crofts.

Bjorklund, B. L., & Bee, H. L. (2008). *The journey of adulthood* (6th ed.). Upper Saddle River, NJ: Prentice Hall.

Blanchard, L. T., Gurka, M. J., & Blackman, J. A. (2006).Emotional, developmental, and behavioral health of American children and their families: A report from the 2003 national survey of children's health. *Pediatrics, 117,* 1202–1212.

Blatner, A. (2005). Psychodrama. In R. J. Corsini & D. Wedding (Eds.), *Current psychotherapies* (7th ed., pp. 399–408). Belmont, CA: Wadsworth.

Blocher, D. (2000). *Counseling: A developmental approach* (4th ed.). Hoboken, NJ: Wiley

Boer, P. M. (2001). *Career counseling over the Internet.* Mahwah, NJ: Lawrence Erlbaum.

Bordin, E. S. (1975). The generalizability of the psychoanalytic concept of the working alliance.

Psychotherapy: Theory, Research, and Practice, 16, 252–260.

Bouchard, S., Payeur, R., Rivard, V., Allard, M., Paquin, B., Renaud, P., & Goyer, L. (2000). Cognitive behavior therapy for panic disorder with agoraphobia in videoconference: Preliminary results. *Cyberpsychology & Behavior, 3*(6), 999–1007.

Bowen, M. (1978). *Family therapy in clinical practice.* New York: Jason Aronson.

Boyd, D. R. (1986). The oughts of is: Kohlberg at the interface between moral philosophy and developmental psychology. In S. Modgil & C. Modgil, *Lawrence Kohlberg: Consensus and controversy* (pp. 43–83). Philadelphia: Falmer Press.

Boyd, V., Hattauer, E., Brandel, I. W., Buckles, N., Davidshofer, C., Deakin, S., Erskine, C., Hurley, G., Locher, L., Piorkowski, G., Simono, R. B., Spivack, J., & Steel, C. M. (2003). Accreditation standards for university and college counseling centers. *Journal of Counseling & Development, 81*(2), 168-177.

Boyle, P. J., & Callahan, D. (1995). Managed care in mental health: The ethical issues. *Health Affairs, 14*(3), 7–22.

Brammer, L. M., Abrego, P. J., & Shostrom, E. L. (1993). *Therapeutic counseling and psychotherapy* (6th ed.). Upper Saddle River, NJ: Prentice Hall.

Braun, S. A., & Cox, J. A. (2005). Managed mental health care: Intentional misdiagnosis of mental disorders. *Journal of Counseling & Development, 83*(4), 425–433.

Brewer, J. M. (1932). *Education as guidance: An examination of the possibilities of curriculum in terms of life activities, in elementary and secondary schools, and colleges.* New York: Macmillan.

Brewer, J. M. (1942). *History of vocational guidance.* New York: Harper & Row.

Brill, A. A. (1938). *The basic writings of Sigmund Freud.* New York: Modern Library.

Brock, G. W., & Barnard, C. P. (1999). *Procedures in family therapy* (3rd ed.). Boston: Allyn & Bacon.

Brock, S. E., Sandoval, J., & Lewis, S. (2001). *Preparing for crises in the schools: A manual for building school crisis response teams* (2nd ed.). New York: Wiley.

Brooks, D. K., & Gerstein, L. H. (1990). Counselor credentialing and interprofessional collaboration. *Journal of Counseling & Development, 68*(5), 477–484.

Broskowski, A., & Eaddy, M. (1994). Community mental health centers in a managed care environment. *Administration and Policy in Mental Health and Mental Health Services Research, 21*(4), 335–352.

Brown, D. (2007). *Career information, career counseling, and career development* (9th ed.). Boston: Allyn & Bacon.

Brown, D., Pryzwansky, W. B., & Schulte, A. C. (2006). *Psychological consultation and collaboration: Introduction to theory and practice* (6th ed.). Needham Heights, MA: Allyn & Bacon.

Brown, J. H., & Brown, C. S. (2002). *Marital therapy: Concepts and skills for effective practice*. Pacific Grove, CA: Brooks/Cole.

Browning, C., Reynolds, A. L., & Dworkin, S. H. (1991). Affirmative psychotherapy for lesbian women. *Counseling Psychologist, 19,* 177–196.

Bruner, J. (1986). *Actual minds, possible worlds*. Cambridge, MA: Harvard University Press.

Bruner, J. (1990). *Acts of meaning*. Cambridge, MA: Harvard University Press.

Bruner, J., & Haste, H. (Eds.). (1987). *Making sense*. London: Methuen.

Buehler, C., & Massarik, F. (Eds.). (1968). *The course of human life*. New York: Springer.

Burbach, D. J., Borduin, C. M., & Peake, T. H. (1988). Cognitive approaches to brief psychotherapy. In T. H. Peake, C. M. Borduin, & R. P. Archer, *Brief psychotherapies changing frames of mind* (pp. 57–86). Newbury Park, CA: Sage.

Burlingame, G. M., & Fuhriman, A. (1990). Time-limited group therapy. *Counseling Psychologist, 18,* 93–118.

Burnett, M. (1979). Understanding and overcoming addictions. In S. Eisenberg & J. E. Patterson (Eds.), *Helping clients with special concerns* (pp. 343–362). Chicago: Rand-McNally.

Butler, R. N. (1963). The life review: An interpretation of reminiscence in the aged. *Psychology, 256,* 65–76.

Butler, R. N. (1975). *Why survive?: Being old in America*. New York: Harper & Row.

Butler, R. N., & Gleason, H. P. (Eds.). (1985). *Productive aging: Enhancing vitality in later life*. New York: Springer.

Cade, B., & O'Hanlon, W. H. (1993). *A brief guide to brief therapy*. New York: Norton.

Calahan, D., Cisin, I. H., & Crossley, H. M. (1969). *American drinking practices: A national study of drinking behaviors and attitudes*. New Brunswick, NJ: Rutgers Center of Alcohol Studies.

Camara, W. J.; Nathan, J. S.; Puente, A. E. (2000). *Psychological test usage: Implications in professional psychology. Professional Psychology: Research and Practice, 31*(2), 141–154.

Caplan, G. (1963). Types of mental health consultation. *American Journal of Orthopsychiatry, 33,* 470–481.

Caplan, G. (1964). *Principles of preventive psychiatry*. New York: Basic Books.

Caplan, G. (1970). *The theory and practice of mental health consultation*. New York: Basic Books.

Caplan, G. (1989). *Population-oriented psychiatry*. New York: Human Sciences Press.

Caplan, G. (1995). Types of mental health consultation. *Journal of Educational and Psychological Consultation, 6*(1), 7–21.

Caplan, G.; Caplan, R. B.; & Erchul, W. P. (1994). Caplanian mental health consultation: Historical background and current status. *Consulting Psychology Journal: Practice and Research, 46*(4), 2–12.

Caplan, G.; Caplan, R. B.; & Erchul, W. P. (1995). A contemporary view of mental health consultation: Comments on "Types of Mental Health Consultation" by Gerald Caplan (1963). *Journal of Educational and Psychological Consultation, 6*(1), 23–30.

Carkhuff, R. (1969). *Helping and human relations* (Vols. 1 & 2). New York: Holt, Rinehart & Winston.

Carkhuff, R. (1971). *The development of human resources*. New York: Holt, Rinehart & Winston.

Carney, J. S., & Granato, L. A. (2000, January 1). The business of counseling: Planning and establishing a private practice. *Counseling and Human Development, 32*(5), n.p.

Carroll, L., Gilroy, P. J., & Ryan, J. (2002). Counseling transgendered, transsexual, and gender-variant clients. *Journal of Counseling and Development, 80,* 131–139.

Carter, B. (1988). Remarried families: Creating a new paradigm. In M. Walters, B. Carter, P. Papp, & O. Silverstein (Eds.), *The invisible web: Gender patterns in family relationships* (pp. 333–368). New York: Guilford Press.

Carter, B., & McGoldrick, M. (1999). Overview: The expanded family life cycle. In B. Carter & M. McGoldrick (Eds.), *The expanded family life cycle* (3rd ed., pp. 1–26). New York: Gardner Press.

Carter, R. (1986). Does Kohlberg avoid relativism? In S. Modgil & C. Modgil, *Lawrence Kohlberg: Consensus and controversy* (pp. 9–20). Philadelphia: Falmer Press.

Casas, J. M., Vasquez, M. J., & Ruiz de Esparza, C. A. (2007). Counseling the Latina/o: A guiding framework for a diverse population. In P. B. Pedersen, W. J. Lonner, J. G. Draguns, & J. E. Trimble (Eds.), *Counseling across cultures* (6th ed., pp. 133–160). Thousand Oaks, CA: Sage.

Cavanaugh, J. C., & Blanchard-Fields, F. (2006). *Adult development and aging* (5th ed.). Belmont, CA: Wadsworth.

Centers for Disease Control and Prevention. (2004). Youth risk behavior surveillance—United States. *Morbidity and Mortality Weekly Report, 53* (SS02), 1–96.

Centers for Disease Control and Prevention. (2006). *School associated violent deaths*. Retrieved April 1,

2007, from http://www.cdc.gov/ncipc/sch-shooting.htm.

Centers for Disease Control and Prevention. (2004). Youth risk behavior surveillance—United States, 2005. *Morbidity & Mortality Weekly Report, 55* (SS-5), pp. 1–108. Atlanta, GA: Author.

Cermak, T. L. (1986). Children of alcoholics and the case for a new diagnostic category of codependency. In R. J. Ackerman (Ed.), *Growing in the shadow: Children of alcoholics* (pp. 23–31). Pompano Beach, FL: Health Communications.

Chamberlain, L. L., & Jew, C. L. (2005) Assessment and diagnosis. In P. Stevens & R. L. Smith (Eds.), *Substance abuse counseling: Theory and practice* (3rd ed., pp. 123–158). Upper Saddle River, NJ: Merrill/Prentice Hall.

Cheston, S. E. (2000). A new paradigm for teaching counseling theory and practice. *Counselor Education & Supervision, 39*(4), 254–269.

Chickering, A. W. (1969). *Education and identity.* San Francisco: Jossey-Bass.

Chickering, A. W., & Reisser, L. (1993). *Education and identity* (2nd ed.). San Francisco: Jossey-Bass.

Chinen, A. (1989). *In the ever after: Fairy tales and the second half of life.* Wilmette, IL: Chiron.

Chodorow, N. (1974). Family structure and feminine personality. In M. Z. Rosaldo & L. Lamphere (Eds.), *Woman, culture, and society.* Stanford, CA: Stanford University Press.

Chodorow, N. (1978). *The reproduction of mothering.* Berkeley: University of California Press.

Clark, M. A., Amatea, E. (2004). Teacher perceptions and expectations of school counselor contributions: Implications for program planning and training. *Professional School Counseling, 8*(2), 132–140.

Clawson, T. W., Henderson, D. A., Schweiger, W. K., & Collins, D. R. (2003). *Counselor preparation 1999–2001: Programs, faculty, trends* (11th ed.). New York: Brunner-Routledge.

Cobia, D. C., & Henderson, D. A. (2007). *Developing an effective and accountable school counseling program.* Upper Saddle River, NJ: Prentice Hall.

Cochran, J. L. (1996). Using play and art therapy to help culturally diverse students overcome barriers to school success. *School Counselor, 43,* 287–298.

Coddington, D. C., Keen, D. J., Moore, K. D., & Clarke, R. L. (1990). *The crisis in health care: Costs, choices, and strategies.* San Francisco, CA: Jossey-Bass.

Cohen, R. J., & Swerdlik, M. E. (2002). *Psychological testing and assessment: An introduction to tests and measurement* (5th ed.). Boston, MA: McGraw-Hill Higher Education.

Colapinto, J. (2000). Structural family therapy. In A. M. Horne (Ed.), *Family counseling and therapy* (3rd ed., pp. 140–169). Belmont, CA: Wadsworth.

Cole, C., & Rodman, H. (1987). When school-age children care for themselves: Issues for family life educators and parents. *Family Relations, 26,* 92–96.

Coles, R. (1970). *Erik H. Erikson: The growth of his work.* Boston: Little, Brown.

Collison, B. B. (2001). Professional associations, standards, and credentials in counseling. In D. C. Locke, J. E. Myers, & E. L. Herr (Eds.), *The handbook of counseling* (pp. 55–68), Thousand Oaks, CA: Sage.

Comer, R. J. (2006). *Abnormal psychology* (5th ed.). New York: Worth Publishers.

Conarton, S., & Silverman, L. D. (1988). Feminist developmental theory. In M. A. Dutton-Douglas & I. E. Walker (Eds.), *Feminist psychotherapies: Integration of therapeutic and feminist systems* (pp. 37–67). Norwood, NJ: Ablex.

Consumer Reports. (1992). *How to resolve the health care crisis: Affordable protection for all Americans.* Yonkers, NY: Author.

Cook, J. E., & Doyle, C. (2002). Working alliance in online therapy as compared to face-to-face therapy: Preliminary results. *CyberPsychology & Behavior, 5,* 95–105.

Cooper, C. C., & Gottlieb, M. C. (2000). Ethical issues with managed care: Challenges facing counseling psychology. *The Counseling Psychologist, 28*(2), 179–236.

Corey, G. (2005). *Theory and practice of counseling and psychotherapy* (7th ed.). Pacific Grove, CA: Brooks/Cole.

Corey, G., & Corey, M. S. (2006). *Groups: Process and practice* (7th ed.). Pacific Grove, CA: Brooks/Cole.

Corey, G., Corey, M. S., & Callanan, P. (2007). *Issues and ethics in the helping professions* (7th ed.) Belmont, CA: Brooks/Cole.

Cormier, W. H., & Cormier, L. S. (2003). *Interviewing and change strategies for helpers: Fundamental skills and cognitive-behavior interventions* (5th ed.). Pacific Grove, CA: Brooks/Cole.

Corr, C. A. (1991–1992). A task-based approach to coping with dying. *Omega, 24*(2), 81–94.

Corsini, R. J. (2008). Introduction. In R. J. Corsini & D. Wedding (Eds.), *Current psychotherapies* (8th ed.). Belmont, CA: Wadsworth.

Cottone, R. R., & Tarvydas, V. M. (2003). *Ethical and professional issues in counseling* (2nd ed.). Upper Saddle River, NJ: Merrill/Prentice Hall.

Council for Accreditation of Counseling and Related Educational Programs (CACREP). (2001). *The 2001 standards.* Retrieved June 19, 2007, from http://www.cacrep.org/2001Standards.html

Coy, D., & Sears, S. (2000). The scope of practice of the high school counselor. In J. Wittmer (Ed.), *Managing your school counseling program: K–12 developmental strategies* (pp. 56–67). Minneapolis, MN: Educational Media.

Craig, R. J. (2003). Assessing personality and psychopathology with interviews. In J. R. Graham, J. A. Naglieri, & I. B. Weiner (Eds.), *Handbook of psychology: Assessment psychology* (Vol. 10, pp. 487–508). Hoboken, NJ: John Wiley & Sons.

Cronbach, L. J. (1990). *Essentials of psychological testing* (5th ed.). New York: Harper & Row.

Crose, R. (1990). Reviewing the past in the here and now: Using Gestalt therapy techniques with life review. *Journal of Mental Health Counseling, 12*(3), 279–287.

Crosson-Tower, C. (2005). Understanding child abuse and neglect (6th ed.). Boston: Allyn & Bacon.

Cummings, E., & Henry, W. E. (1961). *Growing old.* New York: Basic Books.

Cunningham, N. J., & Sandu, D. S. (2000). A comprehensive approach to school-community violence prevention. *Professional School Counseling, 4,* 126–133.

Cutler, D. L., & Huffine, C. (2004). Heroes in community psychiatry: Professor Gerald Caplan. *Community Mental Health Journal, 40*(3), 193–197.

Dabrowski, K. (1964). *Positive disintegration.* Boston: Little, Brown.

Dabrowski, K. (1970). *Mental growth through positive disintegration.* London: Gryf.

Dalley, T., Case, C., Schaverien, J., Weir, F., Halliday, D., Hall, P. N., & Waller, D. (1987). *Images of art therapy: New developments in theory and practice.* New York: Tavistock.

Danzinger, P. R., & Welfel, E. R. (2001). The impact of managed care on mental health counselors: A survey of perceptions, practices, and compliance with ethical standards. *Journal of Mental Health Counseling, 23*(2), 137–150.

Davenloo, H. (Ed.). (1994). *Basic principles and techniques in short-term dynamic psychotherapy.* New York: Spectrum.

Davis, K. M. (2003). Teaching a course in school-based consultation. *Counselor Education and Supervision, 42*(4), 275–285.

Dawson, D. A., Grant, B. F., & Li, T. K. (2005). Quantifying the risks associated with exceeding recommended drinking limits. *Alcoholism, Clinical and Experimental Research, 29*(5), 902–908.

de Shazer, S. (1988). *Clues: Investigating solutions in brief therapy.* New York: Norton.

Delmaestro, S. (1990). Sharing despair: Working with distressed caregivers. In B. Genevay & R. S. Katz (Eds.), *Countertransference and older clients* (pp. 123–135). Newbury Park, CA: Sage.

Department of Health and Human Services (DHHS). (2000). *Mental health: A report of the surgeon general.* Rockville, MD: Author.

Diamond, M., Johnson, P. E., Protti, A. M., Ott, C., & Kajisa, C. (1985). Plasticity in the 904-day-old male rat cerebral cortex. *Experimental Neurology, 87*(2), 309–317.

Dinkmeyer, D. (1967). The counselor as consultant to the teacher. *School Counselor, 14,* 294–297.

Dinkmeyer, D., & Carlson, J. (2006). *Consultation: Creating School-Based Interventions* (3rd ed.). New York: Taylor & Francis Group.

Dinkmeyer, D., & McKay, G. D. (1976). *Systematic training for effective parenting.* Circle Pines, MN: American Guidance Services.

Dinkmeyer, D., Jr., & Dinkmeyer, D., Sr. (1991). Adlerian family therapy. In A. M. Horne & J. L. Passmore (Eds.), *Family counseling and therapy* (2nd ed., pp. 383–402). Itasca, IL: F. E. Peacock.

Dinkmeyer, Jr., D. (2006). School consultation using individual psychology. *Journal of Individual Psychology, 62*(2), 180–187.

Disch, R. (Ed.). (1988). *Twenty-five years of the life review: Theoretical and practical considerations.* New York: Haworth Press.

Dollarhide, C. T. (2003). Partnering with students: Counseling in the three domains. In C. T. Dollarhide & K. A. Saginak (Eds.), *School counseling in the secondary school: A comprehensive process and program* (pp. 133–158). Boston, MA: Allyn & Bacon.

Dollarhide, C. T., & Lemberger, M. E. (2006). "No Child Left Behind": Implications for school counselors. *Professional School Counseling, 9*(4), 295–304.

Dorwart, R. A., & Epstein, S. S. (1993). *Privatization and mental health care: A fragile balance.* Westport, CT: Auburn House.

Dougherty, A. M. (2004). *Psychological consultation and collaboration in school and community settings* (4th ed.). Belmont, CA: Wadsworth.

Dowd, E. T. (2003). Adlerian, cognitive-behavioral, and constructivist psychotherapies: Commonalities, differences, and integration. In R. E. Watts, *Adlerian, cognitive, and constructivist therapies: An integrative dialogue* (pp. 91–106). New York: Springer.

Dowell, D. A., & Ciarlo, J. A. (1983). Overview of the Community Mental Health Centers Program from an evaluation perspective. *Community Mental Health Journal, 19*(2), 95–128.

Dreikurs, R. (1968). *Psychology in the classroom.* New York: Harper & Row.

Dreikurs, R., Lowe, R., Sonstegard, M., & Corsini, R. J. (Eds.). (1959). *Adlerian family counseling: A manual for counseling centers.* Eugene: University of Oregon.

Dreyfus, E. (1962). Counseling and existentialism. *Journal of Counseling Psychology, 9,* 128–132.

Drummond, R. J., & Jones, K. D. (2006). *Appraisal procedures for counselors and helping professions* (6th ed.). Upper Saddle River, NJ: Prentice Hall.

Dryden, W. (Ed.). (1998). *Key issues for counselling in action.* London: Sage.

Dugan, W. E. (1993). *Wood block and toy project: Designed for diversely-abled senior volunteers.* St. Cloud, MN: Retired Senior Volunteer Program.

Dusay, J. M., & Dusay, K. M. (1989). Transactional analysis. In R. J. Corsini & D. Wedding (Eds.), *Current psychotherapies* (4th ed., pp. 405–453). Itasca, IL: F. E. Peacock.

Eaton, D. K., Kann, L., Kinchen, S. A., Ross, J. G., Hawkins, J., Harris, W. A., & et al. (2006). Youth risk behavior surveillance—United States. *Morbidity and Mortality Weekly Report, 55*(SS-5), 1–108.

Efran, J. (2002, May/June). Therapeutic vision. *Psychotherapy Networker, 26*(3), 28–35, 70.

Egan, G. (2007). *The skilled helper: A problem management and opportunity development approach to helping* (8th ed.). Pacific Grove, CA: Brooks/Cole.

Elderhostel. (2007). *What is Elderhostel?* Retrieved August 25, 2007, from http://www.elderhostel.org/about/what_is.asp

Ellis, A. (1973). *Humanistic psychotherapy: The rational-emotive approach.* New York: Julian Press.

Ellis, A. (1992). Brief therapy: The rational-emotive method. In S. H. Budman, M. F. Hoyt, & S. Friedman (Eds.), *The first session in brief therapy* (pp. 36–58). New York: Guilford Press.

Ellis, A. (2000). Rational-emotive behavior: Marriage and family therapy. In A. M. Horne & J. L. Passmore (Eds.), *Family counseling and therapy* (3rd ed., pp. 489–514). Itasca, IL: Peacock.

Ellis, A. (2005). Rational emotive behavior therapy. In R. J. Corsini & D. Wedding (Eds.), *Current psychotherapies* (7th ed., pp. 166–201). Belmont: CA: Thomson Brooks/Cole.

Ellis, A. (2008). Rational–emotive behavior therapy. In R. J. Corsini & D. J. Wedding (Eds.), *Current psychotherapies* (8th ed.). Belmont, CA: Wadsworth.

Ellis, A., & Grieger, R. (1977). *Handbook of rational–emotive therapy.* New York: Springer.

Erchul, W. P., & Martens, B. K. (1997). *School consultation: Conceptual and empirical bases of practice.* New York: Plenum Press.

Erickson, M. H. (1980). *The collected papers of Milton H. Erickson on hypnosis: Vol. 4. Innovative hypnotherapy* (E. L. Rossi, Ed.). New York: Irvington.

Erickson, S. (2005). Etiological theories of substance abuse. In P. Stevens & R. L. Smith (Eds.), *Substance abuse counseling: Theory and practice* (3rd ed., pp. 87–122). Upper Saddle River, NJ: Merrill/Prentice Hall.

Eriksen, K., & Kress, V. (2005). *Beyond the DSM story: Ethical quandaries, challenges, and best practices.* Thousand Oaks, CA: Sage.

Erikson, E. (1950). *Childhood and society.* New York: Norton.

Erikson, E. H. (1963). *Childhood and society* (2nd ed.). New York: Norton.

Erikson, E. H. (1968). *Identity, youth, and crises.* New York: Norton.

Erikson, E. H. (1978). Reflections on Dr. Borg's life cycle. In E. H. Erikson (Ed.), *Adulthood* (pp. 1–32). New York: Norton.

Erikson, E. H. (1980). *Identity and the life cycle.* New York: Norton.

Erikson, E. H. (1982). *The life cycle completed.* New York: Norton.

Erikson, J. M. (1997). *The life cycle completed: Erik H. Erikson.* New York: Norton.

Erk, R. R. (2004). *Counseling treatment for children and adolescents with DSM-IV-TR disorders.* Upper Saddle River, NJ: Pearson/Merrill/Prentice Hall.

EstÈs, C. P. (1992). *Women who run with the wolves.* New York: Ballantine Books.

Ewen, R. B. (2003). *An introduction to theories of personality* (6th ed.). Mahwah, NJ: Lawrence Erlbaum.

Fairbairn, W. R. (1954). *An object-relations theory of personality.* New York: Basic Books.

Farber, L. (1966). *The ways of the will.* New York: Basic Books.

Fenell, D. L., & Weinhold, B. K. (2003). *Counseling families: An introduction to marriage and family therapy* (3rd ed.). Denver: Love.

Fischer, E. H., & Farina, A. (1995). Attitudes toward seeking professional psychological help: A shortened form and considerations for research. *Journal of College Student Development, 36,* 368–373.

Fleshman, B., & Fryrear, J. L. (1981). *The arts in therapy.* Chicago: Nelson–Hall.

Fletcher, A. M. (2001). *Sober for good.* Boston: Houghton Mifflin.

Foley, V. D. (1989). Family therapy. In R. J. Corsini & D. Wedding (Eds.), *Current psychotherapies* (4th ed., pp. 455–500). Itasca, IL: F. E. Peacock.

Forrest, G. G. (1994). *Intensive psychotherapy of alcoholism* (The Master Work Series). Lanham, MD: Jason Aronson.

Foucault, M. (1980). *Power/knowledge: Selected interviews and other writings*. New York: Pantheon Books.

Fowler, J. W. (1981). *Stages of faith: The psychology of human development and the quest for meaning*. San Francisco: Harper & Row.

Fowler, J. W. (1991). Stages in faith consciousness. In F. K. Oser & W. G. Scarlett (Eds.), Religious development in childhood and adolescence [Special issue]. *New Directions in Child Development, 52,* 27–45.

Fowler, J. W. (1995). *Stages of faith: The psychology of human development and the quest for meaning*. New York: HarperOne.

Frame, M. W., & Williams, C. B. (2005). A model of ethical decision making from a multicultural perspective. *Counseling & Values, 49,* 165–179.

Framo, J. L. (1982). *Explorations in marital and family therapy*. New York: Springer.

Frankl, V. (1963). *Man's search for meaning*. New York: Washington Square Press.

Fransella, F., & Dalton, P. (2000). *Personal construct counseling in action* (2nd ed.). London: Sage.

Fransella, F., & Dalton, P. (2000). *Personal construct counselling in action* (2nd ed.). Newbury Park, CA: Sage.

Freeman, M. S. (2001). Innovative alcohol education program for college and university judicial sanctions. *Journal of College Counseling, 4*(2), 179–185.

Freud, A. (1966). *The ego and mechanisms of defense*. New York: International Universities Press.

Freud, S. (1949). *An outline of psychoanalysis* (J. Strachey, Trans.). New York: Norton. (Original work published 1940)

Friedan, B. (1993). *The fountain of age*. New York: Simon & Schuster.

Fromm, E. (1941). *Escape from freedom*. New York: Rinehart.

Fukuyama, M. A., & Sevig, T. D. (1997). Spiritual issues in counseling: A new course. *Counselor Education and Supervision, 36,* 233–244.

Galassi, J., & Akos, P. (2004). Developmental advocacy: Twenty-first century school counseling. *Journal of Counseling & Development, 82,* 146–157.

Gallagher, R. P. (2006). *National Survey of Counseling Center Directors*. Alexandria, VA: International Association of Counseling Services.

Gardner, H. (1993). *Frames of mind: The theory of multiple intelligences*. New York: Basic Books.

Garreau, J. (1988). The integration of an American dream. *Washington Post National Weekly Edition, 5,* 6–8.

Garrett, M. T., (2004). Profile of Native Americans. In D. R. Atkinson (Ed.), *Counseling American minorities: A cross-cultural perspective* (6th ed., pp. 147–170). New York: McGraw–Hill.

Gazda, G. M. (1978). *Group counseling: A developmental approach*. Boston: Allyn & Bacon.

Gazda, G. M. (1989). *Group counseling: A developmental approach* (4th ed.). Boston: Allyn & Bacon.

Gazda, G. M., & Horne, A. (2001). *Group counseling and group psychotherapy: Theory and application*. Boston: Allyn & Bacon.

Gearon, C. J. (2003, February). Visiting the 'kids' gets harder. *AARP Bulletin,* p. 6.

Gelso, C. J., & Carter, J. A. (1985). The relationship in counseling and psychotherapy: Components, consequences, and theoretical antecedents. *Counseling Psychologist, 13,* 155–243.

Gelso, C. J., & Fretz, B. R. (2001). *Counseling psychology* (2nd ed.). Belmont, CA: Wadsworth.

Genevay, B., & Katz, R. S. (Eds.). (1990). *Countertransference and older clients*. Newbury Park, CA: Sage.

Genter, D. S. (1991). A brief strategic model for mental health counseling. *Journal of Mental Health Counseling, 13,* 59–68.

George, R. L., & Cristiani, T. S. (1986). *Counseling theory and practice* (2nd ed.). Upper Saddle River, NJ: Prentice Hall.

Geratz, E. (1995). A biopsychosocial paradigm for counseling clients with AIDS. *Counseling Today, 37,* p. 16.

Gergen, K. J. (1985). The social constructionist movement in modern psychology. *American Psychologist, 40,* 266–275.

Gergen, K. J., & McNamee, S. (2000). From disordering discourse to transformative dialogue. In R. A. Neimeyer & J. D. Raskin, *Constructions of disorder* (pp. 333–349). Washington, DC: American Psychological Association.

Gerig, M. S. (2007). *Foundations for mental health and community counseling: An introduction to the profession*. Upper Saddle River, NJ: Pearson Education.

Gesell, A. (1940). *The first five years of life*. New York: Harper.

Gesell, A. (1948). *Studies in child development*. New York: Harper.

Gibson, R. L., & Mitchell, M. H. (2007). *Introduction to counseling and guidance* (7th ed.). New York: Macmillan.

Gil, E. (1991). *The healing power of play: Working with abused children*. New York: Guilford.

Gilligan, C. (1982). *In a different voice: Psychological theory and Women's development*. Cambridge, MA: Harvard University Press.

Gilligan, C. (2002). *The birth of pleasure*. New York: Alfred A. Knopf.

Gilliland, B. E., & James, R. K. (1997). *Crisis intervention strategies* (3rd ed.). Pacific Grove, CA: Brooks/Cole.

Ginter, E. J. (2000). Private practice. In D. C. Locke, J. E. Myers, & E. L. Herr (Eds.), *The handbook of counseling* (pp. 355–371), Thousand Oaks, CA: Sage.

Gladding, S. T. (2005). *Counseling as an art: The creative arts in counseling* (3rd ed.). Alexandria, VA: American Counseling Association.

Gladding, S. T. (2007). *Family therapy: History, theory, and practice* (4th ed.). Upper Saddle River, NJ: Merrill/Prentice Hall.

Gladding, S. T. (2007). *Counseling: A comprehensive profession* (5th ed.). Upper Saddle River, NJ: Merrill/Prentice Hall.

Gladding, S. T. (2008). *Group work: A counseling specialty* (5th ed.). Upper Saddle River, NJ: Merrill/Prentice Hall.

Gladding, S. T., & Newsome, D. W. (2004). *Community and agency counseling* (2nd ed.). Upper Saddle River, NJ: Merrill/Prentice Hall.

Gladding, S. T., & Veach, L. J. (2003). Community counseling: Leadership opportunities today. In J. D. West, C. J. Osborn & D. L. Bubenzer (Eds.), *Leaders and legacies: Contributions to the profession of counseling* (pp. 65–78). New York: Brunner-Routledge.

Glasser, W. (1998). *Choice theory: A new psychology of personal freedom.* New York: Harper Perennial.

Glosoff, H. L., Herlihy, B., & Spence, E. B. (2000). Privileged communication in the counselor–client relationship. *Journal of Counseling & Development, 78*(4), 454–462.

Glosoff, H. L., & Pate R. H. (2002). Privacy and confidentiality in school counseling. *Professional School Counseling, 6*(1), 20–27.

Glosoff, H. L., Corey, G., & Herlihy, B. (2006). Avoiding detrimental multiple relationships. In B. Herlihy & G. Corey (Eds.), *ACA ethical standards casebook* (6th ed., pp. 209–222). Alexandria, VA: American Counseling Association.

Goldenberg, I., & Goldenberg, H. (2007). *Family therapy: An overview* (7th ed.). Pacific Grove, CA: Brooks/Cole.

Goldman, L. (1972). Tests and counseling: The marriage that failed. *Measurement and Evaluation in Guidance, 4,* 213–220.

Goldman, L. (1982). Assessment in counseling: A better way. *Measurement and Evaluation in Guidance, 15,* 70–73.

Goldman, L. (1990). Qualitative assessment. *Counseling Psychologist, 15,* 205–213.

Goldman, L. (1992). Qualitative assessment: An approach for counselors. *Journal of Counseling & Development, 70,* 616–621.

Goldman, L. (1994). The marriage is over 1/4 for most of us. *Measurement and Evaluation in Counseling and Development, 26,* 217–218.

Goleman, D. (1995). *Emotional intelligence: Why it can matter more than IQ.* New York: Bantam Books.

Goleman, D. (1998). *Working with emotional intelligence.* New York: Bantam Books.

Goode, E. (1998, November 24). How much therapy is enough? It depends. *New York Times,* pp. D1, D10.

Goode, E. (1998, November 24). When is brief therapy enough? *New York Times,* p. 10.

Gould, E., Reeves, A. J., Graziano, M. S. A., & Cross, C. G. (1999, October 15). Neurogenesis in the neocortex of adult primates. *Science, 286*(5439), 548–552.

Gould, M. S., Marracco, F. A., Kleinman, M., Thomas, J. G., Mostkoff, K., Cote, J., & Davies, M. (2005). Evaluating iatrogenic risk of youth suicide screening programs: A randomized controlled trial. *Journal of the American Medical Association, 293*(13), 1635–1643.

Gould, R. (1978). *Transformations: Growth and change in adult life.* New York: Simon & Schuster.

Granello, D. H., & Granello, P. F. (2007). *Suicide: An essential guide for helping professionals and educators.* Boston, MA: Pearson.

Greenhill, L., Pliszka, S., Dulcan, M. K., & the Work Group on Quality Issues. (2002). Practice parameter for the use of stimulant medications in the treatment of children, adolescents, and adults. *Journal of the American Academy of Child and Adolescent Psychiatry, 41*(Suppl.), 26S–49S.

Grief, G. L. (1985). *Single fathers.* Toronto: Heath.

Guterman, J. T., & Kirk, M. A. (1999). Mental health counselors and the Internet. *Journal of Mental Health Counseling, 21,* 300–325.

Hadley, T. R., Culhane, D. P., Mazade, N., & Manderscheid, R. W. (1994). What is a CMHC? A comparative analysis by varying definitional criteria. *Administration and Policy in Mental Health, 21,* 295–308.

Haley, J. (1987). *Problem-solving therapy.* San Francisco: Jossey-Bass.

Haley, J. (1991). *Problem-solving therapy.* San Francisco: Jossey-Bass.

Hall, C. S., Lindzey, G., & Campbell, J. B. (1998). *Theories of personality* (4th ed.). New York: Wiley.

Hall, G. S. (1916). *Adolescence.* New York: Appleton.

Hamburger, Y. A., & Ben-Artzi, E. (2000). The relationship between extraversion and neuroticism and the different uses of the Internet. *Computers in Human Behavior, 16,* 441–449.

Hammersmith, S. K. (1987). A sociological approach to counseling homosexual clients and their families. *Journal of Homosexuality, 13,* 173–190.

Hansen, J. C., Rossberg, R. H., & Cramer, S. H. (1994). *Counseling: Theory and process* (5th ed.). Boston: Allyn & Bacon.

Harrigan, M. P., & Farmer, R. L. (2000). The myths and facts of aging. In R. L. Schneider, N. P. Kropf, & A. J. Kisor (Eds.), *Gerontological social work: Knowledge, service settings, and special populations* (2nd ed., pp. 26–64). Belmont, CA: Brooks/Cole/Thomson Learning.

Harrison, T. (2000). Brief counseling in the K–12 developmental counseling program. In J. Wittmer (Ed.), *Managing your school counseling program: K–12 developmental strategies* (pp. 85–94). Minneapolis, MN: Educational Media.

Hartley, A. (2006). Changing role of the speed of processing construct in the cognitive psychology of human aging. In J. E. Birren & K. W. Schaie (Eds.), *Handbook of the psychology of aging* (6th ed., pp. 183–208). Burlington, MA: Elsevier Academic Press.

Hartley, D., Bird, D. C., Lambert, D., & Coffin, J. (2002, November). *The Role of Community Mental Health Centers as Rural Safety Net Providers* (Working Paper #30). Portland, ME: Edmund S. Muskie School of Public Service. Retrieved June 26, 2007, from http://muskie.usm.maine.edu/Publications/rural/wp30.pdf

Haste, H. (1993). Morality, self, and sociohistorical context: The role of lay social theory. In G. G. Noam & T. E. Wren, *The moral self* (pp. 175–207). Cambridge, MA: MIT Press.

Havighurst, R. J. (1953). *Human development and education.* New York: Longman, Green.

Heathcote, D. (1971). *Drama in the education of teachers.* Newcastle, UK: University Printing.

Heesacker, M., & Prichard, S. (1992). In a different voice revisited: Men, women, and emotion. *Journal of Mental Health Counseling, 14,* 274–290.

Heilbrun, A. B., Jr. (1982). Cognitive factors in early termination: Social insight and level of defensiveness. *Journal of Counseling Psychology, 29,* 29–38.

Herdt, G. (1989). Gay and lesbian youth: Emergent identities and cultural scenes at home and abroad. *Journal of Homosexuality, 17,* 1–42.

Herlihy, B., & Corey, G. (2005). *ACA ethical standards casebook* (6th ed.). Alexandria, VA: American Counseling Association.

Hermann, M. A., & Finn, A. (2002). An ethical and legal perspective on the role of school counselors in preventing violence in schools. *Professional School Counseling, 6*(1), 46–54.

Herr, E. L. (2004). ACA fifty years plus and moving forward. In G. W. Waltz & R. Yep (Eds.), *VISTAS—Perspectives on Counseling 2004* (pp. 15–23). Alexandria, VA: American Counseling Association and Counseling Outfitters/CAPS Press.

Hershenson, D. B., & Berger, G. P. (2001). The state of community counseling: A survey of directors of CACREP-accredited programs. *Journal of Counseling & Development, 79*(2), 188–193.

Hershenson, D. B., Power, P. W., & Waldo, M. (2003). *Community counseling: Contemporary theory and practice.* Prospect Heights, IL: Waveland Press.

Hetzel, R. D., Barton, D. A., & Davenport, D. S. (1994, May). Helping men change: A group counseling model for male clients. *Journal for Specialists in Group Work, 19,* 52–64.

Hillman, J. (1989). *A blue fire: Selected writings.* New York: Harper Perennial.

Hodges, S. (2001). University counseling centers at the twenty-first century: Looking forward, looking back. *Journal of College Counseling, 4*(2), 161–173.

Hoffman, M. A. (1991). Counseling the HIV-infected client: A psychosocial model for assessment and intervention. *Counseling Psychologist, 19,* 467–542.

Hogg, J. A., & Frank, M. L. (1992). Toward an interpersonal model of codependence and contradependence. *Journal of Counseling & Development, 70,* 371–375.

Horne, A. M., & Sayger, T. V. (2000). Behavioral approaches to couple and family therapy. In A. M. Horne (Ed.), *Family counseling and therapy* (3rd ed., pp. 454–488). Belmont, CA: Wadsworth.

Horney, K. (1945). *Our inner conflicts.* New York: Norton.

Hosford, R. E., & DeVisser, L. (1974). *Behavioral approaches to counseling: An introduction.* Washington, DC: APGA Press.

House, R. M., & Holloway, E. L. (1992). Empowering the counseling professional to work with gay and lesbian issues. In S. H. Dworkin & F. J. Gutièrrez (Eds.), *Counseling gay men and lesbians: Journey to the end of the rainbow* (pp. 307–324). Alexandria, VA: American Counseling Association.

Hull, C. (1928). *Aptitude testing.* Yonkers-on-Hudson, NY: World Book.

Ingersoll, R. E. (1997). Teaching a course on counseling and spirituality. *Counselor Education and Supervision, 36,* 224–232.

Ingraham, C., & Meyers, J. (2000). Introduction to multicultural and cross-cultural consultation in schools: Cultural diversity issues in school consultation. *School Psychology Review, 29*(3), 315–319.

Ivey, A. E. (2000). *Developmental therapy.* Sunapee, NH: Author.

Ivey, A. E., & Ivey, M. B. (2007). *Intentional interviewing and counseling: Facilitating client development in a multicultural society* (6th ed.). Pacific Grove, CA: Brooks/Cole.

Ivey, A. E., D'Andrea, M., Ivey, M. B., & Simek-Morgan, L. (2007). *Theories of counseling and psychotherapy: A multicultural perspective* (6th ed.). Boston: Allyn & Bacon.

Jack, D. C. (1991). *Silencing the self: Women and depression.* Cambridge, MA: Harvard University Press.

Jack, D. C. (1999). *Behind the mask: Destruction and creativity in women's aggression.* Cambridge, MA: Harvard University Press.

Jacobi, J. (1973). *The psychology of C. G. Jung* (8th ed.). New Haven, CT: Yale University Press.

Jahoda, M. (1958). *Current concepts of positive mental health.* New York: Basic Books.

Jakubiak, C. H., Jr., & Callahan, J. J., Jr. (1995–1996, Winter). Treatment of mental disorders among nursing home residents: Will the market provide? *Generations, 19,* 39–42.

James, R. K. (2008). *Crisis intervention strategies* (4th ed.). Belmont, CA: Brooks/Cole.

Jellinek, E. M. (1960). *The Disease Concept of Alcoholism.* New Haven, CT: Hillhouse.

Jellinek, M. S. & Nurcombe, B. (1993). Two wrongs don't make a right: Managed care, mental health, and the marketplace. *Journal of the American Medical Association, 270*(14), 1737–1739.

Johnson Institute. (1987). *The family enablers.* Minneapolis, MN: Author.

Johnson, B. A., & Ait-Daoud, N. (2005). Alcohol: Clinical aspects. In J. H. Lowinson, R. Ruiz, R. B. Millman, & J. B. Langrod (4th ed.), *Substance abuse: A comprehensive textbook* (pp. 151–163). Baltimore, MD: Williams & Wilkins.

Johnson, K., (2000). *School crisis management: A hands-on guide to training crisis response teams* (2nd ed.). Alameda, CA: Hunter House.

Jordan, J. V., Kaplan, A. G., Miller, J. B., Stiver, I. P., & Surrey, J. L. (Eds.). (1991). *Women's growth in connection: Writings from the Stone Center.* New York: Guilford Press.

Juliano, T. R. (2005). Women's multiple roles, role balance, and social support as predictors of life satisfaction and mental health (Doctoral dissertation, Columbia University, 2005). *Dissertation Abstracts International, 66*(09), AAT 3188754.

Jung, C. G. (1933). The stages of life. In *Modern man in search of a soul.* San Diego: Harcourt Brace.

Jung, C. G. (1970). *Modern man in search of a soul* (W. S. Dell & C. F. Baynes, Trans.). New York: Harcourt Brace Jovanovich. (Original work published 1933)

Jung, C. G. (1971). *Psychological types* (H. G. Baynes, Trans.; rev. R. F. C. Hull). (Bollingen Series XX, vol. 6). Princeton, NJ: Princeton University Press. (Original work published 1921)

Kaplan, A. G. (1991). Empathic communication in the psychotherapy relationship. In J. V. Jordan, A. G. Kaplan, J. B. Miller, I. P. Stiver, & J. L. Surrey (Eds.), *Women's growth in connection: Writings from the Stone Center* (pp. 44–50). New York: Guilford Press.

Kaplan, A. G., & Klein, R. (1991). The relational self in late adolescent women. In J. V. Jordan, A. G. Kaplan, J. B. Miller, I. P. Stiver, & J. L. Surrey (Eds.), *Women's growth in connection: Writings from the Stone Center* (pp. 122–131). New York: Guilford Press.

Kasl, C. D. (1989). *Women, sex, and addiction: Search for love and power.* New York: Harper & Row.

Katz, R. (1990). Using our emotional reactions to older clients: A working theory. In B. Genevay & R. S. Katz (Eds.), *Countertransference and older clients* (pp. 17–26). Newbury Park, CA: Sage.

Kay, T. (1990). *To dance with the white dog.* New York: Washington Square Press.

Kegan, R. (1982). *The evolving self: Problem and process in human development.* Cambridge, MA: Harvard University Press.

Kegan, R. (1986). Kohlberg and the psychology of ego development: A predominantly positive evaluation. In S. Modgil & C. Modgil, *Lawrence Kohlberg: Consensus and controversy* (pp. 163–181). Philadelphia: Falmer Press.

Kelly, E. W., Jr. (1995). *Spirituality and religion in counseling and psychotherapy: Diversity in theory and practice.* Alexandria, VA: American Counseling Association.

Kelly, G. A. (1955). *A theory of personality: The psychology of personal constructs.* New York: Norton.

Kempler, W. (1973). Gestalt therapy. In R. J. Corsini & D. Wedding (Eds.), *Current psychotherapies* (pp. 251–286). Itasca, IL: F. E. Peacock.

Keyes, C. L. M. (2000). Subjective change and its consequences for emotional well-being. *Motivation and Emotion, 24*(2), 67–84.

Kiesler, C. A. (2000). The next wave of change for psychology and mental health services in the health care revolution. *American Psychologist, 55,* 481–487.

Kirk, B. A., Johnson, A. P., Redfield, J. E., Free, J. E., Michel, J., Roston, R. A., & Warman, R. E. (1971). Guidelines for university and college counseling services. *American Psychologist, 26,* 585–589.

Kitchener, K. S. (1984). Intuition, critical evaluation, and ethical principles: The foundation for ethical decisions in counseling psychology. *Counseling Psychologist, 12,* 43–55.

Klein, M. (1948). *The analysis of self.* New York: International Universities Press.

Knight, B. G. (2004). *Psychotherapy with older adults* (3rd ed.). Thousand Oaks, CA: Sage.

Knowlton, M. (1996, March). *Evolution of a new old age.* Speech delivered at Productive Aging Conference, Vancouver, British Columbia, Canada.

Knox, S., Hess, S. A., Petersen, D. A., & Hill, C. E. (1997). A qualitative analysis of client perceptions of the effects of helpful therapist self-disclosure in long-term therapy. *Journal of Counseling Psychology, 44,* 274–283.

Kocet, M. M. (2006) Ethical challenges in a complex world: Highlights of the 2005 ACA Code of Ethics. *Journal of Counseling & Development, 84,* 228–234.

Kohlberg, L. (1969). Stage and sequence: The cognitive- developmental approach to socialization. In D. Goslin (Ed.), *Handbook of socialization theory and research* (pp. 347–480). Chicago: Rand McNally.

Kohlberg, L. (1981). *Essays in moral development: Vol. 1. The philosophy of moral development.* San Francisco: Harper & Row.

Kohlberg, L. (1984). *Essays on moral development, Vol.2: The psychology of moral development.* San Francisco: Harper & Row.

Kohlberg, L. (1986). A current statement on some theoretical issues. In S. Modgil & C. Modgil, *Lawrence Kohlberg: Consensus and controversy.* Philadelphia: Falmer Press.

Kohlberg, L. (1986a). *Essays on moral development, Vol.3: Education and moral development.* San Francisco: Harper & Row.

Kottman, T. (2004). Play therapy. In A. Vernon, *Counseling children and adolescents* (3rd ed., pp. 111–136). Denver, CO: Love.

Kronick, R. (1991). Health insurance 1979–1989: The frayed connection between employment and insurance. *Inquiry, 28*(4), 318–332.

Kropf, N. P. (2000). Home health and community services. In R. L. Schneider, N. P. Kropf, & A. J. Kisor (Eds.), *Gerontological social work: Knowledge, service settings,*[BIB1] *and special populations* (2nd ed., pp. 167–190). Belmont, CA: Brooks/Cole/ Thomson Learning.

Krumboltz, J. D. (Ed.). (1966). *Revolution in counseling.* Boston: Houghton Mifflin.

Krumboltz, J. D., & Thoresen, C. E. (1976). *Counseling methods.* New York: Holt, Rinehart & Winston.

Kübler-Ross, E. (1969). *On death and dying.* New York: Macmillan.

Kübler-Ross, E. (1974). *Questions and answers on death and dying.* New York: Macmillan.

L'Abate, L., Ganahl, G., & Hansen, J. C. (1986). *Methods of family therapy.* Upper Saddle River, NJ: Prentice Hall.

Lambert, M. J., Shapiro, D. A., & Bergin, A. S. (1986). The effectiveness of psychotherapy. In S. L. Garfield & A. E. Bergin (Eds.), *Handbook of psychotherapy and behavior change* (pp. 157–211). New York: John Wiley.

Landreth, G. L., & Sweeney, D. S. (1997). Child-centered play therapy. In K. J. O'Connor & L. M. Braverman (Eds.), *Play therapy theory and practice: A comparative presentation* (pp. 17–45). New York: John Wiley.

Landreth, G. L., (2002). *Play therapy: The art of the relationship* (2nd ed.). New York: Brunner–Routledge.

Larans, A. (1989). Brief psychotherapy: The multimodal model. *Psychology: A Journal of Human Behavior, 26,* 7–10.

Lawless, L. L., Ginter, E. J., & Kelly, K. R. (1999). Managed care: What mental health counselors need to know. *Journal of Mental Health Counseling, 21*(1), 50–65.

Lawrence, G., & Robinson Kurpius, S. E. (2000). Legal and ethical issues involved when counseling minors in nonschool settings. *Journal of Counseling & Development, 78,* 130–136.

Layne, C. M., & Hohenshil, T. H. (2005). High tech counseling: Revisited. *Journal of Counseling & Development, 83*(2), 222–226.

Lazarus, A. (1976). *Multimodal behavior therapy.* New York: Springer.

Lazarus, A. (1989). Brief psychotherapy: The multimodal model. *Psychology: A Journal of Human Behavior, 26,* 7–10.

Lazarus, A. (2005). Multimodal therapy. In R. J. Corsini & D. Wedding (Eds.), *Current psychotherapies* (7th ed., pp. 337–371). Belmont, CA: Thomson Brooks/ Cole.

Lazarus, A. (2008). Multimodal therapy. In R. J. Corsini & D. Wedding (Eds.), *Current psychotherapies* (8th ed.). Belmont, CA: Wadsworth.

Leibert, T. W. (2006). Making change visible: The possibilities in assessing mental health counseling outcomes. *Journal of Counseling & Development, 84*(1), 108–113.

Leibert, T. W., Archer, J., Munson, J., & York, G. (2006). An exploratory study of client perceptions of internet counseling and the therapeutic alliance. *Journal of Mental Health Counseling, 28*(1), 69–83.

Leitner, L. M., Faidley, A. J., & Celentana, M. A. (2000). Diagnosing human meaning making: An experiential constructivist approach. In R. A. Neimeyer & J. D. Raskin, *Constructions of disorder* (pp. 175–203). Washington, DC: American Psychological Association.

Leong, F. L. T, & Zachar, P. (1999). Gender and opinions about mental illness as predictors of attitudes toward seeking professional psychological help. *British Journal of Guidance and Counselling, 27,* 123–132.

Leong, F. T. L., & Chou, E. L. (2007). Counseling international students and sojourners. In P. B. Pedersen, W. J. Lonner, J. G. Draguns, & J. E. Trimble (Eds.), *Counseling across cultures* (6th ed., pp. 185–208). Thousand Oaks, CA: Sage.

Levine, S. K. (1992). *Poiesis: The language of psychology and the speech of the soul.* Toronto: Palmerston Press.

Levinson, D. J. (1978). *Seasons of a man's life.* New York: Knopf.

Levinson, D. J. (1978). *The seasons of a man's life.* New York: Ballantine Books.

Levinson, D. J. (1986). A conception of adult development. *American Psychologist, 41,* 3–14.

Levinson, D. J., & Levinson, J. D. (1996). *The seasons of a woman's life.* New York: Knopf.

Levitsky, A., & Perls, I. (1970). The rules and games of Gestalt therapy. In J. Fagan & I. Shepherd (Eds.), *Gestalt therapy now* (pp. 140–149). New York: Harper & Row.

Levy, D. M. (1971). Beginning of the child guidance movement. In M. Levitt & B. Rubenstein (Eds.), *The mental health field: A critical appraisal* (pp. 32–39). Detroit: Wayne State University Press.

Lewis, J. A., & Lewis, M. D. (1977). *Community counseling: A human services approach.* New York: Wiley.

Locke, D. (1986). A psychologist among the philosophers: Philosophical aspects of Kohlberg's theories. In S. Modgil & C. Modgil, *Lawrence Kohlberg: Consensus and controversy* (pp. 21–38). Philadelphia: Falmer Press.

Loevinger, J. (1976). *Ego development.* San Francisco: Jossey–Bass.

Lopez, F. G. (1986). Family structures and depression: Implications for the counseling of depressed college students. *Journal of Counseling & Development, 64,* 508–511.

Lounsbury, J., & Vats, G. (2003). The future of middle level education: Optimistic and pessimistic views. *Middle School Journal, 35*(2), 20–38.

Luongo, P. F. (2000). Partnering child welfare, juvenile justice, and behavioral health with schools. *Professional School Counseling, 3,* 308–314.

Lyddon, W. (1999). Forms and facets of constructivist psychology. In R. A. Neimeyer & M. J. Mahoney, *Constructivism in psychotherapy* (pp. 69–92). Washington, DC: American Psychological Association.

Madanes, C. (1981). *Strategic family therapy.* San Francisco: Jossey–Bass.

Mahoney, M. J. (1999). Continuing evolution of the cognitive sciences and psychotherapies. In R. A. Neimeyer & M. J. Mahoney (Eds.), *Constructivism in psychotherapy* (pp. 39–67). Washington, DC: American Psychological Association.

Maki, M. T., & Kitano, H. H. L. (2007). Counseling Asian Americans. In P. B. Pedersen, W. J. Lonner, J. G. Draguns, & J. E. Trimble (Eds.), *Counseling across cultures* (6th ed., pp. 109–133). Thousand Oaks, CA: Sage.

Mann, J. (1973). *Time-limited psychotherapy.* New York: McGraw–Hill.

Marino, T. W. (1996). Grief counseling broadens its definition. *Counseling Today, 39,* 13.

Martire, L. M., Parris Stephens, M. A., & Townsend, A. L. (2000). Centrality of women's multiple roles: Beneficial and detrimental consequences for psychological well-being. *Psychology and Aging, 15*(1), 148–156.

May, R. (1961). *Existential psychology.* New York: Van Nostrand Reinhold.

May, R., & Yalom, I. (2000). Existential psychotherapy. In R. Corsini & D. Wedding (Eds.), *Current psychotherapies* (6th ed., pp. 273–302). Itasca, IL: F. E. Peacock.

McAuliffe, G. J., & Erikesen, K. P. (1999). Toward a constructivist and developmental identity for the counseling profession: The context–phase–stage–style model. *Journal of Counseling & Development, 77,* 267–280.

McClure, R. F., Livingston, R. B., Livingston, K. H., & Gage, R. (2005). A survey of practicing psychotherapists. *Journal of Professional Counseling: Practice, Theory, and Research, 33*(1), 35–46.

McFadden, J. (1996). A transcultural perspective: Reaction to C. H. Patterson's "Multicultural Counseling: From Diversity to Universality." *Journal of Counseling & Development, 74*(3), 232–235.

McGoldrick, M., Pearce, J. K., & Giordano, J. (1982). *Ethnicity and family therapy.* New York: Guilford Press.

McNiff, S. (1988). *Fundamentals of art therapy.* Springfield, IL: Charles C. Thomas.

McWhirter, J. J. (1989). Religion and the practice of counseling psychology. *Counseling Psychologist, 17,* 613–617.

Mead, M. A., Hohenshil, T. H., & Singh, K. (1997). How the DSM system is used by clinical counselors: A national study. *Journal of Mental Health Counseling, 19,* 383–401.

Meade, M. (1993). *Men and the water of life: Initiation and the tempering of men.* San Francisco: Harper.

Meade, M. (2003). *Mosaic Multicultural Foundation* [Brochure]. Seattle: Author.

Meichenbaum, D. (1985). *Stress inoculation training.* New York: Pergamon Press.

Meichenbaum, D. (2007). Stress inoculation training: A preventative and treatment approach. In P. M. Lehrer, R. L. Woolfolk, & D. H. Barlow (Eds.), *Principles and practice of stress management* (3rd ed.). New York: Guilford.

Mendoza, D. W. (1993). A review of Gerald Caplan's theory and practice of mental health consultation. *Journal of Counseling and Development, 71,* 629–635.

Miller, C. (2003). Interviewing strategies. In M. Hersen & S. M. Turner (Eds.), *Diagnostic interviewing* (3rd ed., pp. 47–66). New York: Kluwer Academic/Plenum Publishers.

Miller, I. J. (1996). Managed care is harmful to outpatient mental health services: A call for accountability. *Professional Psychology: Research and Practice, 27*(4), 349-362.

Miller, J. B. (1976). *Toward a new psychology of women.* Boston: Beacon Press.

Miller, J. B., & Stiver, I. P. (1997). *The healing connection: How women form relationships in therapy and in life.* Boston: Beacon Press.

Miller, R. H., & Rollnick, S. (2002). *Motivational interviewing: Preparing people for change.* New York: Guilford Press.

Miltenberger, R. G. (2007). *Behavior modification: Principles and procedures* (4th ed.). Belmont, CA: Wadsworth.

Minuchin, S. T. (1974). *Families and family therapy.* Cambridge, MA: Harvard University Press.

Minuchin, S., Lee, W., & Simon, G. M. (2006). *Mastering family therapy: Journeys of growth and transformation* (2nd ed.). New York: John Wiley.

Mirin, S. M., & Sederer, L. I. (1994). Mental health care: Current realities, future directions. *Psychiatric Quarterly, 65*(3), 161–175.

Modgil, S., & Modgil, C. (1986). *Lawrence Kohlberg: Consensus & controversy.* Philadelphia: Falmer Press.

Moleski, S., & Kiselica, M. (2005). Dual relationships: A continuum ranging from the destructive to the therapeutic. *Journal of Counseling & Development, 83,* 3–11.

Moody, H. R., & Carroll, D. (1997). *The five stages of the soul: Charting the spiritual passages that shape our lives.* New York: Random House.

Moreno, J. L. (1946). *Psychodrama.* Beacon, NY: Beacon Press.

Moreno, Z. T. (1983). Psychodrama. In H. I. Kaplan & B. J. Sadock (Eds.), *Comprehensive group psychotherapy* (3rd ed., pp. 158–166). Baltimore: Williams & Wilkins.

Morran, D. K., Robison, F. F., & Stockton, R. (1985). Feedback exchange in counseling groups: An analysis of message content and receiver acceptance as a function of leader versus member delivery, session, and value. *Journal of Counseling Psychology, 32,* 57–67.

Morrissey, M. (1997). More grandparents raising grandchildren. *Counseling Today, 39,* 1, 4.

Mosak, H. H. (2000). Adlerian psychotherapy. In R. J. Corsini & D. Wedding (Eds.), *Current psychotherapies* (8th ed., pp. 54–98). Belmont, CA: Wadsworth.

Moursund, J., & Kenny, M. C. (2002). *The process of counseling and therapy* (4th ed.). Upper Saddle River, NJ: Prentice Hall.

Mueller, L. A., & Ketcham, K. (1987). *Recovering: How to get and stay sober.* New York: Bantam.

Murphy, L. J., & Mitchell, D. L. (1998). When writing helps to heal: E-mail as therapy. *British Journal of Guidance & Counselling, 26*(1), 25–32.

Myer, R. A., Peterson, S. E., & Stoffel-Rosales, M. (1991). Codependency: An examination of underlying assumptions. *Journal of Mental Health Counseling, 13,* 449–458.

Myers, J. E. (1989). *Adult children and aging parents.* Alexandria, VA: American Counseling Association.

Myers, J. E. (1990). Aging: An overview for mental health counselors. *Journal of Mental Health Counseling, 12*(3), 245–259.

Myers, J. E., & Schwiebert, V. L. (1996). *Competencies for gerontological counseling.* Alexandria, VA: American Counseling Association.

Nansel, T. R., Overpeck, M., Pilla, R. S., Ruan, W. J., Simons-Morton, B., & Scheidt, P. (2001). Bullying behaviors among US youth: Prevalence and association with psychosocial adjustment. *Journal of the American Medical Association, 285*(16), 2094–2100.

Narrow, W. E., Regier, D. A., Norquist, G., Rae, D. S., Kennedy, C., & Arons, B. (2000). Mental health service use by Americans with severe mental illnesses. *Social Psychiatry & Psychiatric Epidemiology, 35*(4), 147–155.

National Alliance for Caregiving and AARP. (2004). *Caregiving in the U. S.* Retrieved January 15, 2008, from http://www.caregiving.org/data/04finalreport.pdf

National Association of Consumer Survivor Mental Health Administrators. (2003). The prevalence of abuse histories in the mental health system. Retrieved September 1, 2007, from http://www.nasmhpd.org/general_files/TRAUMA.HTM

National Association of Social Workers (NASW). (1999). *The NASW Code of Ethics.* Washington, DC: Author.

National Board for Certified Counselors and Center for Credentialing and Education. (2001). *The practice of Internet counseling.* Retrieved June 27, 2007, from http://www.nbcc.org/webethics2

National Highway Traffic Safety Administration (NHTSA) (2000). Traffic safety facts 2000: Alcohol. (Publication No. DOT HS 808 323). Washington, DC: Author.

National Institute on Alcohol Abuse and Alcoholism. (2007). FAQs for the general public. Retrieved January 10, 2008, from http://www.niaaa.nih.gov/FAQs/General-English/default.htm#safe_level

National Institute on Drug Abuse. (n.d.). *Principles of drug addiction treatment: A research based guide.* Retrieved January 15, 2008, from http://www.nida.nih.gov/PODAT/PODATindex.html

National Occupational Information Coordinating Committee (NOICC). (1992). *The national career development guidelines project.* Washington, DC: Author.

National Research Council Panel to Review Risk and Prevalence of Elder Abuse and Neglect (2003). *Elder mistreatment: Abuse, neglect, and exploitation in an aging America.* Washington, DC: Author.

Neimeyer, G. J. (1999). The challenge of change. In R. A. Neimeyer & M. J. Mahoney (Eds.), *Constructivism in psychotherapy* (pp. 111–126). Washington, DC: American Psychological Association.

Neimeyer, R. A. (1995). Client-generated narratives in psychotherapy. In R. A. Neimeyer & M. J. Mahoney (Eds.), *Constructivism in psychotherapy* (pp. 231–246). Washington, DC: American Psychological Association.

Neimeyer, R. A. (1998). Social constructionism in the counselling context. *Counselling Psychology Quarterly, 11*(2), 135–149.

Neimeyer, R. A. (2003). Two paths diverge in a wood: Cognitive–constructivist contrasts and the future evolution of Adlerian psychotherapy. In R. E. Watts, *Adlerian, cognitive, and constructivist therapies: An integrative dialogue* (pp. 122–137). New York: Springer.

Neimeyer, R. A., & Mahoney, M. J. (Eds.). (1999). *Constructivism in psychotherapy.* Washington, DC: American Psychological Association.

Neimeyer, R. A., & Raskin, J. D. (2000). *Constructions of disorder: Meaning-making frameworks for psychotherapy.* Washington, DC: American Psychological Association.

Neimeyer, R. A., & Stewart, A. (1998). Constructivist psychotherapies. *Encyclopedia of Mental Health, 1,* 547–559.

Neugarten, B. L., Havighurst, R., & Tobin, S. (1961). The measurement of life satisfaction. *Journal of Gerontology, 16,* 134–143.

Nishimura, N. J. (1998). Addressing the issues of multiracial students on college campuses. *Journal of College Counseling, 1,* 45–53.

Noam, G. G. (1990). Beyond Freud and Piaget: Biographical worlds—interpersonal self. In T. E. Wren, *The moral domain* (pp. 360–399). Cambridge, MA: MIT Press.

Noam, G. G., & Wren, T. E. (Eds.). (1993). *The moral self.* Cambridge, MA: MIT Press.

Nussbaum, J. F., Pecchioni, L. L., Robinson, J. P., & Thompson, T. L. (2000). *Communication and aging* (2nd ed.). Mahwah, NJ: Lawrence Erlbaum.

Nystul, M. S. (1993). *The art and science of counseling and therapy.* Upper Saddle River, NJ: Merrill/Prentice Hall.

O'Connor, B. P., & Vallerand, R. J. (1994). Motivation, self-determination, and person–environment fit predictors of psychological adjustment among nursing home residents. *Psychology and Aging, 9,* 189–194.

O'Keefe, P. (1988). When the alcoholic refuses treatment. *Alcoholism and Addiction, 9,* 14.

Oetting, E. R., & Beauvais, F. (1988). Common elements in youth drug abuse: Peer clusters and other psychosocial factors. In S. Peel (Ed.), *Visions of addiction: Major contemporary perspectives on addiction and alcoholism* (pp. 141–161). Lexington, MA: Lexington Books.

Osipow, S. H., & Fitzgerald, L. F. (1996). *Theories of career development* (4th ed.). Boston: Allyn & Bacon.

Padula, M. A. (1994). Reentry women: A literature review with recommendations for counseling and research. *Journal of Counseling & Development, 73,* 10–16.

Palfai, T., & Jankiewicz, H. (1996). *Drugs and human behavior* (2nd ed.). Dubuque, IA: William C. Brown.

Palmo, A. J., Shosh, M. J., & Weikel, W. J. (2000). The independent practice of mental health counseling. In D. C. Locke, J. E. Myers, & E. L. Herr (Eds.), *The handbook of counseling* (pp. 653–667), Thousand Oaks, CA: Sage.

Papero, D. V. (2000). The Bowen theory. In A. M. Horne (Ed.), *Family counseling and therapy* (3rd ed., pp. 272–299). Belmont, CA: Wadsworth.

Parsons, F. (1909). *Choosing a vocation.* Boston: Houghton Mifflin.

Parsons, R. D. (1996). The skilled consultant. Boston: Allyn & Bacon.

Parsons, R. D., & Kahn, W. J. (2005). *The school counselor as consultant: An integrated model for school-based consultation.* Belmont, CA: Brooks/Cole.

Pascal, E. (1992). *Jung to live by*. New York: Warner Books.

Passons, W. R. (1975). *Gestalt approaches in counseling*. New York: Holt, Rinehart & Winston.

Patterson, C. H. (1986). *Theories of counseling and psychotherapy* (4th ed.). New York: Harper & Row.

Patterson, G. R. (1971*). Families: Application of social learning to family life*. Champaign, IL: Research Press.

Patterson, G. R., & Guillion, M. E. (1968). *Living with children*. Champaign, IL: Research Press.

Peel, S. (1988). A moral vision of addiction: How people's values determine whether they become addicts. In S. Peel (Ed.), *Visions of addiction: Major contemporary perspectives on addiction and alcoholism* (pp. 203–233). Lexington, MA: Lexington Books.

Perlmutter, M., & Hall, E. (1992). *Adult development and aging* (2nd ed.). New York: Wiley.

Perls, F. (1969). *Gestalt therapy verbatim*. New York: Bantam Books.

Perls, F. S. (1969). *Gestalt therapy verbatim*. Lafayette, CA: Real People Press.

Perls, L. (1976). Comments on the new directions. In E. Smith (Ed.), *The growing edge of Gestalt therapy* (pp. 221–226). New York: Brunner/Mazel.

Perry, W. G. (1970). *Forms of intellectual and ethical development in the college years: A scheme*. New York: Holt, Rinehart & Winston.

Peterson, K. S. (2001, August 6). Grandparents' labor of love. *USA Today,* pp. D1–2.

Phelps, R., Eisman, E. J., & Kohout, J. (1998). Psychological practice and managed care: Results of the CAAP practitioner survey. *Professional Psychology: Research and Practice, 29,* 31–36.

Piaget, J. (1926). *The language and thought of the child*. London: Routledge & Kegan Paul.

Piaget, J. (1932). *The moral judgment of the child*. London: Routledge & Kegan Paul.

Pillemir, K., & Moore, D. W. (1989). Abuse of patients in nursing homes: Findings from a survey of staff. *Gerontologist, 29*(3), 314–320.

Pine, G. J. (1969). The existential school counselor. *Clearing House, 43,* 351–354.

Pistole, M. C., & Roberts, A. (2002). Mental health counseling: Toward resolving identity confusions. *Journal of Mental Health Counseling, 24*(1), 1–19.

Polkinghorne, D. E. (2001). Managed care programs: What do clinicians need? In B. D. Slife, R. N. Williams, & S. H. Barlow (Eds.), *Critical issues in psychotherapy: Translating new ideas into practice* (pp. 121–146). Thousand Oaks, CA: Sage.

Posavac, E. J., & Carey, R. G. (2002). *Program evaluation: Methods and case studies* (6th ed.). Upper Saddle River, NJ: Merrill/Prentice Hall.

Prediger, D. J. (1994). Tests and counseling: The marriage that prevailed. *Measurement and Evaluation in Counseling and Development, 26,* 227–234.

Presbury, J. H., Echtering, L. G., & McKee, J. E. (2002). Beyond brief counseling and therapy: An integrative approach (2nd ed.) . Upper Saddle River, NJ: Merrill/Prentice Hall.

President's Advisory Commission on Asian Americans and Pacific Islanders. (2001). *A people looking forward: Action for access and partnerships in the 21st Century. An interim report to the President*. Washington, DC: Government Printing Office.

Price, R. H., & Lynn, S. J. (1986). *Abnormal psychology* (2nd ed.). Chicago: Dorsey Press.

Prochaska, J. O., & Norcross, J. C. (2006). *Systems of psychotherapy: A transtheoretical analysis* (6th ed.). Pacific Grove, CA: Wadsworth.

Rank, O. (1936). *Will therapy*. New York: Knopf.

Raskin, N. J., & Rogers, C. R. (1995). Person-centered therapy. In R. Corsini & D. Wedding (Eds.), *Current psychotherapies* (5th ed., pp. 128–161). Itasca, IL: F. E. Peacock.

Real, T. (1997). *I don't want to talk about it*. New York: Fireside.

Real, T. (2002). The awful truth. *Psychotherapy Networker, 26,* 34–43, 58.

Remley, T. P., Jr., & Herlihy, B. (2007). *Ethical, legal, and professional issues in counseling* (Updated 2nd ed.). Upper Saddle River, NJ: Merrill/Prentice Hall.

Rencken, R. H. (2000). *Intervention strategies for sexual abuse* (2nd ed.). Alexandria, VA: American Association of Counseling and Development.

Rest, J., Narvaez, D., Bebeau, M. J., & Thoma, S. J. (1999). *Postconventional moral thinking: A neo-Kohlbergian approach*. Mahwah, NJ: Lawrence Erlbaum.

Richmond-Abbott, M. (1992). *Masculine and feminine: Gender roles over the life cycle*. New York: McGraw–Hill.

Riemer-Reiss, M. L. (2000). Utilizing distance technology for mental health counseling. *Journal of Mental Health Counseling, 22,* 189–203.

Rigazio-DiGilio, S. A. (2000). Reconstructing psychological distress and disorder from a relational perspective: A systemic coconstructive–developmental framework. In R. A. Neimeyer & J. D. Raskin, *Constructions of disorder: Meaning-Making Frameworks for Psychotherapy* (pp. 309–332). Washington, DC: American Psychological Association.

Rigazio-DiGilio, S. A. (2007). Family counseling and therapy: Theoretical foundations and issues of practice. In A. E. Ivey, M. D'Andrea, M. B. Ivey., & L. Simek-Morgan, *Theories of counseling and psychotherapy: A multicultural perspective* (6th ed., pp. 429–468). Boston: Allyn & Bacon.

Rigazio-DiGilio, S. A., & Ivey, A. E. (1991). Developmental counseling and therapy: A framework for individual and family treatment. *Counseling and Human Development, 24,* 1–19.

Riger, S., Raza, S., & Camacho, J. (2002). The radiating impact of intimate partner violence. *Journal of Interpersonal Violence, 17*(2), 184–205.

Riley, S. (1997, Winter). Children's arts and narratives: An opportunity to enhance therapy and a supervisory challenge. *The Supervision Bulletin,* 2–3.

Robbins, A. (1980). *Expressive therapy: A creative arts approach to depth-oriented treatment.* New York: Human Sciences Press.

Robinson, T. L. (2005). *The convergence of race, ethnicity, and gender* (2nd ed.). Upper Saddle River, NJ: Merrill/Prentice Hall.

Robinson, T. L., & Howard-Hamilton, M. F. (2005). *The convergence of race, ethnicity, and gender.* Upper Saddle River, NJ: Merrill/Prentice Hall.

Robinson, T. L., & Watt, S. K. (2000). "Where no one goes begging": Converging gender, sexuality, and religious diversity in counseling. In D. C. Locke, J. E. Myers, & E. L. Herr (Eds.), *The handbook of counseling* (pp. 589–599). Thousand Oaks, CA: Sage.

Rochlen, A. B., Zack, J. S., & Speyer, C. (2004). Online therapy: Review of relevant definitions, debates, and current empirical support. *Journal of Clinical Psychology, 60*(3), 269–283.

Rodgers, R. F. (1984). Theories of adult development: Research, status, and counseling implications. In A. D. Brown & R. W. Lent (Eds.), *Handbook of counseling psychology* (pp. 479–519). New York: John Wiley.

Rogers, C. R. (1939). *The clinical treatment of the problem child.* Boston: Houghton Mifflin.

Rogers, C. R. (1942). *Counseling and psychotherapy: Newer concepts in practice.* Boston: Houghton Mifflin.

Rogers, C. R. (1951). *Client-centered therapy: Its current practice, implications, and theory.* Boston: Houghton Mifflin.

Rogers, C. R. (1957). The necessary and sufficient conditions of therapeutic personality change. *Journal of Counseling Psychology, 21,* 95–103.

Rogers, C. R. (1961). *On becoming a person.* Boston: Houghton Mifflin.

Rogers, C. R. (1970). *Carl Rogers on encounter groups.* New York: Harper & Row.

Rogers, C. R. (1973). Some new challenges. *American Psychologist, 28,* 379–387.

Rogers, C. R. (1980). *A way of being.* Boston: Houghton Mifflin.

Romano, J. L., & Skovolt, T. M. (1998). Henry Borow and counseling psychology: A half-century common journey. *Counseling Psychologist, 26,* 448–465.

Rowe, J. W., & Kahn, R. L. (1998). *Successful aging.* New York: Pantheon.

Rudd, S. S., Weissberg, N., & Gazda, G. M. (1988). Looking to the future: Themes from the Third National Conference for Counseling Psychology. *Counseling Psychologist, 16,* 423–430.

Ryff, C. D. (1986). *The failure of successful aging research.* Paper presented at the annual meeting of the Gerontological Society of America, Chicago, IL.

Sadock, B. J., & Sadock, V. A., (2000). *Kaplan and Sadock's comprehensive textbook of psychiatry.* Philadelphia: Lippincott, Williams & Wilkins.

Sampson, J. P., Jr., Kolodinski, R. W., & Greeno, P. P. (1997). Counseling on the information highway: Further possibilities and potential problems. *Journal of Counseling Development, 75,* 203–212.

Samuels, A. (1985). *Jung and the post-Jungians.* New York: Routledge.

Santrock, J. W. (2008). *Life-span development* (11th ed.). New York: McGraw Hill.

Satir, V. M. (1967). *Conjoint family therapy.* Palo Alto, CA: Science and Behavior Books.

Satir, V. M. (1972). *Peoplemaking.* Palo Alto, CA: Science and Behavior Books.

Satir, V. M., & Bitter, J. M. (2000). The therapist and family therapy: Satir's human validation process model. In A. M. Horne (Ed.), *Family counseling and therapy* (3rd ed., pp. 62–101). Belmont, CA: Wadsworth.

Schaef, A. W. (1986). *Codependence: Misunderstood—mistreated.* San Francisco: Harper & Row.

Schaefer, L. C., & Wheeler, C. C. (2004). Guilt in cross gender identity conditions: Presentations and treatment. In U. Leli & J. Drescher (Eds.), *Transgender subjectivities: A clinician's guide* (pp. 117–128). Binghamton, NY: Haworth Medical Press.

Schmall, V. L., Lawson, L., & Stiehl, R. (1993). *Depression in later life: Recognition and treatment.* Corvallis: Oregon State University.

Schmidt, J. J. (1987). Parental objections to counseling services: An analysis. *School Counselor, 34,* 387–391.

Schmidt, J. J. (2003). *Counseling in schools: Essential services and comprehensive programs* (4th ed.). Boston: Allyn & Bacon.

Schulz, R., & Salthouse, T. (1999). *Adult development and aging: Myths and emerging realities* (3rd ed.). Upper Saddle River, NJ: Prentice Hall.

Sears, R., Rudisill, J., & Mason-Sears, C. (2006). *Consultation skills for mental health professionals.* Hoboken, NJ: John Wiley & Sons.

Seligman, L. (1996). *Diagnosis and treatment planning in counseling* (2nd ed.). New York: Plenum Press.

Seligman, L. (2006). *Theories of counseling and psychotherapy: Systems, strategies, and skills* (2nd ed.) . Upper Saddle River, NJ: Merrill/Prentice Hall.

Sexton, T. L., & Whiston, S. C. (1994). The status of the counseling relationship: An empirical review, theoretical implications, and research directions. *Counseling Psychologist, 22,* 6–78.

Shaffer, D. R., & Kipp, K. (2006). *Developmental psychology: Childhood and adolescence* (7th ed.). Belmont, CA: Wadsworth.

Shah, S. A. (1969). Privileged communication, confidentiality, and privacy: Privileged communications. *Professional Psychology, 1,* 56–69.

Sharf, R. S. (2008). *Theories of psychotherapy and counseling: Concepts and cases* (4th ed.). Belmont, CA: Wadsworth.

Shear, M. K., Greeno, C., Kang, J., Ludewig, D., Frank, E., Swartz, H. A., & Hanekamp, M. (2000). Diagnosis of nonpsychotic patients in community clinics. *American Journal of Psychiatry, 157,* 581–587.

Sheehy, G. (1976). *Passages: Predictable crises of adult life.* New York: Bantam.

Sherman, E. (1991). *Reminiscence and the self in old age.* New York: Springer.

Sherman, R., & Dinkmeyer, D. (1987). *Systems of family therapy: An Adlerian integration.* New York: Brunner/Mazel.

Sifneos, P. E. (1987). *Short-term dynamic psychotherapy: Evaluation and technique* (2nd ed.). New York: Springer.

Simon, R. (1997). Fearless foursome. *Family Therapy Networker, 21,* 58–68.

Simon, R. W. (1997). The meanings individuals attach to role identities and their implications for mental health. *Journal of Health and Social Behavior, 38,* 256–274.

Sink, C. A. (2000). Modeling collaboration through caring communities of learners. *Professional School Counseling, 3,* ii–iii.

Skinner, A., & Zack, J. S. (2004). Counseling and the Internet. *American Behavioral Scientist, 48*(4), 434–446.

Skinner, B. F. (1953). *Science and human behavior.* New York: Macmillan.

Skynner, A. C. R. (1981). An open-systems group analytic approach to family therapy. In A. S. Gurman & D. P. Kniskern (Eds.), *Handbook of family therapy* (pp. 39–84). New York: Brunner/Mazel.

Slaikeu, K. A. (1990). *Crisis intervention: A handbook for practice and research* (2nd ed.). Needham Heights, MA: Allyn & Bacon.

Smith, H. B., & Robinson, G. P. (1995). Mental health counseling: Past, present, and future. *Journal of Counseling & Development, 74*(2), 158–162.

Smith, R. L. (2005). Research and contemporary issues. In P. Stevens & R. L. Smith (Eds.), *Substance abuse counseling: Theory and practice* (3rd ed., pp. 339–372). Upper Saddle River, NJ: Merrill/Prentice Hall.

Sommers-Flanagan, J., & Sommers-Flanagan, R. (2003). *Clinical interviewing* (3rd ed.). Hoboken, NJ: John Wiley & Sons.

Speaker, K. M., & Petersen, G. J. (2000). School violence and adolescent suicide: Strategies for effective intervention. *Educational Review, 51*(1), 65–73.

Spilka, B., Hood, W. R., & Gorsuch, R. (1985). *The psychology of religion.* Upper Saddle River, NJ: Prentice Hall.

Stadler, H. A., & Stahl, E. (1979). Trends in community counselor training. *Counselor Education and Supervision, 19,* 42–48.

Stadler, H. A., & Stahl, E. (1979). Trends in community counselor training. *Counselor Education and Supervision, 19*(1), 42–48.

Staude, J. R. (1981). *The adult development of C. G. Jung.* Boston: Routledge & Kegan Paul.

Steenbarger, B. N. (1990). Toward a developmental understanding of the counseling specialty: Lessons from our students. *Journal of Counseling & Development, 68,* 434–437.

Steenbarger, B. N. (1991). All the world is not a stage: Emerging contextualist themes in counseling and development. *Journal of Counseling & Development, 70,* 288–296.

Steenbarger, B. N. (1998). Alcohol abuse and college counseling: An overview of research and practice. *Journal of College Counseling, 1,* 81–92.

Steiner, C. (1974). *Scripts people live: Transactional analysis of life scripts.* New York: Grove Press.

Stevens, P. (2005a). Family therapy and substance abuse treatment. In P. Stevens & R. L. Smith (Eds.), *Substance abuse counseling: Theory and practice,* (3rd ed., pp. 213–238). Upper Saddle River, NJ: Merrill/Prentice Hall.

Stevens, P. (2005b). Individual and group treatment. In P. Stevens & R. L. Smith (Eds.), *Substance abuse counseling: Theory and practice* (3rd ed., pp. 187–212). Upper Saddle River, NJ: Merrill/Prentice Hall.

Stevens, P. (2005c). Introduction to substance abuse counseling. In P. Stevens & R. L. Smith (Eds.), *Substance abuse counseling: Theory and practice* (3rd ed., pp. 1–35). Upper Saddle River, NJ: Merrill/Prentice Hall.

Stevens, P. (2005d). Sustaining behavior change: Relapse prevention strategies. In P. Stevens & R. L. Smith (Eds.), *Substance abuse counseling: Theory and practice* (3rd ed., pp. 291–313). Upper Saddle River, NJ: Merrill/Prentice Hall.

Stevens, R., Smith, R. L., & Garcia, E. E. (2005). Treatment planning and treatment setting. In P. Stevens & R. L. Smith (Eds.), *Substance abuse counseling: Theory and practice* (3rd ed., pp. 159–186). Upper Saddle River, NJ: Merrill/Prentice Hall.

Stevens, R., Smith, R. L., & Capps, F. C. (2005). The major substances of abuse and the body. In P. Stevens & R. L. Smith (Eds.), *Substance abuse counseling: Theory and practice* (3rd ed., pp. 87–122). Upper Saddle River, NJ: Merrill/Prentice Hall.

Stiver, I. P. (1997). What is the role of transference and the unconscious in the relational model? In J. V. Jordan (Ed.), *Women's growth in diversity* (pp. 37–41). New York: Guilford Press.

Stofle, G. S. (2001). *Choosing an online therapist.* Harrisburg, PA: White Hat Communications.

Stone, G. I., & Archer, J., Jr. (1990). College and university counseling centers in the 1990s: Challenges and limits. *Counseling Psychologist, 18,* 539–607.

Strang, R. (1953). *The role of the teacher in personnel work* (4th ed.). New York: Columbia University Teachers College.

Strupp, H. H. (1981). Toward the refinement of time-limited dynamic psychotherapy. In S. H. Budman (Ed.), *Forms of brief therapy* (pp. 219–242). New York: Guilford Press.

Strupp, H. H., & Binder, J. (1984). *Psychotherapy in a new key: A guide to time-limited dynamic psychotherapy.* New York: Basic Books.

Subby, R. (1987). *Lost in the shuffle: The codependent reality.* Pompano Beach, FL: Health Communications.

Substance Abuse and Mental Health Services Administration (SAMHSA). (2007). New study shows American Indians and Alaska Natives continue to have higher rates of alcohol use and illicit drug use disorders than other racial groups. Retrieved August 30, 2007, from http://www.samhsa.gov/newsroom/advisories/0701231626.aspx

Substance Abuse and Mental Health Services Administration (SAMHSA). (2006). *Results from the 2005 national survey on drug use and health: National findings* (DHHS Publication No. SMA 06-4194). Rockville, MD: Author.

Sue, D., Sue, D. W., & Sue, S. (2005). *Understanding abnormal behavior* (8th ed.). Boston: Houghton Mifflin.

Sue, D. W., & Sue, D. (2003). *Counseling the culturally different* (4th ed.). New York: John Wiley.

Sue, D. W., & Sue, D. (2007). *Counseling the culturally diverse: Theory and practice* (5th ed.). New York: John Wiley.

Sue, D. W., Arredondo, P., & McDavis, R. J. (1992). Multicultural competencies/standards: A pressing need. *Journal of Counseling & Development, 70,* 477–486.

Suler, J. (2001). Assessing a person's suitability for online therapy: The ISMHO clinical case study group. *CyberPsychology & Behavior, 4*(6), 675–679.

Summerfeldt, L. J., & Antony, M. M. (2002). Structured and semistructured diagnostic interviews. In M. M. Antony (Ed.), *Handbook of assessment and treatment planning for psychological disorders* (pp. 3–37). New York, NY: Guilford Press.

Super, D. E. (1942). *The dynamics of vocational adjustment.* New York: Harper Brothers.

Super, D. E. (1949). *Appraising vocational fitness by means of psychological tests.* New York: Harper Brothers.

Super, D. E. (1953). A theory of vocational development. *American Psychologist, 8,* 185–190.

Super, D. E. (1955). Transition: From vocational guidance to counseling psychology. *Journal of Counseling Psychology, 2,* 3–9.

Super, D. E. (1990). A life-span, life-space approach to career development. In D. Brown & L. Brooks (Eds.), *Career choice and development: Applying contemporary theories to practice* (pp. 197–261). San Francisco, CA: Jossey-Bass.

Surrey, J. L. (1991). The self-in-relation: A theory of women's development. In J. V. Jordan, A. G. Kaplan, J. B. Miller, I. P. Stiver, & J. L. Surrey (Eds.), *Women's growth in connection: Writings from the Stone Center* (pp. 51–66). New York: Guilford Press.

Surrey, J. L. (1997). What do you mean by mutuality in therapy? In J. V. Jordan (Ed.), *Women's growth in diversity* (pp. 42–49). New York: Guilford Press.

Sweeney, T. (1998). *Adlerian counseling: A practical approach for a new decade* (4th ed.). Muncie, IN: Accelerated Development.

Sweeney, T. J. (1990). Early recollections: A promising technique for use with older people. *Journal of Mental Health Counseling, 12*(3), 260–269.

Sweeney, T. J. (1998). *The Adlerian counselor.* Muncie, IN: Accelerated Development/Taylor & Francis.

Sweeney, T. J. (2001). Counseling: Historical origins and philosophical roots. In D. C. Locke, J. E. Myers, & E. L. Herr (Eds.), *The handbook of counseling* (pp. 3–26). Thousand Oaks, CA: Sage.

Taffel, R. (1993). In praise of countertransference: Harvesting our errors. *Family Therapy Networker, 17,* 52–57.

Tait, C. (2005). Working with selected populations: Treatment issues and characteristics. In P. Stevens & R. L. Smith (Eds.), *Substance abuse counseling: Theory and practice* (3rd ed., pp. 239–265). Upper Saddle River, NJ: Merrill/Prentice Hall.

Tarasoff v. Regents of the University of California, (1976), 17 Cal.3d 425, 551 P.2d 334.

Thomas, M. B. (1992). *An introduction to marital and family therapy: Counseling toward healthier family systems across the life span*. New York: Macmillan.

Thoresen, C. E., & Mahoney, M. J. (1974). *Behavioral self-control*. New York: Holt, Rinehart & Winston.

Thorndike, R. M. (2005). *Measurement and evaluation in psychology and education* (7th ed.). Upper Saddler River, NJ: Merrill/Prentice Hall.

Tolbert, E. L. (1982). *An introduction to guidance* (2nd ed.). Boston: Little, Brown.

Tracey, T. J. (1988). The stages of influence in counseling. In W. Dryden (Ed.), *Key issues for counselling in action* (pp. 63–72). London: Sage.

Trimble, J. E., & Jumper-Thurman, P. (2007). Ethnocultural considerations and strategies for providing counseling services to Native American Indians. In P. B. Pedersen, W. J. Lonner, J. G. Draguns, & J. E. Trimble (Eds.), *Counseling across cultures* (6th ed., pp. 53–92). Thousand Oaks, CA: Sage.

U.S. Census Bureau (2001). Overview of race and Hispanic origin: Census 2000 brief. Retrieved December 20, 2007, from http://www.census.gov/prod/2001pubs/cenbr01-1.pdf

U.S. Census Bureau. (2004). *U.S. interim projections by age, sex, race, and Hispanic origin: 2000 to 2050*. Retrieved April 10, 2007, from http://www.census.gov/ipc/www/usinterimproj

U.S. Census Bureau. (2004a). *Annual estimates of the population by race alone or in combination and Hispanic or Latino origin for the United States and states*. Washington, DC: Author.

U.S. Census Bureau (2004b). Income stable, poverty up, numbers of Americans with and without health insurance rise, Census Bureau reports. Retrieved August 25, 2007, from http://www.census.gov/Press-Release/www/releases/archives/income_wealth/ 002484. html

U.S. Census Bureau (2005). We the people: Blacks in the United States. Retrieved August 25, 2007, from http://www.census.gov/prod/2005pubs/censr-25.pdf

U.S. Census Bureau. (2006a). Facts for features: Hispanic heritage month. Retrieved August 25, 2007, from http://www.census.gov/Press-Release/www/releases/archives/facts_for_features_special_editions/007173.html

U.S. Census Bureau. (2006b). Nation's population one-third minority. Retrieved December 20, 2007, from http://www.census.gov/Press-Release/www/releases/archives/population/006808.html

U.S. Census Bureau, (2007). Projections of the total resident population by 5-year age groups, and sex with special age categories: Middle series, 1999 to 2100. Retrieved August 25, 2007, from http://www.census.gov/population/www/projections/natsum-T3.html

U.S. Census Bureau (2007a). Quickfacts: Race. Retrieved December 20, 2007, from http://quickfacts.census.gov/qfd/meta/long_68184.htm

U.S. Census Bureau. (2007b). The American community—American Indians and Alaska Natives: 2004. Retrieved August 25, 2007, from http://www.census.gov/prod/2007pubs/acs-07.pdf

U.S. Census Bureau. (2007c). The American community—Asians: 2004. Retrieved August 25, 2007, from http://www.census.gov/prod/2007pubs/acs-05.pdf

U.S. Census Bureau. (2007d). The American community—Blacks: 2004. Retrieved August 25, 2007, from http://www.census.gov/prod/2007pubs/acs-04.pdf

U.S. Department of Commerce (2000). *Census bureau says 7 million grade-school children home alone*. U.S. Census Bureau News. Washington DC: Author.

U.S. Department of Education. (2002). Twenty-fourth annual report to Congress on the implementation of the Individuals with Disabilities Education Act. Retrieved April 1, 2007, from http://www.ed.gov/about/reports/annual/osep/2002/index.html

U.S. Department of Education. (2002a). No Child Left Behind Act of 2001. Retrieved March 15, 2007, from http://www.ed.gov/policy/elsec/leg/esea02/index.html

U.S. Department of Education. (2002b). No Child Left Behind Act of 2001: Executive summary. Retrieved March 15, 2007, from http://www.ed.gov/nclb/overview/intro/execsumm.doc

U.S. Department of Health and Human Services (DHHS). (2001). *Mental health: Culture, race, and ethnicity—A supplement to mental health: A report of the surgeon general*. Rockville, MD: Author, Substance Abuse and Mental Health Services Administration, Center for Mental Health Services.

U.S. Department of Health and Human Services, Administration for Children, Youth, and Families (2005). *Child maltreatment 2005*. Retrieved August 15, 2007, from http://www.acf.dhhs.gov/programs/cb/pubs/cm05/cm05.pdf

U.S. Department of Health and Human Services. (2001). Youth violence: A report of the Surgeon General. Rockville, MD: Author.

U.S. Department of Health and Human Services. (2005). *Child maltreatment*. Washington, DC: Author.

U.S. Department of Justice. (2007). Homicide trends in the U.S.: Intimate homicide. Retrieved September 1, 2007, from http://www.ojp.usdoj.gov/bjs/homicide/intimates.htm

U.S. Department of Labor (2006). *Women in the labor force in 2006.* Retrieved August 15, 2007, from http://www.dol.gov/wb/factsheets/Qf-laborforce-06.htm

U.S. Department of Labor, Bureau of Labor Statistics. (2006). College enrollment and work activity of 2005 high school graduates. Retrieved April 1, 2007, from http://stats.bls.gov/news.release/archives/hsgec_03242006.pdf

U.S. Department of Labor. (2006). Counselors. *Occupational outlook handbook, 2006-07.* Indianapolis, IN: JIST Publishing. Retrieved March 15, 2007, from http://www.bls.gov/oco/ocos067.htm

Upcraft, M. L., & Moore, L. V. (1990). Evolving theoretical perspectives of student development. In M. J. Barr, M. L. Upcraft, & Associates, *New futures for student affairs: Building a vision for professional leadership and practice* (pp. 41–68). San Francisco: Jossey–Bass.

Valliant, G. E. (1977). *Adaptation to life.* Boston: Little, Brown.

Van Kaam, A. (1967). Counseling and psychotherapy from the viewpoint of existential psychology. In D. Arbuckle (Ed.), *Counseling and psychotherapy: An overview* (pp. 20–52). New York: McGraw–Hill.

Vander Kolk, C. J. (1985). *Introduction to group counseling and psychotherapy.* Upper Saddle River, NJ: Merrill/Prentice Hall.

VanZandt, C. E. (1990). Professionalism: A matter of personal initiatives. *Journal of Counseling & Development, 68*(3), 243–245.

Vernon, A. (2004). Working with children, adolescents, and their parents: Practical application of developmental theory. In A. Vernon (Ed.), *Counseling children and adolescents* (3rd ed., pp. 1–34). Denver, CO: Love.

Viney, L. L. (1993). *Life stories: Personal construct therapy with the elderly.* Chichester, UK: Wiley.

Vogel, D. E. (1993). *Family physicians and managed care: A view to the 90s.* Kansas City, MO: American Academy of Family Physicians.

von Bertalanffy, L. (1974). General systems theory and psychiatry. In S. Aristi (Ed.), *American handbook of psychiatry* (Vol. 1, pp. 1095–1117). New York: Brace Books.

Vygotsky, L. S. (1962). *Thought and language.* Cambridge, MA: MIT Press. (Original work published 1934)

Vygotsky, L. S. (1978). *Mind in society.* Cambridge MA: Harvard University Press. (Original works published 1930, 1933, 1935)

Walsh, W. B., & Betz, N. E. (2001). *Tests and assessments* (4th ed.). Upper Saddle River, NJ: Prentice Hall.

Walter, J. L., & Peller, J. E. (1992). *Becoming solution-focused in brief therapy.* New York: Brunner/Mazel.

Walters, M., Carter, B., Papp, O., & Silverstein, O. (Eds.). (1988). *The invisible web: Gender patterns in family relationships.* New York: Guilford Press.

Waters, E. B. (1990a). The life review: Strategies for working with individuals. *Journal of Mental Health Counseling, 12,* 270–278.

Waters, E. B. (1990b). Why counseling? *Generations, 14,* 5–6.

Waters, E. B., & Goodman, J. (1990). *Empowering older adults: Practical strategies for counselors.* San Francisco, CA: Jossey-Bass.

Watkins, C. E. (1983). Transference phenomena in the counseling situation. *Personnel and Guidance Journal, 62,* 206–210.

Watts, R. E. (2003). *Adlerian, cognitive, and constructivist therapies: An integrative dialogue.* New York: Springer.

Weakland, J. H., Fisch, R., Watzlawick, P., & Bodin, A. (1974). Brief therapy: Focused problem resolution. *Family Process, 13,* 141–168.

Weeks, G. R., & L'Abate, L. (1982). *Paradoxical psychotherapy: Theory and practice with individuals, couples, and families.* New York: Brunner/Mazel.

Wegscheider-Cruse, S. (1985). *Choicemaking: For co-dependents, spirituality seekers, and adult children.* Pompano Beach, FL: Health Communications.

Welfel, E. R. (2006). *Ethics in counseling and psychotherapy: Standards, research, and emerging issues* (3rd ed.). Belmont, CA: Brooks/Cole.

Wells, R. A. (1994). *Planned short-term treatment* (2nd ed.). New York: Free Press.

White, H. S., Burke, J. D., & Havens, L. L. (1981). Choosing a method of short-term therapy: A developmental approach. In S. H. Budman (Ed.), *Forms of brief therapy* (pp. 243–267). New York: Guilford Press.

White, J., & Flynt, M. (2000). The school counselor's role in prevention and remediation of child abuse. In J. Wittmer (Ed.), *Managing your school counseling program: K–12 developmental strategies* (pp. 149–160). Minneapolis, MN: Educational Media.

White, M., & Epston, D. (1990). *Narrative means to therapeutic ends.* New York: Norton.

Whiteley, J. M. (1984). A historical perspective on the development of counseling psychology as a profession.

In S. Brown & R. Lent (Eds.), *Handbook of counseling psychology* (pp. 3–55). New York: John Wiley.

Wicks-Nelson, R., & Israel, A. C. (2000). *Behavior disorders of childhood*. Upper Saddle River, NJ: Merrill/Prentice Hall.

Wilczenski, F. L. & Coomey, S. M. (2006). Cyber-communication: Finding its place in school counseling practice, education, and professional development. *Professional School Counseling, 9*(4), 327–331.

Williamson, E. G. (1939). *How to counsel students: A manual of techniques for clinical counselors*. New York: McGraw-Hill.

Wittmer, J. (2000). *Managing your school counseling program: K–12 developmental strategies*. Minneapolis, MN: Educational Media.

Wolberg, L. R. (1980). *Handbook of short-term psychotherapy*. New York: Thieme-Stratton.

Wolpe, J. (1958). *Psychotherapy by reciprocal inhibition*. Stanford, CA: Stanford University Press.

Wolpe, J. (1969). *The practice of behavior therapy*. New York: Pergamon.

Wolpe, J. (1973). *The practice of behavior therapy* (2nd ed.). New York: Pergamon Press.

Woodring, P. (1953). *Let's talk sense about our schools*. New York: Pergamon Press.

Woodworth, R. S., & Sheehan, M. (1964). *Contemporary schools of psychology* (3rd ed.). New York: Ronald Press.

Woody, R. H., Hansen, J. C., & Rossberg, R. H. (1989). *Counseling psychology: Strategies and services*. Pacific Grove, CA: Brooks/Cole.

Worden, J. W. (2001). *Grief counseling and grief therapy: A handbook for the mental health professional* (3rd ed.). New York: Springer.

World Health Organization (WHO). (2002). *Gender and mental health*. Geneva, Switzerland: Author.

Worthington, E. L., Jr. (1989). Religious faith across the life span: Implications for counseling and research. *Counseling Psychologist, 17,* 555–612.

Wren, T. E. (Ed.). (1990). *The moral domain: Essays in the ongoing discussion between philosophy and the social sciences*. Cambridge, MA: MIT Press.

Wrenn, C. G. (1962). *The counselor in a changing world*. Washington, DC: American Personnel and Guidance Association.

Wrenn, C. G. (1973). *The world of the contemporary counselor*. Boston: Houghton Mifflin.

Wylie, M. S. (2002). The untold story: Carol Gilligan on recapturing the lost voice of pleasure. *Psychotherapy Networker, 26,* 46–56.

Wylie, M. S., & Simon, R. (2002). Discoveries from the black box. *Psychotherapy Networker, 26,* 26–37, 68.

Yalom, I. D. (1980). *Existential psychotherapy*. New York: Basic Books.

Yalom, I. D. (2002). *The gift of therapy: An open letter to a new generation of therapists and their patients*. New York: Harper Collins.

Yontef, G. M., & Jacobs, L. (2005). Gestalt therapy. In R. J. Corsini & D. Wedding (Eds.), *Current psychotherapies* (7th ed., pp. 299–336). Belmont, CA: Thomson Brooks/Cole.

Young, M. (2005). *Learning the art of helping: Building blocks and techniques*. Upper Saddle River, NJ: Prentice Hall.

Zucal, B. (1992). Gender issues in couples therapy. In J. D. Atwood (Ed.), *Family therapy: A systemic behavioral approach* (pp. 59–69). Chicago: Nelson–Hall.

Zunker, V. G. (2006). *Career counseling: A holistic approach* (7th ed.). Pacific Grove, CA: Brooks/Cole.

Index

successful aging, 234–236
Sue, D. W., 10
suicide
college and university counseling, 290
high school counseling, 266–267
in older adults, 246
privileged communication issues, 28
Suler, J., 314
Sullivan, Harry Stack, 87, 89, 92
summarization, 43
Super, Donald
Buehler's influence on, 65, 199, 201, 231
on career counseling vs. personal counseling, 200
developmental theory, 201
human development applied to career counseling by, 199
influence on college counseling, 276
on older adult development, 231
superego, 87, 88
Surrey, J. L., 66
Sweeney, T. J., 244, 267
symptom measures of outcome, 302
Systematic Training for Effective Parenting (STEP), 181
System for Interactive Guidance Information (SIGI-Plus), 208
systemic cognitive–developmental therapy (SCDT), 82

T
TA (transactional analysis), 151–152
tabula rasa concept, 99
Taffel, R., 137
Taft, Jessie, 5, 94
Tarasoff v. Regents of the University of California (1976), 27
TAT (Thematic Apperception Test), 122
teachers, school consultation with, 171–172
technical eclecticism, 111
technology, counseling and, 13–14
teenagers. *See* adolescence
termination
determining appropriate time for, 143
in family counseling, 191
in group counseling, 159–160
in individual counseling, 142–145
leading up to the last session, 144–145
in mental health and community counseling, 301–302
in older adult counseling, 243
resisting appropriate termination, 143–144
too soon, 143
testing. *See also* assessment; diagnosis
achievement tests, 120
aptitude tests, 119–120, 206

assessment vs., 113
career counseling, 206
in child guidance clinics, 4–5
classification of tests, 116–118
in counseling, history of, 113–115
counseling theories and, 115
criticisms of, 114–115, 117–118
culture-fair and culture-specific tests, 117–118
early movement (1920–1940), 3–4
functions of, 115
intelligence tests, 118–119
interest inventories, 120–121
nonstandardized tests, 116–117
overview, 115–116
personality measures, 121–123, 206
reliability and validity assessment for, 118
Rogers' doubts about reliance on, 6
standardized tests, overview, 117–118
substance abuse questionnaires, 218–219
test, defined, 113
university testing services, 279, 283
vocational interest inventories, 206
"Tests and Counseling: The Marriage That Failed" (Goldman), 114
Thematic Apperception Test (TAT), 122
theoretical integration, 111
theory. *See* counseling theories; human development theories
third force in psychology, 8
third-party reimbursement, 308
Thoresen, C. E., 101
Tillich, Paul, 78
time-limited dynamic psychotherapy (TLDP), 108, 109
time-limited psychotherapy (TLP), 108
Tobin, S., 235
To Dance With the White Dog (Kay), 233, 235
token economy, 100
tone, setting for individual counseling, 129–130
Tracey, T. J., 129
training programs. *See* counselor training programs
trait-and-factor theory of career counseling, 201–202
transactional analysis (TA), 151–152
transactional patterns, 184
transference, 88, 136–137, 241
Transformations: Growth and Change in Adult Life (Gould), 74
transgender clients, 60–61
transtheoretical integrative approach, 111
treatment planning, 300–301
trends in counseling, 12–14, 82–84, 160
trustworthiness, 37
12-step programs, 223–224
typology, Jungian, 93–94